The AI Metaverse Revolution

The AI Metaverse Revolution: Transforming Multi-business Scenarios (Volume 1)

EDITED BY

JEETESH KUMAR
Taylor's University, Malaysia

AND

MANPREET ARORA
Central University of Himachal Pradesh, India

emerald
PUBLISHING

United Kingdom – North America – Japan – India – Malaysia – China

Emerald Publishing Limited
Emerald Publishing, Floor 5, Northspring, 21-23 Wellington Street, Leeds LS1 4DL.

First edition 2025

British Library Cataloguing in Publication Data
A catalogue record for this book is available from the British Library

ISBN: 978-1-83662-583-4 (Print)
ISBN: 978-1-83662-582-7 (Online)
ISBN: 978-1-83662-584-1 (Epub)

Printed and bound by CPI Group (UK) Ltd, Croydon, CR0 4YY

INVESTOR IN PEOPLE

Contents

About the Editors

Jeetesh Kumar is Head of Research at the Faculty of Social Sciences and Leisure Management, Senior Lecturer at the School of Hospitality, Tourism and Events, Associate Director for Information Management & Documentation at the Centre for Research and Innovation in Tourism, and Hub Leader of the 'Responsible Tourism for Inclusive Economic Growth' Sustainable Tourism Impact Lab at Taylor's University, Malaysia. His research areas include Economic Impacts, Economic Modelling, Sustainable Tourism Development, SMART Tourism and Behavioural Studies. He has worked on consultancies and research projects at the national/ international level and authored 80+ publications, including indexed research articles and book chapters. Twelve postgraduate students (Masters and PhDs) have graduated under his supervision, and currently, he is supervising 7 PhD scholars. He is also active in several national and international associations, conferences, and journals. He is also an Associate Editor for the *Asia-Pacific Journal of Innovation in Hospitality and Tourism* and Regional Editor (Asia) for the *Event Management Journal.* He has co-edited four books under CAB International, IGI, and Emerald and is currently editing five books with Emerald, IGI, and Springer. He is an active speaker and has been invited by several institutions in the Philippines, India, Japan, Indonesia, China, Australia, and Pakistan.

Manpreet Arora, a Senior Assistant Professor of Management at the Central University of Himachal Pradesh, Dharamshala, India, brings over 22 years of rich teaching experience. She is a gold medallist and a merit holder. An accomplished academic, she has an impressive publication record, having authored over 33 papers in esteemed national and international journals listed in Scopus, Web of Science and Category journals, alongside contributing to above 65 book chapters in publications by reputed publishers like Emerald, Routledge, CABI, Springer Nature, AAP, and more. She works in the area of microfinance, sustainable development goals, corporate communications and qualitative research. She is supervising Doctoral students and postgraduate students. Her commitment to management research is evident through the editing of eight books from national and international publishers. She is presently working in the area of metaverse, entrepreneurship, and tourism and is editing books of reputed publications like Emerald and IGI. Her impactful contributions showcase a multi-faceted professional excelling in academia, research, and social advocacy.

About the Contributors

Neetha Mary Avanesh, PhD, is an Associate Professor at the School of Business and Management, Christ (Deemed to be University), Bengaluru, India. She has published several research papers, book chapters, and case studies in Elsevier, Emerald, Harvard Business Review and Ivey Publishing. She has five Best Paper Awards and a patent to her credit. Her research interests include succession planning, psychological contract, workplace spirituality, employee wellbeing and social entrepreneurship. She has undertaken short- and medium-term projects with corporate clientele, including those with Smith Kline Beecham Pharmaceuticals (India) Ltd., Bangalore and Whirlpool of India Ltd., Bangalore. She is passionate about designing and developing human-capital management initiatives across the business spectrum.

Sneha Biswas is a dedicated Assistant Professor at Pailan College of Management and Technology, Kolkata, India. Her expertise lies in healthcare management and public health, backed by a Master's in Public Health and a Bachelor's in Hospital Management and currently pursuing PhD in Healthcare Management. With a published book and research article, her passion for research is evident. Her contributions extend to sustainability topics, showcasing her commitment to advancing knowledge in her field. As an author of an international book, her impact transcends national boundaries. Her dedication to excellence makes her a respected figure in academia, poised to continue making significant contributions to healthcare management and public health.

Yasha Bothra is a passionate educator with a PhD in Finance from the Delhi School of Economics, Delhi University. She is currently working as an Assistant Professor at the Sri Venkateswara College, University of Delhi. Her research papers have been published in renowned journals. She likes to work on contemporary topics also. Her research expertise and teaching experience make her a valuable asset to academic communities.

Rituparna Chatterjee is a distinguished academic and seasoned professional heading the Hospital Management Department at Pailan College. With a strong academic background and nine years of combined experience in the hospital industry and academia, she brings a unique blend of practical knowledge and scholarly pursuit. Her expertise in healthcare management is evident in her international book and research interests in sustainability. As a mentor, she is dedicated to nurturing talent and fostering innovation among her students. Her contributions to the field of hospital management are invaluable.

Aarthy Chellasamy is an Assistant Professor with nine years of teaching experience in School of Business and Management Christ (Deemed to be) University, Bangalore, India. She has completed her Bachelor's in Engineering from Avinashi Lingam University, Coimbatore, Master's in International Business Management, and PhD in Technology Marketing from Anna University. Her teaching interests are in the area of management information system, sentiment analysis and opinion mining, business analytics, consumer behaviour, and operations management. She has published more than 70 research papers to her credit in national and international publishers including Emerald, Taylor & Francis, and Springer. She has also presented papers in many national and international conferences to her credit. Her field of research include information technology implementation and its usage, and consumer behaviour in the digital age.

Scott Dewicki, RGBSI Aerospace & Defense, United States of America, is the Programme Manager, Information Technology Services Leader, and Chief architect at RGBSI Aerospace & Defense. He is a highly successful, experienced information technology, supply chain, and engineering professional. He can communicate and collaborate with clients and demonstrate value from C-suite to working level. His cross-sector background includes automotive, aerospace, consumer products, high-tech, life sciences, health care, chemicals, and public sector. In addition to RGBSI Aerospace & Defense, he has worked for Amazon, Gartner, and IBM.

Vaishali Dhiman is an esteemed Research Scholar associated with HPKVBS, School of Commerce and Management Studies, Central University of Himachal Pradesh, India. Her research focusses on entrepreneurship, business incubation, skill development, the metaverse, and exponential technologies. With a keen interest in fostering innovation and economic growth, she delves into the intricacies of entrepreneurial ecosystems, explores strategies for effective business incubation, navigates the dynamics of the metaverse and exponential technologies, and identifies avenues for skill development in emerging industries. She has a good publication record, having authored nine papers in international journals and books with publishers such as Emerald, Sage, Springer Nature, Taylor & Francis groups AAP, and IGI indexed in Scopus. Her profound insights and dedication to advancing knowledge in these fields position her as a valuable asset to the academic community.

Aditya Kumar Divyam is a Research Scholar at Lovely Professional University, Jalandhar, Punjab, India. His research interests encompass sustainability, corporate social responsibility (CSR), and green marketing. He is committed to investigating how businesses can seamlessly integrate *sustainable* practices into their operations while adhering to their social responsibilities. In his recent research, he delves into the intricate dynamics of green purchase intentions, examining the roles of CSR, eco-advertising, and green trust in shaping consumer behaviour within retail sectors. Looking ahead, he aims to further explore innovative strategies that enable businesses to engage in both environmentally friendly and socially responsible practices, thereby contributing to a more sustainable future for industries and communities alike.

Anshul Garg is an accomplished academician and researcher. He works as a Senior Lecturer at Taylor's University in Malaysia. His research expertise includes self-service technologies in the hospitality and restaurant industry, service quality, service clues, hospitality service, human resource management, and waste management. He has successfully published research work in various Scopus- and Web of Science-indexed journals and book chapters in books published by highly recognised publishers (Emerald, CABI, and IGI-Global). He is an editorial board member and reviewer with many reputed and Scopus-indexed journals.

Seema Garg is an Associate Professor in Amity International Business School, Amity University, Noida, India. She has obtained her PhD degree from Jamia Millia Islamia University, Delhi, India. Previously, she has done her MPhil and MSc degrees in Operational Research from the University of Delhi, Delhi, India in the year 2001 and 1997 respectively. Involved in teaching business statistics, operations research, business research methods, decision sciences, business maths, etc. she has significantly contributed to enhancing scientific understanding by participating in number of national and international conferences, symposia, and seminars by participating and chairing technical sessions. Her publications are in the areas of data envelopment analysis, supply chain management, modelling and efficiency optimisation in banking using data envelopment analysis application of DEA. She has pursued research in truly interdisciplinary areas.

Paul Hartman, PhD, RGBSI Aerospace & Defense, United States of America, is President of RGBSI Aerospace & Defense and Adjunct Professor of Data Driven Decisions in the Master's in Analytics programme at Wittenberg University in Springfield, OH. He serves as the contract principal investigator responsible for the design, development, demonstration, and delivery of the groundbreaking Defense Logistics Agency Digital Sustainment Platform and was featured in the top 100 innovators and entrepreneurs magazine. His current research interests include supply chain management and defense acquisition.

Brian Heath, PhD, Wittenberg University, United States of America is an Adjunct Professor of Analytics and the Founder of Heath Analytics. He has taught analytics courses at the graduate level. An author of over 20 publications, his works include *A Survey of Agent-based Modeling Practices (January 1998 to July 2008), Some Insights into the Emergence of Agent-based Modeling, Epistemology of Modeling and Simulation,* and *The History, Philosophy,* and *Practice of Agent-based*

Modeling and the Development of the Conceptual Model for Simulation Diagram. His research explores agent-based modeling, simulation, decision-making, and uses of analysis in organisations.

Mohammad Abu Horaira, an experienced Associate Professor, works at the College of Tourism and Hospitality Management at the International University of Business Agriculture and Technology in Dhaka, Bangladesh. He was born in the Kishoreganj District on 12 July 1980, and received his SSC and HSC from Dhaka Board. In pursuing a higher education, he attended the IIAS School of Management in Darjeeling, India, earning a three-year hospitality and tourism management diploma. To further his education interest, he earned a Bachelor of Arts in Tourism and Hospitality Management and a Master of Business Administration degree with a concentration in Human Resource Management from IUBAT. The American Hospitality Academy made him a Certified Hospitality Educator. 'Tourism-Community Development Nexus: A Case Study of Kuakata' is the topic of his studies for his MPhil degree, which he is currently conducting at Bangladesh University of Professionals, Dhaka, Bangladesh.

Vincent Pang Fook Huat is an accomplished academician and industry expert with an overall experience of 15 years in various portfolios of the industry. He has worked as an Editor and Author of published Culinary Recipe books. He is actively involved in the restaurant scene and is plying his trade in a German-based delicacy restaurant. He is also a competition skills trainer and an international skills medallist.

Ross Jackson, PhD, Wittenberg University, United States of America, is an Associate Professor of Business. He has taught management in large universities and small liberal arts colleges. An author of over 30 publications, his works include *Management in Quandary: A Critique of Organizational Power*, *Haunted Across the Political Spectrum: The Specter of Communism in Two Midcentury American Organizations*, *Nietzsche's Construction of Power: Implications for International Business Ethics*, *Becoming Who You Are Through Authentic Organizational Communication*, and *The Spectacle of Analysis: Analytics as Organizational Propaganda*. His research interests focus on organisational power, analytics, and *détournement*.

P. James Daniel Paul is a Professor in Mittal school of Business. He is known as an Economist, Investment Facilitator, and Analytics Expert with significant experience working with prominent international organisations, including UNIDO, the World Bank, ADB, UKTI, the European Union, PWC, EY, the Murugappa Group, and Skymark. Additionally, his associations with organisations such as CII, SICCI, Tanstia FnF, VIT, Karunya Universities, NIPFP, and BDHC are said to have further shaped his public-oriented perspective. His career, spanning 29 years, reportedly involved contributions to 18 organisations and the successful execution of over 43 projects across 14 countries.

Lokesh Jasrai has PhD in is currently working as Professor in the Marketing Department at Lovely Professional University in Jalandhar, Punjab. With a focus on consumer behaviour and marketing strategy, The author's research portfolio encompasses a diverse range of topics including predicting opinion leadership based on demographics in the mobile telecom services sector, examining e-loyalty among female apparel shoppers in India, developing segmentation typologies for telecom service users using the motivated consumer innovativeness scale, and exploring consumer innovativeness for green consumer durables through factorial designs. With expertise in these areas, the author contributes valuable insights to academia and industry.

Firoj Kabir is an accomplished author, researcher, and Lecturer of the Department of 'Tourism and Hospitality Management' of Daffodil Institute of IT, Dhaka, Bangladesh, with a strong academic background in BBA and MBA majoring in Tourism and Hospitality Management from the University of Dhaka. His passion lies in exploring the intersection of travel and culture. His diverse areas of interest include archaeological tourism, sustainable tourism, and the unique characteristics of Generation Z travellers. Through extensive research and insightful writing, he sheds light on the intricate connections between historical sites, responsible tourism, and the evolving preferences of the next generation of travellers. His work not only enriches the field of tourism but also inspires readers to engage with the world around them in meaningful and responsible ways.

Prabhjeet Kaur is a Doctoral Research Scholar currently perusing PhD in Marketing Domain with Artificial Intelligence powered Customer Relationship Management from Lovely Professional University. The areas of other research are geography plate tectonic movements, E-STEM, higher education, and Morse code. She has already four Scopus-indexed chapter to her achievement from multi-aspects of research interest. In future, she aims to publish more multi-domain topic of interest that are relevant for both industrial and common community growth.

Neeraj Kaushik, PhD, is currently working as an Associate Professor and Head in the Department of Business Administration, National Institute of Technology, Kurukshetra, India. His interest areas are services marketing and research methodology. He has to his credit 60 articles published in Indian and international journals and conferences.

Rupam Konar is the Programme Director for the PhD in Hospitality and Tourism and MSc in Tourism at Taylor's University, Malaysia. He is a Senior Lecturer in the School of Hospitality, Tourism, and Events and serves as a Managing Editor for the Scopus-indexed *Asia Pacific Journal of Innovation in Hospitality and Tourism*. He is also an Associate Director at the Centre for Research and Innovation in Tourism and a Certified Microsoft Innovative Educator. His research focusses on service innovation, delivery, and design in hospitality, with numerous publications and successful research projects.

Manjit Kour has a PhD in Management from Punjab Technical University. Presently, she is working as Professor in the University School of Management, Chandigarh University, Punjab, India. Her specialisation is finance and marketing. Her areas of research interests include business ethics, online marketing, metaverse, corporate finance, and Fintech. She has authored two books and have published 43 research papers in quality journals including Web of Science, ABDC, Scopus, UGC-CARE list. She has presented numerous research papers in various national and international conferences. She is Innovation Ambassador with Ministry of Education, India and has delivered more than 30 expert talks in various seminars and workshops, she is on editorial board of *Journal of Commerce and Accounting* (ABDC-indexed journal). She is active reviewer in various Web of Science and Scopus-indexed journals as well.

Pankaj Kumar is currently working as an Assistant Professor in Faculty of Commerce and Management, United University, Prayagraj, Uttar Pradesh, India. He has completed his PhD in Finance from Faculty of Commerce, Banaras Hindu University and published number of research papers in ABDC and CARE-listed journals.

Sanjeev Kumar is a Professor cum HOD, School of Hotel Management and Tourism, Lovely Professional University, Punjab, India. He holds a Bachelor's degree in Hotel Management from Osmania University. He earned his Master's degree in Tourism Management from Madurai Kamaraj University and his Doctorate from Amity University Rajasthan. He has worked as a teacher for the past 18 years. While in Kuwait, he worked as an Assistant Dining Manager for Gulf Catering Company and other hotels. He has 20 research articles and has presented more than 12 papers at national and international conferences. He supervises six PhD research scholars and has directed many MBA and MSc research projects in hospitality and tourism. He has taken part in several FDPs and workshops. He also travelled throughout the country to attend international and national conferences.

Shweta Kumar, DEng, RGBSI Aerospace & Defense, United States of America, is the Managing member and Senior Technical Director at RGBSI Aerospace & Defense and demonstrates executive level leadership including technical and functional guidance to the team at a tactical and strategic level. She has more than 15 years of broad industry base experience within the automotive, aerospace, and heavy equipment manufacturer industries, implementing engineering and advanced manufacturing solutions for over 100 of RGBSI's Fortune 50/100/1000 customers. She also holds a patent for embedded feature development on hybrid electric vehicles for Chrysler.

Anchal Luthra is the Assistant Professor, AIBS, Amity University, Noida, India. She has done PhD, MBA in HR, MPhil, and MEd She carries rich 12 years' experience of industry, research, and academia. Her area of specialisation is human resource management, data analytics and research methodology. She has presented her research work at various national and international conferences and won two best paper awards along with best Teacher Award and Excellence in research award. She has published research paper in Scopus and ABDC listed journals and successfully delivered two industry consultation projects in the area of HR and is also engaged in academic consultation.

Priyakrushna Mohanty is an Assistant Professor in the Department of Business Administration (Tourism) at Christ University, Bengaluru, India. A former UGC Senior Research Fellow, he earned his PhD in Tourism Studies from Pondicherry University, where he also received the Travel Corporation (India) Gold Medal for academic excellence. In addition to a Master's in Tourism Studies, he holds a Master's in Finance and three PG Diplomas in Rural Development, Research Methodology, and Teaching Skills. With over 30 research papers published and 25 conference presentations, he has also served as an editor for books with leading publishers such as Routledge, Emerald, Springer, and CABI. His expertise spans tourism sustainability, e-tourism, events tourism, sustainable livelihoods, research methodology, and gender issues in tourism.

Hafijull Mondal, PhD Research Scholar, Department of Library and Information Science, Netaji Subhas Open University, Kolkata West Bengal, India, is currently working as Librarian in Elitte Institute of Engineering and Management, Sodepur, West Bengal, Kolkata, India. He has BA Honours (Geography), BLIS, MLIS, ADCA PGDLAN, UGC NET, WB SET Qualified for Assistant Professor. He is having 12 years of experience and 44+ Research Papers presented and published for different national and international journals, national and international seminars, conference, and book chapters. He attended 50+ workshops and webinars on related fields. He is working as a Reviewer in *International Journal of Research and Analytical Reviews* and reviewed a paper in Net Journal and Web of Science-Indexed journal. He is working as an Editor in International Publishers, a book series 'Futuristic Trends in Social Sciences'. He is a member of various professional bodies in India.

Aishwarya Nagarathinam specialises in Human Resource Management and Information Technology, with a Doctorate focussed on 'Mapping the Competency Matrix for Software Professionals in Bangalore'. She is an Assistant Professor at the School of Business and Management, Christ (Deemed-to-be University), Bangalore, where she coordinates the MBA programme and leads the Centre for Artificial Intelligence at the Bannerghatta Road campus. With over nine years of teaching experience, she has published in Scopus, Web of Science, and UGC-indexed journals and presented at national and international conferences. She has authored a book on *Competency Mapping* and contributed three chapters on *Artificial Intelligence*, *Submarine Cables*, and *Business Ethics*. Currently, she is involved in a women's hygiene project under the National Health Mission for the Government of Karnataka. Her research interests include competency mapping, strategic management, and business analytics, and she also provides soft skills training for students.

Kumari Neelam is currently pursuing her PhD in Finance from the Department of Commerce, Mahatma Gandhi Kashi Vidyapith, Varanasi, Uttar Pradesh, India. She has published a number of research papers in ABDC and peer-reviewed journals. Her research interests include corporate finance, financial markets, and investment strategies. Additionally, she has presented her work at various national and international conferences, receiving commendations for her contributions to the field.

Abhishek Kumar Pandey is an Assistant Professor in the Management Department of SMS Lucknow. He did his Doctoral work in Human Resource Management from the Department of Business Administration (LUMBA), University of Lucknow, in 2024. His thesis title was *Succession Management Practices in Corporate Firms in India*. He is also qualified for UGC-NET in management. He has an MBA in dual specialisation – HRM and Marketing – from AKTU, Lucknow. Before MBA, he completed a Bachelor of Science in Maths from the University of Gorakhpur.

Neethiahnanthan Ari Ragavan is the Executive Dean at Taylor's University, leading the Faculty of Hospitality, Food, and Leisure Management. With over two decades of experience in hospitality and tourism, he is a renowned expert in sustainable tourism and service quality management. Holding a PhD in Hospitality and Tourism, he has published extensively in top academic journals and presented at international conferences. Under his leadership, Taylor's University has gained global recognition in hospitality education. He is committed to advancing the field and mentoring future industry leaders.

Kavita Rani has a PhD in Management and presently she is working as Professor in University School of Management, Chandigarh University, Punjab, India. Her specialisation is human resource (HR) management and marketing. Her areas of research interests include HR, metaverse, HR analytics, and marketing analytics.

Premendra Sahu is an Associate Professor of Marketing at MATS University Raipur Chhattisgarh, India. He has a research and teaching experience of more than 15 years. His current research interest targets the analysis of the consumer behaviour of millennials in marketing. He has an expertise in the application of analytics in business, with a specific emphasis in marketing, sustainability, retailing, and e-commerce. He has used many statistical tools in his research including SPSS, Smart-PLS, Excel, and R.

Gopinath Sangaran is an accomplished academician, industry expert, and budding researcher. He is a Senior Lecturer at Taylor's University, Malaysia. His research areas include management, organisational behaviour, and hotel industry-related areas. He has published in Scopus-indexed journals. He is also a competition skills trainer and an international skills competition judge.

Animesh Kumar Sharma is a PhD Research Scholar at Mittal School of Business, Lovely Professional University, Phagwara, Punjab, India and working as

Manager – Marketing and Corporate Communication with Vatika Business Centres Private Limited (A Vatika Group Company), Gurugram, India. His research interest areas include digital marketing, social media marketing, search engine marketing, artificial intelligence, machine learning, data analytics, and the applications of technology in business.

Lekhika Sharma is currently working as a PhD Research Scholar at the Department of Business Administration, National Institute of Technology, Kurukshetra, India. She graduated in Commerce from Panjab University in 2018. She completed her Postgraduation in Commerce from Panjab University in 2020. Her area of interest includes consumer behaviour, immersive technologies, and technology adoption.

Rahul Sharma, Lovely Professional University, India, is a highly accomplished Professor of Marketing with over 14 years of experience in academia. He has a PhD in Marketing and has published over 15 articles in high-quality journals in the field. His research interests include consumer behaviour, business analytics, and digital marketing. In addition to his research, he is also a highly sought-after resource person in various faculty development programmes.

Vinita Sharma is associated with Amity International Business School, Amity University, Noida, India. She has more than two decades of experience in academia. Her areas of expertise include information technology and analytics, artificial intelligence and machine learning, Internet of Things, e-commerce, Big Data analytics, predictive analytics, Python, data visualisation, and business intelligence. She is an active researcher and resource person and has been instrumental in delivering expert lectures, technical workshops. Dr Sharma has published numerous research papers in refereed international journals and presented many papers in international conferences.

Anamica Singh is currently serving Amity University, Noida, India, as Assistant Professor in AIBS. She has a PhD in Management from Birla Institute of Technology, Mesra. Prior to PhD, her academic qualifications include Master of Business Administration from Indian Institute of Information Technology & Management, Gwalior and Bachelor of Technology in Information Technology from J.S.S. Academy of Technical Education, Noida. She comes with a rich industry experience of more than 10 years. She has an academic experience and her areas of expertise include various domains of information technology and management. She has presented various research papers in both national and international conferences. She bags paper publications in Scopus and SCI journals.

Pravin Chandra Singh is currently working as an Assistant Professor MSMSR, MATS University. Prior to MATS University, he was associated with Raffles University, Rajasthan, India. He has done his Doctorate from IM-BHU in Marketing. He has published several research papers in journals of repute like IIM-S, PBRI, etc. He has also participated and published papers in national and international conferences like ISDSI sponsored by IIM-N, ICTSGS-Japan, and Hagia Sophia international conference-Turkey.

Sujay Vikram Singh is a Senior Research Fellow currently pursuing a Doctorate at Banaras Hindu University. He graduated and postgraduated from IHM Lucknow. His research interests include hospitality, CRM, service marketing, service quality, and systematic literature reviews. He has published papers in various handbooks and journals. His recent journal publications include the *International Journal of Market Research* (Sage Publishing) [ABDC-A, Scopus] and the *Journal of Global Information Management* (IGI Publishing) [Scopus, ABDC-A]. He has also been a reviewer for tourism and management journals and has presented and published papers at various national and international conferences and seminars. He has received best paper awards at several conferences, including those held at IHM Bhopal, Subharati University, and Delhi University (https://orcid.org/0000-0002-7113-2698).

Vishal Kumar Singh is working as Assistant Professor, School of Management Science (SMS Varanasi) and completed PhD from Institute of Management Studies, Banaras Hindu University, Varanasi, India. He published the research papers in Scopus, Web of Science, UGC-CARE listed journals, and peer-reviewed journals. He also attended various national and international conferences.

Mohammad Badruddoza Talukder is an Associate Professor, College of Tourism and Hospitality Management, International University of Business Agriculture and Technology, Dhaka, Bangladesh. He completed his PhD in Hotel Management at the School of Hotel Management and Tourism, Lovely Professional University, India. He holds a Bachelor's and a Master's degree in Hotel Management from India. He has been teaching various courses in the Department of Tourism and Hospitality at different universities in Bangladesh since 2008. His research areas include tourism management, hotel management, hospitality management, food and beverage management, and accommodation management, where he has published research papers in well-known journals in Bangladesh and abroad. He is one of the certified trainers from Bangladesh for the Food and Beverage Service Department of the SIEP Project. He became an Honorary Facilitator at Bangladesh Tourism Board's Bangabandhu International Tourism and Hospitality Training Institute.

Rajesh Verma is a Professor and Sr Dean at Mittal School of Business, LPU, overseeing its academic and administrative functions. He holds a PhD in Marketing from Himachal Pradesh University, an MBA from Utkal University, and an Executive Programme in Data-driven Product Management from IIM Lucknow, India. With over 20 years of experience in teaching, research, and consulting, he specialises in business models, strategic management, and political marketing. He has published over 60 research papers, 20 case studies, and 10 books, while guiding several PhD and MPhil students. As an active speaker at national and international conferences, he has conducted numerous executive development programmes for industry and have visited countries like the United Kingdom, Spain, Portugal, Dubai, Nigeria, and Sri Lanka for academic assignments. He is also a recipient of multiple awards, including the UGC Junior Research Fellowship and different grants from UKIERI, ICSSR, DST, etc.

Chen Weimei is currently pursuing a PhD degree in Hospitality and Tourism Management at Taylor's University, where her research interests include the direction of artificial intelligence (AI) in the hospitality industry and the direction of service. As an active PhD student, she has published one article in an international journal and has been invited to participate in several international symposiums. Her research not only delves into cutting-edge topics in the hospitality and tourism industry, but also provides valuable insights into AI and service enhancement in the industry.

Minu Zachariah, PhD, has around 25 years of professional and academic experience in human resource management. She is currently working as Professor at B.M.S. College of Engineering, MBA Department. She has completed PhD in Management from Visvesvaraya Technological University. She has published research papers in reputed national and international journals and is passionate about writing academic cases and book chapters. She was the resource person for FDPs, MDPs for MSMEs, and various other training programmes. She is associated with various autonomous institutions such as BOS and BOE. She upgrades her skills on a continuous basis.

Chapter 1

MetaMinds and Digital Realms: Deciphering Gen Z Consumer Behavior in Metaverse Marketing

Priyakrushna Mohanty, Aarthy Chellasamy and Aishwarya Nagarathinam

Department of Business and Management, Christ (Deemed to be University), Bengaluru, India

Abstract

This conceptual research paper explores the innovative convergence of virtual reality (VR), augmented reality (AR), and digital spaces as it dives into the complex dynamics of Gen Z consumer behavior within the metaverse. Businesses and scholars alike face hurdles in comprehending the complex preferences, motives, and decision-making processes of this generation of digital natives, as traditional marketing tactics undergo a metamorphosis in the aftermath of the metaverse. Understanding the nuances of Gen Z's interactions in this immersive digital world is crucial for businesses looking to connect and engage with this significant consumer generation as the metaverse becomes an increasingly important part of everyday life. Thus, this study also attempts to understand the awareness about metaverse among Gen Z and the challenges faced during the act of purchase in a meta environment.

Keywords: Metaverse; Gen Z; consumer behavior; metaverse marketing; virtual reality; augmented reality

The AI Metaverse Revolution: Transforming Multi-Business Scenarios (Volume 1), 1–13

Published under exclusive licence by Emerald Publishing Limited
doi:10.1108/978-1-83662-582-720251001

Introduction

Extended reality (XR) includes VR, AR, and mixed reality (MR) (Milgram et al., 1995). In XR, humans observe and communicate in full or partial digital environments constructed by technology (Mystakidis, 2022). With the help of multimedia and interactive technologies like XR, MR, AR, and VR integrating with avatars, platforms like Second life, Converse, Mine craft, and Roblox have become very popular. Metaverse is a new paradigm which involves the amalgamation of technology, with an interactive immersive virtual experience which has unlimited number of users (Ball, 2022; Dwivedi et al., 2022). Contribution of Meta to business, society, and individual users is still unexplored, and this buzz has forced organizations to assess the potential usage of meta to enhance customer experience, engagement, and interaction (Dwivedi et al., 2023; Shen et al., 2021). With the advent of the metaverse, people's interactions with the virtual world have undergone a paradigm change in the ever-changing field of digital technology. Gen Z, a new generation of consumers, is leading the charge in defining and molding this revolutionary period as society grows more interconnected through digital platforms. MetaMinds – a phrase designed to capture this generation's cognitive prowess and technological dexterity – move through the digital spaces of the metaverse with ease, upending conventional wisdom about consumer behavior and marketing tactics.

A work by Choi and Choi (2020) has stated that immersive technology will provide realistic shopping experiences and utility value offering unique marketing opportunities. McKinsey Report has stated that virtual product sales through avatar have reached $54 billion market value and predicted the potential benefits brands can gain through this immersive experience. Forever 21 has sold virtual beanies through Roblox and Gucci sold a bag which surpassed the value of a physical bag. Use cases are widespread in new immersive retail, entertainment, sports, and educational experiences. Less talked about applications include virtual employee training and team collaboration with avatars, virtual prototyping, and display of products. The South Korea Government has experimented with virtual Seoul Town and the Mayor Office. Virtual goods economy accounts for 40% of global gaming revenue, and in the future rise of crypto currencies, many intend to create a crypto wallet in a meta environment. On the other side, brands such as Adidas, Nike, Coca-Cola, Louis Vuitton, and Lamborghini have also launched NFT (non-fungible tokens) for self-monetizing and generating another revenue stream (Gautam, 2022). Purchases of digital goods are already in place for ordering a pizza in *de-centrland* for deliveries of actual pizza in the real world. Businesses can acquire insights into successful metaverse marketing tactics by bridging the gap between theoretical ideas and real-world applications, assuring relevancy and resonance with Generation Z's MetaMinds (Wider et al., 2023). Deciphering the nuances of this digital frontier is not only a scholarly endeavor but also a strategic imperative for businesses navigating the changing 21st-century landscape, as society go deeper into our exploration of the metaverse and its profound implications on consumer behavior.

Consequently, Gen Z consumers are considered to be more familiar with virtual worlds, transactions, and goods than previous generations, which are proven evidence from 67% of Roblox users and are under the age group of 16, a whole new generation of meta natives. On the other hand, people still question whether this is a fairytale and will it come true? Hazan et al. (2022) have stated that the metaverse in marketing is highly experimental and may throw unique challenges to marketers. This conceptual research paper explores the innovative convergence of VR, AR, and digital spaces as it dives into the complex dynamics of Gen Z consumer behavior within the metaverse. Businesses and scholars alike face hurdles in comprehending the complex preferences, motives, and decision-making processes of this generation of digital natives, as traditional marketing tactics undergo a metamorphosis in the aftermath of the metaverse. Understanding the nuances of Gen Z's interactions in this immersive digital world is crucial for businesses looking to connect and engage with this significant consumer generation as the metaverse becomes an increasingly important part of everyday life (Gupta, 2023). Thus, this study also attempts to understand the awareness about metaverse among Gen Z and the challenges faced during the act of purchase in a meta environment.

Methodology

With the use of this thematic content analysis methodology, the study aims to provide a theoretical framework for comprehending the intricate interactions between Generation Z consumer behavior and metaverse marketing by extracting important insights from the corpus of existing literature. By using this strategy, we hope to further the current scholarly conversation and offer practical advice to companies attempting to navigate the dynamic field of digital marketing in the metaverse.

In the initial stage, the authors conducted a thorough search of academic journals, research papers, and other publications about the purchasing habits of Generation Z and metaverse marketing. Several popular academic databases, such as Web of Science, Scopus, and Google Scholar, were searched. To make sure that relevant material was included, keywords like "Generation Z," OR "Gen Z," "Metaverse," "Consumer Behaviour," and "Digital Marketing" were used. A collection of inclusion and exclusion criteria was developed in order to preserve the validity and dependability of the literature chosen for study. It was mandatory for the sources to be published in scholarly books, conference proceedings, or peer-reviewed journals. In order to account for the most current advancements in the metaverse and the purchasing habits of Generation Z, the inclusion period was extended to encompass the previous 10 years.

A systematic extraction process was used to gather pertinent data from the chosen literature, with an emphasis on important themes, ideas, and conclusions on Generation Z consumer behavior in the metaverse. Each source's abstract, methodology, findings, and discussions were carefully examined as part of this process. The retrieved data were categorized into main themes and sub-themes using a thematic coding technique. This required going through the literature methodically to find trends, recurrent ideas, and important discoveries. To guarantee accuracy and dependability, themes were discussed within the research team and iteratively developed and validated.

Following that, the synthesized concepts were explained in relation to Generation Z customer behavior and metaverse marketing. This step entailed presenting a thorough summary of the current academic discourse on the topic, identifying underlying trends, and making links across subjects. Strict quality assessment procedures were put in place to guarantee the legitimacy and dependability of the chosen literature. The analysis contained only academically credible, peer-reviewed sources.

Awareness About Metaverse Among Gen Z

According to the 2022 metaverse study, "New Realities: Into the Metaverse and Beyond," which gathered data from more than 3,000 people in the USA, UK, and China aged 16–65, the awareness of the metaverse has more than doubled in a year. Gen Z, the digital natives, who were reared on social media and have always had the world at their fingertips, are best positioned to understand the metaverse since they currently use it and will surely influence how it develops. According to Gartner, Inc., 25% of people will use the metaverse for work, shopping, and other activities at least once a day by 2026. Ipsos collaborated with Nokia to conduct a study on "Gen Z and Metaverse," and the results show that Gen Z are in metaverse for reasons such as virtual experiences, social bonding, status, and the possibility of investing in newer technologies (The Virtual Frontier: Gen Z and the Metaverse, 2022).

Born approximately around the mid-1990s and early 2010s, Generation Z has experienced a world dominated by digital technology. In contrast to earlier generations, they are naturally at ease interacting with social media, navigating online environments, and keeping up with the quickly advancing state of technology. Their innate ability to navigate the digital world places them in a pivotal role in the acceptance and development of the metaverse. Generation Z's exposure to social media platforms is often linked to their awareness of the metaverse (Lamba & Malik, 2022). Social media sites such as YouTube, Instagram, and TikTok are often used to post content about metaverse technology, virtual worlds, and virtual experiences. Their perspectives and understanding of the metaverse are shaped by this experience, which acts as an introduction.

In a study conducted by Vice Media group, 1,000 gamers across Gen Z were surveyed, over which more over half (52%) of Gen Z gamers say they want to make money in the metaverse, and one-third say they want to start careers there, indicating that the age group has higher goals related to these online areas. Over the next five years, 20% of people intend to spend their "fun" budgets, which are set aside for entertainment and leisure, on in-game purchases, with an average annual expenditure of $50 (The Metaverse: Gen Z insights, 2022). Gen Z is excited about the metaverse's potential, especially the chance to interact with others and have fun through wholly virtual experiences, but they are also worried about how it will affect society in the future and how social inequality will prevent the metaverse from being accessible to everyone (Aiello et al., 2022).

The way that Generation Z perceives the metaverse is also greatly influenced by the educational system. A more knowledgeable and technologically adept generation is produced by educational institutions that integrate metaverse conversations, immersive technologies, and virtual learning environments (Tlili et al., 2022). Students are exposed to concepts relating to virtual worlds more and more as curricula change to reflect the digital age (Al-Adwan et al., 2023). The exploration of VRs and parallel dimensions in films, TV series, and books has led to a rise in the popularity of the metaverse in popular culture. Generation Z's knowledge is shaped by cultural influences and media portrayals that offer a variety of viewpoints on the metaverse, from dismal cautionary tales to utopian ideals. Furthermore, the possibility for social interaction and connectivity within the metaverse is consistent with Generation Z's inclination toward digital communication and virtual communities (Longo & Faraci, 2023). A natural interest in the metaverse is fostered by virtual environments that enable socializing, collaboration, and shared experiences, which connect with the social dynamics already present in their life.

The Factors Influencing Purchase Behavior in Gen Z Through Metaverse

Theory of planned behavior (Ajzen, 1991) states that consumer behavior intention is determined by attitude, subjective norms, and perceived behavior control. So, consumer purchase behavior heavily depends on predefined positive or negative attitudes toward virtual products in a meta environment. Purchase behavior in meta is also influenced by the perception that is set by early users (e.g., purchase through meta is tedious, risky) (Bleize & Antheunis, 2019). Perceived ease of use and usefulness also determine the consumer purchase behavior. Technology acceptance model proposed by Davis (1989) holds good for marketing as well. Venkatesh et al. (2003) proposed Unified Theory of Acceptance and Use of Technology model which supports performance, effort expectancy, and social influence shapes behavior intention. Flow theory (Domina et al., 2012) states that perceived enjoyment, control, and concentration are the factors determining the intense focus a user has toward an activity. Consumer purchases get completely immersed in activity where they are unaware of things happening around them. So, in virtual world, consumers are carried away and end up buying. Bleize and Antheunis (2019) have four influential factors: perceived enjoyment, social influence, customization, and ease of use that support customer purchase intention in the virtual world.

Keeping the above theories in mind, it can be deciphered that metaverse offers a vibrant and imaginative environment that profoundly affects Generation Z's purchasing habits. Companies who comprehend and adjust to the distinct elements influencing business in the metaverse stand a good chance of building deep relationships with this market (Longo & Faraci, 2023). The metaverse has a multitude of options for businesses to engage with Generation Z consumers in ways that are consistent with their tastes, beliefs, and digital lives. These opportunities range from immersive experiences to personalized interactions and ethical issues (Alfiras et al., 2023). Understanding and taking advantage of these elements will be essential for brands looking to prosper in this new realm of customer interaction as the metaverse develops.

The *immersive and interactive purchasing experiences* provided by the metaverse go beyond the constraints of conventional e-commerce (Baía Reis & Ashmore, 2022). Gen Z is lured to virtual shops, showrooms, and events in the metaverse that offer a more personalized and interesting buying experience because they are enthusiastic users of cutting-edge digital activities. Virtual try-ons and fittings are made possible by AR technology in the metaverse, giving Generation Z the ability to see things in real time before making a purchase. Their trust in the products they choose is increased, and the ambiguity around virtual transactions is decreased, thanks to this engaging and useful approach to online buying. Furthermore, *authenticity and individual expression* are important to Generation Z (Fontana, 2023). People can create and present their digital personas in the metaverse, which affects their purchase decisions. Brands have a greater chance of gaining Generation Z's interest and allegiance if they reflect their values and esthetic preferences in their digital personas. Also, Generation Z can be drawn in by brands that use storytelling and immersive narratives in the metaverse well (Della Sala, 2023). Their emotional connection to a brand can be influenced, which, in turn, can affect their choice to buy if brands can craft engaging tales and experiences that go beyond conventional advertising techniques.

The *creation of communities and social interactions* is facilitated by the metaverse. Community involvement and peer recommendations are highly valued by Generation Z (Oh et al., 2023). Their purchasing decisions are greatly influenced by social influence in virtual places, such as shared shopping experiences and real-time interactions. In addition, the younger generation, Generation Z, is becoming more aware of ethical and sustainable behavior. Environmentally concerned Gen Z customers are inclined to connect with brands that integrate these values into their virtual commerce strategies, such as programs or products that are eco-friendly in virtual form.

Generation Z is inclined toward gaming; therefore, gamification features like virtual currency, challenges, and prizes within the metaverse appeal to their gaming sensibilities (Belk et al., 2022). Gamification of the shopping experience can increase engagement and encourage specific kinds of behavior. The metaverse presents innovative payment methods, such as blockchain-based transactions and virtual currencies. Because they are frequently among the first to adopt new technology, Generation Z might be more likely to make purchases in the metaverse if they believe the payment options are convenient, safe, and in accordance with their tastes.

An important factor in customizing Generation Z's metaverse buying experience is artificial intelligence (AI). AI-powered algorithms are able to examine user preferences, behaviors, and interactions in order to generate personalized suggestions that improve product relevancy and have an impact on purchasing decisions.

Finally, exclusivity and distinctiveness are valued by Generation Z. Exclusive and limited-edition virtual goods that are accessible within the metaverse can engender a sense of urgency and scarcity that encourages users to make purchases in an effort to obtain desirable and uncommon digital goods.

Challenges Faced by Gen Z While Interacting in Metaverse

Though metaverse comes with abundant opportunities for markets, the challenges posed are also novel. The interface should be user friendly and brands and meta platforms should address infrastructural and technical issues. New technology will always come with threats to data security where customers may hesitate to adopt new technology where it becomes vital for brands to create awareness and trust among consumers. Pospiech (2022) stated that the affordability and accessibility of AR and VR accessories might be a hindrance for user participation and experience which set back brands. Sociocultural issues are also to be considered before brands think about meta in full swing. Also, brands should ensure customer willingness to check whether they are personally equipped with resources and skill set to sail through a meta environment. Content, customer engagement, and media dependency also keep changing when there is a change in platform; this becomes another challenge for marketers. Conventional media strategies may not match with 3D world communication strategies and coexisting in the meta environment is a huge challenge apart from regulatory policies and ethical conduct.

Security Issues Faced Metaverse

Implementing cybersecurity measures in the metaverse might be a huge problem as it is a new technology with a lot of uncertainty. There are risks such as lack of regulations, lack of knowledge about cybersecurity best practices, data collection, and the like (Di Pietro & Cresci, 2021). As no help or support is available in metaverse, NFT theft is bound to happen. User's identities can also be stolen and their avatars can be hacked. Similar to the metaverse, darkverse is on the rise, which is more dangerous than the dark web. Instead of being solely online open discussion threads like in dark web criminal forums, it simulates covert physical meetings. Financial fraud could be another common thing in the metaverse. Because of the massive amount of e-commerce that will take place in these worlds, criminals and criminal organizations will be lured to the metaverse. There will be many people trying to rip off users, steal their money, and seize their digital assets (Chukwunonso et al., 2022). The metaverse is expected to produce a large amount of data, which is fed into it from the real world by means of wearable sensors and other smart devices. These data may include both sensitive information that should always be kept private and very basic information about the user and their environment. The majority of applications employ third-party libraries, which may or may not have access to user-generated data. As a result, it is crucial to understand what the owners of these libraries do with these data and how they store it (Chukwunonso et al., 2022).

The concept of the metaverse has been gaining popularity in recent years, with many people excited about the possibilities it offers. However, with new opportunities come new challenges, and Gen Z is likely to face some significant obstacles as they navigate this digital world. One of the most pressing challenges that Gen Z is likely to face in the metaverse is digital addiction (Bojic, 2022). With the abundance of options for entertainment and engagement, it is easy to get lost in the virtual world, leading to negative impacts on mental and physical health, social skills, and productivity. Another challenge is the issue of cyberbullying. Online harassment, trolling, and hate speech can be just as damaging as in-person bullying, and Gen Z may need to develop strategies for dealing with these issues in the metaverse. Privacy and security concerns are also significant challenges that Gen Z is likely to face in the metaverse (Chang et al., 2022). With so much personal information being collected, users will need to be extra vigilant about protecting their data and taking steps to ensure their safety online.

Economic inequality is another issue that could become a challenge for Gen Z in the metaverse. While the metaverse offers many opportunities for entrepreneurship and wealth creation, access to these opportunities may not be equal, and some Gen Z may be left behind due to economic disparities, lack of resources, or technical skills (Allam et al., 2022). Virtual versus real-world identity is another area of concern for Gen Z in the metaverse. Creating a digital persona that is different from their real-world identity can be confusing and could lead to conflicts. It may be challenging for Gen Z to maintain a balance between virtual and real-world identities, especially as the lines between the two become increasingly blurred.

Finally, the lack of human connection is another challenge that Gen Z may face in the metaverse. While the metaverse offers new ways to connect and collaborate with people from all over the world, it may also lead to a sense of disconnection from the physical world and in-person interactions. The challenges faced by Gen Z in the metaverse are significant, and they will need to develop strategies to navigate this digital world successfully. From digital addiction to economic inequality, privacy concerns, and virtual versus real-world identity, these challenges will require careful consideration and planning to ensure that Gen Z can thrive in the metaverse.

Future Prospects

As a rapidly evolving digital space, metaverse intertwines virtual and physical realities and holds immense potential for shaping the future landscape of consumer behavior. Generation Z, the first generation to grow up fully immersed in digital technologies, is positioned at the forefront of this transformative shift (Burstein, 2013). This section of the article explores the future prospects of Generation Z consumer behavior within the metaverse, examining emerging trends, potential developments, and the implications for businesses and marketers.

As a variety of platforms that cater to various interests and specializations arise, the metaverse is predicted to experience tremendous expansion. It is probable that Generation Z will participate in a variety of metaverse environments, ranging from education and professional networking to gaming and leisure, each of which will have a distinct effect on their purchasing habits (Periyasami & Periyasamy, 2022). Immersion experiences will be increasingly skillfully integrated into the metaverse as AR and VR technology develop. Due to their penchant for cutting-edge digital experiences, Generation Z is expected to adopt AR and VR for social media, entertainment, and commerce, which will further impact their purchasing choices (George et al., 2021).

The metaverse's social commerce is going to play a major role in how Generation Z purchases products. Because Gen Z wants more participatory and community-driven retail experiences, virtual events, influencer marketing, and social interactions within digital spaces will be important factors in influencing purchasing decisions (Kouchih & Mataa, 2023). To draw in Generation Z customers, businesses will need to implement cutting-edge metaverse marketing techniques. This tech-savvy population is likely to be engaged best by immersive brand experiences, gamified and interactive marketing efforts, and partnerships with virtual influencers.

It is anticipated that the metaverse will completely redefine fashion, as Generation Z discovers and embraces virtual identities and digital fashion. Gen Z's perception of and interaction with fashion brands will be impacted by the virtual apparel, accessories, and customization choices available in digital arenas. Gen Z's metaverse experience will be mostly customized thanks to AI-driven personalization. In order to deliver highly personalized recommendations that influence purchase decisions by presenting goods and experiences that align with individual interests, sophisticated algorithms will examine user behavior, preferences, and interactions.

The integration of decentralized finance within the metaverse will introduce new economic models and virtual currencies. Generation Z, accustomed to digital transactions, may actively participate in virtual economies, leading to new considerations for businesses in terms of payment methods and financial transactions within the metaverse (Far et al., 2023).

It is conceivable that the metaverse will play a crucial role in professional growth, training, and education. Generation Z's tastes for professional and educational services may be influenced by their participation in online seminars, networking events, and virtual classrooms within the metaverse, as they pursue ongoing education and skill development.

The increased consciousness of social and environmental issues among Generation Z will permeate the metaverse. Gen Z consumers, who place a high value on ethics, may become more loyal and preferential customers to brands that integrate sustainable and socially responsible activities in virtual environments (Zhang et al., 2023). Generation Z may voice worries about privacy, digital well-being, and the possible drawbacks of prolonged virtual interactions as they become more immersed in the metaverse. Brands that put an emphasis on user control, transparency, and digital wellness features would have an easier time appealing to Gen Z's conscientious consumer tastes.

Conclusion

A new era of consumer engagement is being ushered in by the metaverse, where immersive experiences, virtual try-before-you-buy features, social dynamics, decentralized commerce, personalization, and cutting-edge e-commerce platforms all influence consumers' purchase decisions. Businesses need to change with the times and take advantage of the metaverse's ability to redefine consumer behavior and improve the entire retail experience as this game-changing technology continues to advance. The metaverse, where the lines between the real and virtual worlds are blurred and there are countless opportunities for user exploration and engagement, is where purchasing decisions will be made in the future.

The growing inclination of Gen Z to fully immerse themselves in the metaverse signifies a significant change in the way this generation views and interacts with digital environments. Born into a world where technology is already advancing at a rapid pace, there are a number of social, cultural, and technological reasons why Gen Z is so fascinated with the metaverse. A key factor influencing Gen Z's fascination with the metaverse is their innate ease and competence with technology (Lee et al., 2023). Because Gen Z was raised in a time where social media, cellphones, and instant connectivity were the norm, they have a special digital fluency that makes them more likely to investigate and accept cutting-edge innovations like the metaverse. Gen Z's expectations of a dynamic and participatory digital experience are beautifully aligned with the metaverse's seamless integration of virtual and AR.

Gen Z finds the metaverse to be appealing in more socially connected ways than just technology. In a society when friends and family are separated by physical distances, the metaverse provides a virtual environment where relationships can grow and overcome geographic limitations. The capacity to connect, communicate, and share experiences in a way that mimics the intimacy of in-person relationships is what makes it so alluring. Gen Z finds a sense of community building, self-expression, and creativity in virtual social spaces, which connects with their interconnected worldview and gives them a feel of belongingness.

However, concerns about digital overload and well-being, increased risks of privacy and security breaches, unequal access and connectivity, misinformation and content authenticity issues, pressures related to identity and self-image, the persistence of cyberbullying and online harassment, potential economic disparities in emerging virtual economies, the risk of technology addiction and distraction, uncertainties surrounding the lack of regulation and standards, and the ongoing need to adapt to rapid technological changes are just a few of the many challenges that Generation Z must overcome while navigating the metaverse. These difficulties draw attention to the intricate web of social, ethical, and technological considerations that members of Generation Z must manage as they actively engage with and influence the metaverse's changing environment.

Finally, metaverse offers a dynamic panorama of opportunities and challenges for the future of Generation Z. Generation Z is anticipated to participate in a variety of virtual platforms as the metaverse grows, impacting the development of immersive experiences and social commerce. Consumer behavior may be altered by combining cutting-edge technologies like augmented and VR with creative marketing techniques. But issues with digital health, privacy, and possible access disparities need to be addressed. Participation in virtual markets, digital fashion expression, and personalized encounters are all made possible by the metaverse. It also makes us think about ethical behavior, sustainability, and the necessity of flexible learning environments for professionals and educators. Businesses and policymakers must embrace innovation in order to navigate these opportunities while solving the complex challenges.

References

Aiello, C., Bai, J., Schmidt, J., & Vilchynskyi, Y. (2022). *Probing reality and myth in the metaverse*. McKinsey & Company. https://www.mckinsey.com/industries/retail/our-insights/probing-reality-and-myth-in-the-metaverse

Ajzen, I. (1991). The theory of planned behavior. *Organizational Behavior and Human Decision Processes*, *50*, 179–211. https://doi.org/10.1016/0749-5978(91)90020-T

Al-Adwan, A. S., Li, N., Al-Adwan, A., Abbasi, G. A., Albelbisi, N. A., & Habibi, A. (2023). Extending the technology acceptance model (TAM) to predict university students' intentions to use metaverse-based learning platforms. *Education and Information Technologies*, *28*(11), 15381–15413. https://doi.org/10.1007/s10639-023-11816-3

Alfiras, M., Bojiah, J., Mohammed, M. N., Ibrahim, F. M., Ahmed, H. M., & Abdullah, O. I. (2023). Powered education based on metaverse: Pre- and post-COVID comprehensive review. *Open Engineering*, *13*(1). https://doi.org/10.1515/eng-2022-0476

Allam, Z., Sharifi, A., Bibri, S. E., Jones, D. S., & Krogstie, J. (2022). The metaverse as a virtual form of smart cities: Opportunities and challenges for environmental, economic, and social sustainability in urban futures. *Smart Cities*, *5*, 771–801. https://doi.org/10.3390/smartcities5030040

Baía Reis, A., & Ashmore, M. (2022). From video streaming to virtual reality worlds: An academic, reflective, and creative study on live theatre and performance in the metaverse. *International Journal of Performance Arts and Digital Media*, *18*(1), 7–28. https://doi.org/10.1080/14794713.2021.2024398

Ball, M. (2022). *The metaverse: And how it will revolutionize everything*. National Geographic Books.

Belk, R., Humayun, M., & Brouard, M. (2022). Money, possessions, and ownership in the Metaverse: NFTs, cryptocurrencies, Web3 and Wild Markets. *Journal of Business Research*, *153*, 198–205. https://doi.org/10.1016/j.jbusres.2022.08.031

Bleize, D. N. M., & Antheunis, M. L. (2019). Factors influencing purchase intent in virtual worlds: A review of the literature. *Journal of Marketing Communications*, *25*(4), 403–420. https://doi.org/10.1080/13527266.2016.1278028

Bojic, L. (2022). Metaverse through the prism of power and addiction: What will happen when the virtual world becomes more attractive than reality? *European Journal of Futures Research*, *10*. https://doi.org/10.1186/s40309-022-00208-4

Burstein, D. D. (2013). *Fast future: How the millennial generation is shaping our world*. Beacon Press.

Chang, L., Zhang, Z., Li, P., Xi, S., Guo, W., Shen, Y., Xiong, Z., Kang, J., Niyato, D., Qiao, X., & Wu, Y. (2022). 6G-enabled edge AI for metaverse: Challenges, methods, and future research directions. *Journal of Communications and Information Networks*, *7*(2), 107–121.

Choi, U., & Choi, B. (2020). The effect of augmented reality on consumer learning for search and experience products in mobile commerce. *Cyberpsychology, Behavior and Social Networking*, *23*, 800–805.

Chukwunonso, A. G., Njoku, J. N., Lee, J. M., & Kim, D.-S. (2022). Security in metaverse: A closer look. *Institutes of Communications and Information Sciences*, *10*.

Davis, F. D. (1989). Perceived usefulness, perceived ease of use, and user acceptance of Information Technology. *MIS Quarterly*, *13*, 319–340.

Della Sala, I. (2023). *Mapping the metaverse: Interdisciplinary insights and experimental studies into its implications in the development of attitudes, emotions and behaviors towards high-end fashion products* [Master's degree thesis, Luiss Guido Carli]. http://tesi.luiss.it/37240/

Di Pietro, R., & Cresci, S. (2021). Metaverse: Security and privacy issues. *Metaverse for Industry*, *2*, 281–288.

Domina, T., Lee, S.-E., & MacGillivray, M. (2012). Understanding factors affecting consumer intention to shop in a virtual world. *Journal of Retailing and Consumer Services*, *19*(6), 613–620. https://doi.org/10.1016/j.jretconser.2012.08.001

Dwivedi, Y. K., Hughes, L., Baabdullah, A. M., Ribeiro-Navarrete, S., Giannakis, M., Al-Debei, M. M., Dennehy, D., Metri, B., Buhalis, D., Cheung, C. M. K., Conboy, K., Doyle, R., Dubey, R., Dutot, V., Felix, R., Goyal, D. P., Gustafsson, A., Hinsch, C., Jebabli, I., … Wamba, S. F. (2022). Metaverse beyond the hype: Multidisciplinary perspectives on emerging challenges, opportunities, and agenda for research, practice and policy. *International Journal of Information Management*, *66*. https://doi.org/10.1016/j.ijinfomgt.2022.102542

Dwivedi, Y. K., Hughes, L., Wang, Y., Alalwan, A. A., Ahn, S. J. (Grace), Balakrishnan, J., Barta, S., Belk, R., Buhalis, D., Dutot, V., Felix, R., Filieri, R., Flavián, C., Gustafsson, A., Hinsch, C., Hollensen, S., Jain, V., Kim, J., Krishen, A. S., … Wirtz, J. (2023). Metaverse marketing: How the metaverse will shape the future of consumer research and practice. *Psychology and Marketing*, *40*(4), 750–776. https://doi.org/10.1002/mar.21767

Far, S. B., Rad, A. I., & Asaar, M. R. (2023). Blockchain and its derived technologies shape the future generation of digital businesses: A focus on decentralized finance and the metaverse. *Data Science and Management*, *6*(3), 183–197.

Fontana, F. (2023). The evolution of the flagship store. Re-defining the design of commercial spaces for fashion. *ZoneModa Journal*, *13*(1S), 35–47.

Gautam, V. (2022, November 23). *10 big brands that have dipped their toes into the NFT world.* https://www.indiatimes.com/worth/investment/brands-that-have-entered-nftworld

George, A. H., Fernando, M., George, A. S., Baskar, T., & Pandey, D. (2021). Metaverse: The next stage of human culture and the internet. *International Journal of Advanced Research Trends in Engineering and Technology (IJARTET)*, *8*(12), 1–10.

Gupta, P. (2023). Understanding consumer behavior in virtual ecosystems: Adoption of immersive technologies in metaverse among consumers. In P. Keikhosrokiani (Ed.), *Handbook of research on consumer behavioral analytics in metaverse and the adoption of a virtual world* (pp. 130–152). IGI Global.

Hazan, E., Kelly, G., Khan, H., Spillecke, D., & Yee, L. (2022). *Marketing in the metaverse: An opportunity for innovation and experimentation* (0047-5394).

Kouchih, A., & Mataa, H. (2023). The potential of influencer marketing in the emerging metaverse. In R. Bansal, S. A. Qalati, & A. Chakir (Eds.), *Influencer marketing applications within the metaverse* (pp. 57–77). IGI Global.

Lamba, S. S., & Malik, R. (2022). Into the metaverse: Marketing to Gen Z consumers. In D. Bathla & A. Singh (Eds.), *Applying metalytics to measure customer experience in the metaverse* (pp. 92–98). IGI Global.

Lee, Y.-C., Nguyen, M. N., & Yang, Q. (2023). Factors influencing Vietnamese generation MZ's adoption of metaverse platforms. *Sustainability*, *15*, 14940. https://doi.org/10.3390/su152014940

Longo, M. C., & Faraci, R. (2023). Next-generation museum: A metaverse journey into the culture. *Sinergie Italian Journal of Management*, *41*(1), 147–176.

Milgram, P., Takemura, H., Utsumi, A., & Kishino, F. (1995). Augmented reality: A class of displays on the reality-virtuality continuum. *SPIE Proceedings*, 282–292. https://doi.org/10.1117/12.197321

Mystakidis, S. (2022). Metaverse. *Encyclopedia*, *2*(1), 486–497. https://doi.org/10.3390/encyclopedia2010031

Oh, H. J., Kim, J., Chang, J. J. C., Park, N., & Lee, S. (2023). Social benefits of living in the metaverse: The relationships among social presence, supportive interaction, social self-efficacy, and feelings of loneliness. *Computers in Human Behavior*, *139*, 107498. https://doi.org/10.1016/j.chb.2022.107498

Periyasami, S., & Periyasamy, A. P. (2022). Metaverse as future promising platform business model: Case study on fashion value chain. *Businesses*, *2*(4), 527–545.

Pospiech, L. (2022). 10 Metaverse marketing challenges for affiliate marketers and brands. Retrieved 19 August 2022, from https://zeropark.com/blog/metaverse-marketing-challenges/

Report, the Virtual Frontier. (2022, December 12). *GEN z and the metaverse*. https://www.ipsos.com/sites/default/files/ct/publication/documents/2022-09/nokia-the-virtual-frontier-gen-z-and-the-metaverse-2022.pdf

Shen, B., Tan, W., Guo, J., Zhao, L., & Qin, P. (2021). How to promote user purchase in the metaverse? A systematic literature review on consumer behavior research and virtual commerce application design. *Applied Sciences*, *11*, 11087. https://doi.org/10.3390/app112311087

The Metaverse: Gen Z Insights. (2022). https://www.razorfish.com/articles/perspectives/razorfish-vmg-metaverse-research/on. December 2022.

Tlili, A., Huang, R., Shehata, B., Liu, D., Zhao, J., Metwally, A. H. S., Wang, H., Denden, M., Bozkurt, A., Lee, L. H., Beyoglu, D., Altinay, F., Sharma, R. C., Altinay, Z., Li, Z., Jiahao, L., Ahmad, F., Ying, H., Salha, S., … Burgos, D. (2022). Is metaverse in education a blessing or a curse: A combined content and bibliometric analysis. *Smart Learning Environments*, *9*(1), 24. https://doi.org/10.1186/s40561-022-00205-x

Venkatesh, V., Morris, M. G., Davis, G. B., & Davis, F. D. (2003). User acceptance of information technology: Toward a unified view. *MIS Quarterly*, *27*(3), 425–445. https://doi.org/10.2307/30036540

Wider, W., Jiang, L., Lin, J., Fauzi, M. A., Li, J., & Chan, C. K. (2023). Metaverse chronicles: A bibliometric analysis of its evolving landscape. *International Journal of Human–Computer Interaction*, 1–14. https://doi.org/10.1080/10447318.2023.2227825

Zhang, J., Quoquab, F., & Mohammad, J. (2023). Metaverse tourism and Gen-Z and Gen-Y's motivation: "will you, or won't you travel virtually?" *Tourism Review*, *79*(2), 304–320. https://doi.org/10.1108/TR-06-2023-0393

Chapter 2

Out of the Shadows: Cybersecurity Challenges and Solutions in Organizations

Brian Heath[a], *Ross Jackson*[a], *Scott Dewicki*[b], *Paul Hartman*[b] *and Shweta Kumar*[b]

[a]*Wittenberg University, USA*
[b]*RGBSI Aerospace & Defense, USA*

Abstract

Cyber operates in the shadows. Mission and branding receive attention as cyber threats endanger at the periphery. Cybersecurity challenges are dynamic and form exploitable vulnerabilities. In this chapter, general assumptions of organizational cybersecurity risk in a multi-indentured supply chain network were explored. A risk-based simulation model was developed that approximates cybersecurity risk exposure. These results suggest that improving cybersecurity at the bottom-tier within a supply chain generates system-level improvements, but that these are offset by increased network integration. The cybersecurity landscape demands a proactive approach, incorporating technological and collaborative strategies to safeguard against the shadowy nature of cyber threats.

Keywords: Critical infrastructure; data integrity; network; simulation; supply chain; system vulnerabilities

Introduction

Cyber operates in the shadows. Mission, vision, and branding receive internal attention and form the basis of external awareness (Leuthesser & Kohli, 1997; Ramus & Vaccaro, 2017; Verma, 2009), as cyber threats endanger at the

The AI Metaverse Revolution: Transforming Multi-Business Scenarios (Volume 1), 15–25

Published under exclusive licence by Emerald Publishing Limited
doi:10.1108/978-1-83662-582-720251002

periphery of focus (Borkovich & Skovira, 2019; Hepfer & Powell, 2020; Madnick & Mangelsdorf, 2017). Cybersecurity challenges are dynamic, as adversaries leverage cyberspace to conduct operations that strike with precision and remain concealed (Razaque et al., 2019; Schulzke, 2018; Syed et al., 2022). The ubiquity of cyber technologies has introduced significant vulnerabilities within organizations (Ghelani, 2022; Williams et al., 2020) that can be exploited, causing disruptions that impact organizational performance and stability.

The potential for adversaries to compromise information systems and decrypt sensitive data poses a risk (Allodi & Massacci, 2017; Chronopoulos et al., 2017; Ganin et al., 2020). Modeling is useful to understand this threat. In this chapter, cybersecurity risks in a multi-indentured supply chain network were explored. In terms of functional definitions, in this chapter, cybersecurity risks include the potential unauthorized access, disruption, or damage to information systems, networks, and data, driven by threats such as malware, phishing, and ransomware, which can lead to significant operational, financial, and reputational harm. Whereas a multi-indentured supply chain network is a hierarchical system of interconnected suppliers and manufactures, organized into multiple tiers, where each tier supplies components or services to the next level, ultimately culminating in the production of a final product, with specific elements including prime contractors, subcontractors, and the directional flow of products and information. Assumptions formed the basis for a simulation model that approximates organizational, cybersecurity risk exposure. The results suggest a need for robust cybersecurity measures for long-term organizational viability. Simply responding to emergent threats puts organizations perpetually a step behind the cybersecurity threat. Strategic benefit can be derived by holistically getting ahead of one's adversaries by addressing cybersecurity.

Countering cybersecurity threats is not exclusively or even primarily technological (Ahmad, 2021; Wallace et al., 2021; Wright, 2021). Humans contribute to cyber threats and the efficacy of cybersecurity measures (Hadlington, 2021; Pollini et al., 2022; Zimmermann & Renaud, 2019). As such, the human component of organizations and cybersecurity must be included in any potential solution to this concern. The cybersecurity landscape demands a dynamic and proactive approach, incorporating cutting-edge technologies and collaborative strategies to safeguard against cyber threats' pervasive and shadowy nature. The objective of this chapter is to provide empirical evidence showing that improving cybersecurity at the bottom-tier within a supply chain generates system-level improvements, but that these are offset by increased network integration.

This chapter contains a survey of literature to situate key cybersecurity as a concern in both business and military organizations. Concerns of critical infrastructure, data integrity, supply chains, and system vulnerabilities are explored, as well as research on future considerations in cybersecurity. Following the survey of the literature, the method used to develop the simulation is presented along with the results. The conclusion includes a summary of key findings, limitations, and a call to action.

Cybersecurity

Cybersecurity is complex (Wen et al., 2017; Xu, 2020). Making sense of cybersecurity requires delimitation. There are two contexts in this study: business and defense. These were selected due to their significance (Corallo et al., 2021; Hussain et al., 2020). For this examination, concerns of critical infrastructure, data integrity, supply chains, and system vulnerabilities were explored, as well as research on future considerations. Businesses face multifaceted cybersecurity threats that compromise sensitive data, disrupt operations, and erode customer trust (Kumar, 2023; Schneider, 2022). Data breaches remain a high-level threat due to the value of sensitive information (Adlakha et al., 2019) and the prevalence of human error (Kadena & Gupi, 2021; Nobles, 2018). As organizations adopt remote work models, the attack surface expands, with cybercriminals targeting vulnerable systems connecting to less secure homes or public networks (Furnell & Shah, 2020; Ghirardello et al., 2018). A talent gap exacerbates these vulnerabilities, as a shortage of professionals hinders effective defense against cyber threats (Blažič, 2022; Furnell, 2021).

The proliferation of Internet of Things devices introduces vulnerabilities, making proactive cybersecurity measures more imperative (Andrade et al., 2020; Lu & Da Xu, 2018). Businesses must prepare for the potential impact of quantum computing on encryption methods, which could render current systems vulnerable to breaches (Faruk et al., 2022; Nish et al., 2020). The response to these threats involves robust technical defenses, organizational policies, employee training, and an adaptable culture of cybersecurity awareness.

Cybersecurity has become a defining element of national security, with the protection of National Security Systems, the Department of Defense, and the Defense Industrial Base being paramount (Efthymiopoulos, 2019; Solar, 2020). These networks, vital to military and intelligence operations, must be defended against an array of cyber threats to maintain national defense capabilities. The complexity of the cybersecurity landscape necessitates collaboration, where shared intelligence, resources, and expertise are leveraged to enhance the collective cyber defense (Christensen & Petersen, 2017). International cooperation extends beyond borders, which requires strengthening collective security measures with international allies (Lété & Pernik, 2017).

Developing a skilled cyber workforce through targeted education and training initiatives is essential to address the sophisticated and evolving nature of cyber threats (Dawson & Thomson, 2018; Teoh & Mahmood, 2018). This strategy encompasses a need for anticipation and accurate attribution of cyber threats, which are critical for formulating effective defense and deterrence strategies. Ensuring critical infrastructure cybersecurity is a priority, given that sectors like energy, finance, and transportation are integral to stability and are targets of cyberattacks.

As technology advances, the emergence of artificial intelligence-driven cyber capabilities introduces new strategic considerations (Li, 2018; Mohammed, 2020). The responsible adoption of these technologies must be guided by principles that align with ethical standards. Fostering a culture of cybersecurity awareness is vital for creating a resilient defense against cyber threats (Corallo et al., 2022). The evolving nature of cyber risk management reflects the increasing recognition of cybersecurity as a critical component of organizational strategy and risk assessment. The strategic overview of cybersecurity concerns calls for a comprehensive and adaptive approach that addresses these multifaceted challenges. Several key areas of cybersecurity warrant consideration: critical infrastructure, data integrity, supply chains, and system vulnerabilities.

Critical infrastructure encompasses the essential systems and assets that underpin society's functioning (Dawson et al., 2021). This cybersecurity is paramount because their incapacitation would be debilitating (Spremić & Šimunic, 2018; Viganò et al., 2020). As these systems increasingly rely on interconnected digital networks, they become more vulnerable to cyberattacks that could lead to service disruption, theft of information, or control of systems by unauthorized entities (Ahmed & Khan, 2023). Enhancing the resilience and security of critical infrastructure against cyber threats is a strategic priority, necessitating robust collaboration between government entities, private sector stakeholders, and international partners.

Data integrity refers to data's accuracy, consistency, and reliability throughout its lifecycle, ensuring that information remains unaltered from its original state during storage, transfer, or processing (Doku & Rawat, 2019; Duggineni, 2023). This is crucial for maintaining trust in the systems, as unauthorized alterations could lead to incorrect decisions, financial loss, or damage to reputation. To safeguard data integrity, organizations implement measures such as cryptographic hash functions, access controls, version control systems, and rigorous auditing processes (Sharma & Mittal, 2019; Soomro et al., 2019). These practices help detect and prevent unauthorized data modifications, whether due to malicious activities like cyberattacks and insider threats or unintentional changes stemming from human error. Data integrity is foundational for a comprehensive cybersecurity strategy, as it upholds the trustworthiness of critical data assets.

Supply chain cybersecurity is an aspect of risk management that addresses the need to secure the network of suppliers and third-party vendors integral to an organization's operations (Cheung et al., 2021; Latif et al., 2021). Given that adversaries can exploit supply chain vulnerabilities to gain unauthorized access to systems and data, assessing and mitigating risks associated with third-party products and services is essential. This includes conducting thorough security assessments of suppliers, implementing secure software development practices, and ensuring that hardware and software components are from trusted sources (Chang, 2023; Khan et al., 2022). These measures enhance supply chain resilience, protecting the integrity, confidentiality, and availability of critical infrastructure and sensitive data.

System vulnerabilities are weaknesses in a system's design, implementation, or configuration that, if exploited, can compromise the confidentiality, integrity, or availability of the system and its data (Humayun et al., 2020; Zografopoulos et al., 2023). In cybersecurity, the identification, assessment, and remediation of these vulnerabilities are paramount to protecting systems against attacks (Borky et al., 2019; Yaacoub et al., 2022). Addressing the cybersecurity concerns associated with critical infrastructure, data integrity, supply chain, and system vulnerabilities benefits from considering the emerging cybersecurity threats hiding in the shadows.

The proliferation of cloud computing will continue to transform cybersecurity paradigms, offering scalable solutions for risk mitigation and the potential for enhanced security through specialized third-party services (Ahmad et al., 2021; Arce, 2020). However, the reliance on cloud infrastructures also introduces new vulnerabilities and necessitates robust security protocols to protect against data breaches and unauthorized access (Al Nafea & Almaiah, 2021; Maithili et al., 2018). Remote work extends the security perimeter and requires secure remote access and authentication protocols (Borkovich & Skovira, 2020; Evangelakos, 2020). The cybersecurity talent gap remains a concern, with a shortage of experts to meet growing demand.

There are concerns associated with cybersecurity. This review examined cybersecurity implications associated with critical infrastructure, data integrity, supply chains, and system vulnerabilities. A simulation model can facilitate understanding the complexity of the cybersecurity threat. The method used to generate the simulation model of this study is presented in the following section.

Simulation

Simulation models are computerized simplifications of complex systems (Durán, 2021; Ilagan, 2022), which iterate over simulated time (Karian & Dudewicz, 2020; Szymoniak, 2021). These representations are achieved by combining mathematics, logic, and algorithms with a purpose to explore the dynamics of complex systems that are too difficult to experiment with due to the constraints of cost, time, or ethics (Guillod et al., 2020; Mourtzis, 2020). Their utility is derived by combining analytic elements to investigate what could occur. Analysts gain insights into system dynamics by manipulating inputs and observing the changes in outcomes, identifying key leverage points, and predicting outcomes. This is particularly valuable when dealing with systems that exhibit a high degree of feedback, where small changes have significant and sometimes non-linear effects.

Communication is influenced by context (Reboulet & Jackson, 2021). The context of this study required a constrained exposition of the simulated model. Key model assumptions are as follows:

- The multi-indentured supply chain network consists of three interconnected levels (i.e., top-tier, mid-tier, and bottom-tier), with 5 top-tier, 20 mid-tier, and 175 bottom-tier nodes.
- The degree of interconnectedness within the supply chain can vary from as low as 5% to as high as 80%, with an expected interconnectedness value of 20%.
- Cybersecurity risks increase from the top-tier down to the bottom-tier nodes, with expected propagation rates being 90% for those at tiers below, 50% for those at the same tier level, and 10% for those at tiers above the initial cybersecurity occurrence.

- Simulations were based on 1,000 runs per 1,000 randomly generated networks with a focus on reducing the system-level risk associated with cybersecurity improvements at the bottom tier of the network. A total of 1,000,000 samples were generated.

Validation is often considered critical in determining model accuracy (Sargent, 2010). Within that paradigm, the importance of validation lies in providing confidence that outputs are reliable. Heath and Jackson (2013) indicated that "the act of selling simulation models transforms the process of validation into the game of validation where strategy, sportsmanship, power, and skill overshadows the original intent of demonstrating that the model represents something that is supposedly real" (p. 99). Validation was limited here to the reasonableness of the assumptions, interrelationships, and results.

Simulation models, as powerful tools, serve as laboratories for exploring complex systems, allowing for experimentation and analysis. This simple cybersecurity model provides insight into the potential system-level benefit derived from improving cybersecurity at the lowest echelon within a multi-indentured supply chain network.

Results

The simulation focused on making incremental improvements to bottom-tier organizations in the supply chain and measuring the degree of improvement in system-level outcomes. The degree of improvements ranged from 10% to 90%, and the system-level outcomes were assessed as quartiles. The simulated results are summarized in Table 2.1.

Table 2.1. Percentage Change in Average Number of Simulated Breaches from the Initial Network Position.

		Degree of Network Interconnectivity							
Degree of lowest tier improvement		10%	20%	30%	40%	50%	60%	70%	80%
	0%	0%	10%	24%	40%	64%	95%	128%	174%
	10%	−5%	0%	11%	27%	48%	71%	119%	169%
	20%	−16%	−8%	2%	16%	36%	61%	96%	129%
	30%	−23%	−18%	−9%	4%	22%	46%	80%	109%
	40%	−30%	−25%	−16%	−4%	10%	30%	60%	85%
	50%	−37%	−31%	−24%	−13%	2%	19%	51%	74%
	60%	−40%	−38%	−31%	−20%	−9%	7%	35%	64%
	70%	−48%	−44%	−37%	−29%	−15%	1%	16%	47%
	80%	−54%	−49%	−43%	−34%	−24%	−10%	11%	33%
	90%	−60%	−53%	−48%	−40%	−29%	−16%	5%	22%

The percentage change in simulated breaches occurs across two dimensions, the degree of improvement in the lowest-tier organizations and the increased degree of network interconnectivity. All percentage changes are in relation to the initial network position (i.e., 0% improvement, 10% network interconnectivity). Improvements are derived from increasing the degree of improvement in the lowest-tier organizations. Conversely, increases in the degree of network interconnectivity are associated with increases in the number of breaches. The greatest reduction in simulated breaches (−60%) occurs when network interconnectivity is held constant while improving cybersecurity by 90%. The greatest increase in simulated breaches (174%) occurs when improvements are held constant, and network interconnectivity is increased to 80%. These results suggest that increasing cybersecurity in the lowest-tier organizations is essential for addressing the increased cybersecurity threats associated with increasingly integrated networks.

Small improvements in cybersecurity can generate system-wide effects. Focusing on vulnerabilities posed by small firms can improve network security. However, there is a trade-off between interconnectedness and vulnerability.

Conclusion

Organizations benefit from shining light on the cybersecurity. These results suggest that the degree of connectivity within a network is just as important as improving cybersecurity. If one is going to increase connections among suppliers, one must equivalently improve cybersecurity to counterbalance the threat. This finding suggests a trade-off between efficiencies gained through supply chain integration and costs associated with increased cybersecurity, with the practical implication being that organizations must balance the efficiencies gained from increased supply chain connectivity with the necessary investments in cybersecurity to mitigate the associated risks. These results have limitations.

This model is basic. Refinement of the assumptions would improve precision. The model made use of triangular distributions that suffer from being closed. Making use of asymptotic distributions would generate more plausible values at the extremities. Lastly, this simulation focused on system-level outcomes derived through improvements in bottom-tier organizations. Extending the focus to top- and mid-tier organizations would provide a more complete picture. Whereas these limitations are significant, they do not diminish the key findings. Improvements in system-level outcomes can come from cybersecurity improvements in bottom-tier organizations in supply chain networks.

In the face of escalating threats, it is imperative to adopt a unified cybersecurity strategy. This necessitates a collaborative approach. Military and business organizations must prioritize fostering a culture of cybersecurity. It is crucial to leverage partnerships, share intelligence, and empower action. Together, cybersecurity solutions can be scaled and safeguard against this shadowy threat.

References

Adlakha, R., Sharma, S., Rawat, A., & Sharma, K. (2019, February). *Cyber security goal's, issue's, categorization & data breaches* (pp. 397–402). 2019 International conference on machine learning, big data, cloud and parallel computing (COMITCon).

Ahmad, P. A. (2021). Cyber security is more than just a question of information technology. *Journal of Image Processing and Intelligent Remote Sensing (JIPIRS)*, *1*(02), 1–7.

Ahmad, W., Rasool, A., Javed, A. R., Baker, T., & Jalil, Z. (2021). Cyber security in IoT-based cloud computing: A comprehensive survey. *Electronics*, *11*(1), 16.

Ahmed, S., & Khan, M. (2023). Securing the Internet of Things (IoT): A comprehensive study on the intersection of cybersecurity, privacy, and connectivity in the IoT ecosystem. *AI, IoT and the Fourth Industrial Revolution Review*, *13*(9), 1–17.

Al Nafea, R., & Almaiah, M. A. (2021, July). *Cyber security threats in cloud: Literature review* (pp. 779–786). 2021 International conference on information technology (ICIT).

Allodi, L., & Massacci, F. (2017). Security events and vulnerability data for cybersecurity risk estimation. *Risk Analysis*, *37*(8), 1606–1627.

Andrade, R. O., Yoo, S. G., Tello-Oquendo, L., & Ortiz-Garcés, I. (2020). A comprehensive study of the IoT cybersecurity in smart cities. *IEEE Access*, *8*, 228922–228941.

Arce, D. G. (2020). Cybersecurity and platform competition in the cloud. *Computers & Security*, *93*, 101774.

Blažič, B. J. (2022). Changing the landscape of cybersecurity education in the EU: Will the new approach produce the required cybersecurity skills? *Education and Information Technologies*, *27*(3), 3011–3036.

Borkovich, D. J., & Skovira, R. J. (2019). Cybersecurity inertia and social engineering: Who's worse, employees or hackers? *Issues in Information Systems*, *20*(3), 139–150.

Borkovich, D. J., & Skovira, R. J. (2020). Working from home: Cybersecurity in the age of COVID-19. *Issues in Information Systems*, *21*(4).

Borky, J. M., Bradley, T. H., Borky, J. M., & Bradley, T. H. (2019). Protecting information with cybersecurity. In *Effective model-based systems engineering*. Springer. https://doi.org/10.1007/978-3-319-95669-5_10

Chang, E. C. (2023). *Supplier development framework in supply chain cybersecurity evaluation of small and medium-sized enterprises* [Doctoral dissertation, Massachusetts Institute of Technology].

Cheung, K. F., Bell, M. G., & Bhattacharjya, J. (2021). Cybersecurity in logistics and supply chain management: An overview and future research directions. *Transportation Research Part E: Logistics and Transportation Review*, *146*, 102217.

Christensen, K. K., & Petersen, K. L. (2017). Public–private partnerships on cyber security: A practice of loyalty. *International Affairs*, *93*(6), 1435–1452.

Chronopoulos, M., Panaousis, E., & Grossklags, J. (2017). An options approach to cybersecurity investment. *IEEE Access*, *6*, 12175–12186.

Corallo, A., Lazoi, M., Lezzi, M., & Luperto, A. (2022). Cybersecurity awareness in the context of the Industrial Internet of Things: A systematic literature review. *Computers in Industry*, *137*, 103614.

Corallo, A., Lazoi, M., Lezzi, M., & Pontrandolfo, P. (2021). Cybersecurity challenges for manufacturing systems 4.0: Assessment of the business impact level. *IEEE Transactions on Engineering Management*, *70*(11), 3745–3765.

Dawson, J., & Thomson, R. (2018). The future cybersecurity workforce: Going beyond technical skills for successful cyber performance. *Frontiers in Psychology*, *9*, 744.

Dawson, M., Bacius, R., Gouveia, L. B., & Vassilakos, A. (2021). Understanding the challenge of cybersecurity in critical infrastructure sectors. *Land Forces Academy Review*, *26*(1), 69–75.

Doku, R., & Rawat, D. B. (2019). Big data in cybersecurity for smart city applications. In D. B. Rawat & K. Z. Ghafoor (Eds.), *Smart cities cybersecurity and privacy* (pp. 103–112). Elsevier.

Duggineni, S. (2023). Impact of controls on data integrity and information systems. *Science and Technology, 13*(2), 29–35.

Durán, J. M. (2021). A formal framework for computer simulations: Surveying the historical record and finding their philosophical roots. *Philosophy & Technology, 34*(1), 105–127.

Efthymiopoulos, M. P. (2019). A cyber-security framework for development, defense and innovation at NATO. *Journal of Innovation and Entrepreneurship, 8*(1), 1–26.

Evangelakos, G. (2020). Keeping critical assets safe when teleworking is the new norm. *Network Security, 2020*(6), 11–14.

Faruk, M. J. H., Tahora, S., Tasnim, M., Shahriar, H., & Sakib, N. (2022, May). *A review of quantum cybersecurity: Threats, risks and opportunities* (pp. 1–8). 2022 1st international conference on AI in cybersecurity (ICAIC).

Furnell, S. (2021). The cybersecurity workforce and skills. *Computers & Security, 100*, 102080.

Furnell, S., & Shah, J. N. (2020). Home working and cyber security – An outbreak of unpreparedness?. *Computer Fraud & Security, 2020*(8), 6–12.

Ganin, A. A., Quach, P., Panwar, M., Collier, Z. A., Keisler, J. M., Marchese, D., & Linkov, I. (2020). Multicriteria decision framework for cybersecurity risk assessment and management. *Risk Analysis, 40*(1), 183–199.

Ghelani, D. (2022). Cyber security, cyber threats, implications and future perspectives: A review. *American Journal of Science, Engineering and Technology, 3*(6), 12–19.

Ghirardello, K., Maple, C., Ng, D., & Kearney, P. (2018, March). *Cyber security of smart homes: Development of a reference architecture for attack surface analysis* (pp. 1–10). Living in the Internet of Things: Cybersecurity of the IoT-2018.

Guillod, T., Papamanolis, P., & Kolar, J. W. (2020). Artificial neural network (ANN) based fast and accurate inductor modeling and design. *IEEE Open Journal of Power Electronics, 1*, 284–299.

Hadlington, L. (2021). The "human factor" in cybersecurity: Exploring the accidental insider. In M. Khosrow-Pour (Ed.), *Research anthology on artificial intelligence applications in security* (pp. 1960–1977). IGI Global.

Heath, B. L., & Jackson, R. A. (2013). Ontological implications of modeling and simulation in postmodernity. In A. Tolk (Ed.), *Ontology, epistemology, and teleology for modeling and simulation: Philosophical foundations for intelligent M&S applications* (pp. 89–103). Springer Berlin Heidelberg.

Hepfer, M., & Powell, T. C. (2020). Make cybersecurity a strategic asset. *MIT Sloan Management Review, 62*(1), 40–45.

Humayun, M., Niazi, M., Jhanjhi, N. Z., Alshayeb, M., & Mahmood, S. (2020). Cyber security threats and vulnerabilities: A systematic mapping study. *Arabian Journal for Science and Engineering, 45*, 3171–3189.

Hussain, A., Mohamed, A., & Razali, S. (2020, March). *A review on cybersecurity: Challenges & emerging threats* (pp. 1–7). Proceedings of the 3rd international conference on networking, information systems & security.

Ilagan, J. B. (2022). *The design and use of agent-based modeling computer simulation for teaching technology entrepreneurship*. Proceedings of the 30th international conference on computers in education (Vol. 2, pp. 719–723).

Kadena, E., & Gupi, M. (2021). Human factors in cybersecurity: Risks and impacts. *Security Science Journal, 2*(2), 51–64.

Karian, Z. A., & Dudewicz, E. J. (2020). *Modern statistical, systems, and GPSS simulation*. CRC Press.

Khan, A. W., Zaib, S., Khan, F., Tarimer, I., Seo, J. T., & Shin, J. (2022). Analyzing and evaluating critical cyber security challenges faced by vendor organizations in software development: SLR based approach. *IEEE Access, 10*, 65044–65054.

Kumar, I. (2023). Emerging threats in cybersecurity: A review article. *International Journal of Applied and Natural Sciences, 1*(1), 01–08.

Latif, M. N. A., Aziz, N. A. A., Hussin, N. S. N., & Aziz, Z. A. (2021). Cyber security in supply chain management: A systematic review. *LogForum*, *17*(1), 49–57.

Lété, B., & Pernik, P. (2017). *EU-NATO cybersecurity and defense cooperation: From common threats to common solutions*. German Marshall Fund of the United States.

Leuthesser, L., & Kohli, C. (1997). Corporate identity: The role of mission statements. *Business Horizons*, *40*(3), 59–66.

Li, J. H. (2018). Cyber security meets artificial intelligence: A survey. *Frontiers of Information Technology & Electronic Engineering*, *19*(12), 1462–1474.

Lu, Y., & Da Xu, L. (2018). Internet of Things (IoT) cybersecurity research: A review of current research topics. *IEEE Internet of Things Journal*, *6*(2), 2103–2115.

Madnick, S., & Mangelsdorf, I. B. M. E. (2017). What executives get wrong about cybersecurity. *Sloan Management Review, Winter*, 22–24.

Maithili, K., Vinothkumar, V., & Latha, P. (2018). Analyzing the security mechanisms to prevent unauthorized access in cloud and network security. *Journal of Computational and Theoretical Nanoscience*, *15*(6–7), 2059–2063.

Mohammed, I. A. (2020). Artificial intelligence for cybersecurity: A systematic mapping of literature. *Artificial Intelligence*, *7*(9), 1–5.

Mourtzis, D. (2020). Simulation in the design and operation of manufacturing systems: State of the art and new trends. *International Journal of Production Research*, *58*(7), 1927–1949.

Nish, A., Naumann, S., & Muir, J. (2020). *Enduring cyber threats and emerging challenges to the financial sector*. Carnegie Endowment for International Peace.

Nobles, C. (2018). Botching human factors in cybersecurity in business organizations. *HOLISTICA – Journal of Business and Public Administration*, *9*(3), 71–88.

Pollini, A., Callari, T. C., Tedeschi, A., Ruscio, D., Save, L., Chiarugi, F., & Guerri, D. (2022). Leveraging human factors in cybersecurity: An integrated methodological approach. *Cognition, Technology & Work*, *24*(2), 371–390.

Ramus, T., & Vaccaro, A. (2017). Stakeholders matter: How social enterprises address mission drift. *Journal of Business Ethics*, *143*, 307–322.

Razaque, A., Amsaad, F., Khan, M. J., Hariri, S., Chen, S., Siting, C., & Ji, X. (2019). Survey: Cybersecurity vulnerabilities, attacks and solutions in the medical domain. *IEEE Access*, *7*, 168774–168797.

Reboulet, A., & Jackson, R. A. (2021). Effective communication approaches for decision analytics: An exploration of strategies. In R. Jackson & A. Reboulet (Eds.), *Effective strategies for communicating insights in business* (pp. 13–31). IGI Global.

Sargent, R. G. (2010, December). *Verification and validation of simulation models*. Proceedings of the 2010 winter simulation conference (pp. 166–183).

Schneider, J. (2022). A world without trust: The insidious cyber threat. *Foreign Affairs*, *101*, 22.

Schulzke, M. (2018). The politics of attributing blame for cyberattacks and the costs of uncertainty. *Perspectives on Politics*, *16*(4), 954–968.

Sharma, A. K., & Mittal, S. K. (2019, January). *Cryptography & network security hash function applications, attacks and advances: A review* (pp. 177–188). 2019 Third international conference on inventive systems and control (ICISC).

Solar, C. (2020). Cybersecurity and cyber defence in the emerging democracies. *Journal of Cyber Policy*, *5*(3), 392–412.

Soomro, S., Belgaum, M. R., Alansari, Z., & Jain, R. (2019, August). *Review and open issues of cryptographic algorithms in cyber security* (pp. 158–162). 2019 International conference on computing, electronics & communications engineering (iCCECE).

Spremić, M., & Šimunic, A. (2018, July). *Cyber security challenges in digital economy*. Proceedings of the world congress on engineering (Vol. 1, pp. 341–346). International Association of Engineers.

Syed, N. F., Shah, S. W., Trujillo-Rasua, R., & Doss, R. (2022). Traceability in supply chains: A Cyber security analysis. *Computers & Security*, *112*, 102536.

Szymoniak, S. (2021). Security protocols analysis including various time parameters. *Mathematical Biosciences and Engineering*, *18*(2), 1136–1153.

Teoh, C. S., & Mahmood, A. K. (2018). Cybersecurity workforce development for digital economy. *The Educational Review*, *2*(1), 136–146.

Verma, H. V. (2009). Mission statements – A study of intent and influence. *Journal of Services Research*, *9*(2). 153–172.

Viganò, E., Loi, M., & Yaghmaei, E. (2020). Cybersecurity of critical infrastructure. In M. Christen, B. Gordijn, & M. Loi (Eds.), *The ethics of cybersecurity* (pp. 157–177). https://doi.org/10.1007/978-3-030-29053-5_8.

Wallace, S., Green, K., Johnson, C., Cooper, J., & Gilstrap, C. (2021). An extended TOE framework for cybersecurity adoption decisions. *Communications of the Association for Information Systems*, *47*(2020), 51.

Williams, C. M., Chaturvedi, R., & Chakravarthy, K. (2020). Cybersecurity risks in a pandemic. *Journal of Medical Internet Research*, *22*(9), e23692.

Wen, G., Yu, W., Yu, X., & Lü, J. (2017). Complex cyber-physical networks: From cybersecurity to security control. *Journal of Systems Science and Complexity*, *30*, 46–67.

Wright, B. (2021). Cybersecurity: The forever problem. *Journal of Petroleum Technology*, *73*(07), 26–29.

Xu, S. (2020, November). *The cybersecurity dynamics way of thinking and landscape* (pp. 69–80). Proceedings of the 7th ACM workshop on moving target defense.

Yaacoub, J. P. A., Noura, H. N., Salman, O., & Chehab, A. (2022). Robotics cyber security: Vulnerabilities, attacks, countermeasures, and recommendations. *International Journal of Information Security*, *21*, 115–158.

Zimmermann, V., & Renaud, K. (2019). Moving from a "human-as-problem" to a "human-as-solution" cybersecurity mindset. *International Journal of Human-Computer Studies*, *131*, 169–187.

Zografopoulos, I., Hatziargyriou, N. D., & Konstantinou, C. (2023). Distributed energy resources cybersecurity outlook: Vulnerabilities, attacks, impacts, and mitigations. *IEEE Systems Journal*, *17*(4), 6695–6709.

Chapter 3

Exploring Factors Influencing Purchase Intentions Among Metaverse Enthusiasts: An Investigation in Northern India

Kavita Rani and Manjit Kour

University School of Business, Chandigarh University, Punjab, India

Abstract

The idea of the metaverse has drawn a lot of interest from tech businesses, developers, and other industries wanting to explore new paths for innovation and user involvement as technology develops and connection gets better. This study explores the crucial factors influencing users' purchasing intentions in the distinct socio-cultural setting of Northern India, which includes the states of Delhi, Punjab, and Haryana, in response to the growing interest in the metaverse. A semi-structured questionnaire was used to collect data from 380 respondents from Northern India. The study focuses on five independent variables, namely, perceived usefulness, perceived ease of use, social needs, technical maturity, and perceived privacy risk, while gauging their impact on the dependent variable – metaverse usage intention. The findings of the study reveal that the metaverse is largely influenced by perceived utility, perceived privacy risk, and technical maturity. The complex findings of this study have important implications for both research scholars and marketers who want to understand and improve user interaction tactics in the ever-changing metaverse.

Keywords: Metaverse; purchase intentions; perceived usefulness; technical maturity; perceived privacy risk; Northern India; correlation analysis; regression analysis

The AI Metaverse Revolution: Transforming Multi-Business Scenarios (Volume 1), 27–38

Published under exclusive licence by Emerald Publishing Limited
doi:10.1108/978-1-83662-582-720251003

Introduction

The effective role of technology breakthroughs in numerous domains is to facilitate human life. Since we entered the age of technological revolutions, it has become a necessity. The metaverse is a virtual world where users can communicate in real time with other users and computer-generated settings. The metaverse is a persistent, immersive, networked virtual realm that encompasses several platforms, technologies, and experiences, going beyond conventional notions of virtual reality. The idea of the metaverse is greatly supported by the quick development and growing uptake of supporting technologies including cloud computing, internet connectivity, augmented reality, virtual reality, digital currencies, and NFTs (JP Morgan, 2022). Combining the terms "meta" (a prefix meaning "beyond") and "universe," the term "Metaverse" refers to a collection of various virtual places that blend augmented and virtual reality to represent real life through avatars (Sparkes, 2021). A three-dimensional virtual environment that enables users to interact with digital objects and form social connections is what defines the metaverse through avatars. Additionally, they have unrestricted mobility between virtual environments (Cheng et al., 2022). In 2006, metaverse was primarily researched as the second life setting (Park & Kim, 2022). Although early attempts to develop metaverse-like platforms, like second life, were not very successful, new developments in technology and changing social demands have reignited interest in the metaverse's possibilities. Notably, important figures in the tech sector have recognized the potential of the metaverse. CEO of Facebook Mark Zuckerberg renamed the firm Meta in October 2021 to further emphasize the company's dedication to creating a metaverse, while CEO of Nvidia Jensen Hwang declared the company's ambition to create a metaverse in April 2021 (Srinivasan et al., 2022). Tech behemoths have deliberately constructed their business strategies around metaverse platforms, which are essential for bridging the gap between the virtual and physical worlds. According to Lee et al. (2021), these models facilitate the generation and sharing of value among the enterprises and users in the metaverse ecosystem. When new technology is introduced, it is critical to assess user acceptability and look into potential influences on the technology's uptake.

The metaverse is a dynamic virtual environment that allows people to communicate and interact in real time across a wide range of platforms, technologies, and experiences. It has drawn interest from developers, tech companies, and other industries looking for new ways to innovate in the face of rapidly advancing technology and improved connectivity. Beyond traditional ideas of virtual reality, this permanent and immersive virtual world opens up new avenues for investigation and interaction. Knowing what influences users' purchase intentions is crucial as interest in the metaverse increases. While user behavioral intention has been taken into account in existing theoretical models for information system adoption, the difficulty is in assuring user satisfaction. In the customer-centric age, loyalty and continued usage are largely dependent on a satisfactory user experience; important factors that influence this include system quality, information quality, service quality, collaboration quality, and task-technology fit (Spasojevic & Ilic, 2021). Due to the rapid advancement of technology, it is critical to examine and clarify how these technologies are accepted behaviorally (Yun & Eun). By evaluating Palestinian users' intentions to use metaverse and identifying the elements influencing it and the relationships between these aspects, the goal is to close a gap in the research. This will provide insight into Palestinian users and various behaviors that could influence metaverse usage. The developers of the metaverse technology may be able to encourage users to utilize it and engage with it more effectively if they have a deeper understanding of these elements.

By exploring the unique socio-cultural context of Northern India – which includes Delhi, Punjab, and Haryana – this study fills a significant vacuum. As interest in the metaverse grows, it is critical to investigate and understand the dynamics influencing user behavior within this localized setting. The five independent variables: perceived utility, perceived simplicity of use, social needs, technical maturity, and perceived privacy danger are used in this study, and their effect on the dependent variable, metaverse usage intention, is the focus of the study. The paper's framework is organized as follows: the literature review is covered in next section, then the methodology for determining the factors influencing the adoption of metaverse technology is covered. It is followed by the section on description of results of the study; the conclusion is drawn, and the theoretical contribution is highlighted in last section.

Review of Literature

Metaverse

According to Hudson (2011), the metaverse is an immersive mixed-reality environment that includes virtual worlds in addition to the actual world or augmented real-world data. The metaverse is an amalgam of the actual and virtual worlds that gives unmatched chances for dialog, engagement, and value generation on immersive online platforms (Inceoglu & Ciloglugil, 2022; Wang et al., 2022). While the full metaverse is still a way off, metaverse-like elements can be found on a number of virtual reality platforms, including Fortnite and Pubg. Second life games also have metaverse-like features, allowing users to create avatars that can be used in the metaverse, host in-game events, and create virtual economies. Developers have expanded the possibilities of games with this technology (Karaca & Ilkim, 2021). Dwivedi et al. (2022) divided the uses of a metaverse into two groups in their article. There are two categories for using the metaverse: "metaverse as a tool" and "metaverse as a target." When the metaverse is employed as a tool, problems and challenges in the physical world are fixed. "Metaverse as a target" refers to the ways in which the metaverse itself can perform functions such as metaverse expansion and revenue generation. Compared to the metaverse as a tool, target applications for the metaverse are independent and very dependent on the virtual environment.

When new technology is introduced, it is critical to assess user acceptability and look into potential influences on the technology's uptake. According to Lin and Yeh (2019), the interactivity of virtual reality technology has a favorable impact on users' motivation to use it, supporting the idea that attitudes toward teaching and learning using these technologies should be positively influenced. In their investigation into the factors influencing both the intention to use a virtual reality headset and the intention to make a purchase, Huang and Kao (2015) found that variables like effort expectancy, price effectiveness, and facilitation conditions are the influencing factors that directly affect the intention to make a purchase. Despite its enormous potential and significance, there is presently a dearth of focused research on the metaverse (Liu, 2022). Studies that have already been conducted can be divided into two groups: those that describe and characterize the metaverse and those that look at how it affects different facets of our daily lives and businesses. Important components including avatars, virtual worlds, interactivity, immersion, social cooperation, and permanence are examined in this research. Nevertheless, a thorough comprehension of the metaverse and its consequences remains unachieved (Kye et al., 2021).

Technology Acceptance Model

According to Davis's technology acceptance model (TAM), users' attitudes about technology use are shaped by its perceived usefulness and ease of use, and these attitudes then affect users' intentions to actually use or reject technology (Davis, 1989). Although there are additional factors at play, the two most important factors influencing the adoption or rejection of new technology are perceived utility and perceived ease of use. According to the TAM model, perceived utility and perceived ease of use are the two primary deciding variables. Perceived utility mostly indicates how much a person believes utilizing a certain system will enhance his or her productivity at work, and perceived ease of use primarily indicates how much a person believes a particular system is simple to use a particular system (Moon & Kim, 2001). The TAM has been used in numerous research to examine customers' attitudes about new technologies. Using augmented reality to teach anatomy, the study employed a TAM and discovered that the variables of ease of use, utility, curiosity, and enjoyment had a favorable impact on the intention to use (Jiwon, 2019). Intention to use the metaverse at Seol University was tested using a variety of factors. The results showed that intention to use the metaverse is influenced by perceived usefulness and ease of use, perceived usefulness is influenced by perceived ease of use, perceived playfulness and content quality are influenced by perceived usefulness, and social influence influences both perceived usefulness and intention to use the metaverse (Oh, 2021).

Hypothesis of Study

Based on literature review and TAM, the following hypotheses are proposed for the study:

> *H1*. Perceived usefulness has a significant and direct impact on purchase intention of metaverse users.
>
> *H2*. Technical maturity has a significant and direct impact on purchase intention of metaverse users.

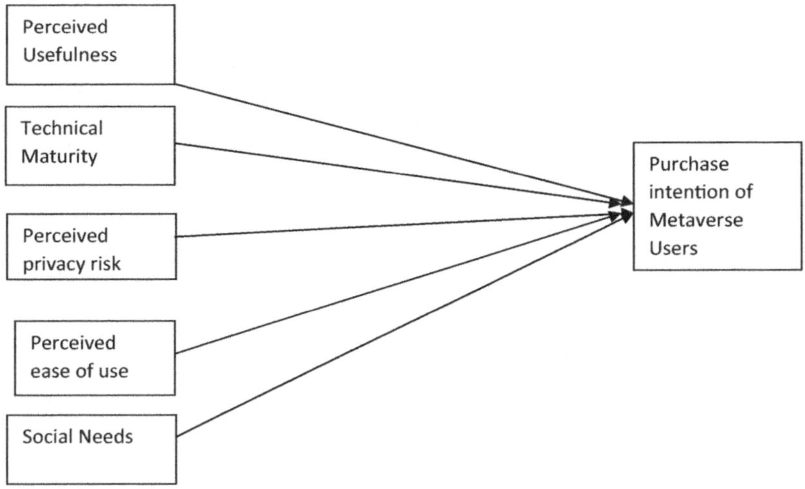

Fig. 3.1. Model of the Study. *Source*: Author's work.

H3. Perceived privacy risk has a significant and direct impact on purchase intention of metaverse users.

H4. Perceived ease of use has a significant and direct impact on purchase intention of metaverse users.

H5. Social needs has a significant and direct impact on purchase intention of metaverse users.

On the basis of hypothesis, a model has been framed as shown in Fig. 3.1.

Methods

For the study, both primary and secondary data were employed. A literature review of internet articles, research papers from the Scopus database, research publications, Google Scholar, and newspapers was conducted using secondary data. In response to the increased interest in the metaverse, this study investigates the critical elements influencing users' purchasing intents in the unique socio-cultural context of Northern India, which encompasses the states of Delhi, Punjab, and Haryana. A semi-structured questionnaire was employed to gather information from 380 participants residing in Northern India. A 42-item Likert scale questionnaire was created and verified. Google Forms was used to administer the survey. 345 completed questionnaires in total were received and utilized in the research. The data were analyzed and interpreted using statistical approaches such as regression analysis, mean, percentage, correlation, and factor analysis. Utilizing SPSS 22, a statistical software, the analysis was completed.

Results and Discussion

The demographic profile of respondents is given in Table 3.1. As can be observed from Table 3.1, the sample used in the study has more of young respondents which points that young people are more interested in new technologies like metaverse.

The primary variables in the study were validated, and construct validity was examined, using factor analysis. Making sure the sample data is adequate is the first stage in the factor analysis process. To verify the same, KMO and Bartlett's test have been utilized. The test is significant at $p < 0.001$, and the KMO statistic (Table 3.2) is determined to be 0.718, indicating the appropriateness of sample data. Thus, it was determined that the data were adequate for factor analysis.

The following stage was employing Varimax rotation in principal component analysis to extract the causative components. Six variables were kept as the primary factors since their Eigen values were greater than 1. Seven scale items were removed from the final questionnaire because they did not load on any of the chosen criteria. As a result, the final questionnaire for analysis contained 35 items. Purchase intention, perceived utility, technical maturity, perceived privacy risk, perceived simplicity of use, and social needs were the six primary criteria identified. Table 3.3 displays the factor loading and Eigen values for the factors.

The Cronbach alpha reliability test was utilized to assess the scale's dependability for the investigation. Scale dependability is indicated by a Cronbach alpha of greater than 0.6 (Hair et al., 2019; Kour & Kaur, 2020; Kour, 2022). Table 3.4 displays the results of the reliability test for the study's scales. Since the Cronbach alpha value for every item falls between 6 and 8, the scale's dependability is deemed adequate.

Table 3.1. Demographic Profile of Respondents.

S. No.	Age	Frequency	Percentage
Age-wise distribution of respondents			
1	Less than 25 years	109	31.6
2	25–35 years	87	25.2
3	35–40 years	78	22.6
4	40–45 years	60	17.4
5	Above 45 years	11	3.2
	Total	345	100%
Gender-wise distribution of respondents			
1	Male	180	52.2
2	Female	165	47.8
	Total	345	100%

Source: Author's work.

Table 3.2. Adequacy of Data (KMO and Bartlett's Test).

Kaiser–Meyer–Olkin measure of sampling adequacy		0.718
Bartlett's test of sphericity	approximately chi-square	3.245E3
	Df	345
	Sig.	0.000

Source: Author's work.

Table 3.3. Factor Analysis.

Construct	**Factor Loadings**	**Eigen Value**	**No. of Items**
Purchase intention	0.703–0.816	2.131	5
Perceived usefulness	0.721–0.803	2.221	7
Technical maturity	0.698–0.791	2.123	6
Perceived privacy risk	0.701–0.814	1.945	5
Perceived ease of use	0.714–0.826	1.765	5
Social needs	0.699–0.845	1.534	6

Source: Author's work.

Table 3.4. Reliability Test.

Variable	**No of Items**	**Cronbach Alpha**
Purchase intention	5	0.642
Perceived usefulness	7	0.801
Technical maturity	6	0.699
Perceived privacy risk	5	0.712
Perceived ease of use	5	0.813
Social needs	6	0.844

Source: Author's work.

To find the connection between purchase intention of metaverse and its antecedents, we have used Pearson's correlation analysis test. The results of Pearson's correlation are shown in Table 3.5. It is found that all the factors, that is, purchase intention, perceived usefulness, technical maturity, perceived privacy risk, perceived ease of use, and social needs have positive and significant association with purchase intention of metaverse users.

The relationship between purchase intention of metaverse users and its antecedents is predicted by using multiple linear regression. The results of multiple linear regression are given in Table 3.6. Perceived usefulness is found to be a positive predictor of purchase intention of metaverse users with beta coefficient of

Table 3.5. Pearson Correlation.

Variable	Perceived Usefulness	Technical Maturity	Perceived Privacy Risk	Perceived Ease of Use	Social Needs	Purchase Intention
Perceived usefulness	1	0.47**	0.21*	0.76*	0.38*	0.44**
Technical maturity	0.67*	0.87*	0.74**	0.53*	0.39*	0.64**
Perceived privacy risk	0.87*	0.43**	1	0.61*	0.63**	0.58**
Perceived ease of use	0.43*	0.66*	0.22*	1	0.34*	0.23*
Social needs	0.75**	0.22*	0.65	0.74*	1	0.45*
Purchase intention	0.61*	0.47**	0.74*	0.56**	0.78	1

Source: Author's work.

*Significant at $p < 0.05$.

**Significant at $p < 0.01$.

Table 3.6. Regression Analysis.

Variable	β	*t*-level	Sign
Constant	0.435	3.657	0.000
Perceived usefulness	0.345	1.523	0.002
Technical maturity	0.435	4.135	0.001
Perceived privacy risk	0.455	7.446	0.000
Perceived ease of use	0.213	9.678	0.342
Social needs	0.342	3.365	0.466

Source: Author's work.

Here, $R^2 = 0.512$, $F = 181.483$, $p < 0.001$.

0.345, and this relationship is found to be significant ($p < 0.001$). Hence, *H1* is supported in our study which states that perceived usefulness has a significant and direct impact on purchase intention of metaverse users. The beta coefficient of technical maturity is 0.345, but this relationship is found to be significant ($p < 0.001$). Hence, *H2* is also supported by our study which means that there is a positive and substantial influence of technical maturity on purchase intention of metaverse users. It is also found that perceived privacy risk is found to be a positive predictor of purchase intention of metaverse users with beta coefficient of 0.455, and this relationship is found to be significant ($p < 0.001$). Hence, *H3* is supported in our study which states that perceived privacy risk has a direct and substantial impact on purchase intention of metaverse users. Perceived ease of use and social needs have positive beta value, but the relationship is not significant; hence, *H4* and *H5* are rejected.

From results of regression analysis, the significant relationship between purchase intention of metaverse users and its antecedents is explained by the following equation:

$$\begin{aligned}&\text{Purchase intention of metaverse users} = 0.435\\&+ 0.345\ (\text{perceived usefulness})\\&+ 0.435\ (\text{technical maturity})\\&+ 0.455\ (\text{perceived privacy risk})\end{aligned} \tag{1}$$

The above regression model (equation 1) has R-squared value of 0.512 which indicates that 51% of purchase intention of metaverse users can be predicted by this model. The model is significant at $p < 0.001$ and has F-value of 181.

Conclusion

This research sought to establish the key drivers of purchase intention among metaverse users in the socio-cultural background of Northern India, focusing on states such as Delhi, Punjab, and Haryana. The study has applied an extended version of the basic premise of the TAM to investigate perceived usefulness, technical maturity, perceived privacy risk, perceived ease of use, and social needs that affect the purchase intentions of metaverse users.

Perceived usefulness became a strong predictor of purchase intention. That supports TAM in showing that when users find the metaverse useful and feel it enhances their digital experience, they will be very much willing to engage in purchase-related activities on the platform. This result underlines the utility's critical role in fostering engagement in emergent technologies. In the future development of metaverse platforms, it will be of paramount importance to emphasize features that enhance user productivity, convenience, and interaction since these drive consumer purchases.

Technical maturity was also in positive relation with purchase intention with statistical significance, which means advanced, stable, and reliable technology is the key to encouraging the adoption of metaverse. Users are most likely to start making purchases in the metaverse when they believe that it is mature and capable of offering them high-quality seamless experiences. It also aligns with other studies done on various digital technologies, showing that technical maturity provides users with trust and confidence to invest their time and money in the platform. The continuous innovations and improvements within the technical capabilities of the metaverse should strongly influence the attraction and retention of users due to its continuously changing nature. On the contrary, it is surprising to see that perceived privacy risk, which should, in theory, stunt the growth of metaverse, influenced purchase intention to be positive. This may be indicative of modern trends in digital spaces where, though people are very much aware of the privacy risks, they still use services they perceive to be useful. This might be interpreted from the paradox to mean that users are becoming more comfortable negotiating the privacy risks or the perceived benefits of the metaverse outweigh concerns. Platforms that find a balance between providing enhanced privacy protections and delivering value to users will have a winning experience in space. This means that, based on findings, metaverse platforms need to further invest in solid security features if they want to convince their users of added value. On the other hand, perceived ease of use and social needs, though being positively related to purchase intention, have not been found to have a statistically significant effect. This result runs somewhat counter to earlier studies, in particular those using the TAM framework, which have generally found ease of use as a very robust predictor of technology adoption. That may be an indication that in the metaverse – with the more techie and younger user base, as was shown in the demographic profile – ease of use is not so crucial. These users may grant more significance to such aspects as novelty, interactiveness, and technical complexity than to simplicity. Besides, the insignificance of social needs can be interpreted in such a way that at this stage of its development, users may position the metaverse as a personal or functional tool rather than a means for social contact.

The model resulting from this analysis explains 51% of the variance in purchase intention, thus showing that while perceived usefulness, technical maturity, and privacy risk represent relevant factors, other elements may also come into play in shaping user behavior inside the metaverse, such as emotional, cultural, or psychological. The overall high R-square value of 0.512 reflects that this model is a fairly great explanation for user behavior and, therefore, a good precursor for further research and development in this domain.

Theoretical Contribution of Study

This study's theoretical contribution stems from its methodical examination of the elements influencing users' purchase intentions in the metaverse within the unique socio-cultural setting of Northern India. This research considerably expands the corpus of knowledge now available on consumer behavior in virtual worlds by improving and expanding on preexisting theoretical frameworks. A significant contribution is the nuanced examination of the TAM, which highlights the importance of perceived utility and stimulates a contemplative dialog about the suitability of perceived ease of use in the context of the metaverse. The study also presents perceived privacy risk as a critical factor, recognizing the critical significance that privacy considerations play in users' decision-making. A more dynamic understanding of technology adoption is made possible by the inclusion of technical maturity as a predictor, highlighting the significance of technological developments in influencing user attitudes. Although social demands and the Northern Indian setting did not show a significant association, this non-significant finding illustrates how cultural differences exist in the significance of social features in virtual environments. In summary, this study contributes to our theoretical knowledge of metaverse adoption and lays the groundwork for future investigations into the nuances of user behavior in a variety of technological and cultural contexts.

Limitations

Although this study offers insightful information, it is not without flaws. First off, the research's geographic focus – exclusively on Northern India – reduces the findings' potential for generalization. To determine wider application, future research could take a more varied range of locales into account. Furthermore, the cross-sectional approach used in this study makes it more difficult to determine causality or track changes in metaverse adoption patterns over time.

References

Cheng, X., Mou, J., Shen, X., de Vreede, T., & Raianer, A. (2022). Call for paper: Opportunities and challenges in the metaverse. *Internet Research*. https://www.emeraldgrouppublishing.com/calls-for-papers/opportunities-and-challenges-metaverse

Davis, F. D. (1989). Perceived usefulness, perceived ease of use, and user acceptance of information technology. *JSTOR*, *13*, 319–340.

Dwivedi, Y. K., Hughes, L., Baabdullah, A. M., Ribeiro-Navarrete, S., Giannakis, M., Al-Debei, M. M., Dennehy, D., Metri, B., Buhalis, D., Cheung, C. M. K., Conboy, K., Doyle, R., Dubey, R., Dutot, V., Felix, R., Goyal, D. P., Gustafsson, A., Hinsch, C., Jebabli, I., … Wamba, S. (2022). Metaverse beyond the hype: Multidisciplinary perspectives on emerging challenges, opportunities, and agenda for research, practice, and policy. *International Journal of Information Management*, *66*, 102542. https://doi.org/10.1016/j.ijinfomgt.2022.102542/

Hair, J. F., Gabriel, L. D. S., Silva, D. D., & Braga, S. (2019). Development and validation of attitudes measurement scales: Fundamental and practical aspects. *RAUSP Management Journal*, *54*, 490–507.

Huang, C.-H., & Kao, Y.-H. (2015). UTAUT2 based predictions of factors influencing the technology acceptance of phablets by DNP. *Mathematical Problems in Engineering*, *1*, 1–23.

Hudson, A. (2011). Librarians in second life and future virtual worlds. In D. Zabel (Ed.), *Reference reborn: Breathing new life into public services librarianship* (pp. 61–77). Libraries Unlimited.

Inceoglu, M. M., & Ciloglugil, B. (2022). *Use of metaverse in education*. International conference on computational science and its applications (pp. 171–184). Springer.

Jiwon, A. (2019). Technology acceptance and influencing factors. *Journal of the Korea Convergence Society*, *10*, 487–494.

Karaca, Y., & Ilkım, M. (2021). Investigation of the attitudes distance education of the faculty of sport science students in the Covid-19 period. *Turkish Online Journal of Distance Education*, *22*(4), 114–129.

Kour, M. (2022). *Impact of pre-purchase trust and health risk on online grocery shopping during COVID-19*. 2022 international conference on disruptive technologies for multidisciplinary research and applications (CENTCON) (pp. 75–80).

Kour, M., & Kaur, R. (2020). Impact of social media marketing on consumer buying behaviour: An empirical study. *International Journal of Advanced Science and Technology*, *29*(11s), 975–984.

Kye, B., Han, N., Kim, E., Park, Y., & Jo, S. (2021). Educational applications of metaverse: Possibilities and limitations. *Journal of Educational Evaluation for Health Professions*, *18*, 18–32.

Lee, L.-H., Braud, T., Zhou, P., Wang, L., Xu, D., Lin, Z., Kumar, A., Bermejo, C., & Hui, P. (2021). *All one needs to know about metaverse: A complete survey on technological singularity, virtual ecosystem, and research agenda*. arXiv preprint arXiv:2110.05352.

Lin, P. H., & Yeh, S. C. (2019). How motion-control influences a VR-supported technology for mental rotation learning: From the perspectives of playfulness, gender difference, and technology acceptance model. *International Journal of Human–Computer Interaction*, *35*, 1736–1746.

Liu, X. (2022). The transformation of the library from the perspective of the metaverse: Space, resources and services. *World Scientific Research Journal*, *8*(8), 21–29.

Moon, J. W., & Kim, Y. G. (2001). Extending the TAM for a World-Wide-Web context. *Information & Management*, *38*, 217–230.

Morgan, J. P. (2022). Opprtunities in the Metaverse. https://www.jpmorgan.com/content/dam/jpm/treasury-services/documents/opportunities-in-the-metaverse.pdf

Oh, J. H. (2021). A study on factors affecting the intention to use the metaverse by applying the extended technology acceptance model (ETAM): Focused on the virtual world metaverse. *Journal of the Korea Contents Association*, *21*, 204–216.

Park, S. M., & Kim, Y. G. (2022). A Metaverse: Taxonomy, Components, Applications, and Open Challenges. *IEEE Access*, *10*, 4209–4251.

Sparkes, M. (2021). What is a metaverse. *New Scientist*, *251*, 18.

Spasojevic, V. L., & Ilic, M. Đ. (2021). *Educational effects of contextual learning in Serbian language classes*.

Srinivasan, R., Jha, A. K., & Verma, N. K. (2022). To talk or not?: An analysis of firm-initiated social media communication's impact on firm value preservation during a massive disruption across multiple firms and industries. *Decision Sciences*, *54*(4), 410–431.

Wang, F.-Y., Qin, R., Wang, X., & Hu, B. (2022). Metasocieties in metaverse: Metaeconomics and metamanagement for metaenterprises and metacities. *IEEE Transactions on Computational Social Systems*, *9*(1), 2–7.

Chapter 4

Metaverse Regulation for Artificial Intelligence: Conceptual Approach for Marketing Domain

Prabhjeet Kaur, Lokesh Jasrai and Aditya Kumar Divyam

Mittal School of Business, Lovely Professional University, Phagwara, India

Abstract

The comprehensive research aims to investigate the complex interplay between artificial intelligence (AI) and marketing regulations. It delves into the evolution of AI in marketing, assesses its contemporary applications, analyzes ethical and legal implications, examines existing regulatory frameworks, and identifies the gaps in AI regulations specific to the marketing domain. The purpose of this research is to provide a deep understanding of the critical need for AI regulation in marketing. This chapter employs a multi-faceted methodology, including literature review, comparative analysis, case studies, and theoretical frameworks. It synthesizes insights from AI policymakers, marketers, ethicists, legal experts, and scholars. It also investigates AI regulations across different countries and evaluates the impact of data privacy regulations such as General Data Protection Regulation (GDPR) on AI in marketing. The research findings highlight the evolution of AI in marketing, showcasing its transformative applications. The study undercovers the ethical and legal challenges posed by AI in marketing and regulations designed to promote different metaverses of AI to marketing domain. In conclusion, this research contributes to the understanding of the role of AI regulation in marketing. It provides a conceptual framework for AI regulation in marketing, incorporating ethical considerations and balancing innovation with consumer protection. The case studies exemplify real-world implications, and recommendations are

The AI Metaverse Revolution: Transforming Multi-Business Scenarios (Volume 1), 39–58

Published under exclusive licence by Emerald Publishing Limited
doi:10.1108/978-1-83662-582-720251004

offered for policymakers and marketers to ensure responsible AI adoption, compliance, and collaboration in the dynamic landscape of AI-driven marketing.

Keywords: AI in marketing; AI regulation; ethical implications; consumer protection; data privacy; metaverse regulations

Introduction

The term metaverse defines the regulatory purpose of AI in the marketing domain. The world has been transformed through AI, with changing patterns in datasets. The rapid advancement of artificial technology has led industrialists and healthcare specialists to adopt emerging technology to solve the digitalization problem in the industrial sectors of finance, marketing, retail, and transportation. Various examples have relayed such incidents worldwide.

The medical field is one of the sectors where AI is used for digital innovation. According to a study from Stanford University, AI can predict, with 90% accuracy, whether a patient will pass away in the hospital. This can help identify patients at significant risk so that they can receive proper care. In the financial sector, AI can detect fraud and predict marketing trends. For example, JPMorgan Chase developed a tool called COiN, which uses machine learning to analyze legal documents and extract meaningful information. This significantly reduces the time to review documents from 360,000 hours (approximately 41 years) to just a few seconds. Patients at considerable risk can be identified using this information, and proper care can be provided. Another example is in the educational sector, where personality and cognitive ability correlate with academic performance. This explains why personality tests increase the validity of learning approaches. Behavioural sciences include psychological assessment which helps enhance user experience with AI applications (Chamorro-Premuzic et al., 2016).

AI systems must be transparent, explainable, and responsible for addressing regulatory and legal issues. According to European Union research, 'AI legislation should be a vital component of the wider digital advancement policy framework, which ought to be founded on human-centric values and principles and aim at maximizing the advantages of AI while reducing the risks' (Chamorro-Premuzic et al., 2016). The authors discussed new technologies that can quickly and affordably predict human work performance. Industrial psychologists focusing on employee behaviour in the workplace have explained that very few studies explored the research aspect of new evaluation methods, leaving multiple aspects for practices with adequate data to judge the effectiveness of the tool.

Background of the Study

AI systems make confident decisions that affect human life. However, such decisions should be explainable, transparent, and accountable. In addition, such a system should comply with ethical and legal standards such as human rights and privacy laws. Therefore, it is essential to develop a comprehensive legal and regulatory framework for AI that addresses these issues. Using the same concept as an identical approach, a similar study proposes a methodological framework in which normative questions have been specified regarding whether such questions relate to the exploration of institutional rules. These rules should be adopted for AI or problematic issues, which should be resolved with the help of existing laws and courts (Petit, 2017).

Significance of the Study

This study suggests a theoretical observation in the digital innovation industry to create a conceptual foundation for AI legislation and regulation (Stathis & van den Herik, 2024). A multidisciplinary method was considered for conceptualizing the framework from legal, ethical, technical, and social perspectives (Ofosu-Ampong, 2024). This study aimed to address the relevant problems that must be solved to create and implement the most effective AI system (Triguero et al., 2024). This study introduces a conceptual framework for AI law and regulation, outlines the current scenario, discusses critical issues, and concludes with crucial contributions. Generative AI-integrated systems can automate routine tasks, predict complex patterns in datasets, and provide insights that were previously impossible to obtain (Sai et al., 2024).

Focus of the Study

Previous studies have specified the metaverse role of AI architecture, which is indirectly related to the development of robust human-centric AI (Yao et al., 2024). Although regulatory frameworks are often viewed as barriers, they can help interpret the aspects positive side of AI usage in the healthcare industry (Vidal et al., 2023). Hence, regulatory guidelines are required to ensure the safety use of AI. Another study suggested that achieving this goal requires a comprehensive assessment of diverse government standards and policies across all continents and establishing national control procedures (Blasch et al., 2019).

Literature Review

Highlights Concerns About AI

Issues related to AI that were raised at the time of its deployment in the public sector have been discussed. It focuses on the difficulties of balancing public law's commitment to reason-giving with AI tool's lack of explainability. Some difficulties enable states to use contemporary AI technologies to increase their system ability, distributive impact, and legitimacy. Previous studies support the public sector's cautious use of AI systems (Freeman Engstrom & Ho, 2021). Although AI is widely employed by the government, most innovations are technical or gradual. The 'AI WATCH' example states that collaborative learning workshops should concentrate on AI and data governance. The activities of the AI Monitor Task need to prioritize areas of policy, such as education, health, safety, security, housing, transit, and agriculture (van Noordt et al., 2020).

AI Progress Towards Human Interaction

The latest trend for trust is related to the occasion of a human-centred approach, which requires an assessment of the user's desire to use specific applications. This trend refers to online virtual systems for gaming hotspots. Research must understand the human-centric approach to technology adoption in order to support particular decisions and identify needs. In this seminar, industry developers brought together experts for intelligent interactions between people and AI in virtual (gaming) settings. It provides documentation of the project and its results, including enhanced AI–human interaction (Ashlock et al., 2023). With an approach towards the human-centric dynamics of AI, the system requires the preparation and control of intelligent segments. This study introduced the need for a model-based control system that combines automated planning and formal specifications.

Technological Aspect Among World Regulatory Bodies

Technologies based on AI are already reviving industries and establishing new economic sectors. Globally, governments and society are attempting to ascertain whether new ethical, legal, and regulatory systems are required to see where AI fits. Governance and policy are crucial to ensure that new technologies such as AI are used to their utmost capacity to benefit humankind while minimizing inherent risks and resolving societal concerns. This chapter offers an overview of some US government initiatives in these areas, as well as the perspectives of the four American Association for the Advancement of Science and Technology Policy for scholars who are working on a variety of AI-related issues (Madhavan et al., 2020). The three primary hazards of using AI data for training are innovation, discrimination, and data quality. It offers guidelines for a GDPR-compliant assurance standard for data collection and AI instruction as well as rules for the reuse of personal data (Hacker, 2021). The following study claims that the five levels of AI law data rules, specific to the application of AI regulations, general AI rules, general non-AI rules, and non-AI rules with the application, constitute a complicated stratigraphy. The mappings are the foundation for creating a grounded framework for classifying AI and its varieties. The study also offers recommendations for organizing AI compliance processes for professionals (Viljanen & Parviainen, 2022). Although AI is moving forward rapidly and changing the world, it poses legal concerns and issues. When evaluating the application of AI across different businesses, regulators must be aware of the legal dangers and difficulties in making wise decisions. Regulators and lawmakers must focus on the lack of legislation limiting the use and advancement of AI, such as autonomous vehicles, in the construction sector (Parveen, 2024).

Multidisciplinary Framework for Incorporating Legal, Ethical, Technical, and Social Perspectives

This study combines the technical, legal, and economic elements of explainability to define the appropriate amount in a particular setting. This study suggests three steps: identifying contextual circumstances, assessing technical resources, and determining production levels for global and local explanations. It stresses that explanations only benefit society when their overall social benefits outweigh their disadvantages (Beaudouin et al., 2020). The complexity of AI systems has raised issues with accountability from moral and legal standpoints. Although further multidisciplinary research is required to strengthen accountability frameworks, the current standards can be used (Boch et al., 2022).

This article offers European Commission (EC) 25 recommendations on regulating AI and data while preparing the Law of AI. It investigates how the impending European AI legal framework might be related to American law, offers a distinct strategy tailored to the incentives and dangers of each business, and makes recommendations on how to implement it. The EC is also developing the Data Act, which is a legal framework for data governance. The worldwide law of AI and data systems should be shaped by the global norms and standards established by EU. The EU needs to offer the rest of the world a distinct North Star, pointing towards a specific goal. It must adopt a comprehensive set of fundamental AI principles, distinguish various economic sectors, and collaborate with nations that adhere to European digital standards (Kop, 2020).

The underlying concepts are relatable to the arguments related to AI protection. AI can change human-based systems in the future, including creativity. Questions about authorship and copyright protection for computer-generated work are addressed in this article. It examines many legislative alternatives, including authorship, public domain status, *sui generis* safeguarding, and rights to publications and distributors (Frosio, 2021). Another study highlighted the proactive idea of modernizing and enhancing legally significant trade in the EU through smart contracting. Initiating such a plan emphasizes a realistic transition path to temper the escalating rush to embed exchanges (Solarte-Vásquez & Nyman-Metcalf, 2017). AI-integrated tools, applications, and software are recognized under an umbrella term that includes a variety of technologies that generate automatic judgements, suggestions, conclusions, or forecasts. Applications with the same characteristics as AI but built on different technologies are called 'algorithmic systems' to avoid creating false associations. Legal protection is necessary when innovations are used and have an impact on people or society as a whole (Thouvenin et al., 2021). The green-bond market study signifies that gathering private and public resources for climate change adaptation and mitigation is known as climate financing. Green bonds are among the many financial instruments used to support investments in climate finance. This study examines the role of policy research in climate financing, green bonds, and the development of green-bond regulations and standards. Additionally, it suggests opportunities for additional study in every one of our specialized fields (Mok et al., 2020).

Existing Regulatory Frameworks for AI in Different Industries

While AI in marketing can enhance customer involvement and decision-making, concerns about data security and consumer privacy still persists. The GDPR tackles this issue through an AI-based data analysis. However, the lack of regulations in obtaining and using AI-based data for predictive analytics generates uncertainty. Transparency and fairness are critical components of AI-powered marketing tactics. This provides experts perspectives with a balanced framework to incorporating it. This framework procures AI's potential while respecting individual rights and data privacy. A well-crafted regulatory framework is required to solve these issues while maintaining consumer trust.

Gap Analysis: Lack of Specific AI Regulations in Marketing

AI in marketing can assist a company's decision-making process and encourage consumer participation. However, attention must be paid to laws that can influence marketing tactics. The two primary issues are customer privacy and data protection. The GDPR aims to address these issues by regulating the data analysis that AI-based systems perform in order to produce personalized information. However, one significant drawback is the manner in which AI-derived data are obtained and applied to predictive analytics (Doshi-Velez & Kim, 2017). This lack of regulation creates uncertainty, making marketers consider the moral implications of their AI implementations and giving consumers concern about how their data are handled.

The context of reports presented by government entities, companies, firms, and individuals must be characterized by transparency and fairness. This is particularly critical in the realm of AI-powered marketing strategies which rely on a multitude of algorithm-based decisions (Albaroudi et al., 2024). System bias raises questions about company compliance with consumer protection regulations. To counter such a deviance, there is a need for a comprehensive framework. This balanced framework requires expert views from policymakers, legal experts, technologists, and marketers. Enabling balanced innovation in expert opinions can leverage the potential of AI, while safeguarding individual rights and data privacy.

The lack of specialized AI regulations in marketing underscores a crucial gap that necessitates prompt attention. A well-crafted regulatory framework must be established to harness AI's potential while preserving ethical tenets and consumer confidence. It should encompass the unique challenges posed by AI in marketing and offer clear guidelines to ensure responsible AI adoption, fair practices, and data protection.

Human-centric AI

Associated Risk with Human-centred AI

From a human-centric standpoint, this study examines how to modify conventional RE approaches to work with AI systems. A case study will be conducted to assess the modelling language after establishing the requirements and specifications and mapping them into one. According to literature, current RE techniques are not used by AI systems (Troussas et al., 2023). This study illustrates how an easy-to-use human-centric probabilistic analysis approach can democratize AI. The contradictions between environmental health and ecosystem vitality were revealed using 2018 environmental performance index information gathered from 180 nations (Papadimitriou et al., 2020). These tensions are exposed using AI-based predictive modelling approaches that have been used for water quality detection and healthcare record maintenance (How et al., 2020; Shah et al., 2021; van Smeden et al., 2022). Semantics and analytics can benefit from forthcoming waves of AI and Internet-of-Things (IoT)-enabled applications. Robotics and AI are being developed from a human-centric viewpoint, enabling us to better comprehend human action and intelligence. Better robotized medical processes, prosthetic and rehabilitative equipment, and human–machine interfaces can be created using research (Heng et al., 2022).

Ethical issues that automated decision-making (ADM) algorithms, such as algorithmic bias, are covered in this commentary. To resolve this issue, one must have a thorough understanding of sociotechnical systems, economic incentives, and individual and organizational behaviour. ADM frameworks that are human-centred and fairness-conscious emphasize the full participation of human decision-makers at every stage of the process. The ethical issues that ADM algorithms encounter, like algorithmic bias, are covered in this commentary. It makes the case that to resolve it, one must have a thorough understanding of sociotechnical systems, economic incentives, and individual and organizational behaviour. For management information system (MIS) researchers, new avenues for future research are made explicit (Adomavicius & Yang, 2022). The use of AI, Virtual Reality (VR), and augmented and virtual reality to improve railway asset management is proposed in this study as a human-centric design approach. This study strives to boost the efficiency and efficacy of the management. This upkeep processes in the railway industry as well as make information relevant, context-aware, and meaningful for end user (Kour et al., 2022). A cutting-edge concept known as 'human-centred artificial intelligence', or 'HCAI', envisions highly automated systems that are also under human control (Costabile et al., 2022).

Owing to its dual nature, AI poses both a danger and a way to safeguard information technology systems and human rights. This study discusses the negative effects of AI on human rights to safeguard information. The negative aspect of the information may limit the principle and its function during the design phase. This idea is believed to enhance AI system security and better match them with human rights. However, this frequently requires improvement in practice. During the design phase, the intended purpose should be carefully evaluated (Fantin & Vogiatzoglou, 2020). This study attempts to assist business decisions with data fusion from web scraping and suggests an approach analysis based on sentiment analysis and machine learning. Supervised learning generates explanations and enhances suggestions using human-focused AI (Kumar et al., 2021). By evaluating embryo quality, AI-based models can reliably predict IVF results. For the embryo-grading process to be as objective and reliable as possible, automatic forecasting models may be necessary. According to a comprehensive review and meta-analysis of 18 published studies, AI-based models may reliably predict live delivery, clinical pregnancy, pregnancy with a heartbeat, and ploidy status (Sfakianoudis et al., 2022). Governments and large corporations are developing AI, which is used in various sectors. This study examined what it takes to be human-centred, how AI is created, and what factors should be considered when developing human-centred AI to achieve sustainable development and the SDGs. It was concluded that other projects and the development of AI methods should employ human-in-the-loop ideas. The expansion of the government's AI expenditures, resolving data and technology biases, and solving data access challenges are among the policy considerations for human-centred AI to assist in achieving the SDGs (Mhlanga, 2022).

Conceptual Framework for Standardized AI Law and Regulation for Digital Innovation Growth in Industry Across the Globe

The study has detailed frameworks from the literature through a thematic approach to highlight the implementation of AI systems. This approach relates to issues such as the clinical usage of AI to create a framework and simultaneously influence multiple individual regulatory goals (TerKonda & Fish, 2023). The criteria-wise general data protection regulation and DDI (data-driven innovation) identification of models, purpose, and concepts are as follows. Table 4.1 provides details on types of data-driven models, with the purpose highlighted in the study and what are the concepts observed. These concepts helped in analyzing the metaverse regulation in different domains of the industry and research development areas. The core concepts like privacy issues, data-driven policies human-centred interaction in technology advancement, and how these data-driven models have been adopted by various studies. To conceptualize the themes related to these literature, manual concepts have been observed.

Case Studies: AI Regulation in Marketing

Case Study 1: AI Regulation in the Insurtech Industry

This case study explains how cutting-edge technologies (AI, deep learning, etc.) have been employed in insurance ecosystems. This case study provides a detailed explanation of the functions of AI in marketing services in the Insurtech sector (Infantino, 2024). Specifically, Lemonade's insurance case shows the contract and indemnity service that the company has been using to cover insurance losses. Lemonade's AI company uses an image of a medical certificate based on optical character recognition (OCR) as a compensation calculation service. The OCR is examined through domestic and international case reports of medical patients, provides safety, and proves the company's security system. These services have introduced the innovative use of AI in the system. These companies have significantly reduced the lead-time for insurance agreements and payments by utilizing machine learning with vast AI-based client data. There are frequent disagreements between

Table 4.1. Classification, Main Definitions, and Contributions to GDA and DDI.

Authors	Type of Data-driven Models	Purpose	Main Concepts Observed
Cheung and She (2016), Imran-Daud et al. (2016), and Zhan et al. (2020)	'Multimedia Information Systems Human Computing Interaction Social and Information Networks'	The study aims to design privacy-setting interfaces for IoT users that can automatically detect sensitive information about user privacy requirements as per the policy of the data publisher	'Real-world data, sensitivity, visibility of information and data management. Developing privacy profiles, privacy default settings, user privacy preferences. Privacy-driven access control, content-driven protection of user publications, textual messages, content'
Karegar et al. (2020)	'Security and Privacy'	The study analyzes the effectiveness, efficiency, user satisfaction, and privacy concerns related to consent form-based user interaction	'User privacy and engagement, user attention and satisfaction, types of interactions'
Malgieri and Custers (2018) and Hall et al. (2021)	'Privacy, Social Network Services Computer Technology Data Design, Data Base Tools'	The studies propose a framework for calculating users' privacy scores, analyzing data privacy rights, and examining issues related to sharing user profiles derived from mobile phone data	'Privacy scores, users in online social networks, privacy issues, privacy risk. Data-driven economy, pricing privacy, user personal data. Privacy risk assessment, risk-users, quality of user profiles, user classification of privacy'

(*Continued*)

Authors	Type of Data-driven Models	Purpose	Main Concepts Observed
Saura et al. (2021)	'Human-Computer Interaction'	The study aims to evaluate the elements that influence user's tendency to control personal data in and outflows, focusing on online privacy	'Privacy controls over data flows, concerns over information privacy, individuals' privacy empowerment'
Quiñones-Gómez et al. (2024) and Qiao and Yin (2019)	'Recommendation with privacy-preservation'	The proposal is to propose a data-driven service and recommend a system like a CDN framework	'Collaborative filtering, context-aware, temporal information of service invocations, privacy, and decision-making'
Yu et al. (2024)	'Data Privacy, Computer Science'	The study proposes a data-driven analysis method that secures user details that are sensitive and according to privacy rules for disclosure of data. It also focuses on evaluating a real online behaviour dataset	'Online user behaviour data, behaviour data, privacy protection, privacy disclosure'
Ishteyaq et al. (2024) and Zhou et al. (2024)	'Technology and communication enhancement'	The studies explore the application of blockchain technology 5G networks and its potential for user data, and the other literature highlights data security and privacy issues	'5G technology, connectivity, users' perceptions, new technologies testing. Cloud storage, user's data security, user's privacy protection, information disclosure, privacy disclosure'

Mohammed and Rozsa (2024)	'Information Systems'	The study aims to explore attributes that influence user's privacy, check devices fitness, and verify data variations	'Information privacy, collecting sensitive data, privacy concerns'
Gupta et al. (2024), Shieh et al. (2024), and Toti and Steils (2024)	'Information Management Computer Privacy & Communication Networks Privacy and data models'	The study proposes a model for analyzing consumer perception of personalized online ads, explains a multi-dimensional data-driven model, and analyzes subjective privacy and awareness evaluation issues using a data-driven model	'Consumer perceptions of ads on the click-through intention, privacy concerns, social content, trust. Privacy preservation, service recommendations, quality ensemble-driven recommendation. User privacy-aware preferences, observable user data, privacy issues of social network behaviours'

policyholders and insurers over indemnity estimation, which was determined with accurate and appropriate compensation, as seen in the case of a UAE company (Abu Yazbek, 2023). In the current case study, AI regulation implementation can be discussed in the insurance industry as per a study by initiating the insurance policy applicability and implementation of certain proceedings until the claimant is completed. This case study highlights that all proceedings should be transparent, so there are no chances of loopholes. These loopholes can be prevented by implementing AI in insurance-related online systems (Kelly et al., 2019). This will provide security to authenticity and other concerns that obligate consumer's hesitation to purchase such a policy (Chen et al., 2022). In the metaverse league, the healthcare sector and healthcare-related insurance policies are covered but yet to be implemented appropriately. This implementation has both positive and negative effects. With the implementation of AI, world nations can obtain an overview of whether loan or charity cases for which money from insurance policies has been issued are correctly used. Another aspect relates to the marketing coverage. Nowadays, transparency can be utilized as one of the metaverse regulations for practical marketing approaches for effective decision-making (Dwivedi et al., 2023).

Case Study 2: Chatbot Potential for Industry

Both consumers and businesses can profit greatly from customized marketing strategies. Chatbots have the potential to revolutionize personalized marketing by collecting, analyzing, and utilizing client data, while facilitating communication (Shanmugam et al., 2023). This comprehensive case study assesses the potential of using chatbots from an industrial viewpoint, highlighting significant advantages, difficulties, and possible next steps that businesses might take when utilizing chatbots for marketing. It is based on the qualitative information gathered from an emerging field company. Our primary findings suggest that chatbots deliver more effective and less invasive consumer approaches and improve customer identification and segmentation (Kaushal & Yadav, 2023). With advanced technology such as AI-integrated chatbots, concerns are related to the development of a legal and regulatory framework. This case study provides a method to create flexible regulations to adapt to the evolving nature of AI technology in metaverse marketing. The case study also addresses the need for a metaverse framework relevance related to questions addressing bureaucratic problems during its implementation. The metaverse regulation states that while establishing AI-enabled advanced technology, clear guidelines and ethical standards should be followed. This regulatory action will reduce potential risks and build trust among the industry that has already adopted blockchain technology (Gadekallu et al., 2022). For industry, the study of Habbal et al. (2024) states that the AI-based 'TRiSM' framework can provide reliability and trustworthiness of this advanced technology adaptation. Benefits and challenges are also present, such as regulatory compliance for stakeholder collaboration. The future of metaverse regulations has been explored in terms of security, fundamentals, and privacy. This metaverse regulation architecture was drafted with countermeasures for future systems (Wang et al., 2023). The option to increase cybersecurity assessments (Radanliev, 2024) requires an evolving landscape of regulatory advancements. This cybersecurity assessment highlights gaps in the existing standards that require improvement. Metaverse regulation has the potential to integrate technologies for industrial production. These challenges include interoperability and future research directions (Zhang et al., 2024).

Case Study 3: Chatbot Potential for Marketing Industry

The numerous uses of AI in marketing are yet to result in mainstream acceptance. However, AI has the potential to change the marketing industry and make it subject to businesses through its application. This study aims to provide an in-depth understanding of the long-term effects of AI on marketing by examining existing applications, prospective use cases, implementation opportunities, and optimization areas. It focuses on the challenges and possible uses for businesses that offer predictions regarding the direction of marketing. These are important for staying competitive in the future. The focus should be on robotic process automation, or RPA (Perret & Heitkamp, 2021). The metaverse will impact marketing that allows businesses to maintain their identities. The adaptation of technology among Generation Z will enhance brand awareness. It is only possible through digital technology, which is AI-powered (Nalbant & Aydın, 2023). The competitive edge will improve the growth in marketing. For mandating AI metaverse regulation in chatbots, organizations need to establish norms that can share values and guidelines that are responsible for technology and data. Regulation related to data usage and its deletion from the decision support system must be impactful (Wirtz & Pitardi, 2023).

Case Study 4: Moral Implication of AI on Minorities in the Organization

There has long been discussion on the moral implications of AI. Scholars and pundits have drawn attention to the shortcomings of AI about women, minorities who are visible, older adults, youth, and Native Americans. There are now several ethical standards and suggestions for AI. These recommendations offer moral precepts and values that prioritize people to direct the development of responsible AI. These rules have no legal force behind them and have no bearing. The time has come to support efforts aimed at regulating AI worldwide, considering human rights and ethical norms while developing AI. The government must step in, and marginalized communities must speak up to ensure AI laws are customized to their needs. This research focuses on the risks that marginalized and minority communities encounter due to technology and discrimination linked to the ethical challenges posed by AI. The following problem also proposes using AI vigilance in a regulatory manner to oversee AI technology use and counter potential harm caused by AI actions. The envisioned AI vigilantes would be individuals or groups more vulnerable to AI's impacts. This well-intentioned initiative aims to cooperate with authorities to prevent the misuse of power (Nwafor, 2021).

Comprehending Regulations, Laws, Policies, and Decisions for Future

Addressing Challenges in the Implementation of AI Regulation in Marketing

As integrating AI in marketing gains momentum, addressing the challenges of implementing effective AI regulation becomes paramount. These challenges emerge from AI technologies' dynamic and evolving nature, the complex marketing landscape, and the need to balance innovation with consumer protection. Navigating these challenges is essential to ensure that AI-driven marketing practices adhere to ethical standards, legal requirements, and societal expectations. One significant challenge lies in the rapid pace of AI advancements. The regulatory landscape must grapple with keeping pace with technological developments to ensure that regulations remain relevant and adaptable. Traditional regulatory approaches may need help to keep up with the agility of AI systems, leading to potential gaps or outdated guidelines. A forward-looking regulatory framework incorporating flexibility and continuous update mechanisms is essential to address this challenge (Zittrain et al., 2017).

The opacity of AI algorithms poses another obstacle. The intricate workings of AI systems often elude clear interpretation, making it challenging to assess their fairness, transparency, and potential biases. Crafting regulations that mandate algorithmic transparency without stifling innovation is a delicate task. Striking a balance between protecting proprietary algorithms and ensuring public accountability requires collaboration between regulatory bodies and industry stakeholders (Diakopoulos, 2016). Furthermore, the global nature of marketing and AI technologies introduces cross-jurisdictional challenges. With varying cultural norms, legal traditions, and levels of AI adoption, harmonizing regulations across jurisdictions becomes complex. The extraterritorial impact of AI-driven marketing campaigns necessitates international cooperation to ensure consistent standards and enforcement mechanisms, as per the European Parliament (2021).

Ethical considerations also play a pivotal role in the regulation of AI. The question of defining and operationalizing ethical AI practices in marketing is multifaceted. Ethical frameworks must accommodate diverse cultural perspectives and uphold universal values. Integrating ethical guidelines into AI regulations requires interdisciplinary collaboration among technologists, ethicists, policymakers, and marketers (Jobin et al., 2019). As AI technologies evolve, so do job displacement and workforce disruption concerns. Striking a balance between AI-driven automation and job preservation poses a challenge for policymakers and regulators. Regulations must encourage innovation while safeguarding livelihoods through measures such as reskilling initiatives and supportive labour policies (Acemoglu & Restrepo, 2019).

Addressing challenges in the implementation of AI regulations in marketing demands a multidimensional approach that considers technological, ethical, and regulatory nuances (Ali et al., 2023). A proactive and collaborative regulatory framework that accounts for AI advancements, transparency, cross-border complexities, ethics, and workforce impacts is essential (Fatima et al., 2020). By recognizing these challenges and embracing adaptability, policymakers can shape a regulatory environment that supports responsible and beneficial AI-driven marketing practices (Dwivedi et al., 2021).

The Need for Cross-disciplinary Collaboration in AI Regulation

The rapid advancement and integration of AI technologies across various industries have underscored the imperative for cross-disciplinary collaboration in shaping effective AI regulation. The multifaceted nature of AI, encompassing technical, ethical, legal, and societal dimensions, necessitates expertise from diverse fields to develop comprehensive regulatory frameworks that are both innovative and responsible technologies, ranging from machine-learning algorithms to neural networks, deeply rooted in computer science and engineering principles. However, the ethical implications of AI decisions, algorithmic biases, and societal impacts transcend technical considerations. Collaboration with ethicists, philosophers, and social scientists is crucial to ensure that AI regulations account for potential consequences and prioritize human values (Floridi & Cowls, 2022). These collaborations facilitate a more holistic understanding of how AI systems interact with and impact individuals, communities, and societies.

Conclusion and Implications for the Future of AI Regulation in Marketing

This study has undertaken a comprehensive theoretical explanation in exploring the relationship between AI and marketing regulation, shedding light on the multifaceted dynamics that shape this evolving landscape. By synthesizing insights from diverse stakeholders, including AI policymakers, marketers, ethicists, legal experts, and scholars, this study has delved into the critical intersection of innovation, consumer protection, and ethical considerations within AI-driven marketing practices. Through an in-depth examination of existing regulatory frameworks, it becomes evident that while AI regulations are emerging in various sectors, they need more specificity when applied to marketing. The gap analysis underscores the absence and need for comprehensive guidelines addressing the nuanced challenges posed by AI-driven marketing. Moreover, exploring AI ethics guidelines emphasizes the centrality of core principles such as transparency, fairness, and accountability in shaping responsible AI deployment. The case studies underscore the practical implications of ethical considerations and data privacy in real-world AI-driven marketing scenarios.

The implications derived from this research hold far-reaching significance for the trajectory of AI regulation in the marketing realm. The proposed guidelines offer actionable recommendations for policymakers and marketers, providing a structured framework to navigate the intricate landscape of AI technologies while upholding consumer rights and ethical norms. Emphasizing transparency, data privacy, fairness, ethical AI practices, and collaborative efforts ensures a holistic approach that strikes a balance between innovation and societal well-being.

Looking ahead, the future of AI regulation in marketing presents a transformative prospect. By integrating continuous monitoring and evaluation mechanisms, regulatory frameworks can swiftly adapt to the rapid evolution of AI technologies. The globalization of markets and the borderless nature of AI require coordinated efforts among jurisdictions, highlighting the paramount importance of cross-border collaboration to establish harmonized and effective regulations.

Beyond regulatory compliance, the implications extend to the marketing ecosystem as a whole. The insights garnered from ethical AI practices and consumer protection principles not only serve as guidelines for marketers but also foster trust and long-lasting relationships with consumers. By adhering to these principles, marketers can cultivate a sense of empowerment, respect, and mutual benefit, thereby nurturing sustainable customer engagement.

In summation, this journey through the realm of AI regulation in marketing has illuminated a path where technological innovation converges with ethical integrity and consumer safeguarding. The insights and recommendations presented in this research provide a compass for steering the course of AI-driven marketing towards an equitable, transparent, and prosperous future. As AI continues to shape the marketing landscape, the principles delineated in this study will serve as guiding beacons, ensuring that AI-driven marketing endeavours create value not only for businesses but also for the broader society and consumers as well.

References

Abu Yazbek, F. H. (2023). *Takaful insurance: A critical evaluation of Takaful business in the UAE and its prospects for growth* [PhD dissertation, University of Hertfordshire].

Acemoglu, D., & Restrepo, P. (2019). Automation and new tasks: How technology displaces and reinstates labor. *Journal of Economic Perspectives, 33*(2), 3–30.

Adomavicius, G., & Yang, M. (2022). Integrating behavioral, economic, and technical insights to understand and address algorithmic bias: A human-centric perspective. *ACM Transactions on Management Information Systems, 13*(3), 34. https://doi.org/10.1145/3519420

Albaroudi, E., Mansouri, T., & Alameer, A. (2024). A comprehensive review of AI techniques for addressing algorithmic bias in job hiring. *AI, 5*(1), 383–404.

Ali, S., Abuhmed, T., El-Sappagh, S., Muhammad, K., Alonso-Moral, J. M., Confalonieri, R., Guidotti, R., Del Ser, J., Díaz-Rodríguez, N., & Herrera, F. (2023). Explainable artificial intelligence (XAI): What we know and what is left to attain trustworthy artificial intelligence. *Information Fusion, 99*, 101805.

Ashlock, D., Maghsudi, S., Liebana, D. P., Spronck, P., & Eberhardinger, M. (2023). *Human-game AI interaction: Report from Dagstuhl Seminar 22251*.

Beaudouin, V., Bloch, I., Bounie, D., Clémençon, S., d'Alché-Buc, F., Eagan, J., Maxwell, W., Mozharovskyi, P., & Parekh, J. (2020). *Flexible and context-specific AI explainability: A multidisciplinary approach*. arXiv preprint arXiv:2003.07703.

Blasch, E., Sung, J., Nguyen, T., Daniel, C. P., & Mason, A. P. (2019). *Artificial intelligence strategies for national security and safety standards*. arXiv preprint arXiv:1911.05727.

Boch, A., Hohma, E., & Trauth, R. (2022). *Towards an accountability framework for AI: Ethical and legal considerations*. Institute for Ethics in AI, Technical University of Munich.

Chamorro-Premuzic, T., Winsborough, D., Sherman, R. A., & Hogan, R. (2016). New talent signals: Shiny new objects or a brave new world? *Industrial and Organizational Psychology*, *9*(3), 621–640. https://doi.org/10.1017/iop.2016.6

Chen, Z., Wu, J., Gan, W., & Qi, Z. (2022, December 17–20). *Metaverse security and privacy: An overview*. 2022 IEEE International Conference on Big Data (Big Data).

Cheung, M., & She, J. (2016). Evaluating the privacy risk of user-shared images. *ACM Transactions on Multimedia Computing, Communications, and Applications*, *12*(4s), 58. https://doi.org/10.1145/2978568

Costabile, M. F., Desolda, G., Dimauro, G., Lanzilotti, R., Loiacono, D., Matera, M., & Zancanaro, M. (2022). *A human-centric AI-driven framework for exploring large and complex datasets*. CEUR workshop proceedings.

Diakopoulos, N. (2016). Accountability in algorithmic decision making. *Communications of the ACM*, *59*(2), 56–62.

Doshi-Velez, F., & Kim, B. (2017). *Towards a rigorous science of interpretable machine learning*. arXiv preprint arXiv:1702.08608.

Dwivedi, Y. K., Hughes, L., Ismagilova, E., Aarts, G., Coombs, C., Crick, T., Duan, Y., Dwivedi, R., Edwards, J., & Eirug, A. (2021). Artificial Intelligence (AI): Multidisciplinary perspectives on emerging challenges, opportunities, and agenda for research, practice and policy. *International Journal of Information Management*, *57*, 101994.

Dwivedi, Y. K., Hughes, L., Wang, Y., Alalwan, A. A., Ahn, S. J., Balakrishnan, J., Barta, S., Belk, R., Buhalis, D., & Dutot, V. (2023). Metaverse marketing: How the metaverse will shape the future of consumer research and practice. *Psychology & Marketing*, *40*(4), 750–776.

Fantin, S., & Vogiatzoglou, P. (2020). *Purpose limitation by design as a counter to function creep and system insecurity in police artificial intelligence*. United Nations Interregional Crime and Justice Research Institute (UNICRI).

Fatima, S., Desouza, K. C., & Dawson, G. S. (2020). National strategic artificial intelligence plans: A multi-dimensional analysis. *Economic Analysis and Policy*, *67*, 178–194.

Floridi, L., & Cowls, J. (2022). A unified framework of five principles for AI in society. In S. Carta (Ed.), *Machine learning and the city: Applications in architecture and urban design* (pp. 535–545). John Wiley & Sons Ltd.

Freeman Engstrom, D., & Ho, D. E. (2021). Chapter 3: Artificially intelligent government: A review and agenda. In R. Vogl (Ed.), *Research handbook on big data law* (pp. 57–86). Edward Elgar Publishing. https://doi.org/10.4337/9781788972826.00009

Frosio, G. (2021). *The Nonexistent A (I) uthor: a Techno-legal Argument Against the Protection of AI-generated Creativity (L'(I) Autore inesistente: una tesi tecno-giuridica contro la tutela dell'opera generata dall'Intelligenza Artificiale)*.

Gadekallu, T. R., Huynh-The, T., Wang, W., Yenduri, G., Ranaweera, P., Pham, Q.-V., da Costa, D. B., & Liyanage, M. (2022). *Blockchain for the metaverse: A review*. arXiv preprint arXiv:2203.09738.

Gupta, S., Paul, J., Stoner, J. L., & Aggarwal, A. (2024). Digital transformation, online advertising, and consumer behaviour. *International Journal of Advertising*, *43*(8), 1–24.

Habbal, A., Ali, M. K., & Abuzaraida, M. A. (2024). Artificial Intelligence Trust, Risk and Security Management (AI TRiSM): Frameworks, applications, challenges and future research directions. *Expert Systems with Applications*, *240*, 122442. https://doi.org/10.1016/j.eswa.2023.122442

Hacker, P. (2021). A legal framework for AI training data – From first principles to the Artificial Intelligence Act. *Law, Innovation and Technology*, *13*(2), 257–301. https://doi.org/10.1080/17579961.2021.1977219

Hall, A., Liu, X. M., & Murphy, D. (2021, 13–16 October). *Integrating andragogy theory into a multidisciplinary curriculum to achieve a connected program for a doctorate in cybersecurity*. 2021 IEEE frontiers in education conference (FIE).

Heng, W., Solomon, S., & Gao, W. (2022). Flexible electronics and devices as human–machine interfaces for medical robotics. *Advanced Materials*, *34*(16), 2107902.

How, M.-L., Cheah, S.-M., Chan, Y.-J., Khor, A. C., & Say, E. M. (2020). Artificial intelligence-enhanced decision support for informing global sustainable development: A human-centric AI-thinking approach. *Information*, *11*(1), 1–24.

Imran-Daud, M., Sánchez, D., & Viejo, A. (2016). Privacy-driven access control in social networks by means of automatic semantic annotation. *Computer Communications*, *76*, 12–25.

Infantino, M. (2024). A comparative study of automated quantification in digital insurance. *International Journal of Digital Law and Governance*.

Ishteyaq, I., Muzaffar, K., Shafi, N., & Alathbah, M. A. (2024). Unleashing the power of tomorrow: Exploration of next frontier with 6G networks and cutting edge technologies. *IEEE Access*, *12*, 29445–29463. https://doi.org/10.1109/ACCESS.2024.3367976

Jobin, A., Ienca, M., & Vayena, E. (2019). The global landscape of AI ethics guidelines. *Nature Machine Intelligence*, *1*(9), 389–399.

Karegar, F., Pettersson, J. S., & Fischer-Hübner, S. (2020). The Dilemma of user engagement in privacy notices: Effects of interaction modes and habituation on user attention. *ACM Transactions on Privacy and Security*, *23*(1), 5. https://doi.org/10.1145/3372296

Kaushal, V., & Yadav, R. (2023). Learning successful implementation of Chatbots in businesses from B2B customer experience perspective. *Concurrency and Computation: Practice and Experience*, *35*(1), e7450.

Kelly, C. J., Karthikesalingam, A., Suleyman, M., Corrado, G., & King, D. (2019). Key challenges for delivering clinical impact with artificial intelligence. *BMC Medicine*, *17*(1), 195. https://doi.org/10.1186/s12916-019-1426-2

Kop, M. (2020). *Shaping the law of AI: Transatlantic perspectives*.

Kour, R., Castaño, M., Karim, R., Patwardhan, A., Kumar, M., & Granström, R. (2022). A human-centric model for sustainable asset management in railway: A case study. *Sustainability*, *14*(2), 1–19.

Kumar, S. A., Nasralla, M. M., García-Magariño, I., & Kumar, H. (2021). A machine-learning scraping tool for data fusion in the analysis of sentiments about pandemics for supporting business decisions with human-centric AI explanations. *PeerJ Computer Science*, *7*, e713.

Madhavan, R., Kerr, J. A., Corcos, A. R., & Isaacoff, B. P. (2020). Toward trustworthy and responsible artificial intelligence policy development. *IEEE Intelligent Systems*, *35*(5), 103–108. https://doi.org/10.1109/MIS.2020.3019679

Malgieri, G., & Custers, B. (2018). Pricing privacy – The right to know the value of your personal data. *Computer Law & Security Review*, *34*(2), 289–303. https://doi.org/10.1016/j.clsr.2017.08.006

Mhlanga, D. (2022). Human-centered artificial intelligence: The superlative approach to achieve sustainable development goals in the fourth industrial revolution. *Sustainability*, *14*(13), 1–22.

Mohammed, A. A., & Rozsa, Z. (2024). Consumers' intentions to utilize smartphone diet applications: An integration of the privacy calculus model with self-efficacy, trust and experience. *British Food Journal*, *126*(6), 2416–2437. https://doi.org/10.1108/BFJ-11-2023-0989

Mok, L. W., Tripathy, A., & Lunven, G. (2020). A multidisciplinary literature review of academic research on the green bond market. *Journal of Environmental Investing*, 100–129.

Nalbant, K. G., & Aydın, S. (2023). Development and transformation in digital marketing and branding with artificial intelligence and digital technologies dynamics in the Metaverse universe. *Journal of Metaverse*, *3*(1), 9–18.

Nwafor, I. E. (2021). AI ethical bias: a case for AI vigilantism (AIlantism) in shaping the regulation of AI. *International Journal of Law and Information Technology*, *29*(3), 225–240.

Ofosu-Ampong, K. (2024). Artificial intelligence research: A review on dominant themes, methods, frameworks and future research directions. *Telematics and Informatics Reports*, *14*, 100127. https://doi.org/10.1016/j.teler.2024.100127

Papadimitriou, E., Neves, A. R., & Saisana, M. (2020). *JRC statistical audit of the 2020 environmental performance index*. Publications Office of the European Union Luxembourg.

Perret, J. K., & Heitkamp, M. (2021). On the potentials of artificial intelligence in marketing – The case of robotic process automation. *International Journal of Applied Research in Management and Economics*, *4*(4), 35–55.

Petit, N. (2017). *Law and regulation of artificial intelligence and robots-conceptual framework and normative implications*. SSRN 2931339.

Qiao, B., & Yin, H. (2019). A data-driven and the deep learning based CDN recommendation framework for ICPs. *Peer-to-Peer Networking and Applications*, *12*(5), 1445–1453. https://doi.org/10.1007/s12083-018-0673-x

Quiñones-Gómez, J. C., Mor, E., & Chacón, J. (2024). Data-driven design in the design process: A systematic literature review on challenges and opportunities. *International Journal of Human–Computer Interaction*, 1–26. https://doi.org/10.1080/10447318.2024.2318060

Radanliev, P. (2024). Integrated cybersecurity for metaverse systems operating with artificial intelligence, blockchains, and cloud computing. *Frontiers in Blockchain*, *7*. https://www.frontiersin.org/journals/blockchain/articles/10.3389/fbloc.2024.1359130

Sai, S., Gaur, A., Sai, R., Chamola, V., Guizani, M., & Rodrigues, J. J. P. C. (2024). Generative AI for transformative healthcare: A comprehensive study of emerging models, applications, case studies, and limitations. *IEEE Access*, *12*, 31078–31106. https://doi.org/10.1109/ACCESS.2024.3367715

Saura, J. R., Ribeiro-Soriano, D., & Palacios-Marqués, D. (2021). From user-generated data to data-driven innovation: A research agenda to understand user privacy in digital markets. *International Journal of Information Management*, *60*, 102331. https://doi.org/10.1016/j.ijinfomgt.2021.102331

Sfakianoudis, K., Maziotis, E., Grigoriadis, S., Pantou, A., Kokkini, G., Trypidi, A., Giannelou, P., Zikopoulos, A., Angeli, I., Vaxevanoglou, T., Pantos, K., & Simopoulou, M. (2022). Reporting on the value of artificial intelligence in predicting the optimal embryo for transfer: A systematic review including data synthesis. *Biomedicines*, *10*(3), 1–20.

Shah, M. I., Alaloul, W. S., Alqahtani, A., Aldrees, A., Musarat, M. A., & Javed, M. F. (2021). Predictive modeling approach for surface water quality: Development and comparison of machine learning models. *Sustainability*, *13*(14), 1–20.

Shanmugam, G., Rajendran, D., Thanarajan, T., Murugaraj, S. S., & Rajendran, S. (2023). Artificial intelligence as a catalyst in digital marketing: Enhancing profitability and market potential. *Ingénierie des Systèmes d'Information*, *28*(6), 1627–1636. https://doi.org/10.18280/isi.280620

Shieh, C.-H., Ling, I. L., & Liu, Y.-F. (2024). The role of privacy-related factors in consumer perceptions of smart advertising. *Journal of Service Theory and Practice*, *34*(2), 216–241. https://doi.org/10.1108/JSTP-11-2022-0252

Solarte-Vásquez, M. C., & Nyman-Metcalf, K. (2017). Smart contracting: A multidisciplinary and proactive approach for the EU digital single market. *TalTech Journal of European Studies*, *7*(2), 208–246. https://doi.org/10.1515/bjes-2017-0017

Stathis, G., & van den Herik, J. (2024). Ethical and preventive legal technology. *AI and Ethics*, 1–18. https://doi.org/10.1007/s43681-023-00413-2

TerKonda, S. P., & Fish, E. M. (2023). Artificial intelligence viewed through the lens of state regulation. *Intelligence-Based Medicine*, *7*, 100088. https://doi.org/10.1016/j.ibmed.2023.100088

Thouvenin, F., Christen, M., Bernstein, A., Braun Binder, N., Burri, T., Donnay, K., Jäger, L., Jaffé, M., Krauthammer, M., & Lohmann, M. (2021). *A legal framework for artificial intelligence*. Position paper.

Toti, J.-F., & Steils, N. (2024). Showing or hiding? The impact of visibility of general conditions of use on retargeted Ad intrusiveness and perceived ethicality of mobile apps. *Journal of Interactive Marketing*, 10949968231221472. https://doi.org/10.1177/10949968231221472

Triguero, I., Molina, D., Poyatos, J., Del Ser, J., & Herrera, F. (2024). General purpose artificial intelligence systems (GPAIS): Properties, definition, taxonomy, societal implications and responsible governance. *Information Fusion, 103*, 102135. https://doi.org/10.1016/j.inffus.2023.102135

Troussas, C., Krouska, A., Koliarakis, A., & Sgouropoulou, C. (2023). Harnessing the power of user-centric artificial intelligence: Customized Recommendations and personalization in hybrid recommender systems. *Computers, 12*(5), 1–13.

van Noordt, C., Misuraca, G., Mortati, M., Rizzo, F., & Timan, T. (2020). *AI Watch-Artificial Intelligence for the public sector: Report of the "1st Peer Learning Workshop on the use and impact of AI in public services"*, Brussels 11–12 February 2020.

van Smeden, M., Heinze, G., Van Calster, B., Asselbergs, F. W., Vardas, P. E., Bruining, N., de Jaegere, P., Moore, J. H., Denaxas, S., Boulesteix, A. L., & Moons, K. G. M. (2022). Critical appraisal of artificial intelligence-based prediction models for cardiovascular disease. *European Heart Journal, 43*(31), 2921–2930. https://doi.org/10.1093/eurheartj/ehac238

Vidal, D. E., Loufek, B., Kim, Y.-H., & Vidal, N. Y. (2023). Navigating US regulation of artificial intelligence in medicine – A primer for physicians. *Mayo Clinic Proceedings: Digital Health, 1*(1), 31–39. https://doi.org/10.1016/j.mcpdig.2023.01.003

Viljanen, M., & Parviainen, H. (2022). AI applications and regulation: mapping the regulatory strata [original research]. *Frontiers in Computer Science, 3*, 1–11. https://doi.org/10.3389/fcomp.2021.779957

Wang, Y., Su, Z., Zhang, N., Xing, R., Liu, D., Luan, T. H., & Shen, X. (2023). A survey on metaverse: Fundamentals, security, and privacy. *IEEE Communications Surveys & Tutorials, 25*(1), 319–352. https://doi.org/10.1109/COMST.2022.3202047

Wirtz, J., & Pitardi, V. (2023). How intelligent automation, service robots, and AI will reshape service products and their delivery. *Italian Journal of Marketing, 2023*(3), 289–300. https://doi.org/10.1007/s43039-023-00076-1

Yao, X., Ma, N., Zhang, J., Wang, K., Yang, E., & Faccio, M. (2024). Enhancing wisdom manufacturing as industrial metaverse for industry and society 5.0. *Journal of Intelligent Manufacturing, 35*(1), 235–255. https://doi.org/10.1007/s10845-022-02027-7

Yu, E., Ye, Z., Zhang, Z., Qian, L., & Xie, M. (2024). A federated recommendation algorithm based on user clustering and meta-learning. *Applied Soft Computing*, 111483. https://doi.org/10.1016/j.asoc.2024.111483

Zhan, T., Yin, K., Xiong, J., He, Z., & Wu, S.-T. (2020). Augmented reality and virtual reality displays: Perspectives and challenges. *Iscience, 23*(8), 1–13.

Zhang, S., Li, J., Shi, L., Ding, M., Nguyen, D. C., Chen, W., & Han, Z. (2024). *Industrial metaverse: Enabling technologies, open problems, and future trends*. arXiv preprint arXiv:2405.08542.

Zhou, Z., Onireti, O., Xu, H., Zhang, L., & Imran, M. (2024). AI and blockchain enabled future wireless networks: A survey and outlook. *Distributed Ledger Technology, 3*(3), 1–30. https://doi.org/10.1145/3644369

Zittrain, J. L., Faris, R., Noman, H., Clark, J., Tilton, C., & Morrison-Westphal, R. (2017). The shifting landscape of global internet censorship (pp. 17–38). Berkman Klein Center Research Publication.

Chapter 5

Beyond Boundaries: Uniting AI and the Metaverse for Tomorrow's Realities

Hafijull Mondal

Department of Library and Information Science, Netaji Subhas Open University, Kolkata, India
Elitte Institute of Engineering and Management, Kolkata, India

Abstract

This chapter explores the intersection of artificial intelligence (AI) and the Metaverse, aiming to understand the potential impact of combining these two transformative technologies. By adopting a multidisciplinary approach, the chapter reviews research in AI, virtual reality (VR), augmented reality (AR), and emerging digital trends. It draws on case studies, theoretical insights, and potential future scenarios to investigate the merging of AI and the Metaverse. The findings highlight how this integration could revolutionize human–machine interactions, enhance immersive experiences, and unlock new possibilities in areas such as gaming, education, healthcare, and business. Additionally, the chapter provides practical guidance for researchers, developers, and policymakers on leveraging AI within Metaverse platforms, designing immersive experiences, and addressing ethical considerations. This work stands out for its originality, offering a novel perspective by synthesizing ideas from diverse fields and inspiring innovative thinking about the future of AI and the Metaverse.

Keywords: Artificial intelligence; Metaverse; virtual reality; augmented reality; human–machine interaction; digital technologies

The AI Metaverse Revolution: Transforming Multi-Business Scenarios (Volume 1), 59–75

Published under exclusive licence by Emerald Publishing Limited
doi:10.1108/978-1-83662-582-720251005

1. Introduction

In the ever-growing field of technology, two key concepts – the Metaverse and AI – are set to change how we interact, learn, work, and view reality. The Metaverse is a shared digital space where people can explore and connect through virtual worlds, combining elements of AR and VR. On the other hand, AI uses algorithms and computational power to mimic human intelligence, helping with tasks, problem-solving, and information processing. The importance of the Metaverse comes from its growth from a simple idea into a powerful digital reality. It's a vast virtual ecosystem where people can engage, create, and interact within a constantly expanding digital world. Once just a part of science fiction, the Metaverse is now a real blend of technology, connectivity, and human imagination.

Meanwhile, AI has evolved from basic logical processes to advanced deep learning systems, expanding what's possible in technology. It's become a widespread tool that enhances human abilities, automates tasks, and improves decision-making across different fields. The merging of AI and the Metaverse marks a crucial point in technological progress. It points to a future where virtual environments are not only immersive but also intelligent, where digital spaces are both interactive and adaptive, and where human experiences go beyond the limits of the physical world.

This chapter aims to explore how these two concepts work together. It will look at their individual roles and highlight how their combination could affect society, the economy, and technological growth. The following sections of this chapter will take a closer look at the Metaverse and AI, examining their development and how they each contribute to the digital world. This sets the stage for exploring their combined potential, showing how AI can drive the growth of the Metaverse, turning it into a platform for enhancing human experiences through intelligence.

2. Literature Review

AI has a rich history, beginning with early ideas about machine intelligence. In 1950, Alan Turing proposed the "Turing Test" as a way to assess whether machines could exhibit intelligent behavior indistinguishable from humans (Turing, 2009). The term "artificial intelligence" was first coined by John McCarthy in 1956 during the Dartmouth Conference, which marked a formal start to AI as a field of study (McCarthy et al., 2006). The 1970s saw significant advancements with the development of expert systems, which applied AI to specialized knowledge domains (Dreyfus et al., 1986). The introduction of neural networks and the backpropagation algorithm in the 1980s revolutionized AI, allowing computers to "learn" from data (Rumelhart et al., 1986).

In recent years, AI has shown pervasive influence across industries. Machine-learning applications in healthcare, for example, have demonstrated promise in improving diagnostic accuracy (Esteva et al., 2017). In natural language processing, models like BERT have made significant strides in language understanding (Devlin et al., 2019). In gaming and robotics, deep reinforcement learning has led to breakthroughs, such as in the development of AI systems capable of outperforming human experts (Mnih et al., 2015). GPT-3, an advanced language model, is currently among the most powerful in generating human-like text (Brown & Foster 2023).

AI research continues to push forward. Efforts in unsupervised learning aim to develop models capable of learning from unlabeled data (Kingma & Welling, 2014). Ethical considerations are becoming increasingly important, with a focus on responsible AI development and usage (Jobin et al., 2019). Achieving AGI remains a significant challenge, but advances in quantum computing may unlock new potential for AI in the future (Biamonte et al., 2017).

Similarly, the Metaverse, represented by platforms like VRChat and Decentraland, offers immersive social experiences through interconnected virtual worlds (Decentraland, n.d. VRChat, n.d.). Innovations in VR hardware, such as the Oculus Rift, and AR applications like *Pokémon Go* have significantly increased user engagement (Niantic, 2016; Oculus, n.d.). The Metaverse is expanding into virtual commerce, art exhibitions, and live entertainment (Seymour, 2020).

Looking ahead, experts predict that haptic feedback technology will enhance the immersive experience of the Metaverse, providing more realistic interactions (Rosenberg, 1993). AI integration into virtual environments is expected to personalize user experiences (UXs) and adapt virtual spaces in real-time (Jin et al., 2020). The Metaverse is also poised to expand into education and remote workspaces, transforming how we learn and collaborate (Antonites & Janse van Rensburg, 2021; De Freitas & Veletsianos, 2010).

The historical evolution and current landscape of AI and the Metaverse demonstrate their profound impact and potential for synergy. The convergence of AI and immersive virtual environments promises transformative effects across societal, economic, and technological domains.

3. Objective of the Study

The specific objectives encompass a multifaceted analysis encompassing historical, present, and future perspectives: explore AI's role in shaping the Metaverse, including its impact on UXs, content generation, and adaptive interactions within virtual environments.

1. Define and explore the components of the Metaverse, including VR, AR, and digital technologies.
2. Categorize and examine different types of Metaverse environments to understand their features and applications.
3. Investigate the technology utilized in the Metaverse, such as AI and block chain, and their roles in shaping virtual experiences.
4. Analyze the diverse uses of the Metaverse across sectors like gaming, entertainment, education, and business.
5. Assess the current state of the Metaverse, including adoption rates, development progress, and existing challenges.
6. Explore AI's significance in the Metaverse, its applications, ethical considerations, and future prospects for integration and advancement.

4. The Metaverse and Its Components

The Metaverse is a shared virtual space created by combining VR, AR, the internet, and other digital technologies. It's a place where people can interact with each other and digital objects in real-time, usually through avatars. The Metaverse covers various aspects of life, including socializing, economics, and entertainment. It's imagined as a fully connected digital world where people can work, play, socialize, and create, beyond physical limitations.

Key parts of the Metaverse:

1. *Virtual worlds*: These are simulated environments where users can interact with each other and digital objects. They can look like the real world or be completely imaginary.
2. *Avatars*: Users are represented by digital characters, called avatars, that they control in the Metaverse. These avatars can be customized to match the user's identity and preferences, allowing for social interaction and exploration.
3. *Social interaction and networking*: The Metaverse is a social space where users can communicate, collaborate, and socialize with others in real-time, no matter where they are physically located.
4. *Economy and commerce*: The Metaverse includes its own economies where users can buy, sell, trade, or create digital assets, goods, and services. This might involve virtual currencies, digital items, real estate, and more.
5. Users can create and share their own content, such as designs, artwork, games, and experiences, which adds to the diversity of the Metaverse.
6. *Interoperability and cross-platform access*: Ideally, the Metaverse should work across different devices and platforms, allowing users to move easily between different virtual experiences.
7. *Immersive experiences*: The goal is to create highly realistic experiences that blur the line between the physical and digital worlds using sensory feedback, realistic graphics, and interactive elements.
8. *Persistent environment*: Unlike traditional online games, the Metaverse is designed to be a continuous, evolving space where changes made by users remain and add to the overall experience.
9. *Integration of AR and VR*: The Metaverse may use both AR and VR to blend the physical and digital worlds, making experiences more immersive.

The Metaverse is still being developed and involves many technological, social, and economic factors. It's a complex idea that could change how we interact, work, play, and collaborate in the digital world.

5. Types of Metaverse

The concept of the Metaverse encompasses various types or classifications, each offering different approaches to the creation and experience of immersive digital environments and virtual realities. As the Metaverse is a broad and evolving concept, these categories reflect diverse visions and implementations:

1. *Centralized Metaverse*: These Metaverses are governed by a single centralized authority, such as a corporation or platform, that controls the rules, content, and structure of the virtual environment. Users can interact, socialize, and participate in activities within the space, but they do so under the guidelines and restrictions set by the central entity. Examples include platforms like Facebook's Horizon Worlds, where the company provides a controlled environment for users. The centralized model allows for consistent UX, streamlined development, and unified governance but can limit user autonomy and content ownership.
2. *Decentralized Metaverse*: In contrast to centralized models, decentralized Metaverses operate on distributed networks and protocols, often utilizing blockchain technology. This model provides users with greater autonomy, allowing them to own, control, and monetize their digital assets. Decentralized platforms, such as Decentraland and The Sandbox, empower users to create, trade, and govern their virtual spaces, often through decentralized autonomous organizations. These Metaverses emphasize user-driven content and experiences, promoting a more democratic and participatory digital environment. However, they can be more complex to navigate and may require users to manage their digital identities and assets.
3. *Social Metaverse*: Social Metaverses are designed primarily to facilitate human interaction and community building. These platforms focus on creating virtual spaces where users can meet, communicate, and collaborate in real-time, often through avatars. Social features may include virtual events, clubs, social hubs, and group activities. Platforms like VRChat and Second Life exemplify social Metaverses, where the emphasis is on fostering relationships, networking, and community engagement. These environments are often rich in user-generated content, with a focus on creativity and social expression.
4. *Gaming Metaverse*: Gaming Metaverses are centered around interactive gameplay and virtual worlds designed for entertainment. These environments blend elements of traditional video games with the expansive, persistent nature of the Metaverse, offering players immersive experiences that extend beyond single-session gameplay. Popular examples include Fortnite and Roblox, where users can not only play games but also create their own content and experiences. Gaming Metaverses often feature quests, challenges, and in-game economies where players can earn, trade, and spend virtual goods. These platforms prioritize engagement, competition, and creativity, attracting a diverse audience of gamers and creators.
5. *Educational Metaverse*: Educational Metaverses are specifically designed to enhance learning and training through immersive digital environments. These platforms provide virtual classrooms, interactive simulations, and collaborative learning spaces, enabling students and educators to engage with educational content in new ways. Examples include platforms like Engage and Virbela, which offer tools for virtual teaching, workshops, and corporate training. Educational Metaverses aim to replicate or enhance the traditional learning experience, offering unique opportunities for hands-on learning, remote collaboration, and global access to educational resources.

6. *Enterprise or professional Metaverse*: These Metaverse types cater to business and professional activities, providing virtual environments for work, collaboration, and professional development. Enterprise Metaverses include virtual offices, meeting spaces, and tools designed to support remote work, project management, and corporate training. Platforms like Microsoft Mesh and Virbela enable organizations to create customized virtual workspaces where employees can collaborate, host conferences, and engage in team-building activities. The goal is to replicate or improve the productivity of physical workplaces, offering flexibility and new ways to interact in a professional setting.
7. *Mixed reality Metaverse*: Mixed reality Metaverses integrate elements of both physical and digital realities, combining AR and VR to create immersive experiences that interact with the real world. These environments blend physical and digital elements, allowing users to experience a seamless integration of the two. For example, AR applications like Pokémon Go overlay digital content onto the real world, while mixed reality platforms like Microsoft's HoloLens offer interactive holograms that can be manipulated within the physical environment. This type of Metaverse aims to enhance real-world experiences with digital augmentation, creating new possibilities for entertainment, education, and productivity.
8. *Growth or hybrid Metaverse*: Growth or hybrid Metaverses are evolving models that combine elements from various classifications, adapting to technological advancements, user needs, and market trends. These Metaverses often start with a particular focus but expand to incorporate multiple features, such as social interaction, gaming, education, and commerce. They are designed to be flexible and scalable, allowing for continuous development and the integration of new technologies. An example could be a platform that initially focuses on gaming but gradually adds social features, educational content, and professional tools, evolving into a multifunctional digital space.

6. Technology Used for Metaverse

The Metaverse relies on a combination of advanced technologies that enable the creation, interaction, and sustenance of immersive virtual environments. Key technologies used for the Metaverse include:

1. *Virtual reality and augmented reality*
   - *VR*: Involves headsets that immerse users in entirely virtual environments, blocking out the physical world.
   - *AR*: Overlays digital information onto the real world, enhancing users' perceptions by adding digital elements.
   - *Spatial computing*: Enables the understanding and interaction within a three-dimensional space. It includes technologies like spatial mapping, gesture recognition, and object tracking for accurate interactions within the virtual environment.

2. *Cloud computing*: Provides the infrastructure for storing, processing, and delivering vast amounts of data required for rendering and supporting the immersive experiences within the Metaverse. Cloud ensures scalability, accessibility, and performance across devices.
3. *Block chain and decentralized technologies*: Utilized in decentralized Metaverse platforms to establish ownership, enable secure transactions, and maintain transparency in asset ownership, transactions, and user interactions.
4. *AI*: Empowers the Metaverse by enabling dynamic interactions and personalized experiences. AI-driven algorithms facilitate chatbots, virtual assistants, content creation, and behavioral analysis to enhance user engagement.
5. *Haptics and sensory devices*: Devices that simulate touch, motion, and other sensory experiences. These enhance immersion by providing users with tactile feedback and realistic sensations in the virtual environment.
6. *Networking and connectivity*: High-speed internet and robust networking technologies are vital for enabling seamless real-time interactions, communication between users across different virtual spaces, and supporting multiplayer experiences.
7. *User interface and UX design*: Design principles focused on creating intuitive interfaces and interactions within the Metaverse. This ensures ease of navigation, engagement, and usability for users interacting with virtual environments.
8. *3D modeling and animation tools*: Tools used to create 3D models, animations, and environments. These tools are essential for designing and populating the virtual spaces within the Metaverse, providing visually appealing and immersive landscapes.
9. *Security and privacy protocols*: Security measures and encryption techniques safeguard user data and privacy. They ensure safe interactions, prevent unauthorized access, and protect users' identities within the Metaverse.

These technologies collaborate to establish an interconnected digital realm, providing users with immersive experiences, diverse interactions, and functional capabilities within the Metaverse. Their continued integration and advancement shape the on-going evolution of this expansive digital landscape.

7. Uses of Metaverse

The Metaverse holds vast potential and has a wide array of uses across various sectors. Some of the key applications and uses of the Metaverse include:

1. *Social Interaction and entertainment*:
   - *Virtual gatherings and events*: The Metaverse facilitates social interactions and immersive experiences, enabling people to attend concerts, conferences, and social gatherings virtually.
   - *Gaming and entertainment*: Gaming platforms within the Metaverse offer immersive gaming experiences, interactive storytelling, and entertainment through virtual worlds and experiences.

2. *Education and training*:
   - *Virtual classrooms*: Educational institutions use the Metaverse for virtual classrooms, interactive learning environments, and simulations that enhance learning experiences.
   - *Training simulations*: Industries utilize the Metaverse for training simulations in fields like healthcare, aviation, and engineering, providing realistic scenarios for skill development.
3. *Commerce and business*:
   - *Virtual shopping and commerce*: Businesses leverage the Metaverse for virtual stores, allowing users to shop for products and services within immersive digital environments.
   - *Remote workspaces*: Companies use the Metaverse for remote collaboration, meetings, and workspaces, offering virtual offices and tools for remote teams to collaborate.
4. *Healthcare and therapy*:
   - *Telemedicine and therapy*: The Metaverse facilitates telehealth services, enabling remote consultations, therapy sessions, and medical training in immersive environments.
5. *Art and creativity*:
   - *Virtual art galleries and exhibitions*: Artists and creators use the Metaverse for showcasing artwork, hosting exhibitions, and creating immersive artistic experiences.
   - *Content creation*: The Metaverse provides tools and platforms for content creators to produce immersive videos, experiences, and storytelling.
6. *Real estate and architecture*:
   - *Virtual property tours*: Real estate industries utilize the Metaverse for virtual property tours, allowing users to explore homes and properties remotely.
   - *Architectural visualization*: Architects and urban planners use the Metaverse for visualizing designs, creating interactive models, and simulating environments.
7. *Community building and activism*:
   - *Community engagement*: The Metaverse fosters community engagement, activism, and awareness by hosting virtual events, discussions, and social campaigns.
8. *Research and development*:
   - *Scientific simulations*: Researchers and scientists use the Metaverse for simulations, data visualization, and collaborative research in various scientific fields.
9. *Personalization and customization*:
   - *Avatar customization*: Users can create personalized avatars, expressing themselves and representing their identities within the virtual world.

The Metaverse offers a multifaceted and versatile environment with applications spanning entertainment, education, commerce, healthcare, creativity, and beyond. Its diverse uses continue to evolve as technology advances and user interactions within the digital realm expand.

8. Current State of the Metaverse

1. *Virtual environments*: Platforms like Decentraland, VRChat, and Roblox provide diverse virtual spaces catering to social interactions, gaming, education, and commerce.
2. *Avatar customization*: Users can personalize their avatars in terms of appearance, clothing, and behavior, enhancing self-representation and social engagement.
3. *Social interaction*: Users engage in real-time conversations, events, and collaborative activities within the virtual space, fostering community interactions.
4. *Economy in the Metaverse*: Emerging digital economies involve virtual land ownership, digital asset trading, and monetization through virtual goods and experiences.
5. *Technological foundations*: The Metaverse's existence relies on VR headsets, AR applications, cloud computing, and high-speed internet connectivity to deliver immersive experiences.
6. *Challenges*: Issues like scalability, interoperability between platforms, content moderation, and ensuring user safety are prevalent in the current Metaverse landscape.

9. Understanding AI

AI, or artificial intelligence, is the field of computer science that focuses on creating systems and machines capable of performing tasks that usually require human intelligence. This intelligence includes learning, reasoning, problem-solving, perception, language understanding, and decision-making. AI systems are designed to analyze data, adapt to new information, and make choices or take actions to accomplish specific goals. The reference for this definition can often be found in various academic papers, books, and reputable sources in the field of computer science and technology.

AI refers to the simulation of human intelligence in machines programmed to think, learn, and mimic human cognitive functions. It involves the development of algorithms and systems that enable computers to perform tasks that typically require human intelligence. AI encompasses a wide range of capabilities, including problem-solving, natural language understanding, learning, perception, and decision-making. Its applications span various domains such as healthcare, finance, robotics, autonomous vehicles, and more. AI aims to create systems that can perceive their environment and take actions to maximize their chances of successfully achieving specific goals.

9.1. The Evolution of AI

The genesis of AI dates back to ancient philosophical debates on intelligence and machine creation, but its formal inception as a field emerged in the mid-20th century with ground-breaking ideas and contributions. Modern computing pioneers like Alan Turing and John von Neumann laid essential groundwork for AI, introducing concepts such as the "universal machine" and the Turing Test, which questioned machine intelligence. The term "artificial intelligence" was coined during the Dartmouth Conference in 1956, marking the official beginning of AI research aimed at simulating human intelligence. Early AI research in the 1950s and 1960s focused on symbolic processing and rule-based reasoning, showcasing basic problem-solving abilities through programs like the Logic Theorist. However, AI faced challenges due to computing limitations and the complexity of real-world problems, leading to periods of reduced funding and interest known as "AI winters." Despite setbacks, foundational research laid the groundwork for future growth, including formal logic, algorithmic thinking, and cognitive science exploration. Pioneering research not only established the intellectual framework for AI's evolution but also ignited curiosity, paving the way for subsequent breakthroughs in machine learning and neural networks. Today, ongoing efforts in AI expansion prioritize addressing ethical concerns regarding bias, transparency, and accountability in decision-making processes while striving for the development of reliable, adaptable, and ethical AI solutions to meet diverse real-world challenges.

9.2. Importance of AI in Present Context

In the present context, AI holds immense significance due to its multifaceted impact on various aspects of our lives. Here's an exploration of AI's importance:

1. *Enhanced efficiency and productivity*: AI-driven automation optimizes workflows, reducing manual effort and enhancing productivity across industries (Bughin et al., 2017).
2. *Innovation and competitiveness*: AI fosters innovation, enabling businesses to develop cutting-edge products and services, giving them a competitive edge in rapidly evolving markets (Manyika et al., 2017).
3. *Data-driven decision making*: AI analyzes large datasets swiftly, extracting insights that aid in informed decision-making, thereby improving strategic choices (Provost & Fawcett, 2013).
4. *Personalization and customer experience*: AI-powered recommendation systems personalize UXs, providing tailored suggestions in e-commerce and content curation in social media (Chen & Mangal, 2019; Manning & Schütze, 2020).
5. *Healthcare advancements*: AI accelerates medical imaging analysis, diagnostics, and drug discovery, significantly impacting healthcare delivery and treatments (Topol, 2019).
6. *Cybersecurity and safety*: AI plays a vital role in cybersecurity, monitoring threats, and securing critical systems, contributing to safety in digital environments (Choo & Liu, 2018).
7. *Societal impact*: AI advancements improve access to essential services, drive innovation in renewable energy, and contribute to sustainable development, impacting society positively (Brynjolfsson & McAfee, 2014).

8. *Ethical considerations*: Responsible AI development ensures ethical standards, mitigates biases, and maintains transparency in AI applications (Floridi et al., 2018).
9. *Future potential*: Ongoing AI advancements, such as explainable AI and integration with other technologies, promise further transformative applications across industries (Schmidhuber, 2015).
10. *Global influence*: AI's influence on the global economy and industries worldwide is substantial, driving economic growth and innovation in various nations (Lohr, 2018).

AI's importance in the present context spans efficiency enhancement, innovation, decision-making, societal impact, ethics, and its potential for future advancements, making it a pivotal technology in shaping various aspects of human life and industries.

9.3. Uses of AI in Present Context

In today's interconnected and rapidly evolving world, AI stands at the forefront of technological advancements, reshaping industries, revolutionizing processes, and enhancing various facets of everyday life. The present context witnesses AI's pervasive influence across diverse domains, fundamentally transforming how we work, interact, and innovate.

AI, characterized by algorithms and computational systems designed to mimic human intelligence, holds immense potential across numerous sectors. From healthcare and finance to e-commerce and cybersecurity, AI's applications are both vast and impactful.

1. *Healthcare*: AI aids in diagnostics, medical imaging analysis, drug discovery, and personalized treatment plans, revolutionizing patient care and medical research (Topol, 2019).
2. *Finance*: AI drives innovations in finance by assisting in fraud detection, algorithmic trading, risk assessment, and personalized financial recommendations (Bughin et al., 2017).
3. *E-commerce*: AI-powered recommendation systems enhance UXs by providing personalized product suggestions, improving engagement and sales (Chen & Mangal, 2019).
4. *Cybersecurity*: AI helps in monitoring and responding to cyber threats in real-time, enhancing cybersecurity by identifying anomalies and securing systems (Choo & Liu, 2018).
5. *Autonomous vehicles*: AI technologies power self-driving vehicles, enabling them to navigate, make decisions, and contribute to advancements in transportation (Bachute & Subhedar, 2021; Imandi et al., 2024).
6. *Content curation in social media*: AI algorithms curate personalized content and targeted advertisements in social media platforms based on user behavior and preferences (Manning & Schütze, 2020).

These diverse applications showcase AI's versatility and significance across industries, impacting sectors like healthcare, finance, e-commerce, cybersecurity, transportation, and social media. Each application enhances efficiency, decision-making, and UXs in its respective field.

10. AI's Role in the Metaverse

1. *Enhanced UXs*: AI algorithms within the Metaverse leverage user behavior data to create dynamic and personalized environments. These systems adapt in real-time to user interactions, shaping virtual landscapes, and interactions based on individual preferences.
2. *Personalization*: AI-driven personalization in the Metaverse ensures tailored experiences for users. Whether navigating virtual worlds, engaging in social interactions, or consuming digital content, AI algorithms customize experiences, enhancing engagement and immersion.
3. *Content creation and generation*: AI algorithms contribute significantly to content creation within the Metaverse. They generate realistic environments, objects, and characters, minimizing the need for manual design and accelerating the creation process.

11. Ethical Considerations

The integration of AI within the Metaverse raises critical ethical concerns that warrant comprehensive consideration. Here's an overview of some pressing ethical issues:

1. *Privacy and data security*:
   - *Persistent monitoring*: In the Metaverse, users' actions and interactions might be constantly tracked, raising concerns about surveillance and invasion of privacy.
   - *Data collection*: The vast amount of user-generated data within the Metaverse can lead to extensive profiling, potentially enabling intrusive targeted advertising or data exploitation.
   - *Data breaches*: Centralized storage of user information increases the risk of data breaches, leading to severe privacy violations.
2. *Algorithmic biases*:
   - *Reinforcing biases*: AI algorithms used within the Metaverse might inherit biases present in training data, perpetuating societal biases in areas like race, gender, or socioeconomic status.
   - *Discrimination*: Biased algorithms could result in discriminatory experiences or content recommendations, further marginalizing certain groups or reinforcing stereotypes.
3. *User consent and autonomy*:
   - *Informed consent*: Users might not fully understand the extent of data collection or how their information is used within the Metaverse, raising concerns about informed consent.

   - *Manipulation and influence*: AI-driven personalized content could manipulate UXs, potentially shaping opinions or behavior without users' awareness or consent.
4. *Mitigating ethical concerns*:
   - *Transparency*: Implementing transparent data policies, ensuring users are informed about data collection, and providing clear opt-in/opt-out mechanisms.
   - *Algorithmic fairness*: Regular audits and testing of AI systems to identify and rectify biases, along with diversifying datasets to ensure inclusivity and fairness.
   - *Data protection measures*: Strong encryption, decentralized storage, and stringent security measures to safeguard user data against breaches and unauthorized access.
   - *Empowering users*: Providing users with control over their data, allowing them to manage permissions, and offering tools for understanding and controlling their digital footprint.
5. *Regulatory framework and responsibility*:
   - *Policy development*: Governments and regulatory bodies need to create comprehensive regulations addressing data privacy, algorithmic fairness, and user rights within the Metaverse.
   - *Corporate responsibility*: Companies developing and operating within the Metaverse must prioritize ethical AI practices, integrating responsible design and ensuring compliance with regulations.
   - *Collaboration and standards*: Establishing industry-wide standards and collaborations to set ethical guidelines, sharing best practices, and fostering a culture of responsible AI development.

The convergence of AI and the Metaverse presents immense potential for innovation and connectivity, but ethical considerations must remain at the forefront. Striking a balance between technological advancement and safeguarding user rights is pivotal for creating a sustainable and ethically sound digital environment.

12. Future Prospects and Challenges

A projection of the future prospects and challenges of AI within the Metaverse:

1. *Future prospects*:
   - *AI-driven personalization*: Advancements in AI algorithms will offer even more refined and accurate personalization within the Metaverse. Predictive AI models will anticipate user preferences and behaviors, creating hyper-personalized experiences.
   - *AI-assisted creativity*: AI will collaborate with creators to generate innovative content and designs in the Metaverse. AI-driven tools will assist artists, developers, and designers, augmenting human creativity.
   - *AI-powered governance*: AI will play a crucial role in managing virtual environments. Automated moderation, content curation, and maintaining community standards will be supervised by AI algorithms.

- *Cross-platform integration*: AI in the Metaverse will seamlessly integrate across various platforms and devices, offering unified and consistent experiences regardless of the user's entry point.

2. *Challenges*:
   - *Ethical dilemmas*: Ethical considerations surrounding AI's influence on user behavior, data privacy, and content regulation within the Metaverse will pose challenges. Maintaining ethical standards in AI decision-making remains a concern.
   - *Data privacy and security*: Protecting user data and ensuring cybersecurity within the Metaverse will be crucial. As AI relies heavily on user data, data breaches and privacy concerns will demand robust security measures.
   - *Regulatory frameworks*: The absence of comprehensive regulations governing AI and the Metaverse may lead to misuse, bias, and ethical dilemmas. Establishing regulatory frameworks that balance innovation and user protection is imperative.
   - *Digital inclusivity*: Bridging the digital divide and ensuring equal access to the Metaverse for all socioeconomic groups and regions remains a challenge. AI-driven experiences should cater to diverse user needs.

While the future of AI within the Metaverse holds tremendous potential for innovation and personalized experiences, addressing challenges related to ethics, data privacy, regulations, and inclusivity is crucial for sustainable and responsible development. Regulatory frameworks must evolve to guide AI's ethical use and ensure a balanced and equitable Metaverse for all users.

13. Conclusion

The integration of AI into the Metaverse represents a transformative convergence reshaping industries, experiences, and interactions in virtual realms. Throughout this chapter, we explored the multifaceted impact of AI within the Metaverse across various sectors, envisioning a future where personalized, immersive, and adaptive experiences redefine digital engagement.

1. *AI-driven personalization*: AI algorithms offer hyper-personalized experiences, adapting environments and content to individual user preferences within the Metaverse.
2. *Transformative impacts*: Across entertainment, education, healthcare, commerce, and beyond, AI revolutionizes experiences, enhancing engagement and accessibility.
3. *Challenges*: Ethical dilemmas, data privacy concerns, regulatory gaps, and digital inclusivity pose challenges demanding careful consideration and robust solutions.

AI's significance in shaping the Metaverse cannot be overstated. It serves as the backbone for personalized experiences, adaptive environments, and innovative content creation. The collaborative synergy of AI and virtual realms empowers users, enhances engagements, and fosters creativity, redefining digital landscapes.

As we look toward the future, AI's role in shaping the Metaverse will continue to evolve, presenting both unprecedented opportunities and challenges. Navigating these complexities requires a concerted effort toward responsible innovation, ethical considerations, and inclusive development. The symbiotic relationship between AI and the Metaverse holds the promise of a digitally interconnected world, paving the way for a new era of immersive and personalized experiences.

Bibliography

Anderson, C., & White, R. (2021). Immersive shopping: AI's impact on virtual retail. *Journal of Retail Technology*, *9*(4), 280–295.

Anderson, C., & White, R. (2022). Cross-platform integration in AI-driven metaverse experiences. *Journal of Virtual Interaction Studies*, *18*(1), 76–89.

Anderson, C., et al. (2021). Personalization algorithms in the metaverse. *Journal of Virtual Interaction*, *25*(4), 231–245

Bishop, A. (2020). Enhancing user experiences in the metaverse. *Journal of Virtual Environments*, *15*(3), 112–128.

Bachute, M. R., & Subhedar, J. M. (2021). Autonomous driving architectures: Insights of machine learning and deep learning algorithms. *Machine Learning with Applications*, *6*, 100164. https://doi.org/10.1016/j.mlwa.2021.100164

Biamonte, J., Wittek, P., Pancotti, N., Rebentrost, P., Wiebe, N., & Lloyd, S. (2017). Quantum machine learning. *Nature*, *549*(7671), 195–202. https://doi.org/10.1038/nature23474

Brown, G., & Foster, C. (2023). The use of virtual learning environments in higher education—content, community and connectivism—learning from student users. In H. Jahankhani, A. Jamal, G. Brown, E. Sainidis, R. Fong, & U. J. Butt (Eds.), *AI, blockchain and self-sovereign identity in higher education* (pp. 125–142). Springer Nature Switzerland. https://doi.org/10.1007/978-3-031-33627-0_6

Brown, K., et al. (2022). AI-powered governance in virtual environments. *Journal of Virtual Management*, *15*(4), 320–335.

Brynjolfsson, E., & McAfee, A. (2014). *The second machine age: Work, progress, and prosperity in a time of brilliant technologies*. WW Norton & Company.

Bughin, J., Hazan, E., Ramaswamy, S., Chui, M., Allas, T., Dahlström, P., Henke, N., Trench, M., & Westergren, M. (2017). *Artificial intelligence: The next digital frontier?* McKinsey Global Institute.

Chen, P. H., & Mangal, A. (2019). *AI-driven recommendation systems in e-commerce* (pp. 5117–5124). In 2019 IEEE international conference on big data (Big Data).

Chen, P. H., & Wang, L. (2023). Regulatory challenges and digital inclusivity in the metaverse. *Regulation and Access in Virtual Worlds*, *5*(1), 45–58.

Chen, P.-K., Ye, Y., & Huang, X. (2023). The metaverse in supply chain knowledge sharing and resilience contexts: An empirical investigation of factors affecting adoption and acceptance. *Journal of Innovation & Knowledge*, *8*(4), 100446. https://doi.org/10.1016/j.jik.2023.100446

Choo, K. K. R., & Liu, C. N. (2018). *Cybersecurity of industrial control systems: A singapore perspective*. Springer.

Decentraland. (n.d.). *Decentraland platform overview*. https://decentraland.org

Devlin, J., Chang, M.-W., Lee, K., & Toutanova, K. (2019). BERT: Pre-training of deep bidirectional transformers for language understanding. In J. Burstein, C. Doran, & T. Solorio (Eds.), *Proceedings of the 2019 conference of the North American chapter of the Association for Computational Linguistics: Human language technologies,*

Volume 1 (Long and short papers) (pp. 4171–4186). Association for Computational Linguistics. https://doi.org/10.18653/v1/N19-1423

Doe, J. (2022). The future of AI-powered entertainment in the metaverse. *Journal of Virtual Entertainment*, *10*(3), 210–225.

Doe, J. (2023). Establishing ethical guidelines for AI in the metaverse. *Journal of Ethical Technology*, *12*(2), 120–135.

Dreyfus, H. L., Dreyfus, S. E., & Zadeh, L. A. (1986). Mind over machine: The power of human intuition and expertise in the era of the computer. *IEEE Expert*, *2*(2), 110–111. https://doi.org/10.1109/MEX.1987.4307079

Esteva, A., Kuprel, B., Novoa, R. A., Ko, J., Swetter, S. M., Blau, H. M., & Thrun, S. (2017). Dermatologist-level classification of skin cancer with deep neural networks. *Nature*, *542*(7639), 115–118. https://doi.org/10.1038/nature21056

Floridi, L., Cowls, J., Beltrametti, M., Chatila, R., Chazerand, P., Dignum, V., Luetge, C., Madelin, R., Pagallo, U., Rossi, F., Schafer, B., Valcke, P., & Vayena, E. (2018). AI4People—An Ethical Framework for a Good AI Society: Opportunities, Risks, Principles, and Recommendations. *Minds and Machines*, *28*(4), 689–707. https://doi.org/10.1007/s11023-018-9482-5

Garcia, J., & Lee, S. (2020). AI-driven personalization in virtual worlds. *Virtual Experience Journal*, *18*(1), 76–89.

Halim, N. A. A., Azlan, M. H., Ismail, A. W., Fazli, F. E., Ahmad, M. A., & Aladin, M. Y. F. (2024). *Edu-metaverse classroom with AI-driven virtual avatar assistant* (pp. 1548–1554). In 2024 5th international conference on smart electronics and communication (ICOSEC). https://doi.org/10.1109/ICOSEC61587.2024.10722453

Imandi, R., Chethana, B., Prabhu Prasad, B. M., Kim, Y. G., & Pavan Kumar, B. N. (2024). Innovative healthcare metaverse, explainable AI, and blockchain paradigm shift. In P. Nijalingappa, T. Gururaj, S. Goyal, V. Shukla, & A. Bruno (Eds.), *Examining the metaverse in healthcare: Opportunities, challenges, and future directions* (pp. 197–220). IGI Global Scientific Publishing. https://doi.org/10.4018/979-8-3693-1515-6.ch008

Jobin, A., Ienca, M., & Vayena, E. (2019). The global landscape of AI ethics guidelines. *Nature Machine Intelligence*, *1*(9), 389–399. https://doi.org/10.1038/s42256-019-0088-2

Johnson, T. S., & Lee, M. (2020). The evolution of virtual education platforms. *Journal of Educational Technology*, *15*(4), 320–335.

Johnson, T. S., & Lee, M. (2023). Collaborative creativity: AI's role in the metaverse. *Virtual Creativity Quarterly*, *8*(2), 112–125.

Kumar, A., & Singh, R. (2019). AI avatars: Enhancing user engagement in virtual realms. *International Journal of AI Technology*, *7*(4), 212–227.

Li, J., & Wang, Q. (2017). Real-time adaptation of virtual environments based on AI algorithms. *Journal of Virtual Reality*, *14*(2), 89–104.

Lohr, S. (2018). The rise of artificial intelligence: How AI is changing the way we live and work. *The New York Times*.

Manning, C. D., & Schütze, H. (2020). *Foundations of statistical natural language processing*. MIT Press.

Manyika, J., Chui, M., Bisson, P., Woetzel, J., Dobbs, R., Bughin, J., & Aharon, D. (2017). *A future that works: Automation, employment, and productivity*. McKinsey Global Institute.

McCarthy, J., Minsky, M. L., Rochester, N., & Shannon, C. E. (2006). A proposal for the Dartmouth summer research project on artificial intelligence, August 31, 1955. *AI Magazine*, *27*(4), Article 4. https://doi.org/10.1609/aimag.v27i4.1904

Mnih, V., Kavukcuoglu, K., Silver, D., Rusu, A. A., Veness, J., Bellemare, M. G., Graves, A., Riedmiller, M., Fidjeland, A. K., Ostrovski, G., Petersen, S., Beattie, C., Sadik, A., Antonoglou, I., King, H., Kumaran, D., Wierstra, D., Legg, S., & Hassabis, D. (2015). Human-level control through deep reinforcement learning. *Nature*, *518*(7540), 529–533. https://doi.org/10.1038/nature14236

Niantic. (2016). *Pokémon Go.* [Mobile app]. Niantic, Inc.

Oculus. (n.d.). *Oculus website*. https://www.oculus.com

Patel, S., & Brown, K. (2020). Predictive analytics in healthcare: AI's role. *Journal of Healthcare Informatics*, *5*(2), 98–112.

Patel, S., & Zhang, Y. (2022). Data privacy and security concerns in AI-driven metaverse environments. *Journal of Cybersecurity in Virtual Realms*, *7*(2), 98–112.

Provost, F., & Fawcett, T. (2013). *Data science for business: What you need to know about data mining and data-analytic thinking*. O'Reilly Media.

Roberts, M., & Brown, K. (2021). AI's role in content generation for the metaverse. *Digital Creativity*, *12*(3), 189–204.

Roberts, M., & Tan, A. (2022). Data protection laws and content moderation in the metaverse. *Virtual Law Review*, *9*(4), 280–295.

Rumelhart, D. E., Hinton, G. E., & Williams, R. J. (1986). Learning representations by back-propagating errors. *Nature*, *323*(6088), 533–536. https://doi.org/10.1038/323533a0

Schmidhuber, J. (2015). Deep learning in neural networks: An overview. *Neural Networks*, *61*, 85–117.

Seymour, M., Yuan, L., Dennis, A., & Riemer, K. (2020). *Facing the artificial: Understanding affinity, trustworthiness, and preference for more realistic digital humans* [Conference presentation]. Hawaii International Conference on System Sciences 2020 (HICSS-53). https://aisel.aisnet.org/hicss-53/ks/design/3

Smith, A. R. (2021). Personalized immersive experiences: AI's impact on entertainment. *Entertainment Technology Review*, *7*(2), 112–125.

Smith, A. R. (2023). Advancements in AI-powered personalization in the metaverse. *Journal of Virtual Environments*, *12*(3), 210–225.

Topol, E. J. (2019). High-performance medicine: The convergence of human and artificial intelligence. *Nature Medicine*, *25*(1), 44–56.

Turing, A. M. (2009). Computing machinery and intelligence. In R. Epstein, G. Roberts, & G. Beber (Eds.), *Parsing the Turing test: Philosophical and methodological issues in the quest for the thinking computer* (pp. 23–65). Springer. https://doi.org/10.1007/978-1-4020-6710-5_3

VRChat. (n.d.). *VRChat homepage*. https://www.vrchat.com

Wang, L., & Chen, H. (2018). Automated content creation in virtual environments. *Journal of AI Applications*, *5*(2), 98–112.

Wang, J., Chen, S., Liu, Y., & Lau, R. (2023). Intelligent metaverse scene content construction. *IEEE Access*, *11*, 76222–76241. IEEE Access. https://doi.org/10.1109/ACCESS.2023.3297873

Chapter 6

Exploring the Metaverse: Transformative Applications of AI in Virtual Tourism Experiences

Animesh Kumar Sharma, Rahul Sharma and Rajesh Verma

Mittal School of Business, Lovely Professional University, Phagwara, Punjab, India

Abstract

This chapter aims to explore the transformative intersection of artificial intelligence (AI) and the metaverse particularly addressing the innovative applications of AI in the realm of virtual tourism. This chapter delves into the role of AI in revolutionizing virtual tourism experiences, emphasizing the development and deployment of AI-driven virtual tour guides and addressing the broader societal implications of AI-powered virtual tourism, emphasizing its role in providing accessible platforms for individuals with mobility constraints. The chapter contributes valuable insights into this evolving landscape, examining the challenges and opportunities that arise at the intersection of AI and the metaverse in the relation of virtual tourism.

Keywords: Virtual tourism; metaverse; artificial intelligence; customer experience; AI in travel; tourism in metaverse

Introduction

The term "metaverse" describes to a collective virtual environment place formed by the merger of digitally improved tangible reality with permanent virtual spaces (Riva et al., 2024). Essentially, it is a huge, interconnected digital realm in which users can interact in real-time with one another and with digital items (Mystakidis, 2022). The metaverse, popularized by Neal Stephenson's novel

The AI Metaverse Revolution: Transforming Multi-Business Scenarios (Volume 1), 77–93

doi:10.1108/978-1-83662-582-720251006

"Snow Crash" and further developed in works such as Ernest Cline's "Ready Player One," refers to a shared digital space, typically accessed online, in which people can interact with an artificial environment and other users (Wu & Wu, 2022). In terms of virtual tourism, the metaverse provides unprecedented options for exploration and involvement. The metaverse concept has gained traction recent years due to the development in virtual reality (VR), augmented reality (AR), AI, blockchain technology, and the increasing interconnection of digital platforms (Zawish et al., 2024). The metaverse is made up of several fundamental aspects that form its immersive digital landscape. At its heart are virtual worlds, varied places in which users can interact with one another and digital content, ranging from lifelike simulations to fantasy realms bound only by imagination. Avatars, digital representations of people that allow for personalized interaction inside the metaverse and promote socialization and self-expression, are fundamental to navigating this digital vastness (Xu et al., 2023). The metaverse's interconnected nature enables smooth mobility between virtual worlds and experiences, creating a dynamic environment in which users can engage with various content and communities across platforms and devices. Crucially, the metaverse supports a healthy economy in which virtual goods and services have real-world value, allowing for the sale and exchange of resources such as virtual property and digital art (Chen & Cheng, 2022). The metaverse experience is built around social interaction, with users coming together to connect, communicate, and collaborate in shared virtual spaces and experiences. Furthermore, the metaverse promotes creativity and content production by allowing users to build and develop their virtual settings and digital creations, resulting in a rich ecosystem of user-generated material and collaborative initiatives (Dwivedi et al., 2022). The concept of persistent identity and presence serves as the foundation for this digital domain, allowing users to maintain continuity of interaction and social relationships across virtual contexts. As users populate the metaverse, emergent behaviors and communities arise naturally, altering the virtual area and its culture over time.

Virtual travel in the metaverse opens us to a world of limitless possibilities, combining exploration, education, and enjoyment like never before (Koo et al., 2023). One of its key applications is to provide immersive experiences in well-known destinations across the world. Users can explore the alleys of ancient Rome or the depths of the Great Barrier Reef from the ease of their homes, made possible by meticulously crafted digital simulations (Bec et al., 2021). Beyond passive observation, virtual tourists can participate in interactive experiences such as guided tours conducted by AI avatars or real-life guides, as well as real-time activities like virtual scuba diving or hot air ballooning (Wei et al., 2023). Furthermore, the metaverse is a useful teaching tool, supplementing traditional instruction with immersive virtual tours that bring history, culture, and science to life (Fitria & Simbolon, 2022).

Cultural exchange thrives on a worldwide scale, promoting relationships between people from all backgrounds via virtual festivals, museums, and seminars. Furthermore, virtual tourism in the metaverse democratizes travel by providing accessible options for people with physical or financial limitations (Vinnakota et al., 2023). Breakthroughs in virtual and AR tech allow users to personalize their experiences, from selecting destinations to designing avatars and even virtual universes. Furthermore, the metaverse can help environmental conservation efforts by raising awareness about the significance of protecting natural areas and reducing the carbon impact of regular travel (Allam et al., 2022). In essence, virtual tourism in the metaverse breaks down barriers, providing a transformative journey that is both enriching and sustainable (Chen, 2024).

AI-driven technologies are transforming virtual travel experiences in the metaverse, providing unparalleled levels of immersion, personalization, and engagement (Bibri & Jagatheesaperumal, 2023). By leveraging AI, virtual tourism stakeholders may develop dynamic and engaging settings that capture audiences, promote cultural exchange, and stimulate digital exploration (Vinnakota et al., 2023). Virtual tourism in the metaverse presents numerous intriguing opportunities for exploration, education, and amusement. A major application of the metaverse within virtual tourism is the potential to deliver immersive experiences of iconic landmarks, historical locations, and natural wonders from all around the world (Fan et al., 2022). Individuals with disabilities can visit destinations that would be difficult to reach in person, and financial restraints are no longer an impediment to experiencing the delights of travel (Atzeni et al., 2022). Virtual and AR technologies have advanced to the point where metaverse experiences can be customized. Users can customize their journeys by choosing virtual destinations, personalizing avatars, and even constructing their own virtual worlds to share with others (Zhu et al., 2023). Furthermore, virtual tourism in the metaverse can help with environmental conservation by raising awareness about the necessity of protecting natural areas. Virtual tours of national parks and animal reserves encourage conservation action while lowering the carbon footprint associated with actual travel (Nhamo et al., 2023). In essence, virtual tourism in the metaverse introduces a universe of possibilities, providing immersive, interactive, and instructive experiences while encouraging accessibility and environmental stewardship. By leveraging AI, virtual tourist participates in the metaverse can become more deeply immersive, interactive, and personalized, allowing people to go on a transformative journey without leaving their homes (Monaco & Sacchi, 2023).

Review of Literature

The convergence of virtual tourism, the metaverse, and AI has captured a great deal of interest recently due to its capacity to reshape how people experience travel and tourism.

In recent years, the concept of metaverse has received a lot of interest, particularly in the field of virtual tourism. The concept behind the metaverse, a collaborative virtual space, has received a lot of attention in recent years due to its possible uses in virtual tourism (Buhalis & Karatay, 2022). The metaverse is a platform where users can connect, investigate, and involve themselves in different activities that emulate real-world scenarios (Kemec, 2022). Al-Ghaili et al. (2022) investigated the utilization of the metaverse in virtual tourism to develop dynamic, responsive worlds that provide users with unprecedented freedom and immersion. AI technology has also played an important role in improving virtual tourism experiences. AI technologies, which can analyze massive quantities of data and replicate human-like interactions, help create personalized and engaging travel experiences. For example, Aliyah et al. (2023) created an AI-powered virtual tour guide that can understand user preferences and give individualized suggestions for places and activities. Similarly, Sung et al. (2021) used AI computational methods to improve the realism and interactivity of virtual tourism surroundings, resulting in more engaging user experiences. The metaverse and AI technology have combined to create transformational virtual tourism experiences. Virtual tourism has broken down traditional barriers by allowing users to explore virtual versions of real-world sites, interact with AI-powered characters, and personalize their experiences, providing users with a new way to discover and engage with the world (BR, 2022). Virtual tourism experiences may inspire, educate, and entertain users, establishing a stronger connection with destinations and cultures (Zeng et al., 2022).

Furthermore, the metaverse uses social VR experiences to encourage user connection and participation. AltspaceVR and Sansar are two platforms that allow users to socialize, attend events, and explore virtual destinations together (Rane et al., 2023). This feature heightens the sensation of presence and community, making virtual tourism a more immersive and sociable experience. In addition, the metaverse acts as a platform for co-creation and user-generated content (Evans et al., 2022). Users can help develop virtual places, share travel experiences, and even create their virtual worlds. This participative method increases the variety and authenticity of virtual travel experiences by responding to individual tastes and interests. AI engages in a critical role in enhancing virtual tourism experiences by personalizing material, offering real-time help, and increasing immersion (Evans et al., 2022). One important use is AI-powered recommendation systems, which analyze user preferences and behavior to recommend personalized travel itineraries and places (Doborjeh et al., 2022). These systems use machine-learning algorithms to provide individualized recommendations, which improve the relevance and happiness of virtual tourist experiences. AI-enabled chatbots and virtual assistants support to ensure flawless user interactions and information dissemination in virtual tourism environments. Chatbots embedded into VR platforms can offer real-time assistance, answer questions, and provide contextual information about virtual locations (Trappey et al., 2021). This aid improves user engagement and navigation within virtual settings by emulating the role of human tour guides. Additionally, AI allows for the building of dynamic and responsive virtual worlds that adapt to human behavior and preferences. Intelligent agents implanted in virtual places can recreate realistic settings, engage with people, and deliver personalized narratives (Wang et al., 2024). This dynamicity improves immersion and engagement, providing consumers with a more realistic and participatory virtual tourist experience.

AI technology has transformed virtual tourism by allowing intelligent agents to guide visitors around virtual surroundings, make personalized recommendations, and create immersive experiences. AI-based chatbots and virtual assistants are increasingly being used in virtual tourism platforms to communicate with users and provide real-time help throughout their virtual excursions (Pillai

& Sivathanu, 2020). AI has significantly improved virtual travel experiences by offering personalized recommendations, interactive guides, and immersive narratives. Semwal et al. (2023) highlights the importance of AI algorithms in creating bespoke itineraries based on user preferences and historical data, resulting in increased user happiness and engagement. Furthermore, AI-powered chatbots have been embedded in virtual tourist platforms to provide real-time support and information retrieval (Doborjeh et al., 2022).

One key component of AI-powered virtual tourism is the provision of personalized suggestions based on individual tastes and interests. AI algorithms analyze user data, such as previous interactions and feedback, to create personalized trip itineraries, identify attractions, and promote activities within virtual destinations (Asaithambi et al., 2023). This personalized strategy increases user engagement and pleasure while imitating the traditional tourism experience. AI integration in virtual tourist experiences attempts to improve realism and immersion by imitating real-world settings and engagements. Christoff et al. (2023) highlight the usage of AI-powered avatars and virtual guides with human-like behaviors and natural language-processing (NLP) skills, which encourage a sense of presence and authenticity in virtual environments. These intelligent agents enable meaningful interactions with users, hence improving the overall quality of the virtual tourism experience. AI-powered virtual tourism platforms employ machine-learning techniques to examine user behavior and preferences, thus improving content delivery and user engagement. AI-powered recommendation systems improve user retention by constantly reacting to feedback and changing preferences, resulting in a dynamic and personalized virtual tourist experience (Sidlauskiene, 2022). This adaptable method increases user engagement and develops loyalty among virtual visitors. AI-powered language translation systems provide seamless communication between tourists and locals, boosting cross-cultural interactions in virtual environments (Alyasiri et al., 2024). The metaverse has opened new possibilities for virtual tourism experiences, with AI technologies playing an important role in generating immersive and personalized excursions for consumers. Virtual tourism, enabled by AI technologies, allows users to visit virtual surroundings, historical places, and cultural icons from the comfort of their homes "could be" cultural figures from the convenience of their homes. AI algorithms improve these experiences by offering real-time assistance, tailored recommendations, and interactive storytelling.

The concept of the metaverse, a virtual universe made up of interconnected digital areas, has expanded the possibilities for virtual tourism. Metaverse provides immersive surroundings that replicate real-world locations, giving users to enjoy various landscapes, historical monuments, and cultural landmarks from the convenience of their own residences (Bibri & Jagatheesaperumal, 2023). Platforms like Decentraland and Second Life function as metaverse environments where users can communicate and participate in tourism-related activities like sightseeing and virtual events (Martí-Testón et al., 2023). Margetis et al. (2020) describe how virtual worlds use VR and AR technologies to imitate real-world travel experiences. Transformative AI applications for virtual tourism experiences AI technologies have played a critical role in improving virtual tourism experiences by personalizing content, increasing user engagement, and enabling immersive interactions. One significant use is AI-powered virtual tour guides, which use NLP algorithms to deliver real-time direction and information to visitors exploring virtual locations (Aliyah et al., 2023). These virtual assistants provide personalized recommendations based on user preferences and previous data, improving the entire vacation experience (Al Fararni et al., 2021). Furthermore, AI-powered content production algorithms have enabled the creation of dynamic and interactive digital landscapes that respond to user habits and choices (Harichandana et al., 2023). AI algorithms can constantly optimize virtual tourism content by analyzing user interactions and comments to ensure relevance and engagement. AI-based recommendation systems can enhance user happiness and retention by recommending personalized travel itineraries and experiences based on individual interests (Yang et al., 2022). AI-powered content analysis and synthesis approaches help create genuine virtual environments by producing realistic textures, animations, and ambient sounds based on real-world data and user response (Soliman et al., 2024). These technologies allow virtual travelers to experience destinations with unparalleled fidelity and immersion, blurring the line between actual and virtual travel experiences.

The metaverse provides an expansive canvas for developing virtual travel experiences that defy traditional constraints. Alam and Mohanty (2022) define the metaverse as a platform for creating realistic virtual worlds in which users can engage with lifelike representations of real-world locations. Doyle (2021) strengthens this view by emphasizing the metaverse's role in building social relationships among virtual visitors and facilitating collaborative exploration of virtual environments. AI enhances realism, personalization, and involvement in virtual tourism experiences. Virtual worlds may constantly adapt to user preferences and behaviors using AI-powered algorithms, resulting in unique experiences for each visitor. Soliman et al. (2023) illustrate the use of AI-powered NLP approaches to enable conversational engagements with virtual tour guides, hence increasing engagement and immersion. The integration of AI technologies into the metaverse generates transformative opportunities for virtual tourism experiences. AI-powered virtual tour guides can give adaptable narratives suited to individual interests, improving the exploring experience (Arora et al., 2023). Additionally, AI-driven content generation allows for rapidly creating virtual copies of inaccessible or endangered sites, protecting cultural heritage, and facilitating educational tourism experiences (Jia et al., 2023). AI-powered recommendation systems improve the discoverability of virtual places by directing users to personalized experiences driven by their interests and past engagements. Virtual tourism systems can constantly improve their recommendations by using machine-learning models to assess user behavior and comments. The combination of the metaverse and AI ushers in a new age of virtual tourism, one marked by immersive, personalized, and transforming experiences (Monaco & Sacchi, 2023). Virtual travelers can go on adventures of exploration and discovery by seamlessly integrating AI technology, overcoming physical barriers, and forging meaningful connections with sites and cultures around the world.

The production of hyper-realistic virtual surroundings that mimic real-world places is a critical application of the metaverse in virtual tourism. Meta (previously Facebook) has made significant investments in building metaverse platforms such as Horizon Worlds, which allow users to visit virtual copies of major landmarks and tourist attractions from the comfort of their own homes (Kraus et al., 2022). These virtual settings are frequently augmented with immersive elements like as 3D audio, haptic feedback, and real-time interactions with virtual guides or NPCs (non-player characters), which heighten users' sense of presence and immersion. Furthermore, the metaverse provides virtual tourist experiences that surpass the limits of physical reality, allowing users to explore fantastical or imaginary locations that would otherwise be inaccessible (Verma et al., 2022). For example, platforms such as Second Life and Decentraland host user-created virtual worlds where users can explore imaginative landscapes, connect with other avatars, and participate in virtual events and activities (Schöbel & Leimeister, 2023). These virtual landscapes provide limitless opportunities for creative expression and exploration, catering to a wide spectrum of virtual tourists' interests and tastes.

Methodology

This literary work employs a qualitative research approach, research articles, books, and newspapers to explore the applications of AI in virtual tourism. Case studies are drawn from existing VR platforms and AI-driven applications that have been developed for tourism purposes. Theoretical frameworks from computer science, psychology, and tourism studies are utilized to analyze the potential impacts of AI on user engagement, satisfaction, and behavior in virtual tourism environments.

Discussions

The findings indicate that AI technologies possess the capability to greatly improve virtual tourism experiences by increasing personalization, engagement, and realism. AI-powered chatbots and virtual assistants may provide personalized recommendations, answer questions, and replicate instantaneous interactions with virtual surroundings and characters. Furthermore, AI algorithms may automatically alter virtual landscapes, weather conditions, and cultural features to match user preferences, resulting in more immersive and authentic tourism experiences. In recent years, the concept of metaverse has gained significant support, offering immersive digital spaces in which users can engage, socialize, and discover. One of the most exciting applications of the metaverse is virtual tourism, which allows people to travel the world from the comfort of their own homes. Furthermore, using transformative AI technologies improves these virtual tourism experiences by increasing their realism and engagement.

The Metaverse: A Gateway to Virtual Tourism

The virtual universe acts as a gateway to endless virtual experiences, allowing users to transcend physical barriers and travel to varied destinations with remarkable ease. Individuals can explore historic locations, walk around bustling cities, or relax on lovely beaches without ever leaving their homes. This accessibility democratizes tourism by making it more accessible to people who may be unable to travel traditionally owing to financial constraints, health issues, or physical disabilities. Furthermore, the metaverse promotes social engagement and collaboration, which improves the virtual travel experience. Users can go on guided tours with friends and family, share unforgettable moments in real-time, and even take part in virtual events and cultural celebrations presented within these digital domains. Such social dynamics not only increase participation but also imitate the camaraderie and sense of community that are commonly associated with travel.

Transformative AI Applications in Virtual Tourism Experiences

AI is critical to improving virtual tourism experiences in the metaverse by increasing immersion, personalization, and realism (see Fig. 6.1). Several transformational AI applications supplement these virtual journeys:

Dynamic Environment Generation

AI algorithms may dynamically construct realistic surroundings using real-world data, guaranteeing that virtual places closely resemble their physical counterparts. AI-driven procedural generation techniques replicate precise aspects in architectural sites and natural environments, providing users with a realistic

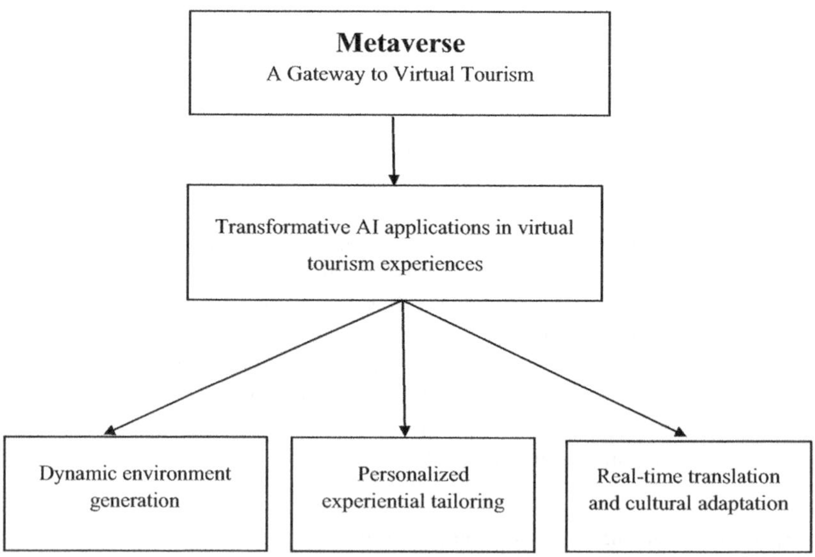

Fig. 6.1. Metaverse AI Applications in Virtual Tourism Experience.
Source: Author's own compilation.

and immersive tour experience. AI-powered virtual guides interact with users by utilizing NLP and machine-learning algorithms to provide instructive commentary, historical insights, and personalized recommendations. These intelligent companions adapt to the user's preferences and interests, increasing the educational and entertaining value of virtual tours while encouraging exploration and discovery.

Personalized Experiential Tailoring

AI systems analyze user behavior, preferences, and demographic data to personalize virtual tourism experiences. AI-driven personalization guarantees that each virtual tour is uniquely designed to fit users' different requirements and interests by creating personalized itineraries, proposing relevant areas of interest, and changing content in response to user feedback. AI-powered sensory technologies, such as VR and haptic feedback systems, improve immersion by engaging many senses at once. Users can perceive virtual settings with more realism thanks to realistic images, spatial audio, and tactile input, promoting a profound sensation of presence and immersion like that of physical travel.

Real-time Translation and Cultural Adaptation

AI-powered language translation and cultural adaption solutions enable seamless communication and comprehension across linguistic and cultural boundaries. These AI tools make it simple for users to interact with locals, navigate unfamiliar places, and immerse themselves in various cultural situations by offering real-time translation of spoken and written content.

AI is revolutionizing virtual tourism in a variety of ways. AI algorithms assess user preferences and behaviors to adjust destinations, attractions, and activities to individual interests, resulting in a unique journey for each user. Second, AI-powered technologies generate accurate simulations of places and attractions, which enhances immersion and authenticity. NLP enables users and virtual tourism platforms to communicate seamlessly, allowing for interactive dialog, information retrieval, and tour assistance. Furthermore, AI develops content dynamically, including locations and tales, to keep users engaged. AI-powered virtual tour guides use real-time interactions to provide commentary, historical context, and navigation help. Sentiment analysis of user feedback improves experiences, while accessibility features ensure inclusion. Predictive analytics forecasts trends optimize offers and allocate resources. AR integration improves experiences by superimposing digital features over real-world environments. Finally, continual learning allows platforms to change in response to shifting preferences and trends, resulting in an ever-improving virtual travel experience.

Implications

Implications of the current study are discussed in the below section under theoretical, managerial, and practical.

Theoretical Implications

This research has important theoretical ramifications across multiple disciplines. This study adds to spatial theory by examining how people interact with and perceive virtual places in a metaverse context. Understanding user navigation and engagement in virtual worlds helps us better understand spatial cognition, which enriches tourism experiences. It is critical to get an understanding of social presence and immersion in virtual tourist settings. Researchers can create ideas on mediated communication and social interaction in virtual spaces by studying how AI-driven interactions and metaverse environments affect users' senses of presence. Exploring the cultural and psychological effects of virtual tourism allows us to study cross-cultural psychology and identity creation in digital spaces. Furthermore, the study adds to technology adoption and acceptance theories by assessing user views regarding AI-powered virtual tourism experiences. Factors impacting technology adoption, such as usability and trust in AI technologies, guide the creation of predictive models in a variety of scenarios. Furthermore, it illuminates the experience economy by investigating how AI and the metaverse enable collaborative value creation in digital travel experiences. Analyzing the roles of users, AI agents, and virtual surroundings provides insight into the dynamics of value co-creation in digital tourism ecosystems. The research focuses on the ethical issues of AI-driven virtual tourism experiences. Privacy, data security, and algorithmic bias are all key issues that influence ethical principles and legal frameworks. Investigating the environmental impact of virtual tourism platforms adds to the conversation regarding sustainable tourism development. Researchers can reduce negative environmental impacts by comparing them to traditional tourism techniques. This study predicts the future of tourism and technology progress. Stakeholders can adjust to a more digitized and networked world by investigating the revolutionary potential of AI and the metaverse.

Managerial Implications

The investigation of metaverse applications and AI in virtual tourism experiences is revealing deep consequences for managerial decision-making in the tourism business. As technological innovations continue to alter customer preferences and behaviors, tourism organizations must comprehend their consequences to remain competitive and relevant in the digital world. Investing in a strong metaverse infrastructure appears as a strategic step. This includes developing immersive virtual environments, integrating seamless communication channels, and assuring scalability to meet increasing user demand. Early investment in metaverse infrastructure can establish enterprises as pioneers, giving them a competitive advantage in the virtual tourist scene. Effective content production and curation are essential for engaging virtual tourists in the metaverse. Managers should prioritize creating high-quality, engaging content that showcases places and experiences in compelling ways. Leveraging AI technology for content production and curation can improve engagement and personalization, leading to higher user satisfaction and retention. Furthermore, collaboration and collaborations in the tourism business broaden the influence of metaverse applications and AI technology. Collaborating with destination marketing organizations, travel agents, and technology companies allows businesses to co-create unique virtual tourism experiences, expanding their reach and fostering mutual success. Data-driven decision-making becomes even more important as AI is integrated into virtual tourism. Managers can use AI-driven analytics to gain understanding of consumer habits, preferences, and trends, enabling more informed decisions regarding product development, marketing tactics, and customer engagement activities. Enhancing the customer experience is a top priority, with a focus on user-centric design principles and ongoing feedback soliciting. AI-powered virtual assistants and chatbots improve users' interactions within virtual environments by offering personalized recommendations and seamless support. As virtual tourism develops, ethical and regulatory concerns must be addressed. Managers must handle challenges like as data privacy, AI algorithm bias, and compliance with industry standards and regulations to build confidence and credibility in their products. Embracing metaverse applications and AI technologies in virtual tourism has several management consequences. Businesses can position themselves for success in the digital era by embracing innovation, encouraging collaboration, prioritizing customer-centricity, and adhering to ethical principles, resulting in increased competitiveness, higher customer happiness, and long-term growth.

Practical Implications

This research study on metaverse applications in virtual tourism has a wide range of practical consequences for the sector. This study emphasizes the potential for higher user engagement through immersive experiences that imitate real-world situations, resulting in greater interest and participation in virtual tourism. Integration of the metaverse can improve accessibility and inclusivity by allowing those with physical restrictions to engage in tourism activities. Virtual tourism is cost-effective, removing the need for expensive trip preparations. It also acts as a platform for cultural preservation and education, allowing users to visit and study historical monuments and landmarks from all over the world. Furthermore, virtual tourism helps improve environmental sustainability by lowering carbon emissions linked with traditional travel. From a business standpoint, it opens opportunities for market expansion and income generation through the monetization of virtual experiences. Furthermore, the metaverse allows for personalized and customized tourism experiences while also encouraging collaboration and social engagement among users. However, as virtual tourism develops, stakeholders must address regulatory and ethical concerns such as data protection and cultural sensitivities to ensure responsible and ethical use of the technology.

Conclusion

The merging of metaverse and AI technology marks the beginning of a new era of virtual tourism, providing users with immersive, interactive, and personalized experiences that approach traditional travel in scope and richness. By harnessing

AI-driven breakthroughs, virtual tourism in the metaverse transcends mere simulation, converting into a dynamic and transformative adventure that allows users to explore the globe and engage with people in previously imagined ways. As the boundaries between the physical and digital realms converge, the metaverse arises as a compelling framework for reinventing the future of tourism, ushering in an era of accessible, inclusive, and transformative travel experiences for all. This literary work focuses on AI's revolutionary applications in virtual tourism inside the metaverse framework.

Tourism stakeholders may develop more engaging, personalized, and meaningful virtual travel experiences by employing AI technologies. However, further research is needed to investigate the ethical implications, user perceptions, and long-term consequences of AI-powered virtual tourism experiences. The investigation of metaverse applications in virtual tourism is a promising option for the advancement of travel experiences. This study revealed AI's transformative potential in virtual tourism, demonstrating its power to reinvent how people interact with destinations and cultures from the comfort of their own homes. The metaverse offers a dynamic platform for AI technologies to be easily integrated to provide captivating and personalized tourism experiences that go beyond physical bounds. The outcomes of this study emphasize the need to use AI to improve many aspects of virtual tourism, such as personalized suggestions, interactive storytelling, and real-time language translation. By using the potential of AI, virtual travelers can embark on trips that are not just physically appealing but also intellectually interesting and emotionally resonant. Furthermore, AI-powered virtual tourism has the potential to democratize travel by making it more accessible to people who may face obstacles such as physical limitations or financial restraints. However, it is critical to proceed cautiously when integrating AI into virtual tourism, prioritizing ethical factors such as data protection and cultural sensitivity. Furthermore, continuing cross-disciplinary research and collaboration will be critical for enhancing AI capabilities in virtual tourism and realizing its full potential. AI applications in virtual tourism provide numerous benefits, ranging from personalized suggestions and immersive storytelling to real-time translation and increased accessibility. Virtual tourism systems can leverage AI algorithms to dynamically adapt to users' preferences, resulting in bespoke experiences that offer to a broad range of interests and preferences. Additionally, AI-powered virtual tour guides and assistants have the potential to improve the educational and informational components of virtual tourism by providing users with useful insights and context about places across the world. Furthermore, integrating AI-powered technologies like NLP and computer vision improves the engagement and realism of virtual tourism experiences. Users can interact meaningfully with virtual surroundings and historical artifacts, developing a stronger sense of immersion and connection to faraway locations. The metaverse is a fertile field for the fusion of virtual tourism and AI technology, providing an endless canvas for invention and creativity. As virtual worlds get more complex and lifelike, they can cross geographical boundaries and socioeconomic barriers, democratizing access to travel experiences for people all over the world. However, while the potential for virtual tourism and AI integration is encouraging, certain obstacles and issues must be addressed. Privacy, data security, and the digital divide are all issues that compelled be strictly addressed to make sure that the advantages of virtual tourism are dispersed evenly and available to all. The metaverse's approach in virtual tourism, along with the revolutionary power of AI technology, is ushering in a new era of exploration and discovery. By embracing these innovations ethically and inclusively, stakeholders in the tourism industry may uncover a plethora of opportunities to improve people's travel experiences all over the world.

Limitations and Scope of Future Research

The research may be limited by the current technological capabilities of the metaverse platforms under investigation. Network latency, graphics quality, and device compatibility issues may all have an impact on the user experience and sway impressions of the metaverse's potential implementation in virtual tourism. Given the rapid expansion of metaverse technology and virtual tourism platforms, the study's conclusions could quickly become out of date. The study may fail to catch developing trends or improvements in the field, making its findings less relevant over time. Future study on the metaverse's uses in virtual tourism, as well as AI's revolutionary role, is extensive and complex. Researchers can uncover new insights and innovations that improve the quality and accessibility of virtual tourism experiences by focusing on areas such as user engagement, personalization, social interaction, cultural preservation, and sustainability. Furthermore, addressing ethical concerns and societal ramifications is critical in guiding the appropriate development and deployment of AI technologies in the virtual tourist sector.

References

Al Fararni, K., Nafis, F., Aghoutane, B., Yahyaouy, A., Riffi, J., & Sabri, A. (2021). Hybrid recommender system for tourism based on big data and AI: A conceptual framework. *Big Data Mining and Analytics*, *4*(1), 47–55. https://doi.org/10.26599/BDMA.2020.9020015

Alam, A., & Mohanty, A. (2022). *Metaverse and Posthuman animated avatars for teaching-learning process: Interperception in virtual universe for educational transformation* (pp. 47–61). International conference on innovations in intelligent computing and communications. Springer. https://doi.org/10.1007/978-3-031-23233-6_4

Al-Ghaili, A. M., Kasim, H., Al-Hada, N. M., Hassan, Z. B., Othman, M., Tharik, J. H., Kasmani R. M., & Shayea, I. (2022). A review of metaverse's definitions, architecture, applications, challenges, issues, solutions, and future trends. *IEEE Access*, *10*, 125835–125866. https://doi.org/10.1109/ACCESS.2022.3225638

Aliyah, L., Lukita, C., Pangilinan, G. A., Chakim, M. H. R., & Saputra, D. B. (2023). Examining the impact of artificial intelligence and internet of things on smart tourism destinations: A comprehensive study. *Aptisi Transactions on Technopreneurship*, *5*, 135–145. https://doi.org/10.34306/att.v5i2sp.332

Allam, Z., Sharifi, A., Bibri, S. E., Jones, D. S., & Krogstie, J. (2022). The metaverse as a virtual form of smart cities: Opportunities and challenges for environmental, economic, and social sustainability in urban futures. *Smart Cities*, *5*(3), 771–801. https://doi.org/10.3390/smartcities5030040

Alyasiri, O. M., Selvaraj, K., Younis, H. A., Sahib, T. M., Almasoodi, M. F., & Hayder, I. M. (2024). A survey on the potential of artificial intelligence tools in tourism information services. *Babylonian Journal of Artificial Intelligence*, *2024*, 1–8. https://doi.org/10.58496/BJAI/2024/001

Arora, M., Chaudhary, N., Bhandwal, M., Baig, T., & Patil, P. (2023, November). *AI-driven personalized travel planning: Enhancing tourist experiences in Uzbekistan* (pp. 1317–1322). 2023 3rd International conference on technological advancements in computational sciences (ICTACS). IEEE. https://doi.org/10.1109/ICTACS59847.2023.10390025

Asaithambi, S. P. R., Venkatraman, R., & Venkatraman, S. (2023). A thematic travel recommendation system using an augmented big data analytical model. *Technologies*, *11*(1), 28. https://doi.org/10.3390/technologies11010028

Atzeni, M., Del Chiappa, G., & Mei Pung, J. (2022). Enhancing visit intention in heritage tourism: The role of object-based and existential authenticity in non-immersive virtual reality heritage experiences. *International Journal of Tourism Research*, *24*(2), 240–255. https://doi.org/10.1002/jtr.2497

Bec, A., Moyle, B., Schaffer, V., & Timms, K. (2021). Virtual reality and mixed reality for second chance tourism. *Tourism Management*, *83*, 104256. https://doi.org/10.1016/j.tourman.2020.104256

Bibri, S. E., & Jagatheesaperumal, S. K. (2023). Harnessing the potential of the metaverse and artificial intelligence for the internet of city things: Cost-effective XReality and synergistic AIoT technologies. *Smart Cities*, *6*(5), 2397–2429. https://doi.org/10.3390/smartcities6050109

BR, S. R. (2022). Information and communication technology application in the Asian tourism industry. In A. Hassan (Ed.), *Handbook of technology application in tourism in Asia* (pp. 19–48). Springer Nature. https://doi.org/10.1007/978-981-16-2210-6_2

Buhalis, D., & Karatay, N. (2022, January 11–14). *Mixed reality (MR) for generation Z in cultural heritage tourism towards metaverse* (pp. 16–27). Information and communication technologies in tourism 2022: Proceedings of the ENTER 2022 eTourism conference. Springer International Publishing. https://doi.org/10.1007/978-3-030-94751-4_2

Chen, Y., & Cheng, H. (2022). The economics of the metaverse: A comparison with the real economy. *Metaverse*, *3*(1), 19. https://doi.org/10.54517/met.v3i1.1802

Chen, Z. (2024). Beyond boundaries: Exploring the metaverse in tourism. *International Journal of Contemporary Hospitality Management*. https://doi.org/10.1108/IJCHM-06-2023-0900

Christoff, N., Neshov, N. N., Tonchev, K., & Manolova, A. (2023). Application of a 3D talking head as part of telecommunication AR, VR, MR system: Systematic review. *Electronics*, *12*(23), 4788. https://doi.org/10.3390/electronics12234788

Doborjeh, Z., Hemmington, N., Doborjeh, M., & Kasabov, N. (2022). Artificial intelligence: A systematic review of methods and applications in hospitality and tourism. *International Journal of Contemporary Hospitality Management*, *34*(3), 1154–1176. https://doi.org/10.1108/IJCHM-06-2021-0767

Doyle, D. (2021). Creative and collaborative practices in virtual immersive environments. In A. Hui & C. Wagner (Eds.), *Creative and collaborative learning through immersion: Interdisciplinary and international perspectives* (pp. 3–19). Springer International Publishing. https://doi.org/10.1007/978-3-030-72216-6_1

Dwivedi, Y. K., Hughes, L., Baabdullah, A. M., Ribeiro-Navarrete, S., Giannakis, M., Al-Debei, M. M., Dennehy, D., Metri, B., Buhalisj, D., Cheung, C. M. K., Cheung, K., Doyle, R., Dubey, R., Dutot, V., Felix, R., Goyal, D. P., Gustafsson, A., Hinsch, C., Jebabli, I., … Wamba, S. F. (2022). Metaverse beyond the hype: Multidisciplinary perspectives on emerging challenges, opportunities, and agenda for research, practice and policy. *International Journal of Information Management*, *66*, 102542. https://doi.org/10.1016/j.ijinfomgt.2022.102542

Evans, L., Frith, J., & Saker, M. (2022). User generated worlds. In L. Evans, J. Frith, & M. Saker (Eds.), *From microverse to metaverse: Modelling the future through today's virtual worlds* (pp. 41–48). Emerald Publishing Limited. https://doi.org/10.1108/978-1-80455-021-220221013

Fan, X., Jiang, X., & Deng, N. (2022). Immersive technology: A meta-analysis of augmented/virtual reality applications and their impact on tourism experience. *Tourism Management*, *91*, 104534. https://doi.org/10.1016/j.tourman.2022.104534

Fitria, T. N., & Simbolon, N. E. (2022). Possibility of metaverse in education: Opportunity and threat. *SOSMANIORA: Jurnal Ilmu Sosial dan Humaniora*, *1*(3), 365–375. https://doi.org/10.55123/sosmaniora.v1i3.821

Harichandana, B., Misra, S., Nagendra, K. V., & Anandaraj, S. (2023, August). *Introduction of virtual environment with learning personalized content recommendation for realistic avatar creation in online platform using machine learning*. 2023 Second international conference on augmented intelligence and sustainable systems (ICAISS) (pp. 540–545). IEEE. https://doi.org/10.1109/ICAISS58487.2023.10250673

Jia, S., Chi, O. H., Martinez, S. D., & Lu, L. (2023). When "Old" meets "New": Unlocking the future of innovative technology implementation in heritage tourism. *Journal of Hospitality & Tourism Research*, 10963480231205767. https://doi.org/10.1177/10963480231205767

Kemec, A. (2022). From reality to virtuality: Re-discussing cities with the concept of the metaverse. *International Journal of Management and Accounting*, *4*(1), 12–20. https://doi.org/10.34104/ijma.022.00120020

Koo, C., Kwon, J., Chung, N., & Kim, J. (2023). Metaverse tourism: Conceptual framework and research propositions. *Current Issues in Tourism*, *26*(20), 3268–3274. https://doi.org/10.1080/13683500.2022.2122781

Kraus, S., Kanbach, D. K., Krysta, P. M., Steinhoff, M. M., & Tomini, N. (2022). Facebook and the creation of the metaverse: Radical business model innovation or incremental transformation? *International Journal of Entrepreneurial Behavior & Research*, *28*(9), 52–77. https://doi.org/10.1108/IJEBR-12-2021-0984

Margetis, G., Apostolakis, K. C., Ntoa, S., Papagiannakis, G., & Stephanidis, C. (2020). X-reality museums: Unifying the virtual and real world towards realistic virtual museums. *Applied Sciences*, *11*(1), 338. https://doi.org/10.3390/app11010338

Martí-Testón, A., Muñoz, A., Gracia, L., & Solanes, J. E. (2023). Using WebXR metaverse platforms to create touristic services and cultural promotion. *Applied Sciences*, *13*(14), 8544. https://doi.org/10.3390/app13148544

Monaco, S., & Sacchi, G. (2023). Travelling the metaverse: Potential benefits and main challenges for tourism sectors and research applications. *Sustainability*, *15*(4), 3348. https://doi.org/10.3390/su15043348

Mystakidis, S. (2022). Metaverse. *Encyclopedia*, *2*(1), 486–497. https://doi.org/10.3390/encyclopedia2010031

Nhamo, G., Dube, K., Chapungu, L., & Chikodzi, D. (2023). Quest for NetZero emissions in South African national parks: A tourism perspective. *Heliyon*, *9*(6), 16410. https://doi.org/10.1016/j.heliyon.2023.e16410

Pillai, R., & Sivathanu, B. (2020). Adoption of AI-based chatbots for hospitality and tourism. *International Journal of Contemporary Hospitality Management*, *32*(10), 3199–3226. https://doi.org/10.1108/IJCHM-04-2020-0259

Rane, N., Choudhary, S., & Rane, J. (2023, November 1). Metaverse for enhancing customer loyalty: Effective strategies to improve customer relationship, service, engagement, satisfaction, and experience. *Service, Engagement, Satisfaction, and Experience*. https://dx.doi.org/10.2139/ssrn.4624197

Riva, G., Wiederhold, B. K., & Mantovani, F. (2024). Searching for the metaverse: Neuroscience of physical and digital communities. *Cyberpsychology, Behavior, and Social Networking*, *27*(1), 9–18. https://doi.org/10.1089/cyber.2023.0040

Schöbel, S. M., & Leimeister, J. M. (2023). Metaverse platform ecosystems. *Electronic Markets*, *33*(1), 12. https://doi.org/10.1007/s12525-023-00623-w

Semwal, R., Tripathi, N., Rana, A., Chauhan, A., Bhutani, V., & Gupta, K. (2023, December). *Conceptual integration of AI for enhanced travel experience*. In 2023 10th IEEE Uttar Pradesh section international conference on electrical, electronics and computer engineering (UPCON) (Vol. 10, pp. 1044–1048). IEEE. https://doi.org/10.1109/UPCON59197.2023.10434463

Sidlauskiene, J. (2022). What drives consumers' decisions to use intelligent agent technologies? A systematic review. *Journal of Internet Commerce*, *21*(4), 438–475. https://doi.org/10.1080/15332861.2021.1961192

Soliman, M., Al-Shanfari, L. S., & Gulvady, S. (2023). Sensory marketing and accessible tourism: An AI-generated article. *ROBONOMICS: The Journal of the Automated Economy*, *4*, 53–53. https://journal.robonomics.science/index.php/rj/article/view/53

Soliman, M. M., Ahmed, E., Darwish, A., & Hassanien, A. E. (2024). Artificial intelligence powered metaverse: Analysis, challenges and future perspectives. *Artificial Intelligence Review*, *57*(2), 36. https://doi.org/10.1007/s10462-023-10641-x

Sung, E. C., Bae, S., Han, D. I. D., & Kwon, O. (2021). Consumer engagement via interactive artificial intelligence and mixed reality. *International Journal of Information Management*, *60*, 102382. https://doi.org/10.1016/j.ijinfomgt.2021.102382

Trappey, A. J., Trappey, C. V., Chao, M. H., Hong, N. J., & Wu, C. T. (2021). A vr-enabled chatbot supporting design and manufacturing of large and complex power transformers. *Electronics*, *11*(1), 87. https://doi.org/10.3390/electronics11010087

Verma, S., Warrier, L., Bolia, B., & Mehta, S. (2022). Past, present, and future of virtual tourism—a literature review. *International Journal of Information Management Data Insights*, *2*(2), 100085. https://doi.org/10.1016/j.jjimei.2022.100085

Vinnakota, S., Mohan, M. D., Boda, M. J., Askarzai, W., Devkota, M. P., Shetty, M. S., Wangmo M T., & Choden, M. T. (2023). Venturing into virtuality: Exploring the evolution, technological underpinnings, and forward pathways of virtual tourism. *Educational Research (IJMCER)*, *5*(6), 08–49.

Wang, Y., Wang, L., & Siau, K. L. (2024). Human-centered interaction in virtual worlds: A new era of generative artificial intelligence and metaverse. *International Journal of Human–Computer Interaction*, 1–43. https://doi.org/10.1080/10447318.2024.2316376

Wei, W., Baker, M. A., & Onder, I. (2023). All without leaving home: Building a conceptual model of virtual tourism experiences. *International Journal of Contemporary Hospitality Management*, *35*(4), 1284–1303. https://doi.org/10.1108/IJCHM-12-2021-1560

Wu, B., & Wu, B. (2022). Metaverse: The world reimagined. In *Blockchain for teens: With case studies and examples of blockchain across various industries* (pp. 267–313). Apress. https://doi.org/10.1007/978-1-4842-8808-5_7

Xu, C., Zhong, R., Li, C., & Yan, X. (2023). From fiction to reality: Harnessing the power of imaginative narratives to shape the future of the metaverse. *Journal of Metaverse*, *3*(2), 108–120. https://doi.org/10.57019/jmv.1277525

Yang, F. X., Li, Y., Li, X., & Yuan, J. (2022). The beauty premium of tour guides in the customer decision-making process: An AI-based big data analysis. *Tourism Management*, *93*, 104575. https://doi.org/10.1016/j.tourman.2022.104575

Zawish, M., Dharejo, F. A., Khowaja, S. A., Raza, S., Davy, S., Dev, K., & Bellavista, P. (2024). AI and 6G into the metaverse: Fundamentals, challenges and future research trends. *IEEE Open Journal of the Communications Society*, *5*, 730–778. https://doi.org/10.1109/OJCOMS.2024.3349465

Zeng, Y., Liu, L., & Xu, R. (2022). The effects of a virtual reality tourism experience on tourist's cultural dissemination behavior. *Tourism and Hospitality*, *3*(1), 314–329. https://doi.org/10.3390/tourhosp3010021

Zhu, C., Wu, D. C. W., Hall, C. M., Fong, L. H. N., Koupaei, S. N., & Lin, F. (2023). Exploring non-immersive virtual reality experiences in tourism: Empirical evidence from a world heritage site. *International Journal of Tourism Research*, *25*(3), 372–383 https://doi.org/10.1002/jtr

Chapter 7

Metaverse Adoption Among Banking Users: A Developing Nation's Perspective

Anamica Singh, Anchal Luthra, Seema Garg and Vinita Sharma

Amity International Business School, Amity University, India

Abstract

Metaverse banking transitions online banking to a virtual realm, allowing customers to access services and interact virtually. While metaverse adoption is advantageous, research primarily focuses on gaming, education, and sports, neglecting banking. Current IT models lack focus on personal, voluntary adoption like metaverse banking. To address this, a new UTAUT2 model integrates performance, effort, social influence (SI), trust, and financial resources. Validated through 500 users from Punjab National Bank and Bank of Maharashtra, it proposes new constructs for metaverse banking adoption. Future research should expand to include cultural variations across banks and countries, especially in developing nations, for a comprehensive understanding.

Keywords: Metaverse; UTAUT2; users' intention; banking; information technology; financial resources

Introduction

Science fiction to technology, the metaverse is a buzzword that has become quickly most talked emerging technology. Many industries are rigorously exploring use cases of how to get the profits of metaverse and leverage the opportunities. Financial services are a no exception to explore the infinite possibilities of metaverse (Ooi et al., 2023). Metaverse has exceptional potential to propel banks to the next level of engaging customer experiences.

The AI Metaverse Revolution: Transforming Multi-Business Scenarios (Volume 1), 95–114

Published under exclusive licence by Emerald Publishing Limited
doi:10.1108/978-1-83662-582-720251007

The metaverse has garnered significant attention and enthusiasm in 2021 due to the substantial expenditures and strong commitment shown by global corporations toward metaverse-related large-scale initiatives. Consequently, a multitude of organizations across diverse sectors have shown a keen interest in the metaverse idea, leading them to engage in initiatives related to the metaverse (Duan et al., 2021), with a special focus on capturing market opportunities within their respective industries. These firms may effectively use the metaverse due to its decentralized nature, which is devoid of exclusive ownership or restrictions by individuals, countries, or enterprises. Consequently, this openness facilitates the seamless implementation of novel concepts. Given these considerations, coupled with the versatile capabilities of the metaverse that can effectively meet the diverse needs of customers across various industries, it is logical for businesses, irrespective of their field, to actively engage in research, development, and provision of metaverse-related products and services to their clientele (Tan et al., 2023). The gaming, art, and music sectors have prominently adopted these goods and services. It is worth noting that other industries are also present in this domain; however, their progress has been comparatively sluggish, and they have not yet unveiled ground-breaking products associated with the metaverse (Pew Research Center, 2022).

Building some metaverse goods inherently requires a greater amount of time, and the process of optimizing their potential is even more time-consuming (Damar, 2021). Hence, it is imperative to allocate significant attention to industries that are experiencing a lag in metaverse-related innovations. This is due to the potential for additional innovative opportunities and long-term profitability that businesses in these industries could both offer and attain, irrespective of their current level of advancement. In contemporary discourse within the banking sector, there has been much deliberation around the provision of financial services by banks inside the metaverse. This discourse has subsequently given rise to the conceptualization and popularization of the term "metaverse banking." The phrase in question has lately surfaced and lacks a precise and universally accepted meaning at now. The phrase in question may seem to possess a straightforward interpretation, thus leading to its frequent colloquial reference as "banking" inside the metaverse. However, the need is to put forward a more general definition that comprises the basic factors of metaverse banking. It would be uncommon to encounter a lack of a succinct description if its implementation were to become more prevalent in the future. While it cannot be certain that metaverse banking will emerge as a predominant financial service shortly, banks need to acknowledge the potential possibilities associated with metaverse banking. Neglecting these chances may fail to stay abreast of developments in the banking industry (Pai, 2023).

This paper aims to provide an elucidation of the idea of metaverse banking and investigate its prospective developments by directing a comprehensive assessment of appropriate information from prior studies. Prior research neglected the need to elucidate the concept of metaverse banking and mostly omitted the word when examining banking inside the metaverse, either owing to its nascent nature or underestimation of its long-term prospects. Therefore, the motivation for this research stems from the identified gap, as the authors acknowledge the significant untapped value inherent in both the idea and capacity of metaverse banking.

There is a growing trend among banks to enhance and broaden their digital presence. Both domestic and global banks allocate significant resources toward the implementation of digitalization strategies in order to minimize the need for customers to physically visit bank branches. Consequently, a significant number of financial resources were allocated toward the development of mobile applications that prioritize consumer needs, facilitating convenient access to services while on the move. This involved the migration of applications to cloud servers, the establishment of payment platforms, the facilitation of cryptocurrency storage and trading, the enhancement of cybersecurity measures, and the reconfiguration of the underlying architectural requirements to a centralized data warehouse (Özkaynar, 2022; Sasubilli et al., 2022). Digital architecture is the current avenue of investment in AI. AI is a major factor used in digital chatbot development for customer service. For example, artificial intelligence (AI) is usually engaged with those applications that have the digital chat bots which can handle customer inquiries effectively as well as being the one implementing the machine-learning algorithms that can intelligently identify the potential of the customer to be upsold and cross-sold. By developing these technologies, the investors' aim is to develop technologies that can be used to provide personalized services for high-net-worth customers, thus supporting their long-term retention (Giang Barrera & Shah, 2023).

Digital innovations have revved up the customer's transactional experience. It is evident that the absence of personal interaction with customers has noticeably affected the overall process (Özkaynar, 2022). As a result of the digitization of services, several banks have implemented downsizing strategies for their physical locations. This is mostly attributed to the widespread use of online platforms, which have significantly decreased the frequency of in-person client visits to the bank. There is a decrease in bank personnel and physical presence, and in the end, the bank as a brand gets more alienated from the customers (Özkaynar, 2022). According to Özkaynar (2022), customer–bank talk will take place in those banks that use virtual reality (VR) and augmented reality (AR) for service provision. Inside the framework of AR and VR, users are being exposed to three-dimensional virtual environment. However, they also get to experience physical simulations that replicate real-life activities with the help of specialized electronic devices, like gloves and headgear. Whether bells and whistles have been added or VR still stands on its own, the merging of VR and AR that resulted in metaverse is taking place, and it is here. Metaverse can be seen as an AR concept of the next generation in which high tech can be applied by banks; withal, the customer's human-centric approach can be preserved while the deeper personalization goal is achieved.

The current study seeks to analyze how the metaverse influences the various functional aspects of the Indian economy's financial transactions. The present work also wants to find the understanding of how the metaverse would work on the customer's trust for technology and the emergence of engagement in the banking sector. The outcome of this research is projected to recast the metaverse image where it is described as the next stage of the internet revolution presenting a broad exposure of interconnected experiences. The metaverse is seen as a dynamic design space that allows one to repurpose experiences through very different platform ecosystem that would come. The metaverse will, additionally, make transitions become so smooth between the virtual and the physical worlds that only virtual simulations will be needed to produce goods and services which are then transformed into concrete results. The general trend toward greater integration and interconnection is predicted to be largely off-course in the present setup.

Literature Review and Theoretical Background

The best-known big players in the fields of commerce, banking, financial services and metaverse are gaming, media, and entertainment are highly foreseen (Tan et al., 2023). The metaverse would provide users with the ability to own or rent digital holdings, necessitating the availability of financial services and reliable payment infrastructure (Dwivedi et al., 2022). Ethereum blockchain utilization on the Decentral and platform exemplifies the capacity to generate, purchase, and trade virtual land, digital assets, and properties showcasing the possibility for novel business models centered on virtual domains within the sectors of financial services (Ghosh et al., 2024). Within the domain of metaverse, individuals are afforded the chance to get digital goods, including footwear from esteemed companies like as Nike and garments from high-end fashion establishments like Gucci, to augment their virtual residences and avatars (Lee et al., 2024).

Metaverse concepts encompass the integration of physical domains as well as virtual, offering financial and banking companies the opportunity to cultivate a collaborative atmosphere with their clientele. With the help of digital banking solutions that utilize a three-dimensional aspect, and a feeling of presence, intimacy and human warmness can be still better realized. For example, this can be a buyer that live-interacts with a human customer service rep "embodied" as a real avatar or a simple chat between a consultant or a video call. The possible impact of the metaverse on financial and banking services is still uncertain. But, it is very important for the banks to actively experiment with this change and see if it can help create more attractive, more excited customers by immersing them into the virtual space (Abbott et al., 2022; Dwivedi et al., 2022).

Metaverse in Banking

In terms of adopting new technologies, the Indian banking sector has always been in the forefront. Hence, a crucial aspect of the digital India initiative lies in the banking sector's embrace of digital technology and its capacity to facilitate the expansion of digital payment systems. The establishment of digital banking ecosystems such as UPI and IMPS by the National Payment Corporation of India has led to a significant rise in the use of contactless payments. Consequently, the Indian digital economy currently constitutes more than 70% of the nation's current gross domestic product. Instead of implementing cryptocurrencies or other alternative currencies that are considered assets rather than currencies according to Indian regulatory policies, Bharatmeta incorporates built-in APIs to seamlessly interface with the digital public infrastructure established for payment purposes. Bharatmeta has successfully created and implemented dedicated virtual branches for Punjab National Bank and Bank of Maharashtra, to offer easy financial services to its customers. The potential of generative AI to revolutionize content generation and boost collaboration via immersive experiences inside the metaverse establishes a strong complementarity between the two. In line with this, the meticulously crafted three-dimensional virtual branches facilitate consumers in accessing the banks' lounge and acquiring authenticated information about the banks' financial offerings such as deposits, loans, government programs, digital initiatives, and so forth. Additionally, it offers users a customized and interactive banking experience.

The main purpose of the extended Unified Theory of Acceptance and Use of Technology 2 (UTAUT2) is to supply a precise outline for realizing the approval of technology from the customer's perspective. Consequently, in the search for a framework that covers all the possible factors that can cause the intention of using mobile banking and consumer acceptance among Indian customers, UTAUT2 has been identified as the theoretical basis for coming across the conceptual model used in this research. The main constructs contained in the UTAUT2 model, specifically performance expectation (PE), effort expectancy, SI, hedonic motivation, and pricing value, have been asserted as direct factors causing consumers to feel comfortable with Bharat Meta banking.

UTAUT: The UTAUT, which was introduced by Venkatesh et al. (2003), is a synergism of eight well-known models that can refine the prognostic skill of a model. Some theoretical foundations all apply to the significance of PE that is definitely UTAUT. Initially, the concept of benefits and efficacy was put forward by Davis (1989) and Rogers (1995), respectively. Davis et al. (1989) investigated extrinsic motivation, Thompson et al. (1991) looked into task fit, and Bandura (1986) inferred outcome expectations as a part of the theories. PE in UTAUT is arguably easier to understand and would be justified by all of the previous theories. The term "performance expectation" explains the extent to which people believe that a particular piece of technology can leverage/enable good performance (Venkatesh & Davis, 2000). A user's contribution in the ease of use may be evident by the number of actions they perform to make the application user-friendly and compatibility of the application with the user's development (Nguyen, 2023). Specifically, factors like the perceived usability of the technology, its reputation, subjective norm, and SIs are all evidence social impact. This principle, in particular, indicates the opportunity by which the user's key influencers endorse the utilization of the technology (Nguyen, 2023; Venkatesh & Davis, 2000). Compatibility is the major factor along with behavioral control and enabling conditions (Ajzen, 1991), these constructions are essentially parts of user perception which is tightly connected to a technology's organizational and technical support availability (Venkatesh & Davis, 2000).

As far as UTAT is concerned, there are three main types of thorough investigations. Following the recommendation of Chang and Tung (2008), Giang Barrera and Shah (2023) set out to assess UTAUT's efficacy in nontraditional settings. The researchers also aimed to improve UTAUT's applicability by including more components, following the suggestion of Venkatesh et al. (2012). Wong et al.

(2020) also suggested that UTAUT constructs should include predicate information. However, when applied to organizational settings, with an emphasis on employees' adoption of technology, Venkatesh et al. (2012) voiced reservations about the model's theoretical underpinnings. Regulated by several factors like the modes of behavior and social play, the domestic usage of technology takes on a different character (Schlachter et al., 2018).

There is a lack of valid and clear reasons for users' acceptance with reference to financial metaverse services in the UTAUT model. This is because people having financial services are the prospects for these services. The way the people want everything to happen determines their decisions, not just functionality. The work of the client base of financial services in the metaverse is viewed through a UTAMT lens with some basic concepts. To begin with, there is a concept of metaverse performance expectation (MPE), which is all about what the customers believe in the metaverse they can employ the said financial services and what they gain from employing the services. It is almost the same as the original theory of "performance expectancy (PE)" numerous customers were being satisfied with, in the previous UTAUT. The next part is known as the metaverse's effort expectation (MEE). This research investigates the perceived ease of fintech inside the metaverse as one of its dimensions. Similarly, the "the effort expectancy construct" of UTAUT is measured by means of the idea of MEE that revolves around how much trouble the users believe they are going to experience in metaverse banking services. The third component is metaverse social influence, which will analyze how social factors impact the adoption of metaverse financial services by consumers. Likewise, the case discussed here is similar to the "social influence" dimension of UTAUT's acceptance and use of technology in theory. It is all about SI theory research into how their mates' behaviors and attitudes will affect their choices of whether to use and integrate new technology. The last part is about metaverse facilitating conditions. The provision of resources and support is upstream to ensure the effective use of financial metaverse services. Among the UTAUT, the same idea is seen in the course of the "Facilitating Conditions" concept, it brings external conditions as an important factor in the ease of use of technology for users. Metaverse trust (MET) and metaverse financial resources are two new crucial parts that are incorporated in the study, it also takes into account the influence of customers' personal traits. The UTAUMT framework is a new look at variables that could impact metaverse adoption in the financial sector and it includes six main ideas. By considering this technique, the emphasis is shifted from technology to users, and the requirement of a clearer understanding of their requirements is stressed. One new approach for studying how people in the metaverse use financial services is the "Unified Theory of Acceptance and Use of Metaverse Technology" (UTAUMT).

Conceptual Framework

Banking services and metaverse: Bloomberg Intelligence (2021) is of the view that in order to move from traditional banking to metaverse banking, a number of factors must be taken into account, such as technological adaptability, strategic partnerships, customer education, and a future-oriented approach. Banks need to move fast with the latest trends in the metaverse and update their services more often to fit the changing preferences of virtual clients. In the current age, people are availing some of the banking services like online banking, mobile banking, virtual banking, and online payment systems, which the users can attend to at any time, thanks to the technical and internet advancements (Czímer et al., 2022). Online and mobile banking are more widely used and accepted by clients compared to traditional types of banking (Abu Daqar et al., 2020). To help grasp the bigger picture of the banking industry and the role of metaverse, we will define terms like "online banking," "mobile banking," and "metaverse banking" so that we can distinguish between these services. The term "online banking services" refers, in the simplest terms, to any service that a bank provides to its clients that is accessible 24/7 over the internet. Some examples of what online banking services entail include the replacement of paper-based transactions with electronic ones and the provision of quick information and transactions via the bank's website and mobile devices. The provision of financial services via mobile devices, including smartphones and tablets, through the use of specialized mobile apps or websites that are suited for mobile use, is also known as mobile banking (Zhou et al., 2021). With it, users may safely and easily manage their bank accounts, make transactions, and access a range of banking services from any mobile device. Zhou et al. (2021) note that mobile banking differs from online banking in terms of security measures, user experience, features, mobility of devices, and features. A web browser is required to access online banking. Mobile banking, on the other hand, makes use of mobile-optimized websites or specialized applications for use on mobile devices (Sharma et al., 2020). More convenient access, a streamlined interface for touch screens and smaller displays, and mobile-only capabilities like push alerts and mobile check deposits are all benefits of mobile banking (Zhou et al., 2021). Mobile banking applications may provide further security features, such as biometric verification, on top of the security protections already used by internet banking. More and more of these services are popping up, but banks will need to conduct more advertising to get people to use them (Saeed & Reehan, 2021). Online banking's benefits have also been the subject of substantial research (Abu Daqar et al., 2020; Srivastava, et al., 2023). Despite the advantages, adoption is still not certain (Morgan, 2022). As a result, advertising the services effectively is essential. The loss of branch banking among consumers, particularly millennials, has created a competition for conventional banking services from online and mobile banking (Malaquias & Hwang, 2016; Srivastava, et al., 2024). Traditional banks may opt to diversify their products and services or create new digital banking solutions in light of these threats. Those are fair measures that traditional banks may take to adapt to customers' evolving demands, says J.P. Morgan (2022).

Customers in a metaverse banking setting may access their accounts and services without leaving the virtual world, all while interacting with avatars (Birch, 2022). The metaverse ecosystem may provide them the ability to transact, see account balances, move money, and participate in other financial activities.

Customers will likely get real-time assistance and guidance from virtual assistants as they navigate their financial demands in a highly tailored experience.

Integrating the ease of online banking with the thrilling experience of VR, metaverse banking might provide a fresh and engaging approach to money management (Pai, 2023). While the idea of metaverse banking is still in its infancy, the reality for customers will change as banks and technology continue to innovate. Zhao et al. (2022) state that banks and their customers will lead the charge in digital banking and help create exciting new frameworks in the financial industry by adopting this innovative technology.

The financial services business has seen a dramatic shift due to the widespread use of internet banking, which has increased accessibility, piqued consumer interest, and prompted the development of new technological solutions. The term "metaverse banking services" is first used in this research; they refer to monetary dealings that take place in the metaverse. A metaverse is a VR setting where users may interact with one other and computer-generated environments. As an expansion of traditional banking services, "metaverse banking" takes place in the digital realm. However, as a result of major developments in this field, Vietnamese financial institutions have reached a unanimous agreement that the metaverse will play a crucial role in the banking industry's future.

Metaverse and financial resources: A person's level of financial flexibility is defined by the amount of money they are willing to sacrifice in order to use metaverse banking services. This money may come from a variety of sources, including the cost of equipment, transaction fees, and bank-specific costs. According to Ooi and Tan (2016), one reason innovations don't get adopted more often is because individuals can't afford them. According to Alnagrat et al. (2022), in order for extended reality (XR) software and hardware applications to work properly and provide an immersive experience in the metaverse, a variety of input devices are required, including personal computers, cell phones, head mounted displays, sensors (such as sensory gloves), and more. Although there may be some difficulties with the necessary technology, it is important to remember that technology is always improving and become easier to use. We anticipate that the accessibility, cost, and network infrastructure of devices will all increase in tandem with the development of the metaverse and associated technologies. This will pave the way for more widespread usage of metaverse financial services. The high cost of the technology may make metaverse adoption unaffordable for consumers with constrained or limited financial means. Consequently, the adoption would be more difficult to use and have fewer practical advantages. They suggest using creative pricing and marketing techniques to get more people to utilize cutting-edge electronics (Mishra et al., 2023). If banks can lower the cost of accessing metaverse technologies VR and AR devices will be given to a greater number of consumers in a way that will make them more accessible, or financial support or subsidies will be given, this will make consumers perceive using metaverse based banking services as affordable, and they will want to use it.

Metaverse and customer's trust: To "trust" is to have faith that other people will be forthright and true to their word. Kind, honest, and knowledgeable bank employees encourage customers to use their services in the metaverse (Al-Saedi et al., 2020). Establishing confidence in the metaverse of financial services is harder for banks than in conventional banking. The metaverse, with its emphasis on digital interactions and virtual surroundings, adds additional layers to the problem of trust perception. Thus, MET is vital in the online realm. Without it, it's impossible to establish trust and maintain relationships. In contrast to online financial services, which do not include any human contact between the buyer and seller, the metaverse may provide banks new methods to communicate with their clients in immersive and engaging ways. In addition, the many components of this technology have a broad variety of vulnerabilities, which represent both current and future dangers to users' security and privacy (Sillaber et al., 2016). Since XR data breaches may pose invisible threats to a user, hence the lack of user interaction, timely identification is of paramount importance to government agencies and high-tech companies (Abu et al., 2018). VR gadgets and software can only function properly if the data are available and protected while it is on transit, the media is at rest, and the user has a smooth experience. The exposure of sensitive financial data results in monetary losses. The occurrence of thefts of virtual assets in the metaverse or illegal access to user accounts is among the potential scenarios of security breaches (Kulal et al., 2022). Banks and service providers in the metaverse space must converge user educational initiatives, strict protocols, and regulatory compliance as the primary strategies to pre-empt and examine privacy, and security problems. Financial institutions would be wise to build secure systems with artificial exposures and expose the risks and vulnerabilities of XR technology to aid its reasonable creation, development, and protection (Qamar et al., 2023). The research study (Liébana-Cabanillas et al., 2020) pointed out that customers are more apt to adopt new technologies when they feel comfortable with them. They proposed that the willingness to the technology would be increased by the program developed to protect consumer data that are used for risk management and compliance purposes.

Performance expectancy and metaverse: The job performance of individual is largely influenced by some extrinsic motivating factors. For example, social standing which is related to money income is a significant source of extrinsic motivation (CFI Team). A similar concept is used in this study to describe people's faith in the usefulness of different tech tools when it comes to using metaverse financial services: MPE. Metaverse financial services may use customer data and preferences to provide individualized and tailored experiences. Clients could have a digital banking experience all of themselves, along with, for example, using financial planning tools, getting personalized advice, and encountering key financial data. Customer engagement and satisfaction are both, indeed, improved by this level of customization, which, in turn, is more likely to result in good performance.

Effort expectancy and metaverse: The difficulty of using Information Technologies or Information Systems is called MEE in the article of Venkatesh et al. (2003). MEE considers the key principles and particularly depicts the learning and usage barriers of metaverse financial services that potential users face (Chang et al., 2024). It is a lot more complicated to figure out and then utilize the metaverse than it is to use traditional banks. On the other hand, metaverse banking services can accelerate and automate many banking processes, thus, reducing labor and human intervention to a minimum. In the virtual room, you can perform such operations as creating an account, applying for a loan, or transferring money swiftly and effortlessly. This makes banking that much more efficient and comfortable for clients by the reduction of the effort required to perform these actions. These turn positive overtures from those who would switch to others. The research argues that one of the most prominent factors of technology acceptance is ultimately users' effort anticipation (Al-Saedi et al., 2020). Metaverse financial service systems are less likely to be welcomed by users/clients in the condition of the inconvenient statement.

Metaverse and facilitating condition: An MFC is analogous to the facilitating condition that Venkatesh et al. (2003) described as the extent to which a user feels that the system's organizational and technological infrastructure is in place to enable its usage. With the help of metaverse financial services and the cooperation of banks and service providers, MFC explains how a technological breakthrough in the metaverse may fit in with the expectations, tastes, beliefs, and habits of its potential customers. A lot of people use financial services in the metaverse. Online service is already being embraced by consumers, with banking as part of their everyday life. On the other hand, if future technologies are comparable and meet comparable demands, good experiences with existing forms of technology may be more readily transferred. Because the metaverse relies on PCs and mobile devices, customers are more likely to sign up if they are comfortable with these tools and know that they can get help from financial institutions if they run into problems. According to the IS/IT literature (Tarhini et al., 2016), MFC has a beneficial effect on the adoption of new technologies. It follows that consumers would have an outstanding experience if financial services in the metaverse were structured to make their usage easier. This, in turn, would provide the impression that utilizing banking services in the metaverse is supported.

Metaverse and social influence: SI plays a significant role when individuals' decisions regarding technology use are shaped by the opinions and behaviors of others (Dang et al., 2022). Examples of this include the subjective norm in TAM2 and the social norms in TRA. Although forecasting the usage of new technology is a difficult thing to do, SI is identified as a determining factor. A presentation of the name of a metaverse banking service in front of a group of friends, family members, or colleagues is likely to attract potential users. What people see in their social groups may be another factor that will increase their ambition to try. Consequently, interaction with the media platforms or virtual communities is devoted to the metaverse or money talks. Different people's views and opinions, thus, come into play, and this directly influences decision processes. Engagements such as single posting on the website about the metaverse or joining chats related to finance debates are means that inflect individuals' minds and drive them to adopt. Engaging in online discussions, listening to reviews, or watching user-generated content are examples of such activities that expose individuals to a range of perspectives, experiences, and advice on obtaining and using metaverse banking services that lead finally to influencing their attitudes and intentions to adopt. Previous studies on technological adoption have revealed the beneficial role of the social environment on people's aspirations for embracing new technology (Nguyen et al., 2022).

Metaverse in banking services and behavioral intention use: An individual's adoption behavior can be defined as a very specific set of outward behaviors that can be objectively observed in a given context or toward a certain task (Ajzen, 1991). Through the development of the idea of Ajzen (1991), the term "adoption of metaverse banking services" is used to describe people's initial usage and participation of VR- and AR-based financial services in an alternative world/ metaverse for everyday financial activities. Customers' banking habits and routines will be integrated into the process as they adopt, use, and integrate these services. When customers opt to use metaverse banking services, it involves them using them in various ways such as for financial transactions, interacting with others, and other experiences. The ones in metaverse banking services have more chances for showing the usability and consumers like their services without any problems. Customers that are highly positive in the technology field, meaning being at ease with it, and having a good impression of it, the more likely will be that they use it. Those who believe in new technologies and are eager to attempt these new things will generally foresee to use mobile financial services via metaverse. A successful adoption process is shown when clients continue to use these services for their continuing financial demands, demonstrating that they find value in them. They use the framework of acceptance perspectives in information technology with the main idea that both BI and UB are connected (Baptista & Oliveira, 2015).

Discussion

The interaction of the banking goals of users with the metaverse in a developing nation and the setting of this issue had become quite a fascinating multivalent and multilayered thing, as it was always intertwined with the social, economic, and technological obstacles they may encounter. Education, accessibility, trust issues, and cultural breaches are additional significant elements that must be treated to ensure a good and all-around outing for users inside the virtual banking. Metaverse has the potential of helping to include financial large numbers via the use of virtual banking service. One can use digital platforms to get access to finance the same way as to any business service, through transactions, and personal finance management, and the like. This virtual environment gives way to the physical impossibility of being everywhere and cumbersome hardware. To make the metaverse a conducive place to financial service provision, less developed areas should focus on creating accessibility and building a secure digital infrastructure. This encompasses guaranteed internet connection, low-cost gadgets, and user-friendly interfaces. There is of course some space for the government and financial institutions to join their forces for mutual investment in the metaverse enabling infrastructure, thereby making the technology available to a greater extent. The future release of virtual currencies and financial tools may even be achieved by the metaverse. Emphasizing the financial literacy program would greatly assist in educating people about the possible dangers as well as benefits they might incur from digital assets. The government and the banks could produce these instructional programs, and they could provide people with the necessary skills to manage their finances through the virtual environment of the metaverse.

The two main aspects, which are cyber security and trust, are the key terms that correspond to security considerations in both conventional banking systems and the metaverse. It, indeed, is a must for developing countries to allot resources toward the establishment and maximization of straightforward cybersecurity protocols that ensure the financial data and transactions of their customers are safe. The issuance of regulation is a fundamental process to protect the user's rights in the virtual world and to keep the integrity of the financial transaction systems stable, thus creating a degree of trust the users can rely on. There is a negative potential of causing social deterioration in societies, but the metaverse may, on the other hand, also allow developing countries, especially its people, to succeed economically. The economic upliftment of a person through virtual entrepreneurship and the creation of digital assets as well as involvement in virtual economies may be feasible. Governments can act as the conservatives of such activities and hence be the reason for the creation of new job openings and the spreading out of economic development.

User expectations and intentions: For disadvantaged users in developed countries, the onset of the digital era might be a joy since it primarily facilitates financial services. The metaverse points to the future world of individuals with the reality of a virtual space in which property acquisition is possible. First of all, the metaverse is a virtual world in which clients can reproduce essentially any aspect of the real world, including money and finance, without any limitations attached to space and time. Users might have an idea of the meta world in which more and more people are without the use of the traditional banking services that they are used to having, or the quantities are very limited. With the existence of the metaverse, the banks are lost, and this might permit certain people to decide on adopting a more comprehensive range of financial products as well as services. Economic consumers are building their wish lists by considering the use of low-cost banking systems. Interconnectedness in the metaverse could, indeed, lower the costs and fees of transactions, in this way, to make financial services more affordable for many of us. A lot of people are supposed to have some expectations about the introduction of new financial instruments and services that are shaped especially around their different needs. This can refer to decentralized financial solutions as well as virtual assets.

Challenges and concerns: It is the issue of digital literacy that might become a problem for individuals in poor places that the issue of digital literacy may give problems to users in the poor countries. Some technical skills are a prerequisite to comprehend and move around the metaverse properly. In addition, joint efforts are the key to ensuring easy and comfortable interaction of customers with virtual financial services. It is to be emphasized that trust and security are the primary aspects of the establishment of virtual financial systems. Suchlike are the users' fears about the safety of their financial data and transactions done inside the metaverse may be objected to, especially among those who are not specialized in working with virtual peripherals. Apart from the limited internet connection and inadequate infrastructure, it can also prevent consumers from the full experience of virtual banking. The problem of the fact that access to reliable internet services is not evenly distributed should be solved so that people from the whole planet use them. The desire for metaverse banking by the people can be positively or negatively affected by the cultural norms and attitudes toward virtual platforms. The concern over possible objecting or resistance to the adoption of these technologies may come up; therefore, it is imperative to ensure that virtual services mirror the expectations of the community which they are designed for.

User-centric strategies: The education of the user should be an important part of the process of learning and training in the context of education. Simulations and instructional programs have the potential to help users understand the metaverse, virtual banking, and the advantages that come with these platforms. The creators of the easy-to-use interfaces are the top priority. To address the varying degrees of digital literacy among consumers, the virtual banking experience needs to be simple and uncomplicated in its design. The fulfillment of conscious participation and communication with local stakeholders is the most important element that guarantees the successful implementation of initiatives. The consideration of the needs and concerns of the consumers in developing countries might be a direction that would help the metaverse banking services to develop faster. The key features of cost and availability must be made sure of. The involvement of financial organizations and developers is crucial in jointly making virtual banking services affordable and accessible for different segments of the users.

Potential impact: The metaverse can bestow economic empowerment onto people via the provision of avenues for virtual entrepreneurship, the development of digital assets, and engagement in virtual economies. The use of virtual banking has the potential to facilitate and strengthen financial connectedness within communities. Enhanced accessibility to financial resources and more chances for cooperation and trade inside the metaverse might potentially provide advantageous outcomes for users. The implementation of metaverse financial services has the potential to provide employment opportunities in sectors associated with virtual finance, hence fostering regional economic development.

The figures can speak a lot about the penetration on technologies in banking sector. The online banking penetration in India is forecast in 2024 to amount to 45.02%.

The advancement in terms of technology in banking system in the form of metaverse will raise few concerns:

- It can be though that the youth will have an enjoyable experience with the metaverse in otherwise mundane financial transactions?
- Will metaverse prove to be a helpful model for enhancing customer experiences, enabling better ease of banking and opening newer sources of revenue generation such as investments in NFTs, cross-selling of insurance policies, etc.?

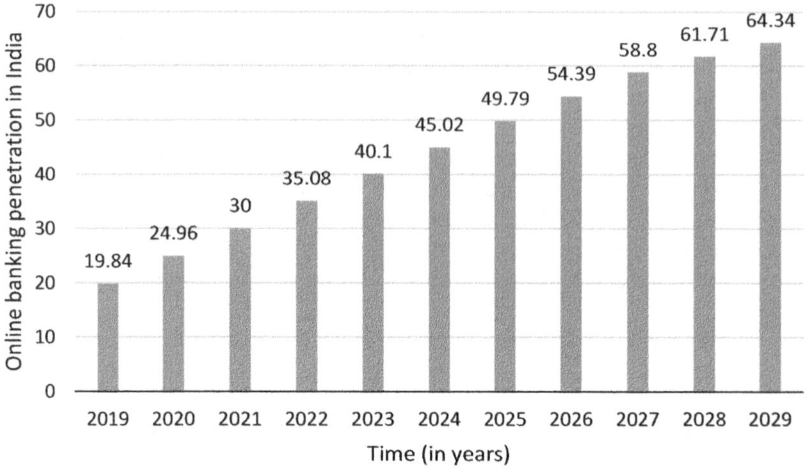

Fig. 7.1. Banking Forecast (Authors' work). Statista Market insights, World Bank, Eurostat, January 2024.

- With metaverse banks may eliminate multiple points of customer interactions, saving massive transactional costs as all activities which can be undertaken by one single banking employee avatar?
- User experiences in virtual environment provide high immersive experience, utilizing and collecting data for personalization and behavioral analysis raises ethical questions?
- The metaverse raises significant privacy and data protection concerns?
- The metaverse distributed data landscape in banking sector raises concerns about who owns and controls the data?

Through metaverse, banks can enable complicated and personalized services to a customer's avatar. These services include:

- Withdrawal of funds from virtual ATM's or branches to virtual wallets.
- High touch customer services to visit virtual branches.
- Avatar advisory for appointment and consultation purposes.
- Real time house tour with the help of mortgage broker.
- Convenience of purchasing and discussing customized financial products.
- Taking part in bank sponsored community programs and attend events.
- Seek help with virtual assistants.

Conclusion

In summary, the incorporation of the metaverse into the banking industry, as seen by users in developing countries, presents both opportunities and challenges. The user's intents and expectations are influenced by a strong inclination toward improved accessibility (Conner & Norman, 2022), more financial inclusivity, economically efficient solutions, and the introduction of novel financial products. Nevertheless, the effective implementation of virtual banking (Park & Kang, 2021) in the metaverse necessitates the resolution of several significant obstacles, including but not limited to issues pertaining to digital literacy, trust and security, restricted internet accessibility, and cultural acceptability (Whitehead et al., 2023). The implementation of user education programs is recommended in order to augment digital literacy (Blevins, 2018) and acquaint consumers with the metaverse and virtual banking interfaces. This will enable users to interact with these pioneering platforms effectively and assertively. The prioritization of simplicity and user-friendliness should be central to the design of virtual banking interfaces. The optimization of the virtual banking experience in terms of intuitiveness may serve as a means to address the disparity among users with diverse degrees of technical competence (Dotsenko, 2021). The active involvement with local communities is necessary in order to get a comprehensive awareness of cultural intricacies (Latif, 2020) and meet societal expectations. This would enable the development of metaverse financial services that are tailored to meet the distinct requirements of consumers residing in poor countries.

It is essential to prioritize accomplishments aimed at enhancing the affordability and accessibility of virtual banking services for a wide range of users. This encompasses the resolution of concerns pertaining to discrepancies in internet accessibility and infrastructure.

The establishment of confidence in virtual financial systems (Koziuk, 2021) is of utmost importance. The implementation of effective security mechanisms, clear communication, and adherence to legal frameworks may engender user trust in the safety of their financial transactions inside the metaverse. The effective implementation of metaverse banking has the potential to yield significant effects, such as fostering economic empowerment, enhancing financial connectedness, and generating employment opportunities, so making a valuable contribution to local economic progress. In brief, the incorporation of the metaverse into the banking industry of emerging economies necessitates a comprehensive strategy that takes into account the distinct requirements and apprehensions of its users. By placing a strong emphasis on education, user-centric design, community participation, affordability, and trust-building, stakeholders have the opportunity to facilitate a favorable and all-encompassing virtual banking experience (PNB ONE: Elevating Banking to an All-encompassing Experience, n.d.). This, in turn, enables users in developing countries to fully harness the revolutionary capabilities of the metaverse.

References

Abbott, M., Murray, J., & Guenther, D. (2022). *How the metaverse will change digital marketing*. Accenture. https://bankingblog.accenture.com/banking-in-the-metaverse-the-next-frontier

Abu, M., Rahayu, S., Ariffin, D. A., & Robiah, Y. (2018). An enhancement of cyber threat intelligence framework. *Journal of Advanced Research in Dynamical and Control Systems*, *10*, 96–104.

Abu Daqar, M. A. M., Arqawi, S., & Karsh, S. A. (2020). Fintech in the eyes of millennials and generation Z (the financial behavior and Fintech perception). *Banks and Bank Systems*, *15*(3), 20–28.

Ajzen, I. (1991). The theory of planned behavior. *Organizational Behavior and Human Decision Processes*, *50*(2), 179–211. https://doi.org/10.1016/0749-5978(91)90020-T

Akour, I. A., Al-Maroof, R. S., Alfaisal, R., & Salloum, S. A. (2022). A conceptual framework for determining metaverse adoption in higher institutions of gulf area: An empirical study using hybrid SEM-ANN approach. *Computers and Education: Artificial Intelligence*, *3*, 100052.

Almarzouqi, A., Aburayya, A., & Salloum, S. A. (2022). Prediction of user's intention to use metaverse system in medical education: A hybrid SEM-ML learning approach. *IEEE Access*, *10*, 43421–43434.

Alnagrat, A., Che Ismail, R., Syed Idrus, S. Z., & Abdulhafith Alfaqi, R. M. (2022). A review of extended reality (XR) technologies in the future of human education: Current trend and future opportunity. *Journal of Human Centered Technology*, *1*(2), 81–96.

Al-Saedi, K., Al-Emran, M., Ramayah, T., & Abusham, E. (2020). Developing a general extended UTAUT model for Mpayment adoption. *Technology in Society*, *62*, 101293.

Alvarez-Risco, A., Del-Aguila-Arcentales, S., Rosen, M. A., & Yáñez, J. A. (2022). Social cognitive theory to assess the intention to participate in the Facebook metaverse by citizens in Peru during the COVID-19 pandemic. *Journal of Open Innovation: Technology, Market, and Complexity*, *8*(3), 142.

Bandura, A. (1986). *Social foundations of thought and action: A social cognitive theory*, Prentice Hall.

Baptista, G., & Oliveira, T. (2015). Understanding mobile banking: The unified theory of acceptance and use of technology combined with cultural moderators. *Computers in Human Behavior*, *50*, 418–430. https://doi.org/10.1016/j.chb.2015.04.024

Birch, K. (2022). JP Morgan is first leading bank to launch in the metaverse. *FinTech Magazine*. https://fintechmagazine.com/banking/jp-morgan-becomes-the-first-bank-to-launchin-the-metaverse

Blevins, B. (2018). Teaching digital literacy composing concepts: Focusing on the layers of augmented reality in an era of changing technology. *Computers and Composition*, *50*, 21–38.

Bloomberg Intelligence. (2021). *Metaverse may be $800 billion market, next tech platform*. Bloomberg. https://www.bloomberg.com/professional/blog/metaverse-may-be-800-billion-market-next-tech-platform/

BNP Paribas. (2017). *BNP Paribas, contributing to the development of virtual reality*. https://group.bnpparibas/en/press-release/bnp-paribas-contributing-development-virtual-reality

Buhalis, D., Lin, M. S., & Leung, D. (2023). Metaverse as a driver for customer experience and value co-creation: Implications for hospitality and tourism management and marketing. *International Journal of Contemporary Hospitality Management*, *35*(2), 701–716.

Chan, Y. K., Tang, Y. M., & Teng, L. (2023). A comparative analysis of digital health usage intentions towards the adoption of virtual reality in telerehabilitation. *International Journal of Medical Informatics*, *174*, 105042.

Chang, S. C., & Tung, F. C. (2008). An empirical investigation of students' behavioural intentions to use the online learning course websites. *British Journal of Educational Technology*, *39*(1), 71–83.

Chang, Y., Wang, Y.-Y., & Tsai, H.-J. (2024). The metaverse in green building concept learning, creative design performance, and learning engagement. *Sustainability*, *16*, 6264. https://doi.org/10.3390/su16146264

Chekembayeva, G., Garaus, M., & Schmidt, O. (2023). The role of time convenience and (anticipated) emotions in AR mobile retailing application adoption. *Journal of Retailing and Consumer Services*, *72*, 103260.

Conner, M., & Norman, P. (2022). Understanding the intention-behavior gap: The role of intention strength. *Frontiers in Psychology*, *13*, 923464. https://doi.org/10.3389/fpsyg.2022.923464

COVID-19 pandemic: A systematic literature review. (2021). *Research Journal of Finance and Accounting*, *12*(18), 1–5.

Czímer, B., Dietz, M., László, V., & Sengupta, J. (2022). *The future of banking: A $20 trillion opportunity*. McKinsey. https://www.mckinsey.com/industries/financial-services/our-insights/the-future-of-banks-a-20-trillion-dollar-breakup-opportunity

Damar, M. (2021). Metaverse shape of your life for future: A bibliometric snapshot. *Journal of Metaverse*, *1*(1), 1–8.

Dang, D. T. V., Nguyen, L., & Nguyen, A. H. D. (2022). Extending UTAUT2 in mobile money adoption and actual use behavior: An empirical research in Vietnam during the Covid-19. *Industrielle Beziehungen. Zeitschrift Für Arbeit, Organisation Und Management*, *10*(4).

Davis, F. D. (1989). Perceived usefulness, perceived ease of use, and user acceptance of information technology. *MIS Quarterly: Management Information Systems*, *13*(3), 319.

Davis, F. D., Bagozzi, R. P., & Warshaw, P. R. (1989). User acceptance of computer technology: A comparison of two theoretical models. *Management Science*, *35*(8), 982–1002.

Dotsenko, N. A. (2021, June). Technology of application of competence-based educational simulators in the informational and educational environment for learning general technical disciplines. *Journal of Physics: Conference Series*, *1946*(1), 012014.

Duan, H., Li, J., Fan, S., Lin, Z., Wu, X., & Cai, W. (2021, October). Metaverse for social good: A university campus prototype. In *Proceedings of the 29th ACM international conference on multimedia* (pp. 153–161). ACM.

Dwivedi, Y. K., Hughes, L., Baabdullah, A. M., Ribeiro-Navarrete, S., Giannakis, M., Al-Debei, M. M., Dennehy, D., Metri, B., Buhalis, D., Cheung, C. M. K., Conboy, K., Doyle, R., Dubey, R., Dutot, V., Felix, R., Goyal, D. P., Gustafsson, A., Hinsch, C., Jebabli, I., … Wamba, S. F. (2022). Metaverse beyond the hype: Multidisciplinary perspectives on emerging challenges, opportunities, and agenda for research, practice and policy. *International Journal of Information Management*, *66*, 102542.

FiinResearch. (2022). *Vietnam banking report 2022*. https://fiinresearch.vn/Store/ReportDetails?id=165025

Finextra. (2016). *Citi taps microsoft hololens for virtual reality trading*. Finextra. https://www.finextra.com/newsarticle/28712/citi-taps-microsoft-hololens-for-virtual-reality-trading

Ghosh, A., Lavanya, Hassija, V., Chamola, V., & El Saddik, A. (2024). A survey on decentralized metaverse using blockchain and Web 3.0 technologies, applications, and more. *IEEE Access*, *12*, 146915–146948. https://doi.org/10.1109/ACCESS.2024.3469193

Giang Barrera, K., & Shah, D. (2023). Marketing in the metaverse: Conceptual understanding, framework, and research agenda. *Journal of Business Research*, *155*, 113420. https://doi.org/10.1016/j.jbusres.2022.113420

Hollensen, S., Kotler, P., & Opresnik, M. O. (2023). Metaverse – The new marketing universe. *Journal of Business Strategy*, *44*(3), 119–125.

Immonen, M., & Sintonen, S. (2015). Evolution of technology perceptions over time. *Information Technology and People*, *28*(3), 589–606.

Jafar, R. M. S., Ahmad, W., & Sun, Y. (2023). Unfolding the impacts of metaverse aspects on telepresence, product knowledge, and purchase intentions in the metaverse stores. *Technology in Society*, *74*, 102265.

Jeong, H., Yi, Y., & Kim, D. (2022). An innovative e-commerce platform incorporating metaverse to live commerce. *International Journal of Innovative Computing, Information and Control*, *18*(1), 221–229.

Jeong, S. H., & Kim, H. K. (2023). Effect of trust in metaverse on usage intention through technology readiness and technology acceptance model. *Tehnički vjesnik*, *30*(3), 837–845.

Koziuk, V. (2021). Confidence in digital money: Are central banks more trusted than age is matter?. *Investment Management and Financial Innovations*, *18*, 12–32. https://doi.org/10.21511/imfi.18(1).2021.02

Kulal, S., Li, Z., & Tian, X. (2022). Security and privacy in virtual reality: A literature review. *Issues in Information Systems*, *23*(2), 185–192.

Lan, N. (2022). Sound prospects for metaverse in Vietnam. *VnEconomy*. https://vneconomy.vn/sound-prospects-for-metaverse-in-vietnam.htm

Latif, A. S. (2020). The importance of understanding social and cultural norms in delivering quality health care – A personal experience commentary. *Tropical Medicine and Infectious Disease*, *5*(1), 22. https://doi.org/10.3390/tropicalmed5010022

Lee, L. H., Braud, T., Zhou, P. Y., Wang, L., Xu, D., Lin, Z., Kumar, D., Bermejo, C., & Hui, P. (2024). All one needs to know about metaverse: A complete survey on technological singularity, virtual ecosystem, and research agenda. *Foundations and Trends® in Human–Computer Interaction*, *18*(2–3), 100–337.

Lee, U. K., & Kim, H. (2022). UTAUT in metaverse: An "Ifland" case. *Journal of Theoretical and Applied Electronic Commerce Research*, *17*(2), 613–635.

Liébana-Cabanillas, F., Japutra, A., Molinillo, S., Singh, N., & Sinha, N. (2020). Assessment of mobile technology use in the emerging market: Analyzing intention to use m-payment services in India. *Telecommunications Policy*, *44*(9), 102009.

Liébana-Cabanillas, F., Marinković, V., & Kalinić, Z. (2017). A SEM-neural network approach for predicting antecedents of m-commerce acceptance. *International Journal of Information Management*, *37*(2), 14–24.

Malaquias, R. F., & Hwang, Y. (2016). An empirical study on trust in mobile banking: A developing country perspective. *Computers in Human Behavior*, *54*, 453–461.

Mishra, V., Tiwari, V., Singh, H., & Singh, P. (2023). Cutting-edge digital marketing: navigating the future. https://doi.org/10.13140/RG.2.2.34480.74240

Morgan, J. P. (2022). *Understanding the metaverse economy*. JPMorgan Chase & Co. https://www.jpmorgan.com/insights/research/understanding-the-metaverse

Nguyen, H.-B., & Nguyen, L.-T. (2021). Factors influence Blockchain adoption in supply chain management among companies based in Ho Chi Minh City. In *Proceedings of the conference towards ASEAN chairmanship 2023* (T-A-C 23 2021) (pp. 1–13). Indonesia.

Nguyen, L. T., Dwivedi, Y. K., Tan, G. W. H., Aw, E. C. X., Lo, P. S., & Ooi, K. B. (2022). Unlocking pathways to mobile payment satisfaction and commitment. *Journal of Computer Information Systems*, *63*(4), 998–1015.

Nguyen, L., Nguyen, D., Ngoc, K. N.-N., & Duc, D. T. V. (2023). Blockchain adoption in logistics companies in Ho Chi Minh City, Vietnam. *Cogent Business & Management*, *10*(2), 1–24.

Oh, J. H. (2021). A study on factors affecting the intention to use the metaverse by applying the extended technology acceptance model (ETAM): Focused on the virtual world metaverse. *The Journal of the Korea Contents Association*, *21*(10), 204–216.

Ooi, K.-B., & Tan, G. W.-H. (2016). Mobile technology acceptance model: An investigation using mobile users to explore smartphone credit card. *Expert Systems with Applications*, *59*, 33–46. https://doi.org/10.1016/j.eswa.2016.04.015

Ooi, K.-B., Tan, G., Aw, E., Cham, T.-H., Dwivedi, Y., Dwivedi, R.,Hughes, L., Kar, A., Loh, X-M., Mogaji, E., Phau, I., & Sharma, A. (2023). Banking in the metaverse: A new frontier for financial institutions. *International Journal of Bank Marketing*, 41. https://doi.org/10.1108/IJBM-03-2023-0168

Özkaynar, K. (2022). Marketing strategies of banks in the period of metaverse, block-chain, and cryptocurrency in the context of consumer behavior theories. *International Journal of Insurance and Finance*, *2*(1), 1–12.

Pai, S. (2023). Banking on the metaverse. *Forbes*. https://www.forbes.com/sites/forbestechcouncil/2022/03/15/banking-onthe-etaverse/?sh=7783b2ea6068

Park, S., & Kang, Y. J. (2021). A study on the intentions of early users of metaverse platforms using the technology acceptance model. *Journal of Digital Convergence*, *19*(10), 275–285.

Pew Research Center. (2022). *The metaverse in 2040*. https://www.pewresearch.org/internet/2022/06/30/the-metaverse-in-2040/

PNB ONE: Elevating Banking to an All-encompassing Experience. (n.d.). *Times of India*. https://timesofindia.indiatimes.com/spotlight/pnb-one-elevating-banking-to-an-all-encompassing-experience/articleshow/104312959.cms

Qamar, S., Anwar, Z., & Afzal, M. (2023). A systematic threat analysis and defense strategies for the metaverse and extended reality systems. *Computers and Security*, *128*, 103127.

Rogers, E. (1995). *Diffusion of innovations*. Free Press.

Saeed, M. A., & Reehan, A. (2021). Using online banking among COVID-19 pandemic: A systematic literature review. *Research Journal of Finance and Accounting*, *12*(18), 1–5.

Schlachter, S., Mcdowall, A., Cropley, M., & Inceoglu, I. (2018). Voluntary work-related technology use during non-work time: A narrative synthesis of empirical research and research agenda. *International Journal of Management Reviews*, *20*, 825–846. https://doi.org/10.1111/ijmr.12165

Sekaran, U., & Bougie, R. (2010). *Research methods for business: A skill-building approach*. John Wiley & Sons.

Sharma, R., Singh, G., & Sharma, S. (2020). Modelling internet banking adoption in Fiji: A developing country perspective. *International Journal of Information Management*, *53*, 102116.

Sillaber, C., Sauerwein, C., Mussmann, A., & Breu, R. (2016). Data quality challenges and future research directions in threat intelligence sharing practice. In *Proceedings of the 2016 ACM on workshop on information sharing and collaborative security* (pp. 65–70). ACM.

Smart, J., Cascio, J., & Paffendorf, J. (2007). *Metaverse roadmap: Pathways to the 3D web*. Metaverse, A Cross-industry Public Foresight Project. http://metaverseroadmap.org/

Srivastava, A., Nalluri, M., Lata, T., Ramadas, G., Sreekanth, N., & Vanjari, H. B. (2023, December). Scaling AI-driven solutions for semantic search. In *2023 International conference on power energy, environment & intelligent control (PEEIC)* (pp. 1581–1586). IEEE.

Srivastava, A., Pandey, P., Verma, P., Sharma, V., Sharma, A., & Kotecha, R. M. (2024). Advancements in intelligent transport systems across various modes of transportation. In *2024 International conference on intelligent systems for cybersecurity (ISCS)*, Gurugram, India (pp. 1–7). IEEE. https://doi.org/10.1109/ISCS61804.2024.10581362

Statista. (n.d.). *Digital connectivity indicators: Banking – India*. https://www.statista.com/outlook/co/digital-connectivity-indicators/banking/indi

Tambiama, M., Polona, C., Maria, N., & Pol, L. (2022). *Metaverse opportunities, risks and policy implications*. European Parliamentary Research Service. https://www.europarl.europa.eu/RegData/etudes/BRIE/2022/733557/EPRS_BRI(2022)733557_EN.pdf

Tan, G. W.-H. H., Aw, E. C.-X. X., Cham, T.-H. H., Ooi, K.-B., Dwivedi, Y. K., Alalwan, A. A., Balakrishnan, J., Chan, H. K., Hew, J.-J., Hughes, L., Jain, V., Lee, V. H., Lin, B., Rana, N. P., & Tan, T. M. (2023). Metaverse in marketing and logistics: The state of the art and the path forward. *Asia Pacific Journal of Marketing and Logistics*, *35*(12), 2932–2946.

Tarhini, A., El-Masri, M., Ali, M., & Serrano, A. (2016). Extending the UTAUT model to understand the customers' acceptance and use of internet banking in Lebanon. *Information Technology and People*, *29*(4), 830–849.

Thompson, R. L., Higgins, C. A., & Howell, J. M. (1994). Influence of experience on personal computer utilization: Testing a conceptual model. *Journal of Management Information Systems*, *11*(1), 167–187.

Toraman, Y. (2022). User acceptance of metaverse: Insights from technology acceptance model (TAM) and planned behavior theory (PBT). *EMAJ: Emerging Markets Journal*, *12*(1), 67–75.

Vatnani, R., & Verma, S. (2014). Comprehensive framework for internet banking adoption: An empirical analysis in the Indian context. *International Journal of Business Information Systems*, *15*(3), 307–324.

Venkatesh, V., & Davis, F. D. (2000). A theoretical extension of the technology acceptance model: Four longitudinal field studies. *Management Science*, *45*(2), 186–204.

Venkatesh, V., Morris, M. G., Davis, G. B., & Davis, F. D. (2003). User acceptance of information technology: Toward a unified view. *MIS Quarterly*, *27*(3), 425.

Venkatesh, V., Thong, J. Y. L., & Xu, X. (2012). Consumer acceptance and use of information technology: Extending the unified theory of acceptance and use of technology. *MIS Quarterly: Management Information Systems*, *36*, 157–178. https://doi.org/10.2307/41410412.

Whitehead, L., Talevski, J., Fatehi, F., & Beauchamp, A. (2023, February 28). Barriers to and facilitators of digital health among culturally and linguistically diverse populations: Qualitative systematic review. *Journal of Medical Internet Research*, *25*, e42719. https://doi.org/10.2196/42719. PMID: 36853742; PMCID: PMC10015358.

Wong, L. W., Leong, L. Y., Hew, J. J., Tan, G. W. H., & Ooi, K. B. (2020). Time to seize the digital evolution: Adoption of blockchain in operations and supply chain management among Malaysian SMEs. *International Journal of Information Management*, *52*, 101997.

Yuen, K. F., Koh, L. Y., Tan, L. Y. H., & Wang, X. (2023). The determinants of virtual reality adoption for marine conservation. *Technology in Society*, *72*, 102170.

Zainurin, M. Z. L., Masri, M. H., Besar, M. H. A., & Anshari, M. (2023). Towards an understanding of metaverse banking: A conceptual paper. *Journal of Financial Reporting and Accounting*, *21*(1), 178–190.

Zhao, Y., Jiang, J., Chen, Y., Liu, R., Yang, Y., Xue, X., & Chen, S. (2022). Metaverse: Perspectives from graphics, interactions and visualization. *Visual Informatics*, *6*(1), 56–67.

Zhou, Q., Lim, F. J., Yu, H., Xu, G., Ren, X., Liu, D., Wang, X., Mai, X., & Xu, H. (2021). A study on factors affecting service quality and loyalty intention in mobile banking. *Journal of Retailing and Consumer Services*, *60*, 102424.

Chapter 8

Democratizing Immersive Learning

Rajesh Verma and P. James Daniel Paul

Lovely Professional University, India

Abstract

The metaverse, a fusion of digitally augmented physical reality and virtual spaces, has rapidly evolved from a niche concept into a global phenomenon. This chapter explores the democratization of immersive learning through Spark AR Studio, focusing on its potential to reshape education within the metaverse. It traces the development of metaverse marketing from early platforms like Second Life to modern environments such as Roblox and Fortnite, showing how advancements in virtual reality (VR) and augmented reality (AR) have transformed consumer engagement. The study applies consumer behavior theories, including Maslow's Hierarchy of Needs, the Theory of Planned Behavior, and the Decision-making Process, to understand how AR and the metaverse address social needs, influence attitudes, and improve decision-making. Additionally, Consumer Engagement and Self-concept Theories illustrate how personalized experiences foster brand loyalty and self-expression. Social Identity Theory is also discussed to highlight the influence of virtual communities on identity formation. The research examines the metaverse's impact on business and education, emphasizing both the opportunities for innovation and the challenges related to security, privacy, and usability. Works by Arora (2024) and Kumar et al. (2024a, 2024b) are cited to stress the importance of aligning academic research with practical applications. This chapter contrasts AR and VR technologies, highlighting AR's ability to blend real-world experiences with immersive elements, particularly benefiting children and society. By utilizing Spark AR Studio, educators and marketers can develop interactive,

The AI Metaverse Revolution: Transforming Multi-Business Scenarios (Volume 1), 115–130

doi:10.1108/978-1-83662-582-720251008

data-driven strategies, promoting inclusive access to engaging educational content and innovative approaches in the digital era.

Keywords: AR Studio; Spark; metaverse; immersive learning application; Facebook; Instagram

Introduction

The metaverse, a collective virtual shared space created by the convergence of virtually enhanced physical reality and physically persistent virtual space, has rapidly emerged as a transformative platform in digital marketing. Initially, a niche concept in gaming, the metaverse has evolved into a global ecosystem, attracting industries from fashion to real estate, education, and retail, as brands recognize its potential to create immersive, interactive experiences for consumers. This chapter explores the evolution of metaverse marketing, tracing its roots from early virtual environments to the sophisticated, data-driven strategies employed today.

Early Developments: The Foundation of Virtual Worlds

The metaverse's marketing potential began with early virtual platforms like Second Life, launched in 2003. This platform allowed users to create avatars, socialize, and build virtual assets. Brands like Adidas and Coca-Cola were among the first to experiment with virtual storefronts, enabling users to explore branded experiences in a digital environment. However, the marketing efforts were often rudimentary, focusing on brand visibility rather than consumer engagement.

By the mid-2010s, advances in VR and AR began to reshape virtual spaces. The introduction of AR applications such as Pokémon Go demonstrated the potential for blending physical and digital worlds, opening new opportunities for interactive marketing. Brands like IKEA capitalized on AR's potential with their Place app, allowing users to visualize furniture in their own homes.

The Rise of Immersive Marketing

The next phase of metaverse marketing emerged with more immersive platforms like Roblox and Fortnite, which incorporated VR, AR, and mixed reality experiences. These platforms enabled brands to create highly engaging and gamified content that resonated with younger audiences. For example, Fortnite's collaborations with brands like Nike and Marvel showcased how in-game events, product drops, and branded experiences could drive both digital and physical sales.

By integrating blockchain technology and non-fungible tokens (NFTs), brands began to monetize virtual assets. Virtual real estate in the metaverse, particularly in platforms like Decentraland and The Sandbox, became hot commodities, and brands like Gucci and Louis Vuitton used NFTs to sell exclusive virtual goods. NFTs enabled brands to offer consumers a sense of ownership over digital assets, whether they were limited-edition items or virtual representations of physical products.

Current Trends in Metaverse Marketing

Several key trends are driving the evolution of marketing strategies in the metaverse today:

- *Personalized experiences and AI-driven content*: As AI continues to evolve, marketers are leveraging generative AI models to create personalized content at scale. Companies use AI to analyze user data, tailoring experiences to individual preferences. Digital twins of customers enable more accurate and relevant marketing, from personalized avatars to virtual fashion recommendations.
- *Virtual influencers and brand ambassadors*: Virtual influencers, like Lil Miquela, are becoming a significant trend in metaverse marketing. These computer-generated characters engage with audiences on platforms like Instagram and TikTok, promoting brands in a highly targeted manner. Virtual influencers are free from human constraints, allowing brands to create consistent messaging and maintain a continuous presence across platforms.
- *Event-based marketing and virtual concerts*: Event-based marketing, particularly virtual concerts, has gained significant traction in the metaverse. Platforms like Fortnite and Roblox have hosted virtual concerts featuring artists such as Travis Scott and Ariana Grande, where millions of users attended simultaneously. These events provide immersive brand sponsorship opportunities and generate massive user engagement, transforming marketing into a participatory experience.
- *NFTs and virtual goods*: The use of NFTs continues to reshape the way brands engage with consumers. Companies are offering exclusive virtual merchandise, collectibles, and experiences that can only be accessed through ownership of NFTs. These digital assets allow brands to monetize their presence in the metaverse while giving users a sense of exclusivity and ownership. For instance, Nike's Cryptokicks offers virtual sneakers as NFTs, with the potential for real-world wearability in the future.
- *Metaverse commerce*: Direct-to-avatar (D2A) commerce has emerged as a new model in metaverse marketing, where brands sell digital items directly to user avatars. Virtual fashion brands like The Fabricant are creating digital-only clothing that users can wear in the metaverse. This shift toward digital goods is also fueled by concerns over sustainability, as virtual products offer an eco-friendly alternative to physical goods.

As the metaverse continues to grow, the integration of 5G technology, artificial intelligence, and VR will drive further advancements in marketing strategies. The metaverse offers limitless possibilities for consumer interaction, enabling brands to create immersive experiences that go beyond traditional media. The convergence of the Internet of Things (IoT) with metaverse marketing will enable seamless interactions between physical and digital environments, blurring the lines between the real and virtual worlds.

In summary, the metaverse represents the future of marketing, providing unprecedented opportunities for brands to engage with consumers in dynamic, immersive, and personalized ways. As technological advancements continue to push the boundaries of virtual environments, marketers will need to adapt and innovate, creating strategies that align with the evolving landscape of the metaverse. By embracing these new trends, brands can foster deeper connections with their audiences and unlock new revenue streams in the digital age. In the following section, we would review some of the consumer behavior theories with a focus on the AR and metaverse generation Z. In this chapter, some of the consumer behavior theories relating to the AR and metaverse used by gen z and review of similar literature are presented.

Review of Literature

Consumer behavior theories explain how people make purchasing decisions and interact with brands. With the rise of AR and the metaverse, these theories are crucial for understanding Generation Z's consumption patterns.

Maslow's Hierarchy of Needs: Maslow's theory outlines human motivations from basic needs to self-actualization. AR and the metaverse help Generation Z meet social and esteem needs by offering interactive and immersive experiences that enhance self-expression and creativity.

Theory of Planned Behavior: This theory posits that attitudes, subjective norms, and perceived control influence consumer behavior. AR and the metaverse shape Generation Z's attitudes toward brands through engaging experiences and peer influences, while also enhancing perceived control through user-friendly technologies.

Decision-making Process: The decision-making process involves problem recognition, information search, evaluation, purchase, and post-purchase behavior. AR assists Generation Z in visualizing products and making informed choices, while the metaverse provides immersive evaluation and community-driven feedback.

Consumer Engagement: Consumer Engagement Theory focuses on meaningful interactions that build loyalty. AR and the metaverse offer interactive and personalized experiences that resonate with Generation Z, leading to greater brand loyalty and advocacy.

Self-concept Theory: Self-concept Theory suggests that consumer behavior is influenced by self-perception and presentation. AR and the metaverse allow Generation Z to shape their self-concept through personalized avatars and virtual experiences, aligning with their ideal self-image.

Social Identity Theory: This theory explores how individuals' self-concept is influenced by social groups. The metaverse and AR enable Generation Z to connect with communities and enhance their social identity through virtual group interactions and shared experiences.

AR and the metaverse offer unique insights into Generation Z's consumer behavior, addressing their social and self-fulfillment needs, influencing decision-making, and enhancing engagement. Understanding these dynamics is essential for brands looking to connect with this digital-native generation effectively.

Arora (2024) discusses how the metaverse is transforming business, disrupting traditional models and creating new opportunities for growth and innovation. The chapter highlights the metaverse's impact on the global economy, focusing on job creation, new industries, markets, and revenue streams. It also emphasizes the need for collaboration to bridge the gap between academic research and practical applications, ensuring real-world impact. However, the lack of standardized frameworks poses challenges for integrating the metaverse safely and effectively into everyday life, with concerns about security, privacy, and usability.

Kumar et al. (2024 a, 2024b) highlight the challenges of navigating the metaverse in business and education. As companies seek new ways to engage customers and educators explore immersive learning, there is a lack of literature in these areas. Their book, *Exploring the Use of Metaverse in Business and Education*, fills this gap by offering a structured framework for understanding the metaverse's complexities. Each chapter covers foundational technologies, academic research, practical applications, and future challenges, providing businesses with strategies for marketing and e-commerce and educators with tools to enhance virtual learning experiences.

Kumar et al. (2024a, 2024b) highlight the challenges of understanding the metaverse in the evolving fields of business and education. As businesses explore virtual engagement and educators seek immersive learning solutions, there is a lack of literature on these topics. *Exploring the Use of Metaverse in Business and Education* addresses this gap by offering a framework that covers essential technologies, academic research, and practical applications. The book provides strategies for businesses to use the metaverse for marketing and e-commerce, while helping educators create engaging virtual learning environments.

Chandel and Arora (2024) examine the social, economic, and environmental impacts of the metaverse, highlighting its alignment with various UN Sustainable Development Goals (SDGs). Their study explores how the metaverse can transcend borders and promote sustainability, contributing to the ethical development of digital technologies. By analyzing the metaverse's potential to support inclusive, equitable, and sustainable growth, the chapter provides insights for policymakers and businesses. The authors emphasize the need to balance innovation with global sustainability as the metaverse evolves.

Dhiman and Arora (2024) highlight the growing recognition of the metaverse's potential by entrepreneurs as it evolves into a virtual space for interaction. Their study uses a bibliometric analysis of the Scopus database (2005–2023) to explore research patterns, collaborations, and thematic trends connecting the metaverse and entrepreneurship. The findings reveal a sharp rise in publications after 2020, reflecting increased interest in the metaverse's entrepreneurial impact, with a diverse and collaborative global research community. Key themes include big data, blockchain, AI, and VR, offering insights into the metaverse's influence on entrepreneurship.

Rathore and Arora (2024) explore how the metaverse, blending the physical and digital worlds, is disclosed in sustainability and integrated reports. The study focuses on select Indian companies from the Nifty 100 index that mention metaverse technologies in their reports. It analyzes the extent of these disclosures and highlights initiatives involving IoT, AI, and VR technologies aimed at improving productivity, operational efficiency, and workplace safety in major Indian industries.

Ranjitha and Venkatesh (2024) discuss how rapid modernization has transformed how people learn, communicate, and share information online though interaction still relies on traditional tools like keyboards and mice. While emerging technologies like social networking, video conferencing, and AR applications contribute to digital transformation, they are limited by conventional barriers such as insufficient network support. The metaverse, a digital representation of the real world, offers a more immersive experience through virtual avatars and complex user interactions. As big tech companies advance this space, the metaverse will expand beyond gaming and social media to include economic systems and digital applications. The chapter explores these developments and their role in digital transformation.

Cerdá-Boluda et al. (2024) explore the integration of technology and human interaction in the metaverse, focusing on virtual shopping in the fashion industry. The study uses scanned virtual hands and infrared sensors to track user hand movements, creating a natural interaction in a metaverse environment. Tested with Meta Quest 2 and utilizing blockchain and NFTs for transactions, the solution garnered positive feedback from 250 in-person participants and 120 remote users. The findings offer valuable technical insights for future metaverse implementations.

Chamola et al. (2024) explore how Generative AI can support the metaverse by creating dynamic, interactive, and personalized content at scale. They analyze AI models that generate different types of content, such as text, images, video, 3D visuals, audio, and gaming and discuss various use cases for each in the metaverse. The study highlights the potential of Generative AI to not only enhance user experiences but also create revenue opportunities for individuals and organizations. Despite challenges, the chapter concludes that Generative AI is key to realizing the full potential of the metaverse.

The collective body of research underscores the transformative impact of the metaverse across various sectors, from business and education to sustainability and entrepreneurship. Arora (2024) and Kumar et al. (2024a, 2024b) highlight the potential of the metaverse to drive innovation, create new markets, and enhance educational and business engagement, while acknowledging challenges related to security and standardized frameworks. Chandel and Arora (2024) emphasize the metaverse's role in supporting the UN SDGs, promoting equitable growth and sustainable development. Studies by Dhiman and Arora (2024) and Rathore and Arora (2024) reveal the metaverse's rising influence on entrepreneurship and corporate disclosures in India, demonstrating its growing integration into real-world applications. Collectively, these studies provide a comprehensive overview of the metaverse's evolving role in shaping the future of digital transformation and economic progress.

Ball (2022) aims to explore the transformative potential of the metaverse in reshaping digital ecosystems and user interactions. The study employs a multidisciplinary approach, analyzing case studies and emerging technologies like VR, AR, and blockchain to understand the metaverse's development. Key findings reveal significant opportunities for immersive engagement and economic growth, alongside challenges in interoperability, data privacy, and equitable access.

Cheremnykh (2024) investigates the integration of AR within the fashion industry, focusing on how brands utilize AR to enhance customer engagement and experience. The study examines various applications, such as virtual try-ons, AR fashion shows, and interactive brand narratives, highlighting the technology's role in bridging physical and digital retail spaces. Key findings suggest that AR not only elevates consumer interaction but also offers significant opportunities for brands to differentiate

Egliston and Carter (2024) critically examine the pervasive myths surrounding VR technologies, aiming to demystify the exaggerated claims often propagated by the tech industry. Their analysis spans various sectors, including gaming, human resources, policing, and the military, to assess VR's actual impact and potential. The authors conclude that, while VR offers notable possibilities, its purported benefits are frequently overstated, with significant concerns related to privacy, control, and social exclusion.

Tourist Guide with Augmented Reality (2023): This chapter explores the development of an AR application designed to enhance the tourism experience by providing interactive and immersive information about tourist attractions.

Augmented Reality and Virtual Reality

Both AR and VR are technologies that alter our perception of the world but in fundamentally different ways (Table 8.1).

While AR operates seamlessly on mobile devices, VR necessitates the use of a specialized VR headset. AR enhances the real-world environment by overlaying digital elements, allowing users to remain aware of their surroundings. In contrast, VR immerses users in a fully simulated environment, effectively blocking out the real world, which can have psychological implications for users, particularly those engaged in prolonged gaming sessions.

Table 8.1. Similarities and Differences Between AR and VR.

Feature	**AR**	**VR**
Environment	Real world with digital overlays	Completely simulated world
Device	Smartphone, tablet, headset (optional)	VR headset required
User awareness	Maintains awareness of real surroundings	Blocks out real surroundings
Applications	Education, marketing, gaming (partially real-world), information visualization	Gaming, training simulations, entertainment, design visualization

Despite their differences, AR and VR share many applications across various fields. However, AR presents distinct advantages, particularly for children and society, where concerns about VR addiction are increasingly prevalent. The benefits of AR, including its ability to enhance real-world awareness while providing immersive experiences, make it a valuable tool in various contexts.

As this is a textbook chapter, we will outline the steps to create an AR experience and an Instagram reel using Spark AR Studio. Additionally, we will compare the user experiences of Facebook and the metaverse, highlighting the unique aspects of each platform.

Facebook (now Meta), Instagram, and Spark AR Studio are all products within the expansive ecosystem created by Mark Zuckerberg. This raises the question: Are these platforms competing against each other, or are they targeting distinct audiences? In this chapter, we explore this dynamic by analyzing the unique value propositions of each platform, particularly focusing on the process of creating immersive experiences with Spark AR and within the metaverse. Additionally, we provide a detailed comparison of the user experiences on Instagram and Facebook to illustrate how these platforms serve different purposes within the broader Meta ecosystem (Fig. 8.1).

From the block diagram, it becomes evident that while Meta and Facebook share similarities in their overarching goals of fostering social connectivity and digital interaction, they cater to different user experiences. Similarly, Instagram and Spark AR Studio, though both integral to the Meta ecosystem, serve distinct purposes. Instagram is primarily a social media platform focused on content sharing and discovery, offering a user-friendly environment for everyday interactions. In contrast, Spark AR Studio is a more specialized tool designed for the creation of immersive AR experiences, catering to content creators, marketers, and developers who seek to push the boundaries of digital engagement (Table 8.2).

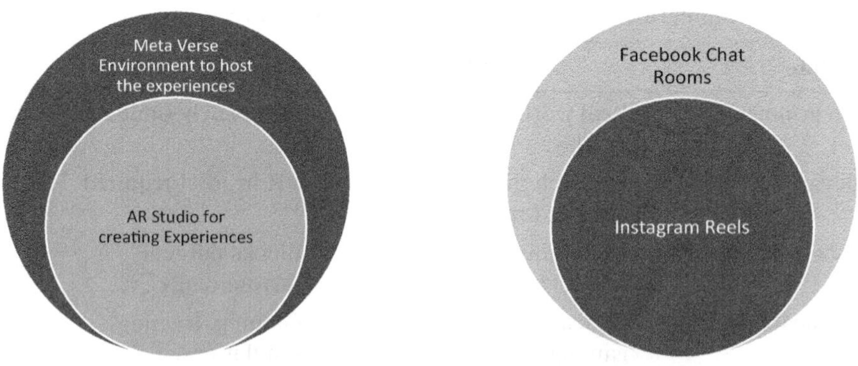

Fig. 8.1. AR Studio and Metaverse.

Table 8.2. Instagram Versus Spark AR Studio.

Feature	Instagram	Spark AR Studio
Purpose	Social media platform for sharing photos and videos	AR creation tool for mobile devices
Focus	Content sharing, discovery, and social connection	Building interactive AR experiences
Content type	Static photos and videos, live streams	3D objects, animations, visual effects
User-generated content	Primarily user-generated photos and videos	Requires some design knowledge and planning
Technical expertise	No coding required, user-friendly interface	Lower barrier to entry, but some learning curve
Output	Feed posts, stories, reels	AR filters and effects for mobile devices
Target audience	Broad social media users	Content creators, marketers, educators
Monetization	Through advertising and influencer marketing	Indirectly through brand promotion in AR filters
Ownership	Owned by Meta (formerly Facebook)	Owned by Meta (formerly Facebook)

While Instagram is a social media platform designed for the general public, Spark AR Studio is a more advanced tool focused on creating AR experiences for mobile devices. In essence, Instagram caters to the everyday user, offering a straightforward and accessible interface for sharing content. On the other hand, Spark AR Studio, though accessible to younger users and hobbyists, is more technically oriented and geared toward professionals who aim to develop and commercialize sophisticated AR experiences for their clients.

Spark AR Studio

Meta's Spark AR Studio is a robust platform for creating AR experiences, offering a comprehensive suite of tools and resources. This powerful platform enables the design and deployment of AR content that can reach a vast and diverse audience across multiple devices.

Key Applications of Spark AR Studio

Spark AR Studio empowers users to create immersive AR experiences across various fields. Some notable applications include:

- *Education*: Spark AR Studio enables the development of interactive 3D models, simulations, and virtual field trips, enriching traditional learning methods and significantly enhancing student engagement.
- *Medicine*: The platform can be used to create visually compelling AR experiences that aid in patient education, offering detailed visualizations of anatomical structures and medical procedures.
- *Tourism*: Travel agencies can leverage Spark AR Studio to craft immersive virtual tours, inspiring wanderlust and allowing potential travelers to explore destinations virtually before making their travel decisions.
- *Automotive technical marketing*: Complex technical concepts, such as vehicle components and functionalities, can be vividly brought to life through interactive AR experiences, providing users with a dynamic and engaging way to explore these intricate details.

These examples highlight just a few of the potential applications of Spark AR Studio. The platform's versatility allows for the creation of AR overlays that can serve informative, educational, and entertaining purposes, making it a valuable tool across a wide range of industries (Table 8.3).

Uses of Spark AR Studio

- Create educational experiences by designing interactive 3D models, simulations, and virtual field trips that enrich the learning process and significantly boost student engagement.
- Enhance marketing and communication through the development of AR filters and effects that promote products, showcase key features, or create captivating ad campaigns that resonate with audiences.
- Visualize complex concepts using interactive AR overlays, allowing users to explore and understand intricate technical information in a dynamic and engaging manner.
- Facilitate remote learning and training by creating AR experiences for virtual demonstrations or procedural training, effectively overcoming geographical barriers and making learning accessible from anywhere.
- Boost tourism and travel experiences by developing immersive virtual tours that enable potential visitors to explore destinations in a compelling way, sparking interest and inspiring real-world travel.

An interesting application of Spark AR Studio that students have explored is creating training programs for children featuring popular cartoon characters like Superman, making learning both fun and interactive.

Spark AR Studio empowers users to create engaging AR experiences for mobile devices. Below is a breakdown of the steps involved.

Table 8.3. Facebook Versus Metaverse.

Feature	Facebook	Metaverse
Purpose	Social networking, content sharing, communication	Richly immersive virtual world for social interaction, work, entertainment, and more
Focus	Connecting existing people and communities	Building a new VR with interconnected experiences
Accessibility	Primarily accessed through mobile app and web browser	Requires specialized hardware like VR headsets (potentially evolving)
User experience	Primarily 2D interface with text, images, and videos	3D virtual environment with avatars representing users
Interaction	Sharing content, commenting, messaging, joining groups	Immersive interactions like attending virtual events, playing games, collaborating in workspaces
Content creation	User-generated content (photos, videos, text)	Diverse content creation tools for building virtual experiences (potentially user-generated and developer-created)
Control and ownership	Data largely controlled by Facebook, limited user ownership of content	Potential for decentralized ownership of virtual assets and experiences
Current stage	Mature and widely used platform	Early stage of development, evolving concept
Future potential	May evolve toward more immersive experiences	Could become a major platform for future social interaction and virtual activities

- *Download and install Spark AR Studio*: Head over to https://spark.meta.com/download/ and download the latest version compatible with your operating system. Once downloaded, follow the on-screen instructions to install the software.
- *Start a new project*: Upon launching Spark AR Studio, you'll be greeted with the option to create a new project. Click on '**New Project**'. You'll be presented with a few project template options. Choose '**Blank Project**' for maximum creative freedom.
- *Explore the interface*: Familiarize yourself with the workspace. The central area is the **Viewport**, where you'll see a live preview of your AR experience. The left-hand side houses the **Scene** and **Properties** panels. The Scene panel lists all

elements in your project, while the Properties panel lets you edit the selected element's properties. The top toolbar provides various tools for manipulating objects, adding effects, and testing your experience.

- *Add a Face Tracker*: Many AR experiences involve interaction with a user's face. To enable this, drag and drop the '**Face Tracker**' element from the library (bottom left) into the Scene panel.
- *Import 3D objects and assets*: Click on the '**Import**' button in the top toolbar. You can import various assets like 3D models, images, and sounds to enhance your experience. It is much easier to save the objects as PNG and then imports them. In Spark AR, the images and videos are called as assets.

Once imported, you can drag and drop these assets into the Scene panel to position them within your AR view.

- *Apply materials and textures*: To customize the appearance of your imported assets, select the asset in the Scene panel. In the Properties panel, you can adjust material properties like color, texture, and lighting to achieve the desired look.
- *Animate and add interactions*: Spark AR Studio allows you to animate your objects and create interactive experiences. You can use the Patch Editor (accessed from the top toolbar) to visually program animations and interactions without needing to code. Alternatively, for simpler animations, you can utilize the built-in animation tools within the Properties panel of the selected object.
- *Test your experience*: Throughout the creation process, you can test your AR experience in real-time using the simulator window (top right corner). This simulates how the experience will appear on a mobile device. For a more realistic test, you can connect your mobile device and preview the experience directly on it using the '**Test on Device**' option in the top toolbar.
- *Export and share*: Once you're satisfied with your creation, you can export it for others to experience. Click on '**Export**' in the top toolbar and follow the on-screen instructions. Spark AR Studio allows you to export your experience for various platforms like Facebook and Instagram, where users can access and interact with it through their mobile apps.

Spark AR Studio offers a vast library of tutorials and resources to help you learn and explore its functionalities. Consider the target audience and purpose of your experience when designing it.

Start with a simple concept and gradually build upon it as you gain experience. By following these steps and exploring the vast capabilities of Spark AR Studio, you can create immersive and engaging AR experiences that can revolutionize learning, marketing, and entertainment.

Examples of how Spark AR can create superior virtual experiences:

- *Interactive product visualizations*: Imagine trying on clothes virtually through an AR filter before buying them online, offering a more interactive experience than static product images.

- *Educational AR scavenger hunts*: Museums or historical sites could develop AR experiences that guide visitors through exhibits with interactive elements, surpassing the limitations of static displays.
- *Location-based AR games*: AR experiences can transform real-world locations into interactive game environments, offering a more immersive experience than traditional mobile games.

Our current digital landscape, dominated by flat screens and social media feeds, provides a vast array of information and opportunities for connection. However, it also has its limitations. Traditional educational methods often struggle to fully engage students, especially in a world where geographically dispersed teams face significant challenges in collaboration. Additionally, social media interactions, while widespread, frequently lack the depth and nuance of real-world connections.

The metaverse seeks to address these limitations by envisioning a richly immersive virtual world where users, represented by avatars, can interact in real time, breaking free from the constraints of the physical world. Imagine:

- *Education*: Students embarking on virtual field trips to distant lands, exploring the intricacies of the human body in 3D, or conducting experiments in meticulously simulated environments. This immersive approach fosters deeper understanding and greater engagement with learning.
- *Work*: Global teams collaborating seamlessly in virtual workspaces, brainstorming ideas on shared digital whiteboards, or attending meetings in immersive conference rooms – transcending the barriers of physical location and time zones.
- *Social connection*: Friends and family gathering in vibrant virtual spaces, attending live concerts, playing interactive games, or simply catching up – creating shared experiences that transcend physical boundaries and bring people closer together, regardless of where they are in the world.

The potential benefits of the metaverse extend far beyond these foundational areas. It holds the promise of transforming:

- *Healthcare*: Revolutionizing remote consultations, virtual therapy sessions, and even surgical training, with patients and professionals engaging in richly detailed, interactive environments that enhance understanding and outcomes.
- *E-commerce*: Allowing users to virtually try on clothing, explore products in 3D, or customize items like cars within a fully interactive digital showroom, elevating the online shopping experience to new heights.
- *Virtual tourism*: Offering immersive virtual tours of far-flung destinations, enabling people to explore iconic landmarks like the Great Wall of China or dive into the depths of the Great Barrier Reef, all from the comfort of their homes.
- *Entertainment and social events*: Enabling people to virtually attend large-scale events, such as concerts or conferences, alongside thousands of participants from across the globe – each one represented by a unique avatar in a shared virtual space.

- *Enhanced learning and training*: Facilitating the creation of immersive learning environments where students and professionals can explore complex subjects, such as human anatomy or surgical procedures, in interactive 3D simulations that provide unparalleled hands-on experience.
- *Product design and prototyping*: Allowing designers and engineers to develop interactive AR prototypes, enabling users to virtually interact with products before they are physically produced, thus streamlining the design process and reducing time to market.
- *Social media engagement*: Elevating user creativity and brand awareness by designing playful, interactive AR filters that capture the imagination and encourage deeper engagement on social media platforms.
- *Fitness and wellness*: Providing remote fitness classes and mental health treatments in engaging virtual environments, allowing people to participate in group activities or one-on-one sessions with professionals from anywhere in the world.
- *Aviation and surgical training*: Imagine a flight school creating a virtual cockpit where students can experience real-time pilot training alongside a virtual instructor. Similarly, in an operating room, a surgeon could guide a procedure, while the identities of patients and medical professionals are protected using Spark AR Studio's advanced masking techniques.

The metaverse is not just an extension of our current digital experience; it is a reimagining of how we interact with the world and each other. By harnessing the power of immersive technology, the metaverse has the potential to reshape industries, enhance learning and social connections, and open up new avenues for creativity and innovation.

Analysis

Beyond the Surface

While the table provides a clear overview of the key differences between Facebook and the metaverse, a deeper analysis reveals additional nuances:

- *Community dynamics*: Facebook's focus on connecting existing communities often leads to a more homogenous user base. The metaverse, with its potential for creating entirely new virtual worlds, could foster more diverse and inclusive communities.
- *Economic implications*: The metaverse's potential for decentralized ownership of virtual assets could create new economic opportunities, such as virtual real estate or digital collectibles. Facebook, as a centralized platform, has limited scope for such economic activity.
- *Educational and training applications*: The immersive nature of the metaverse could revolutionize education and training by providing realistic simulations and collaborative learning experiences. Facebook, while useful for sharing information, lacks the same level of immersion.

- *Privacy and security concerns*: The metaverse, with its potential for tracking user behavior and collecting vast amounts of data, raises significant privacy and security concerns. Facebook has faced similar scrutiny, but the scale and nature of data collection in the metaverse could be even more extensive.

Conclusion

The metaverse represents a paradigm shift in digital interaction, offering a more immersive, interconnected, and potentially economically significant experience compared to traditional social networking platforms like Facebook. However, its development is still in its early stages, and significant challenges related to accessibility, privacy, and regulation must be addressed.

As the metaverse continues to evolve, it is likely to have a profound impact on various aspects of our lives, including social interactions, work, education, and entertainment. It is crucial to monitor its development and engage in thoughtful discussions about its potential benefits and risks.

Key Takeaways

- The metaverse offers a more immersive and interactive experience than Facebook.
- The metaverse has the potential to create new economic opportunities and foster diverse communities.
- Privacy and security concerns are significant challenges that need to be addressed.
- The metaverse's development is still in its early stages, and its full potential remains to be seen.

By understanding these key points, we can better appreciate the transformative potential of the metaverse and its implications for the future of digital interactions.

References

Arora, M. (2024). Metaverse metamorphosis: Bridging the gap between research insights and industry applications. In C. Aurora (Ed.), *Research, innovation, and industry impacts of the metaverse* (pp. 275–286). IGI Global.

Ball, M. (2022). *The metaverse: And how it will revolutionize everything*. Liveright Publishing.

Cerdá-Boluda, J., Mora, M. C., Lloret, N., Scarani, S., & Sastre, J. (2024). Design of virtual hands for natural interaction in the metaverse. *Sensors*, *24*(3), 741.

Chamola, V., Sai, S., Bhargava, A., Sahu, A., Jiang, W., Xiong, Z., Niyato, D., & Hussain, A. (2024). A comprehensive survey on generative AI for metaverse: Enabling immersive experience. *Cognitive Computation*, *16*, 3286–3315. https://doi.org/10.1007/s12559-024-10342-9

Chandel, M., & Arora, M. (2024). Metaverse perspectives: Unpacking its role in shaping sustainable development goals – A qualitative inquiry. In N. Chandel (Ed.), *Research, innovation, and industry impacts of the metaverse* (pp. 62–75). IGI Global.

Cheremnykh, P. (2024). *Gaming the metaverse: User experience analysis and insights from Fortnite*.

Dhiman, V., & Arora, M. (2024). Current state of metaverse in entrepreneurial ecosystem: A retrospective analysis of its evolving landscape. In A. Chang (Ed.), *Exploring the use of metaverse in business and education* (pp. 73–87). IGI Global.

Egliston, B., & Carter, M. (2024). 'The metaverse and how we'll build it': The political economy of meta's reality labs. *New Media & Society*, *26*(8), 4336–4360.

Guide, A. B. S. (2023). *Hands-on augmented reality development with meta Spark Studio*. Apress.

Kumar, J., Arora, M., & Erkol Bayram, G. (Eds.). (2024a). *Exploring the use of metaverse in business and education*. IGI Global.

Kumar, J., Arora, M., & Erkol Bayram, G. (Eds.). (2024b). *Research, innovation, and industry impacts of the metaverse*. IGI Global.

Ranjitha, M., & Venkatesh, S. (2024). An urban revolution: Effect of the metaverse on the perceptions of urban audience. *IEEE Transactions on Network Science and Engineering*, *11*(4), 3577–3584.

Rathore, S., & Arora, M. (2024). Sustainability reporting in the metaverse: A multi-sectoral analysis. In A. Chang (Ed.), *Exploring the use of metaverse in business and education* (pp. 147–165). IGI Global.

Chapter 9

Factors Influencing Adoption of Metaverse Platform: Gen Z Perspective

Pravin Chandra Singh[a], Abhishek Kumar Pandey[b], Premendra Sahu[a], Vishal Kumar Singh[b], Sujay Vikram Singh[c], Kumari Neelam[d] and Pankaj Kumar[e]

[a]*MATS University, India*
[b]*School of Management Sciences, India*
[c]*Banaras Hindu University, India*
[d]*Mahatma Gandhi Kashi Vidyapith University, India*
[e]*United University, India*

Abstract

This chapter examines Generation Z metaverse platform acceptance. This study examined participants' use intentions using the extended unified theory of acceptance and use of technology (UTAUT2) paradigm. The study exclusively covers Delhi NCR and considers games platform in metaverse; hence, conclusions can only be applied to games platform. Several factors influence consumers' intention to use metaverse platforms. This category includes performance expectations, effort expectations, social influence, facilitating conditions, hedonic motivation, price value, and habit. This research also shows a strong correlation between behavioral intention and use behavior with respect to metaverse in gaming platform use.

Keywords: Metaverse platform; games platform; behavioral intention; use behavior; UTAUT2

The AI Metaverse Revolution: Transforming Multi-Business Scenarios (Volume 1), 131–148

Published under exclusive licence by Emerald Publishing Limited
doi:10.1108/978-1-83662-582-720251009

1. Introduction

The profound impact of computer technology on our daily lives cannot be underestimated, especially given remarkable developments that have improved human relationships and communication paradigms. The rise of the metaverse as a market due, in large part, to the COVID-19 epidemic is emblematic of this kind of technical development. The term "Metaverse" is derived from the combination of "meta" (meaning beyond) and "universe." It refers to a highly advanced virtual environment that offers a level of interaction that goes beyond traditional video conferencing (Richter & Richter, 2023). The scope of the metaverse extends beyond gaming and is expected to change various aspects of our daily lives, potentially becoming a worldwide hub for a wide range of events and interactions. There were humble beginnings to technical innovation, which were defined by the rise in popularity of personal computers, the internet, and mobile devices. Apart from the immersive experiences offered by the metaverse, the integration of decentralized digital assets like non-fungible tokens (NFTs) via blockchain technology is a critical factor in augmenting platform adoption. This promotes a more robust and open digital economy by enabling users to safely own, sell, and transfer virtual goods across gaming platforms. It is anticipated that blockchain adoption would further quicken metaverse involvement as companies investigate blockchain's potential for promoting trust and guaranteeing data security (Singh et al., 2024). Presently, however, technological innovation is pervasive. Augmented reality (AR) and virtual reality (VR) are paving the way for the metaverse, which is set to revolutionize our online interactions across various domains such as education, business, remote work, and entertainment (Buhalis et al., 2023). Recent research indicates a growing fascination with the metaverse. Approximately 48% of internet users worldwide show a strong desire to interact in this virtual realm, with live entertainment playing a big role (Petrosyan, 2022). Further investigation into the elements that influence the adoption of the metaverse platform among Generation Z is required, particularly in the dynamic Indian market. This is especially true among the younger generation. The limited comprehension is amplified by the rise of blockchain technology and NFT (Linh, 2022). As business progressively explores metaverse platforms, there is a noticeable difference in the rate at which Gen Z and older generations are adopting them. Thus, this study delves into a comprehensive examination of the metaverse platform (games), with a specific emphasis on the intricacies of its acceptance across generations Z in the Indian context.

1.1. Metaverse in Gaming Platform

The rise of the metaverse has brought about a fresh era of captivating digital encounters, distorting the lines between the virtual and physical realms. In this vast digital world, gaming platforms play a significant role, acting as central hubs for socializing, entertainment, and business. With the rapid advancement of virtual environments and the increasing interconnectedness of gaming platforms, the metaverse landscape is being significantly influenced, leading to enhanced user engagement (Karapakdee & Wannapiroon, 2023). Within the metaverse, gaming platforms provide users with a wide range of experiences, including traditional multiplayer games, interactive social spaces, and virtual events. These platforms utilize cutting-edge graphics, spatial audio, and immersive technologies to create captivating environments that engage users and encourage social connections. By utilizing customizable avatars, collaborative gameplay, and shared experiences, gaming platforms foster significant interactions and the development of communities within the metaverse. Furthermore, gaming platforms provide a rich environment for experimentation and innovation, pushing the limits of what can be achieved in virtual environments by introducing new features and functionalities. With the ever-changing demands and preferences of users within the metaverse, gaming platforms are constantly adapting. They explore user-generated content, virtual economies, cross-platform integration, and AR experiences to stay ahead. Aside from entertainment, gaming platforms within the metaverse also offer promising prospects for generating income and conducting business (Kaur et al., 2023).

1.2. Gen Z and Metaverse Platform

The convergence of artificial intelligence (AI) and the metaverse open up many intriguing possibilities to gain insights into and anticipate user behavior among the Gen Z demographic group. Gen Z individuals have a distinct advantage in influencing and being influenced by emerging technologies due to their digital native status. Generation Z, which includes those born between the middle of the 1990s and the beginning of the 2010s, has reached adulthood during a period that is characterized by rapid technological advancement and continuous connectedness (Zhang et al., 2024). They possess unique preferences and behaviors that set them apart from previous generations. Young individuals of the current generation possess exceptional skills in maneuvering through digital platforms, actively participating in social media content, and actively seeking out experiences that seamlessly blend the physical and virtual realms (Mandal et al., 2024). AI-powered virtual assistants and recommendation systems have the potential to greatly improve convenience, customization, and social connectivity in virtual spaces. However, there may be concerns regarding privacy, data security, and algorithmic bias that could impact trust and willingness to interact with metaverse platforms (Lv, 2023). As AI becomes more integrated into the metaverse, businesses, marketers, and developers must gain a deep understanding of Gen Z user behavior. This knowledge will enable them to create engaging and inclusive virtual experiences. Understanding the younger generation's preferences, expectations, and concerns is crucial for stakeholders to effectively utilize AI in the metaverse (Pricope Vancia et al., 2023). This will facilitate the development of trust and involvement among this vital group, which will be advantageous to some extent.

1.3. Theoretical Framework

1.3.1. Unified Theory of Acceptance and Use of Technology

The unified theory of acceptance and use of technology, also known as UTAUT, is a theoretical framework that seeks to explain and predict individuals' acceptance and usage of technology. Developed by Venkatesh et al. (2003), UTAUT integrates various existing theories and models, such as the technology acceptance model (TAM), the theory of reasoned action, and the theory of planned behavior. UTAUT2 offers a comprehensive framework for understanding individuals' interactions with and perceptions of technology. The model elucidates the individuals' behavioral intention in a manner that is more comprehensible to external parties (Tamilmani et al., 2021). As per the UTAUT2 framework, the inclination to employ experienced a notable surge of 18%, while the level of acceptance toward the technology exhibited a commendable rise of 12%. The statement underscores the advantages that technology bestows upon consumers, as elucidated by Tamilmani et al. (2021). The current investigation endeavors to elucidate the various factors that exert influence on the intentions of individuals residing in India to engage with metaverse platforms. The UTAUT2 model has been selected as the theoretical framework for the present investigation. It is worth noting that several previous studies have, indeed, established the UTAUT2 model as a highly dependable framework for conducting similar investigations (Faqih & Jaradat, 2021; Gharaibeh et al., 2021; Yang et al., 2022).

2. Literature Review and Hypothesis Development

2.1. *Performance Expectancy*

As per the UTAUT2 framework, the notion of "performance expectation" pertains to an individual's conviction regarding the efficacy of technology in facilitating the attainment of their objectives. The notion presented here aligns with the fundamental principles elucidated in both the innovation resistance model and the TAM. Prior research employing the UTAUT2 model has exhibited a positive association between customers' perception of technological advantages and their anticipations of performance outcomes (Venkatesh et al., 2012). Upon careful examination of the discussions, we have successfully formulated a hypothesis:

> *H1*. Performance expectancy positively influences the intention to use the metaverse platform.

2.2. *Effort Expectancy*

Effort expectation evaluates the level of ease with which users can utilize new technologies or systems (Venkatesh et al., 2012). Prior studies have shown that this expectancy can influence individuals' inclination to embrace novel technology (Martins et al., 2014). An individual's perception of the amount of difficulty that relates to the design and execution of a system is referred to as their "effort expectancy." This can have an impact on customer behavior, particularly when assessing the perceived level of exertion needed. When customers contemplate embracing a novel product or technology, they frequently require comprehension of its operation or acquisition of knowledge on how to utilize them. Ramírez-Correa et al. (2019) demonstrated that the level of ease users perceives when using online games has an impact on their intentions to engage with them. From the following discussions, we hypothesized:

> *H2*. Effort expectancy has a positive impact on behavioral intention to use metaverse platform.

2.3. Social Influence

The concept of social influence is an essential component of UTAUT2, which is comparable to the concept of reasoned conduct in many respects (Martin & Icek, 1975). Individuals frequently think that their surroundings exert a substantial impact on their talents. The notion of critical mass suggests that individual actions and behaviors are influenced by group decisions, highlighting the significant role of social impact in personal choices (Marwell et al., 1989). When it comes to technology improvements and system changes, individuals frequently choose to follow the majority opinion of their peers (Mütterlein et al., 2019). Therefore, social influence is acknowledged as a powerful force in influencing decisions regarding new technologies, directing individuals toward educated assessments in the adoption of products and services. From the following discussions, we hypothesized:

> *H3*. Social influence has a significant positive impact on behavioral intention to use metaverse platform.

2.4. Facilitating Condition

Facilitating conditions, within the framework of technology adoption, refer to an individual's cognitive perception concerning the existence of crucial organizational support and technological infrastructure that are considered indispensable for the prosperous implementation and integration of innovative technologies. Essentially, the statement concerns the evaluation of an individual's level of assurance in acquiring the requisite support for a particular technological pursuit. The concept mentioned above possesses an inherent capacity to endow individuals with the means to enhance their capabilities through the acquisition of indispensable skills and knowledge. Consequently, this enables them to proficiently harness the potential of technology. Furthermore, by drawing upon the UTAUT2 framework, one can discern that the presence of facilitating conditions has a notable influence on both the practical implementation of technology and the inclination to embrace it; furthermore, it has been discovered that individuals who have confidence in the preparedness of the organizational and technological infrastructure are more likely to adopt technology (Venkatesh et al., 2012). Under optimal conditions, it is commonly held that consumers may demonstrate a heightened propensity for embracing AR. Similarly, a recent scholarly inquiry carried out by Bower et al. (2020) has successfully demonstrated the beneficial results arising from these specific circumstances in relation to promoting a tendency toward the utilization of VR in educational environments and online gaming. After conducting a thorough analysis of the preceding discussions, we have effectively developed a hypothesis:

> *H4*. Facilitating conditions has a significant positive impact on behavioral intention to use metaverse platform.

2.5. Hedonic Motivation

The pleasure individuals experience when using new technology and services is known as hedonic motivation (Venkatesh et al., 2012). This concept suggests that the significance of internal drive outweighs external incentives when it comes to embracing new technology. Furthermore, this component is significant for forecasting consumers' openness to new technologies, and it has also been associated with increased satisfaction and loyalty (Vieira et al., 2018). Based on the following discussions, we formulated a hypothesis:

> *H5*. Hedonic motivation has a significant positive impact on behavioral intention to use metaverse platform.

2.6. Price Value

The degree a product or service improves a user's experience and increases their economic benefits in proportion to the related financial expenses determines its price (Venkatesh et al., 2012). Having the necessary means to access a service increases people's likelihood of intending to use it. Nevertheless, the cost of integrating new technology remains a significant consideration for users (Baptista & Oliveira, 2015). Based on the following discussions, we formulated a hypothesis:

> *H6*. Price value has a significant positive impact on behavioral intention to use metaverse platform.

2.7. Habit

Behaviors that are carried out on their own accord based on previous experiences of learning are known as habits (Limayem et al., 2007). These habits can direct future behavior since they have been imprinted via repetition. Previous studies show that habit-based incentives are linked to media consumption motives and can significantly impact the likelihood that people will learn performance-oriented abilities. According to empirical research, these routine behaviors have a big impact on how users intend to behave, which affects things like playing video games online or using AR and VR glasses (Ramírez-Correa et al., 2019). From the following discussions, we hypothesized:

> *H7*. Habit has a significant positive impact on behavioral intention to use metaverse platform.

2.8. Behavioral Intention and Use Behavior

Behavioral intention is intricately connected to the level of trust that individuals place in technology and their propensity to continue using it in subsequent situations. This is because individuals tend to be more likely to continue using technology (Rachmawati et al., 2020). When considering intentions, it is of utmost importance to consider how individuals perceive their preparedness to utilize technology. The study places significant emphasis on the cruciality of employing technology on a regular and consistent basis after its acceptance, as highlighted by Wu et al. (2022). Previous scholarly investigations have conclusively demonstrated that the utilization of mobile payment systems is influenced by the conceptual framework known as behavioral intention, as evidenced by the work of Gupta and Arora (2020). The observation is substantiated by the scholarly investigations carried out by Owusu Kwateng et al. (2019), Palas et al. (2022), Sahu et al. (2024), and Wu et al. (2022). Thus, a hypothesis has been duly formulated:

> *H8*. Behavioral intention significantly impacts user behavior to use metaverse platform.

2.9. Conceptual Framework

Fig. 9.1 presents a conceptual framework that elucidates the links between several independent factors and their impact on behavioral intention, which, in turn, affects use behavior. Several factors influence a user's intention to engage in a certain behavior, which, in turn, determines the actual usage of that behavior. This model is based on the (insert applicable theoretical model, e.g., UTAUT).

Performance expectancy: This is a measure of how much a person thinks using a specific system or service would help them perform better. Higher behavioral intention formation is thought to be more likely when performance expectations are higher (*Hypothesis 1 – H1*).

Effort expectancy: The simplicity of use of the system or service is referred to as the effort expectancy. The likelihood that people will form a good behavioral intention increases with how easy and simple they consider the system to be (*Hypothesis 2 – H2*).

Social influence: This variable indicates the degree to which people's opinions about how to use the system are impacted by those of others (friends, family, or social groupings, for example). It is anticipated that social influence will positively affect behavioral intention (*Hypothesis 3 – H3*).

Facilitating conditions: The resources and supports provided by the environment or outside parties to users that increase the likelihood of system or service adoption are known as facilitating conditions. More conducive settings are thought to result in stronger behavioral intention (*Hypothesis 4 – H4*).

Hedonic motivation: This variable relates to how much fun or satisfaction one has when utilizing the system. Higher hedonic motivation is proposed to have a favorable influence on behavioral intention (*Hypothesis 5 – H5*).

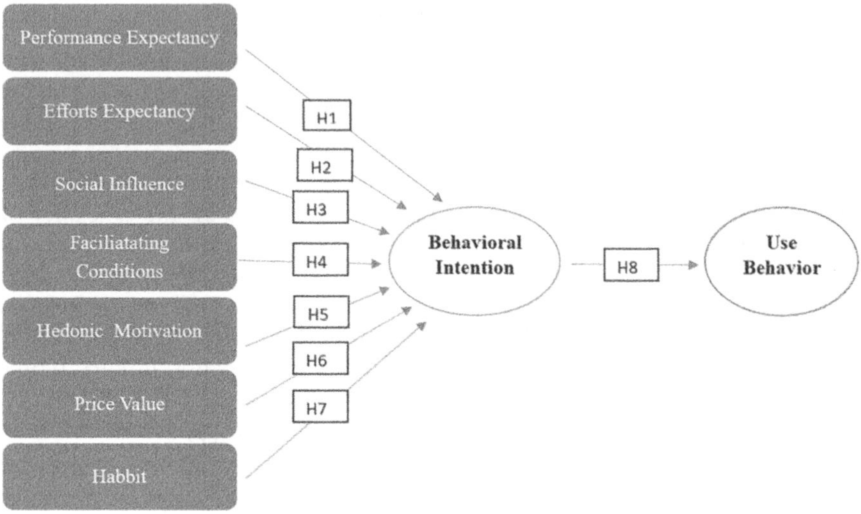

Fig. 9.1. Conceptual Framework. *Source*: Venkatesh et al. (2012).

Price value: The cost–benefit analysis people make before adopting a system is related to price value. Behavioral intention (*Hypothesis 6 – H6*) is predicted to be positively impacted if the perceived value is greater than the cost.

Habit: The term "habit" describes how acclimated people are to utilizing a system, with past behavior reinforcing future usage. Habit is thought to have a favorable impact on behavioral intention (*Hypothesis 7 – H7*).

Behavioral intention and use behavior: Lastly, it is suggested that behavioral intention directly influences use behavior (*Hypothesis 8 – H8*). This implies that those who have stronger behavioral intentions are also more likely to actually use those intentions.

3. Research Methodology

3.1. Data Collection

The present study gathered data from a sample of persons residing in the Delhi-NCR area, with a particular focus on members of Generation Z who demonstrate a keen interest in video gaming platforms. This study's main goal was to examine the variables that affect the metaverse platform's uptake, especially in the gaming industry. A structured questionnaire intended to measure a variety of factors, including performance expectancy, effort expectancy, social influence, facilitating conditions, hedonic motivation, price value, habit, and behavioral intention, was used in the survey approach to collect data. A total of 271 valid responses were received and used for analysis.

3.2. Construct Measurement

The items for the study were adopted from following sources (Table 9.1). To guarantee validity and reliability, the measuring items for the constructs were modified

Table 9.1. Construct with Items.

Construct	No of Items	Source
Performance expectancy	3	Jinseok (2021) and Venkatesh et al. (2012)
Effort expectancy	3	Venkatesh et al. (2012) and Wu and Lee (2017)
Social influence	3	Jinseok (2021) and Venkatesh et al. (2012)
Facilitating conditions	3	Jinseok (2021), Venkatesh et al. (2012), and Wu and Lee (2017)
Hedonic motivation	3	Jinseok (2021), Venkatesh and Zhang (2010), and Wu and Lee (2017)
Price value	3	Venkatesh et al. (2012) and Wu and Lee (2017)
Habit	3	Venkatesh et al. (2012)
Behavioral intention	3	Venkatesh et al. (2012)
Use behavior	3	Venkatesh et al. (2012)

Source: Literature review.

from reliable sources in the literature. The total number of items in each concept was measured on a 5-point Likert scale, with 1 denoting "strongly disagree" and 5 denoting "strongly agree." The specifics for each construct are as follows:

Performance expectancy (3 items): Indicates how much a person thinks they will improve their work performance by using the metaverse platform (Venkatesh et al., 2012).

Effort expectancy (3 items): Evaluates the metaverse platform's usability (Venkatesh et al., 2012).

Social influence (3 items): Measures people's perception of how much influential people think they should use the metaverse platform (Venkatesh et al., 2012).

Facilitating conditions (3 items): The metaverse platform's perceived availability of resources and support is reflected in the three components that make up the facilitating conditions (Venkatesh et al., 2012).

Hedonic motivation (3 items): Measures the enjoyment or fun received from utilizing the metaverse platform (Venkatesh et al., 2012).

Price value (3 items): Evaluates the platform's value in relation to its financial cost (Venkatesh et al., 2012).

Habit (3 items): Indicates how much people utilize the platform automatically as a result of prior use (Limayem et al., 2007).

Behavioral intention (3 items): Measures the likelihood of using the metaverse platform in the future (Venkatesh et al., 2012).

Use behavior (3 items): Evaluates how the metaverse platform is really used (Venkatesh et al., 2012).

3.3. Respondents Profile

The study involved 271 respondents from the Delhi-NCR region. The participants in this study were individuals who had a strong interest in video games. Here are the demographic characteristics of the subjects: the study had a majority of male participants, accounting for 65% of the total, while the remaining 35% were female. The study focused on consumers aged 18–60, with a significant portion falling within the 18–25 age range.

4. Data Analysis

The data analysis was done using a two-step process EFA and CFA; SPSS and AMOS were used for data analysis and relationship testing. KMO value is 0.832 which is above the prescribed value of 0.6 (Field, 2009); χ^2 = 4,980.171; DF= 351, and $p <$ 0.001 (Table 9.2) which reflect that there is an appropriate correlation between the statements for doing principal component analysis. All the observed variables have a factor loading of more than 0.50 which is above the prescribed value (Table 9.3). The composite average Cronbach values of all constructs are above the prescribed values of ≤0.70 (Cronbach, 1951) shows the internal consistency (Table 9.4).

Table 9.2. KMO Value.

Kaiser–Meyer–Olkin measure of sampling adequacy		0.832
Bartlett's test of sphericity	Approximately Chi-square	4,980.171
	Df	351
	Sig.	0.000

Source: Analysis output.

Table 9.3. Factor Loading and Cronbach Alfa.

Construct	**Items**	**Factor Loading**
Performance expectancy		
	I find metaverse platform useful in my daily life	0.649
	Using metaverse platforms helps me accomplish tasks more efficiently	0.760
	Utilizing metaverse platforms boosts my productivity	0.851
Effort expectancy		
	I find it easy to learn how to use metaverse platforms	0.828
	My interactions with metaverse platforms are clear and straightforward	0.777
	I can easily master the use of metaverse platforms	0.806

Table 9.3. (*Continued*)

Construct	Items	Factor Loading
Social influence		
	People who matter to me believe I should use metaverse platforms	0.851
	People who shape my decisions feel I should utilize metaverse platforms	0.855
	People whose views I respect suggest I engage with metaverse platforms	0.867
Facilitating conditions		
	I possess the necessary resources to utilize metaverse platforms	0.949
	I have the essential knowledge to use metaverse platforms	0.928
	When facing challenges with metaverse platforms, I can seek assistance	0.950
Hedonic motivation		
	Engaging with metaverse platforms is intriguing	0.886
	Using metaverse platforms is pleasurable	0.670
	Interacting with metaverse platforms is amusing	0.771
Price value		
	Metaverse platforms are priced reasonably	0.936
	Metaverse platforms offer good value for money	0.885
	Metaverse platforms deliver commendable value for their price	0.913
Habit		
	Engaging with metaverse platforms has become habitual for me	0.888
	It feels natural for me to use metaverse platforms	0.950
	I use metaverse platforms spontaneously, without premeditation	0.952
Behavioral intention		
	I intend to use the metaverse platform in the next months	0.773
	I predict I would use the metaverse platform in the next months	0.803
	I plan to use the metaverse in the next months	0.687
Use behavior		
	I sometimes use metaverse platform	0.882
	I often use metaverse platform to play games	0.729
	I regularly use metaverse platform to play games	0.875

Source: Analysis output.

4.1. SEM Analysis

SEM was employed to examine the structural model of the hypothesized conceptual research model. Table 9.5 presents the structural model's estimations, C.R., S.R., *P*-values, and significance level based on the SEM. The conclusion of the hypothesis lists each of the route coefficients, which represent the relative importance of the influencing components. The variances of all seven variables were computed, and it was discovered that the average variance is more than the calculated maximum variances; however, the shared variance is less than the average and maximum variances (AVE > MSV > ASV). The goodness of fit value is around approximately 0.90, whereas badness of fit index is less than 0.10. According to the indices, SEM is still within acceptable boundaries and may be

Table 9.4. Cronbach's Alpha Value.

Cronbach's Alpha	No of Items
0.889	27

Source: Analysis output.

Table 9.5. Direct Effect of Dependent and Independent Variables.

Direct Relationship	Estimate	S.E.	C.R.	*P*-Value	Significance
Behavioral intention ← Performance expectancy	0.219	0.051	4.291	*	Significant
Behavioral intention ← Effort expectancy	0.120	0.042	2.825	0.005	Significant
Behavioral intention ← Social influence	0.508	0.036	4.389	*	Significant
Behavioral intention ← Facilitating conditions	−0.087	0.054	−1.600	0.110	In significant
Behavioral intention ← Hedonic motivation	0.383	0.062	6.186	*	Significant
Behavioral intention ← Price value	0.703	0.033	5.170	*	Significant
Behavioral intention ← Habit	0.301	0.047	4.152	*	Significant
Use behavior ← Behavioral intention	0.535	0.123	4.336	*	Significant

Source: Analysis output.

considered a feasible model (Hair et al., 2010). All the hypotheses were supported by the prescribed values except *H4*.

Table 9.5 demonstrates the direct effects, respectively. The diagram presented in Fig. 9.2 illustrates the route diagram for the structural equation model. According to the conducted study, it has been determined that several factors, namely, performance expectancy, effort expectancy, social influence, hedonic motivation, price value, and habit, exert a noteworthy influence on the

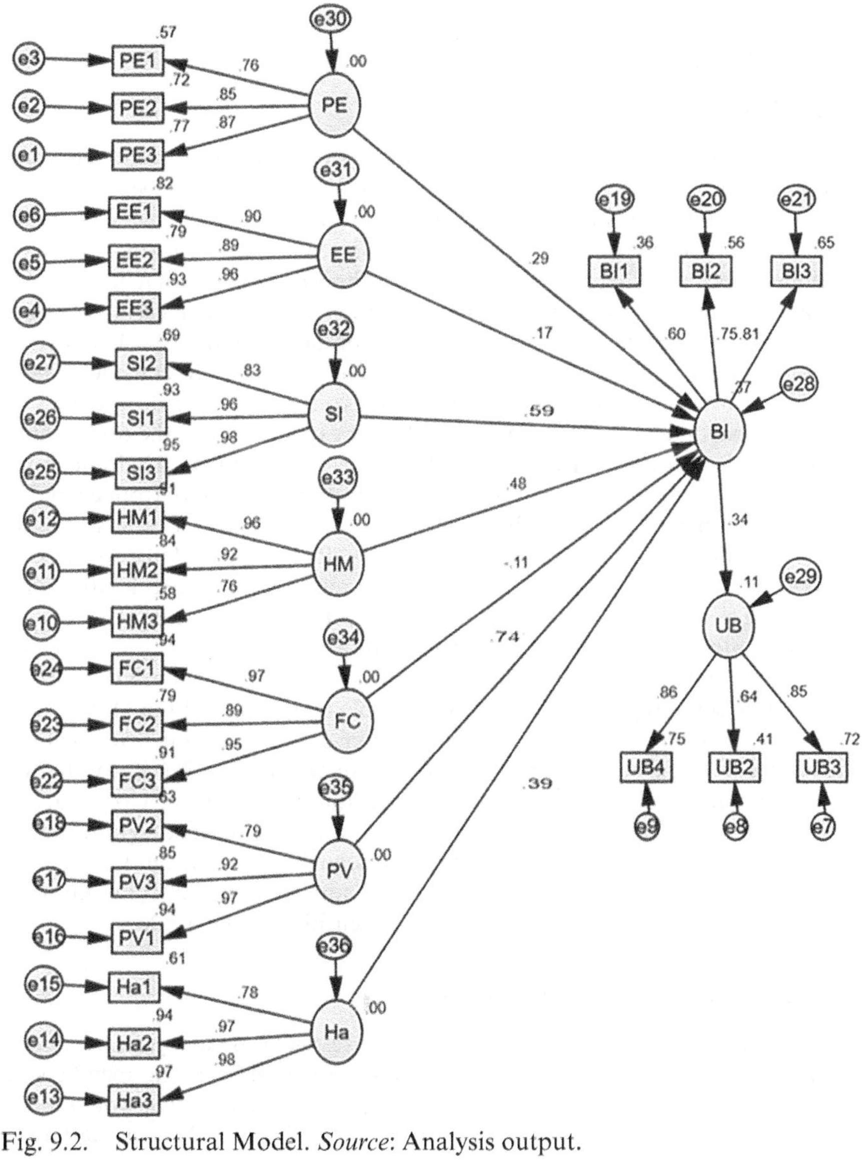

Fig. 9.2. Structural Model. *Source*: Analysis output.

consumer's behavioral intention when it comes to embracing metaverse platforms, particularly those related to gaming. Nevertheless, it has been observed that the presence of facilitating conditions does not exert a substantial impact on individuals' behavioral intention to embrace metaverse platforms. Furthermore, it is worth noting that this study provides substantial evidence to support the notion that there exists a robust and favorable association between one's behavioral intention and their actual usage behavior in the context of embracing a metaverse gaming platform.

5. Conclusions

5.1. Findings

The primary purpose of this investigation was to acquire a thorough comprehension of the diverse factors that wield influence on the degree of interest displayed by individuals belonging to the Generation Z demographic in India, in relation to their involvement with the metaverse gaming platform. The study mentioned above has provided insight into the observation that individuals belonging to the younger demographic group tend to consider various factors when deciding to participate in the metaverse for gaming purposes. The factors mentioned above encompass various aspects that are crucial to consider. These include performance expectations, which refer to the anticipated outcomes or results of a particular action or behavior. Effort expectancy, on the other hand, pertains to the perceived ease or difficulty of performing a task. Hedonic motivation involves the pleasure or enjoyment that individuals derive from engaging in a specific behavior. Social influence refers to the impact that others have on an individual's attitudes, beliefs, and behaviors. Price value relates to the perceived worth or value of a product or service in relation to its cost. Lastly, habit refers to the tendency to engage in behavior repeatedly, often without conscious thought or effort. Furthermore, the present study aims to explore the impact of behavioral intention on the manifestation of actual use behavior. The findings of this study serve to elucidate that the variable of behavioral intention exerts a significant influence on usage behavior. After conducting our investigation, it has come to our attention that the only factor within the Gen Z population that was unequivocally dismissed was the facilitating condition. Upon careful observation, it becomes evident that the correlation of utmost significance is established between the price value and the behavioral intention. Conversely, the correlation between the effort expectancy and the behavioral intention to utilize the metaverse for gaming purposes is identified as the weakest.

5.2. Theoretical and Managerial Implications

The purpose of this academic inquiry was to investigate the many elements that have an impact on the adoption of the metaverse platform among members of the Generation Z cohort. To providing a theoretical framework that would direct the analysis and interpretation of the data, the UTAUT2 model was used. One is presented with several noteworthy developments. The study we conducted at the forefront of employing the UTAUT2 model to acquire profound understandings regarding the inclination to embrace the metaverse platform in India. According to the results, most of the variables significantly affect the propensity to use the platform. However, it is worth noting that facilitating condition (*H4*) does not exhibit a significant influence in this regard. This not only demonstrates that the UTAUT2 paradigm is still relevant, but it also helps us get a deeper understanding of the elements that play a role in the adoption of the metaverse. The metaverse is on the verge of reshaping the boundaries of the gaming realm, allowing businesses to accurately identify and attract their intended audience. The results of our research are crucial for businesses, providing detailed insights into their potential customers. Based on our research, the following practical consequences are of utmost importance: In terms of managerial consequences, metaverse service providers should use their resources to ensure that the targeted customers develop a positive correlation between belief factors and the metaverse platform, particularly the gaming platform. The economic considerations, performance expectations, and potential obstacles associated with the transition all influence the adoption decisions of users. As a result, it is imperative for organizations to enhance platform functionalities and implement state-of-the-art technology to guarantee a smooth user experience. To engage a wide range of users, it is essential to curate eclectic content that represents exceptional service quality. Therefore, it is imperative for organizations to give precedence to content innovation to consistently captivate users. The economic, temporal, and psychological components of adopting a new platform are the most important and influential factors in user choices. Considering this, it is of the utmost importance for businesses to exercise prudence with respect to the amount of time and mental resources that users devote to becoming familiar with fresh platforms in addition to the cost ramifications. The significance of customized strategies is emphasized by the generational gaps in expectations. Organizations should take use of technical improvements to improve the quality of their metaverse goods and services to improve the quality of user engagement among their users. Comprehending the numerous factors that impact user decisions regarding adoption in the metaverse continues to be of paramount importance across generations. The prioritization of cost-effectiveness throughout periods of change is significant and can be addressed through the development of resilient approaches that cultivate a deep user connection with the digital domain of a brand.

5.3. Limitations and Scope for Future Research

This study has several intrinsic limitations, one of which is that it does not take into account the inclusion of moderating elements that are fundamental to the UTAUT2 model. It has been shown that age has a huge influence on the adoption of technology. This is due to the fact that different age groups have different kinds of viewpoints and experiences in life. Gender often exerts a significant influence on the dynamics of technological interaction, as individuals of different genders may display distinct tendencies when it comes to the utilization of technology. The level of familiarity or prior experience an individual possesses with a particular platform can exert a notable influence on both its rate of adoption and the overall public perception surrounding it. Given that the UTAUT2 framework acknowledges the significance of these variables, their exclusion in the current study presents a potential avenue for further exploration. Further investigation should contemplate the incorporation of these moderating variables, thereby enabling a more intricate and multifaceted comprehension of the adoption of metaverse platforms. Considering the identified constraints, future research endeavors should strive to incorporate the previously mentioned variables and perspectives. Upon further examination, it is evident that delving deeper into this investigation has the potential to not only corroborate the conclusions drawn from this study but also contribute to the current corpus of scholarly works pertaining to the utilization and reception of the metaverse platform.

References

Baptista, G., & Oliveira, T. (2015). Understanding mobile banking: The unified theory of acceptance and use of technology combined with cultural moderators. *Computers in Human Behavior*, *50*, 418–430. https://doi.org/10.1016/j.chb.2015.04.024

Bower, M., DeWitt, D., & Lai, J. W. (2020). Reasons associated with preservice teachers' intention to use immersive virtual reality in education. *British Journal of Educational Technology*, *51*(6), 2215–2233.

Buhalis, D., Leung, D., & Lin, M. (2023). Metaverse as a disruptive technology revolutionising tourism management and marketing. *Tourism Management*, *97*(1), 104724.

Cronbach, L. J. (1951). Coefficient alpha and the internal structure of tests. *Psychometrika*, *16*(3), 297–334. https://doi.org/10.1007/BF02310555

Faqih, K. M. S., & Jaradat, M. I. R. M. (2021). Integrating TTF and UTAUT2 theories to investigate the adoption of augmented reality technology in education: Perspective from a developing country. *Technology in Society*, *67*, 101787. https://doi.org/10.1016/j.techsoc.2021.101787

Field, A. (2009). *Discovering statistics using SPSS*. Sage.

Martin, F., & Icek, A. (1975). *Belief, attitude, intention, and behavior: An introduction to theory and research*. Addison-Wesley.

Gharaibeh, M. K., Gharaibeh, N. K., Khan, M. A., Karim Abu-Ain, W. A., & Alqudah, M. K. (2021). Intention to use mobile augmented reality in the tourism sector. *Computer Systems Science and Engineering*, *37*(2), 187–202. https://doi.org/10.32604/csse.2021.014902

Gupta, K., & Arora, N. (2020). Investigating consumer intention to accept mobile payment systems through unified theory of acceptance model: An Indian perspective. *South Asian Journal of Business Studies*, *9*(1), 88–114. https://doi.org/10.1108/SAJBS-03-2019-0037

Hair, F. J., Black, C. W., Babin, J. B., & Amderson, E. R. (2010). *Multivariate data analysis* (7th ed.). Pearson Prentice Hall.

Jinseok. (2021). An empirical study on the factors influencing acceptance intention of extended reality: Application of the UTAUT2 model. *Journal of the Society for Digital Contents*, *22*(1), 1101–1114.

Karapakdee, J., & Wannapiroon, P. (2023). Immersive digital storytelling learning experience with a metaverse gamification game platform to enhance game developer competency. *International Journal of Information and Education Technology*, *13*(6), 890–898. https://doi.org/10.18178/ijiet.2023.13.6.1884

Kaur, J., Lavuri, R., Parida, R., & Singh, S. V. (2023). Exploring the impact of gamification elements in brand apps on the purchase intention of consumers. *Journal of Global Information Management*, *31*(1), 1–30. https://doi.org/10.4018/JGIM.317216

Limayem, M., Hirt, S. G., & Cheung, C. M. K. (2007). How habit limits the predictive power of intention: The case of information systems. *MIS Quarterly*, *31*(4), 705–737. http://www.jstor.orgStableURL:http://www.jstor.org/stable/25148817

Linh, V. (2022, January 7). *"Metaverse" before the opportunity to take off in 2022*. Bloomberg.

Lv, Z. (2023). Generative artificial intelligence in the metaverse era. *Cognitive Robotics*, *3*(1), 208–217.

Mandal, S., Paul, J., Kotni, V. V. D. P., & Chintaluri, M. G. (2024). The orientation of Gen Zs towards metaverse tourism. *Journal of Destination Marketing & Management*, *32*(1) , 100871.

Martins, C., Oliveira, T., & Popovič, A. (2014). Understanding the internet banking adoption: A unified theory of acceptance and use of technology and perceived risk application. *International Journal of Information Management*, *34*(1), 1–13. https://doi.org/10.1016/j.ijinfomgt.2013.06.002

Marwell, G., Oliver, P. E., & Prahl, R. (1989). *Social networks and collective action: A theory of the critical mass*. III I.

Mütterlein, J., Kunz, R. E., & Baier, D. (2019). Effects of lead-usership on the acceptance of media innovations: A mobile augmented reality case. *Technological Forecasting and Social Change*, *145*, 113–124. https://doi.org/10.1016/j.techfore.2019.04.019

Owusu Kwateng, K., Osei Atiemo, K. A., & Appiah, C. (2019). Acceptance and use of mobile banking: An application of UTAUT2. *Journal of Enterprise Information Management*, *32*(1), 118–151. https://doi.org/10.1108/JEIM-03-2018-0055

Palas, J. U., Sorwar, G., Hoque, M. R., & Sivabalan, A. (2022). Factors influencing the elderly's adoption of mHealth: An empirical study using extended UTAUT2 model. *BMC Medical Informatics and Decision Making*, *22*(1), 1–21. https://doi.org/10.1186/s12911-022-01917-3

Petrosyan, A. (2022, July 7). *Main reasons for joining the metaverse worldwide*. Statista.

Pricope Vancia, A. P., Băltescu, C. A., Brătucu, G., Tecău, A. S., Chițu, I. B., & Duguleană, L. (2023). Examining the disruptive potential of Generation Z tourists on the travel industry in the digital age. *Sustainability (Switzerland)*, *15*(11), 1–19. https://doi.org/10.3390/su15118756

Rachmawati, I. K., Bukhori, M., Majidah, Y., Hidayatullah, S., & Waris, A. (2020). Analysis of use of mobile banking with acceptance and use of technology (Utaut). *IJSTR*, *9*(8), 534–540. www.ijstr.org

Ramírez-Correa, P., Rondán-Cataluña, F. J., Arenas-Gaitán, J., & Martín-Velicia, F. (2019). Analysing the acceptation of online games in mobile devices: An application of UTAUT2. *Journal of Retailing and Consumer Services*, *50*, 85–93. https://doi.org/10.1016/j.jretconser.2019.04.018

Richter, S., & Richter, A. (2023). What is novel about the Metaverse? *International Journal of Information Management*, *73*, 1–11. https://doi.org/10.1016/j.ijinfomgt.2023.102684

Sahu, P., Singh, P. C., Divya, K., Singh, S. V., Bakshi, S., Kumari N., Kumar, P., Keshari, U. (2024). Examine the adoption of blockchain technology among tourists: An emerging economy perspective. In R. Srivastava, V. Rana, & M. Faiz (Eds.), *Exploring the world with blockchain through crypto-travel* (Vol. 1, pp. 17–32). IGI-Global. https://doi.org/10.4018/979-8-3693-6562-5

Singh, V. K., Keshari, A., Singh, D., Singh, P. C., & Gautam, A. (2024). Blockchain technology and election transparency: An application of E-voting mechanism. *Pacific Business Review International*, *16*(8), 35–3. www.pbr.co.in

Tamilmani, K., Rana, N. P., Wamba, S. F., & Dwivedi, R. (2021). The extended unified theory of acceptance and use of technology (UTAUT2): A systematic literature review and theory evaluation. *International Journal of Information Management*, *57*(1) , 1–40.

Venkatesh, V., Smith, R. H., Morris, M. G., Davis, G. B., Davis, F. D., & Walton, S. M. (2003). User acceptance of information technology: Toward a unified view. *MIS Quarterly*, *27*(3), 425–478.

Venkatesh, V., Walton, S. M., & Thong, J. Y. L. (2012). Consumer acceptance and use of information technology: Extending the unified theory of acceptance and use of technology. *MIS Quarterly*, *36*(1), 157–178. http://about.jstor.org/terms

Venkatesh, V., & Zhang, X. (2010). Unified theory of acceptance and use of technology, US vs. China. *Journal of Global Information Technology Management*, *13*(1), 5–27.

Vieira, V., Santini, F. O., & Araujo, C. F. (2018). A meta-analytic review of hedonic and utilitarian shopping values. *Journal of Consumer Marketing*, *35*(4), 426–437. https://doi.org/10.1108/JCM-08-2016-1914

Wu, P., Zhang, R., Luan, J., & Zhu, M. (2022). Factors affecting physicians using mobile health applications: An empirical study. *BMC Health Services Research*, *22*(1), 1–14. https://doi.org/10.1186/s12913-021-07339-7

Wu, R., & Lee, J. (2017). The comparative study on third party mobile payment between UTAUT2 and TTF. *Distribution Science Research*, *15*(11), 5–19.

Yang, F., Ren, L., & Gu, C. (2022). A study of college students' intention to use metaverse technology for basketball learning based on UTAUT2. *Heliyon*, *8*(9), 1–15. https://doi.org/10.1016/j.heliyon.2022.e10562

Zhang, J., Quoquab, F., & Mohammad, J. (2024). Metaverse tourism and Gen-Z and Gen-Y's motivation: "will you, or won't you travel virtually?" *Tourism Review*, *79*(2), 304–320. https://doi.org/10.1108/TR-06-2023-0393

Chapter 10

Utopian Dreams or Dystopian Realities: Navigating Ethics in the Metaverse

Lekhika Sharma[a], Neeraj Kaushik[a], Yasha Bothra[b] and Manpreet Arora[c]

[a]*National Institute of Technology, India*
[b]*Sri Venkateswara College, University of Delhi, India*
[c]*Central University of Himachal Pradesh, India*

Abstract

The metaverse is rapidly evolving, presenting transformative opportunities for business, economics, and society. However, like any civic space, it requires well-defined regulations, ethical standards, and legal frameworks to ensure responsible development. A disturbing incident of gang rape reported in the metaverse in early 2024 in London has sparked widespread concern. This event has ignited discussions around security risks, ethical dilemmas, legal implications, and jurisdictional boundaries in virtual spaces. One of the key concerns is the potential for exploitation, manipulation, and abuse within these platforms. While some literature addresses these issues, comprehensive exploration remains limited. This study investigates public perceptions surrounding such incidents, specifically focusing on recent events within the Facebook metaverse. By analyzing reviews and comments from various social media platforms, this research employs text analysis techniques, including topic modeling and sentiment analysis (SA), to uncover user concerns. The findings offer valuable insights into how individuals perceive these platforms' safety and ethical issues, providing practical implications for software developers and policymakers.

Keywords: Metaverse; metaverse ethics; dark side; ethical concerns; rape in virtual world

The AI Metaverse Revolution: Transforming Multi-Business Scenarios (Volume 1), 149–163

Published under exclusive licence by Emerald Publishing Limited
doi:10.1108/978-1-83662-582-720251010

1. Introduction

Several facets of human life have shifted from the physical to the digital realm because of the tremendous changes in the technological environment during the past four decades. This change in our everyday lives, interpersonal interactions, and commercial dealings has been made possible by the advent of personal technological devices, the internet, and portable communication technology. This wave of digital transformation is driven by the core notion of computerizing the components, activities, and processes of the physical world. The metaverse is a post-reality cosmos that permits multimodal interactions with digital objects and virtual environments by combining digital virtuality with physical reality. It is the next version of the internet, where we are involved in it instead of merely seeing it. Real-time communication and dynamic interactions with digital items are made possible by this networked, social web of immersive social spaces. The metaverse has converted the two-dimensional, flat internet into an immersive, three-dimensional world (Tugtekin, 2022). It is a communal virtual shared place formed by the confluence of virtually improved physical reality, augmented reality (AR), and the internet. It is now viewed as the next generation of the internet. It promises to completely transform the way people connect with technology and one another, erasing boundaries between the real and digital worlds and providing countless opportunities for creativity, participation, and teamwork in virtual settings. But at the same time, some studies talk about the dark side of this technology (Dwivedi et al., 2023). Additionally, there have been certain incidents that compel investigation into the shadowy side of this utopian, dreamlike technology, such as the gang rape case that occurred within the metaverse and made headlines in London during the first week of 2024.

2. Review of Literature

2.1. History of Metaverse

The concept of the "metaverse" was first introduced in science fiction in Neal Stephenson's 1992 book Snow Crash (Joshua, 2017; Stephenson, 1992). The online multimedia platform, Second Life, emerged in 2003 and introduced the early virtual environments offering people a taste of the possibilities that virtual spaces may offer for social interaction, business, and creativity. These platforms laid the groundwork for the metaverse by enabling users to construct virtual properties, create avatars, and participate in a digital market (Richter & Richter, 2023). Several innovative technologies are integrated into the metaverse (Lee et al., 2021; Yang et al., 2022). Virtual reality (VR), AR, and blockchain technological developments drove the metaverse's growth as technology developed. Immersion technology and VR headsets have made it possible to create more lifelike and captivating virtual experiences. Non-fungible tokens, which enable the buying, selling, and trading of unique digital assets inside these virtual marketplaces, have brought new methods for controlling digital ownership and transactions to the blockchain and cryptocurrency arena. As Facebook rebranded as Meta in 2021, it spurred a wave of curiosity around the idea of the metaverse (Fig. 10.1). The idea of the metaverse is to create an interactive, fully immersive

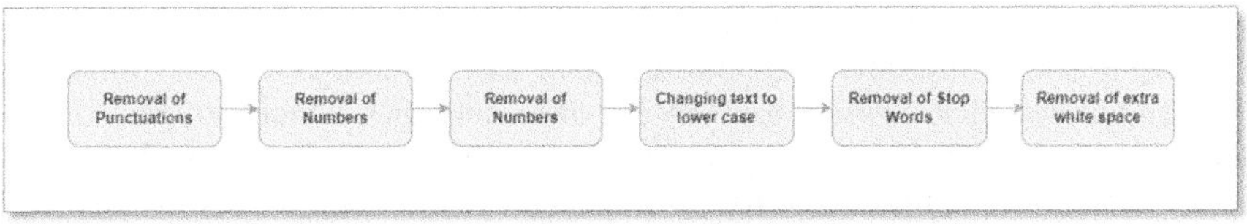

Fig. 10.1. Text Preprocessing. *Source*: Author's own creation.

digital cosmos that allows virtual and real worlds to coexist together (Weinberger, 2022).

2.2. Recent Upsurge in Metaverse Activities

Everything from customer experience to omnichannel sales and marketing, product innovation, and community development is impacted by the metaverse. Many big organizations are stepping up their research into how the metaverse may create a drastically altered world in the next 10 years. Alcántara and Coffee (2022) predicted that the metaverse's economy will generate $800 billion by 2025 and $2.5 trillion by 2030. Start-ups, well-known brands, venture capital, private equity, and large technology businesses are all attempting to take advantage of the metaverse possibility. Another report by Grand View Research (2022) highlighted that metaverse's market size will be worth more than $678 billion by the end of 2030. Hence, businesses that are at the forefront of the metaverse adoption curve also want to allocate a sizeable portion of their digital investment budgets to it. But trust and risk considerations relating to economics, data, governance (including cybersecurity), digital identity, user experience, and persistence – are important for the responsible use of the metaverse (PwC, 2023).

2.3. Metaverse – Virtual Dystopia

With the adoption of the metaverse, a variety of illegal activities have also surfaced, creating new difficulties for law enforcement organizations throughout the globe. Along with its promises and benefits, the metaverse also has a dark side that needs to be explored and understood. Financial fraud, fraud, and more heinous crimes like sexual misbehavior and harassment are all possible in the metaverse (Bovenzi, 2023; Seo et al., 2023; Wu et al., 2023). These crimes frequently make use of the immersive nature of VR to mentally and emotionally harm their victims (Graham Cluley, 2022). The absence of control in VR is a worry shared by safety activists (Crawford & Smith, 2022)

2.3.1. Issues in Metaverse-anonymity

In recent years, the idea of anonymity in the metaverse has drawn attention and raised concerns. When it comes to social networks, using pseudonyms or anonymity makes the network more appealing (Wang & Wang, 2023). With the metaverse's growing potential and appeal, anonymity may let people express themselves freely without worrying about criticism or negative consequences. However, the problem of anonymity also presents several difficulties. In the metaverse, anonymity has also resulted in a lack of responsibility for one's activities, which can give rise to undesirable behaviors like trolling, cyberbullying, and harassment. Additionally, people may feel more motivated to act in ways they would not in real-life encounters when they are anonymous, which can lead to a sense of dehumanization and detachment. Additionally, the idea of anonymity is the source of the phenomena known as "crowd" and "herd" behavior. The propensity for members of a group to follow the beliefs and actions of the majority is known as "crowd behavior," and it frequently results in herd mentality, the loss of personal autonomy, and the inability to think critically. These difficulties show how important it is to regulate and give serious thought to anonymity in the metaverse.

2.3.2. Privacy Concerns

In addition to outlining the current challenges to human rights, Mitrushchenkova (2022) tackles the philosophical and legal challenge of determining the primary changes occurring to an individual's "self." According to the study, there are already significant changes in the concept of personal identity that are occurring on both a qualitative and dimensional level, meaning that numerous identities exist in addition to multidimensional ones. There are significant ethical and legal ramifications to these changes. Cheong has also mentioned that there needs to be some method to grant legal personhood to avatars in the metaverse (Cheong, 2022). The issue of privacy is getting increasingly pressing because of the widespread monitoring and data collection methods that offer little room for protecting your personal information.

2.3.3. Lack of Control and Jurisdiction

The metaverse, a platform made up of digital twins, simulated settings, and cutting-edge reality technologies that defy contemporary comprehension, is covered in this study. Flavián et al. (2023) express worries about high-end technology businesses monopolizing the metaverse, which may result in a loss of control and detrimental effects on society. It underlines how crucial it is to be watchful to keep the metaverse from turning into everyone's worst fear. It urges actions to prevent the possible adverse effects of the metaverse's development and demands a critical analysis of the way it is now organized. There are several drawbacks to metaverse learning environments and emphasis is needed on prudence in their creation and application (Flavián et al., 2023; Liao et al., 2022; Zhang et al., 2021).

The virtual settings are global and decentralized; therefore, jurisdiction over metaverse crimes is complicated. Because players in the metaverse can be located anywhere in the globe, traditional legal systems that are centered on geographic borders have difficulty in handling crimes that take place in the virtual world. (Treleaven et al., 2023). There are major obstacles in determining which country's laws apply, who can prosecute, and how to implement court orders (Bovenzi, 2023).

The literature review illuminates that the metaverse provides a world of limitless opportunities, but it also brings with it important moral, social, and psychological issues that should not be disregarded. Ultimately, the metaverse can only be fully realized as a force for good if its dark side is acknowledged and confronted. To gain a deeper understanding of the public's perception and concerns regarding metaverse security, we have conducted a case study focusing on recent incidents that occurred on a metaverse platform.

3. The Landmark Case

At the onset of the initial week of January 2024, the headlines captured a startling incident of a 16-year-old girl who was sexually attacked on the metaverse platform. The adolescent was reportedly wearing a VR headset in an immersive game when she was allegedly raped by a group of men. The girl's avatar, or digital character, is said to have been gang-raped by online strangers, leaving the girl distraught. The police are reportedly looking into this case as their first virtual sexual offense (Sales, 2024). Like a victim of physical rape, this child also suffered from psychological trauma. According to a senior officer familiar with the case, "There is an emotional and psychological impact on the victim that is longer-term than any physical injuries."

UK Home Secretary James Cleverly also expressed support for the girl, emphasizing the severity of the incident and highlighting the need for addressing such offenses in the virtual realm. He stated, "I know it is easy to dismiss this as being not real, but the whole point of these virtual environments is they are incredibly immersive" (Team & Team, 2024).

The National Police Chiefs' Council's Child Protection and Abuse Investigation Lead, Ian Critchley, warned "The metaverse creates a gateway for predators to commit horrific crimes against children" (Team & Team, 2024).

The world-first case has raised eyebrows over the inadequacy of existing laws in addressing virtual offenses. Since police and prosecutors are currently dealing with a massive backlog of real rape cases, the inquiry into the landmark case has raised concerns about the offenses happening on the virtual platforms (Sharma, 2024). This incident sparked discussions among people and raised crucial questions regarding the safety and ethical considerations within virtual environments (TheoFarrant, 2024).

Therefore, in our study, we aimed to translate these discussions into qualitative analysis to understand people's opinions and perspectives on the metaverse and ethical concerns. To comprehensively evaluate the current state of affairs, this paper sets forth specific research questions:

> *RQ1*. What are the predominant lexical elements observed in the discourse on news platforms and social media platforms?
>
> *RQ2*. How do the general public and experts perceive the security of the metaverse, and what insights (topics) can be extracted from it?
>
> *RQ3*. What are the various sentiments and emotions that individuals associate with the Metaverse?

Despite the limited existing literature on the negative aspects of the metaverse, focusing primarily on conceptual and empirical studies, this is our first and foremost attempt to capture the genuine perspectives of individuals on the negative side of the metaverse over news and social media platforms such as Twitter, Reddit, and Instagram.

4. Research Methodology

4.1. Sources

In covering recent events, newspapers and blog press provide insights into the opinions surrounding news entities (people, places, things). So, in our analysis, we integrated insights from top news articles worldwide. Simultaneously, we directly gauged public perceptions by including viewpoints from individuals on prominent social media platforms like Twitter, Reddit, and Instagram. The study is designed to comprehensively explore these diverse perspectives, combining insights from these sources. As the study is centered around the above-mentioned case, our analysis focused on a specific timeframe, namely, from January 1st to January 25th. We limited the duration to ensure a comprehensive examination of the different perspectives within this defined period. We constructed a comprehensive dataset by collecting top newspaper articles and utilizing various methods for social media platforms, specifically searching with the term "metaverse" to include all relevant information in the corpus. The strategy involved downloading "top" rated posts of all time and complementing the dataset with "hot" and recent top-rated posts to cover emerging topics.

4.2. Text Analysis

Text analysis is a method for drawing insightful conclusions from unstructured text data. It is also referred to as text mining or content analysis. It entails text parsing to produce structured data, which facilitates information management and interpretation (Qualtrics, 2024). Text analysis is essential for many applications, including SA, translation, and automated summary creation. Text analysis enables the conversion of qualitative details into quantitative insights by transforming unstructured text into structured data (Kirchhoff, 2023).

In any text analysis, certain fundamental steps are essential. These steps typically involve preprocessing text, determining the frequency of words within documents to identify word correlations and more. An open-source language "R" studio provides the environment for statistical computing and graphics and offers a range of packages such as tm, SnowballC, ggplot2, and word cloud. These packages are specifically designed to facilitate the aforementioned text-processing steps (Fig. 10.1).

To begin, we load the data by creating a collection of documents using the Corpus () function and the tm library. The text is then preprocessed, which includes deleting common words, numbers, and punctuation that doesn't add to our analysis. Finally, we can carry out additional text mining operations like stemming, tokenization, and word frequency calculations to extract valuable information from the text. We also convert the text to lowercase and eliminate any excess whitespace. As will be explained below, we have included topic modeling and SA in our study.

4.2.1. Topic Modeling

Topic modeling is a statistical technique used to uncover patterns in word usage and organize a large corpus into groups, known as topics, that share a common focus (Vayansky & Kumar, 2020). It is widely applied in various fields, particularly in natural language processing. It helps us understand the main themes or subjects present in a large collection of documents, making it easier to organize and summarize information. In this study, we applied latent Dirichlet allocation (LDA), a popular topic modeling approach introduced by Blei et al. (2003). LDA simplifies each document by treating it as a "bag of words" and creates a term vocabulary based on word frequency. It then classifies topics and assigns documents to them based on the probability distribution of words.

4.2.2. Sentiment Analysis

SA is a computational method for understanding the opinions, sentiments, and subjectivity expressed in text (Taboada, 2016). Its core aim is to discern and analyze opinions expressed in natural language texts. It is a valuable tool for monitoring attitudes, sentiments, and beliefs about locations, goods, or services expressed on various online platforms. In this study, we utilized the NRC Lexicon developed by Mohammad and Turney (2013) for SA. This lexicon categorizes text into two sentiments (positive and negative) and eight emotions (anger, fear, anticipation, trust, surprise, sadness, joy, and disgust). We selected this lexicon for its comprehensive word coverage and the range of emotions it covers.

5. Results and Analysis

5.1. Research Question 1: Visualization Analysis

Text mining techniques enable the identification of frequently occurring terms in documents or paragraphs of text. A word cloud, also known as a text cloud, is a picture of text data. Compared to manual data presentation, these are more visually appealing (Chintalapudi et al., 2021). The word cloud analysis visually represents the frequency of words mentioned in discussions related to the incident. The larger and bolder a word appears in the cloud, the more frequently it has been discussed. In this context (Fig. 10.2), "virtual," "rape," and "people" stand out prominently, indicating that these are central topics in the conversations. Additionally, the presence of words like "game," "police," and "metaverse" suggests that discussions cover aspects related to gaming, law enforcement, and the metaverse platform. As you move toward smaller and less emphasized words, the cloud includes terms like "harassment," "god," "love," "world," and "avatar," providing a nuanced view of the varied themes within the discourse.

Fig. 10.2. Common Word Cloud. *Source*: Author's own creation.

The word cloud comparison (Fig. 10.3) suggests a distinct emphasis in news coverage and public discussions on the metaverse. News outlets tend to concentrate on broader themes such as the concept of the "metaverse," its "virtual" nature, and associated concerns like "safety," "crime," "technology," and "psychology." On the contrary, public discussions on social media platforms seem to be more focused on personal viewpoints and experiences, expressing sentiments through words like "bad," "leave," "call," and "harassment." This divergence indicates that news reports provide a comprehensive overview, while public discourse on social media platforms reflects individual reactions and opinions on specific aspects of the metaverse.

5.2. Research Question 2: Topic Modeling

Topic modeling serves as a valuable tool in information retrieval where large amounts of textual data can be automatically arranged, deciphered, and summarized using this method (Abdelrazek et al., 2023). Each topic represents a clear and understandable idea within the collection of textual information. Topic modeling subsequently furnishes a latent yet interpretable representation of documents based on the identified topics (Crain et al., 2012). With topic modeling algorithms LDA, we identified the underlying five major topics (themes) as well as subtopics and trends in a large corpus of text (Fig. 10.4).

Fig. 10.3. Comparison Cloud. *Source*: Author's own creation.

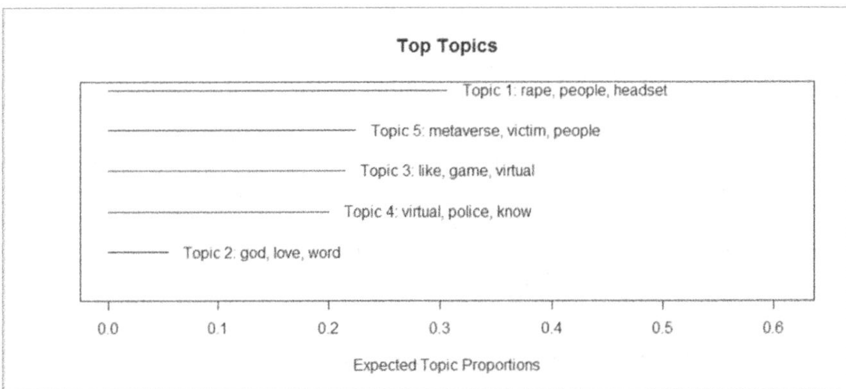

Fig. 10.4. Predicting Numbers of Topics in Text Data. *Source*: Author's own creation.

Topic 1: Online Harassment and Safety Concerns in Metaverse

This topic primarily revolves around discussions related to online harassment, safety concerns, and user accountability within the metaverse. The presence of words like "rape," "harassment," and "headset" suggests that users are engaging in conversations that highlight negative experiences, safety challenges, and the need for accountability in virtual spaces. The concept of creating a safer and more respectful metaverse environment seems to be a central theme.

Topic 2: Spiritual and Emotional Discourse in Metaverse

This topic explores the spiritual and emotional dimensions discussed within the metaverse. Words like "god," "love," and "spirit" indicate that users are engaging in conversations related to spiritual experiences, emotional connections, and the overall impact of virtual interactions on individuals' emotional well-being. This topic reflects a diverse range of sentiments and experiences within the metaverse.

Topic 3: User Experiences and Real-life Integration in Metaverse

Focusing on user experiences, this topic encapsulates discussions about virtual life, real-life integration, and the overall perception of the metaverse. The presence of words like "virtual," "life," and "real" suggests that users are actively sharing their experiences, exploring the integration of virtual elements into their daily lives, and reflecting on the balance between virtual and real-world interactions. It sheds light on the multifaceted nature of user engagement in the metaverse.

Topic 4: Policing and Legal Considerations in the Metaverse

This topic delves into discussions related to policing, legal considerations, and actions taken within the metaverse. The inclusion of words like "virtual," "police," and "crimes" indicates that users are engaging in conversations about law enforcement, legal aspects, and the need for regulations within virtual environments. It suggests a growing awareness and discourse around maintaining order and ensuring ethical behavior in the metaverse.

Topic 5: Victim Narratives, Ethical, and Privacy Concerns in Metaverse Usage

This topic revolves around narratives of victims, ethical concerns, and user behavior in the metaverse. The presence of words like "metaverse," "victim," and "police" suggests that users are discussing ethical considerations, potential victims of misuse, and the role of law enforcement in addressing ethical concerns within virtual spaces. Privacy concerns related to protecting users from potential victimization and ethical considerations are part of this topic.

From the above, it is clear that the metaverse emerges as a complex digital landscape where users navigate safety, spirituality, integration, legality, and ethical considerations. Understanding these diverse aspects is vital to guide the metaverse's development, making it a user-friendly environment that encourages positive experiences and tackles emerging challenges.

5.3. Research Question 3: Sentiment Analysis

SA is a multidisciplinary domain that combines statistical methods, natural language processing, and computational linguistics (Misuraca et al., 2020). We utilized the R-package "Syuzhet" to conduct SA, attributing either "positive" or "negative" valence or categorizing emotions such as "anger," "anticipation," "disgust," "fear," "joy," "sadness," "surprise," and "trust" to each word.

The SA portrays a complex emotional landscape, with an overall negative sentiment prevailing, closely followed by positive expressions (Fig. 10.5). The emotions of "sadness" and "fear" are notably dominant, indicating prevalent discussions on worrisome or distressing aspects of the metaverse. Additionally, there

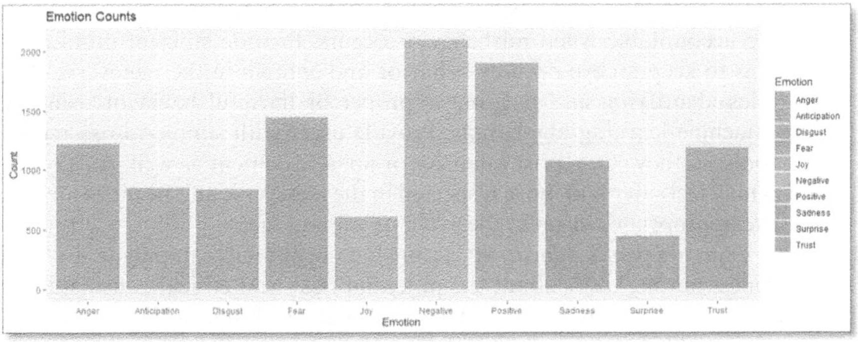

Fig. 10.5. Sentiment Analysis Plot. *Source*: Author's own creation.

is a considerable presence of "disgust," "anticipation," and "anger," suggesting a diverse range of strong reactions and expectations within the community. While positive emotions like "joy" and "surprise" are present, they take a backseat to the more frequently expressed negative sentiments. Understanding the dynamics of online conversations in this rapidly changing digital space is made possible by the insights provided by this nuanced emotional analysis, which highlights the complex nature of user perceptions and concerns in the metaverse.

6. Solutions

Metaverse is being condemned for possible risks it brings with reference to monitoring and carelessness (Crawford & Smith, 2022). Efforts should be made to build a metaverse that enhances rather than abuses lives by promoting a sane strategy that puts ethics, equity, and well-being first. Proactive action is required to mitigate the hazards and adverse effects that anonymity in the metaverse may have. This may entail putting in place procedures for user authentication, monitoring user conduct and material, and giving users the means to report offensive or abusive behavior. Drawing from an in-depth analysis of expert and public perspectives, it is evident that certain steps are necessary to address the current situation. These steps include:

1. *Regulation and ethical standards*: Establish clear regulations and ethical guidelines for the metaverse, covering areas such as user conduct, content moderation, data privacy, and security. These standards should be developed in collaboration with stakeholders, including technology companies, policymakers, and user advocacy groups, to ensure they are comprehensive and effective. Additionally, regularly evaluate and update regulations and ethical standards to adapt to the evolving nature of the metaverse and emerging technologies through audits, reviews, and consultations with stakeholders to ensure that regulations remain effective and relevant.
2. *User authentication and monitoring*: Establish user authentication procedures to confirm users' identities in the metaverse. This can help deter anonymous

and potentially dangerous behavior and offer a way to track down and hold people accountable when misbehavior occurs. Provide efficient monitoring systems to keep an eye on user behavior and content in the metaverse. This includes identifying and flagging improper or harmful behavior using AI and machine-learning algorithms. Provide users with simple-to-use reporting tools, so they can report offensive or abusive content as well. As a result, users may feel safer and more respected in the metaverse and be more inclined to take appropriate action in the event of misconduct.

3. *User awareness and education*: Launch educational campaigns to raise awareness among users about the potential risks and ethical considerations associated with the metaverse. These campaigns should focus on promoting responsible behavior, digital citizenship, and the importance of respecting others' rights and privacy. Provide users with educational resources and guidelines to promote responsible behavior and ethical conduct within the metaverse.
4. *Enforcement and jurisdiction*: Work closely with law enforcement agencies, policymakers, and jurisdictional authorities to address virtual offenses and enforce regulations within the metaverse. This includes sharing information and data to aid in investigations, as well as providing training and resources to law enforcement personnel on virtual crime detection and prevention. Additionally, engage policymakers and jurisdictional authorities to ensure that regulations are aligned with legal frameworks and that jurisdictional issues are addressed effectively.
5. *Research and development*: Invest in research and development to continuously improve the safety and ethical standards of the metaverse. This includes exploring new technologies and methodologies for content moderation, user authentication, and data privacy protection.

These steps, when implemented in a coordinated and comprehensive manner, can help address the security and ethical challenges posed by the metaverse, ensuring a safer and more responsible virtual environment for all users.

7. Conclusion

To sum up, the metaverse is a rapidly evolving digital landscape with immense potential to reshape various aspects of society. However, as with any new technology, it also brings with it a range of ethical, legal, and security challenges that need to be addressed. The recent gang rape case within the metaverse has highlighted the importance of understanding and mitigating these risks. Through text analysis, we have gained valuable insights into public perceptions and concerns regarding the metaverse's security and ethical implications.

Our study has identified key themes and topics that are central to these discussions, including online harassment, safety concerns, spiritual and emotional dimensions, user experiences, legal considerations, and victim narratives. We have also conducted SA to understand the emotional landscape of these discussions, revealing a complex mix of negative and positive sentiments. Based on our findings, we have proposed a set of solutions to address the current challenges. These steps, when implemented in a coordinated and comprehensive manner, can help ensure a safer and more responsible metaverse for all users.

In conclusion, the metaverse holds great promise, but it is essential to address the associated risks and challenges to realize its full potential. By taking proactive measures and working together, we can create a metaverse that enhances lives and promotes ethics, equity, and well-being in this new digital frontier.

References

Abdelrazek, A., Eid, Y., Gawish, E., Medhat, W., & Hassan, A. (2023). Topic modeling algorithms and applications: A survey. *Information Systems, 112*, 102131.

Alcántara, A., & Coffee, P. (2022, June 15). Metaverse spending to total $5 trillion in 2030, McKinsey predicts. *WSJ.* https://www.wsj.com/articles/metaverse-spending-to-total-5-trillion-in-2030-mckinsey-predicts-11655254794

Blei, D. M., Ng, A. Y., & Jordan, M. I. (2003). Latent Dirichlet allocation. *Journal of Machine Learning Research, 3*, 993–1022.

Bovenzi, G. M. (2023). *Meta crimes: Criminal accountability for conducts in the Metaverse.* ACM Web Conference 2023 – Companion of the World Wide Web Conference, WWW 2023. https://doi.org/10.1145/3543873.3587535

Cheong, B. C. (2022). Avatars in the metaverse: Potential legal issues and remedies. *International Cybersecurity Law Review, 3*(2), 467–494. https://doi.org/10.1365/s43439-022-00056-9

Chintalapudi, N., Battineni, G., & Amenta, F. (2021). Sentimental analysis of COVID-19 tweets using deep learning models. *Infectious Disease Reports, 13*(2), 329–339.

Crain, S. P., Zhou, K., Yang, S., & Zha, H. (2012). Dimensionality reduction and topic modeling: From latent semantic indexing to latent Dirichlet allocation and beyond. In C. Aggarwal & C. Zhai (Eds.), *Mining text data* (pp. 129–161). Springer. https://doi.org/10.1007/978-1-4614-3223-4_5

Crawford, A., & Smith, T. (2022). Metaverse app allows kids into virtual strip clubs – BBC News. *BBC News.*

Dwivedi, Y. K., Kshetri, N., Hughes, L., Rana, N. P., Baabdullah, A. M., Kar, A. K., Koohang, A., Ribeiro-Navarrete, S., Belei, N., Balakrishnan, J., Basu, S., Behl, A., Davies, G. H., Dutot, V., Dwivedi, R., Evans, L., Felix, R., Foster-Fletcher, R., Giannakis, M., … Yan, M. (2023). Exploring the darkverse: A multi-perspective analysis of the negative societal impacts of the metaverse. *Information Systems Frontiers, 25*(5). https://doi.org/10.1007/s10796-023-10400-x

Flavián, C., Ibáñez-Sánchez, S., Orús, C., & Barta, S. (2023). The dark side of the metaverse: The role of gamification in event virtualization. *International Journal of Information Management*, 102726. https://doi.org/10.1016/j.ijinfomgt.2023.102726

Graham Cluley. (2022, November 4). *Crime in the metaverse – Police face new challenges in a virtual world.* https://www.bitdefender.com/blog/hotforsecurity/crime-in-the-metaverse-police-face-new-challenges-in-a-virtual-world/

Grand View Research. (2022, September). *Metaverse market size, share & trends analysis report by product, by platform, by technology (blockchain, virtual reality (VR) & augmented reality (AR), mixed reality (MR)).* https://www.grandviewresearch.com/industry-analysis/metaverse-market-report

Joshua, J. (2017). Information bodies: Computational anxiety in Neal Stephenson's snow crash. *Interdisciplinary literary studies*, *19*(1), 17–47. https://doi.org/10.5325/intelitestud.19.1.0017

Kirchhoff, A. (2023). *Unleashing the power of text analysis: Understanding the basics – About JSTOR*. About JSTOR. https://about.jstor.org/blog/unleashing-the-power-of-text-analysis/

Lee, L.-H., Braud, T., Zhou, P., Wang, L., Xu, D., Lin, Z., Kumar, A., Bermejo, C., & Hui, P. (2021). *All one needs to know about metaverse: A complete survey on technological singularity, virtual ecosystem, and research agenda*. ArXiv, abs/2110.05352. https://api.semanticscholar.org/CorpusID:238634091

Liao, S., Wu, J., Bashir, A. K., Yang, W., Li, J., & Tariq, U. (2022). Digital twin consensus for blockchain-enabled intelligent transportation systems in smart cities. *IEEE Transactions on Intelligent Transportation Systems*, *23*(11), 22619–22629. https://doi.org/10.1109/TITS.2021.3134002

Misuraca, M., Forciniti, A., Scepi, G., & Spano, M. (2020). *Sentiment analysis for education with R: Packages, methods and practical applications*. arXiv preprint arXiv:2005.12840.

Mitrushchenkova, A. N. (2022). Personal Identity in the metaverse: Challenges and risks. *Kutafin Law Review*, *9*(4), 793–817. https://doi.org/10.17803/2313-5395.2022.4.22.793-817

Mohammad, S. M., & Turney, P. D. (2013). Crowdsourcing a word – Emotion association lexicon. *Computational Intelligence*, *29*(3), 436–465.

Nancy Jo Sales. (2024, January 5). *A girl was allegedly raped in the metaverse. Is this the beginning of a dark new future?* https://www.theguardian.com/commentisfree/2024/jan/05/metaverse-sexual-assault-vr-game-online-safety-meta

PwC. (2023). *Beyond the hype: what businesses can really expect from the metaverse in 2023*.

Qualtrics. (2024). *The definitive guide to text analysis*. Qualtrics. https://www.qualtrics.com/experience-management/research/text-analysis/

Richter, S., & Richter, A. (2023). What is novel about the metaverse? *International Journal of Information Management*, *73*. https://doi.org/10.1016/j.ijinfomgt.2023.102684

Sales, N. J. (2024, January 8). A girl was allegedly raped in the metaverse. Is this the beginning of a dark new future? *The Guardian*. https://www.theguardian.com/commentisfree/2024/jan/05/metaverse-sexual-assault-vrgame-online-safety-meta

Seo, S., Seok, B., & Lee, C. (2023). Digital forensic investigation framework for the metaverse. *Journal of Supercomputing*, *79*(9), 9467–9485. https://doi.org/10.1007/s11227-023-05045-1

Stephenson, N. (1992). *Snow crash*. Bantam Book.

Sharma, A. (2024, January 3). *16-year-old UK girl virtually "gang-raped" in metaverse game, probe on*. https://www.indiatoday.in/world/story/metaverse-teen-virtual-reality-gangraped-men-game-uk-police-investigation-2483486-2024-01-03

Taboada, M. (2016). Sentiment analysis: An overview from linguistics. *Annual Review of Linguistics*, *2*, 325–347.

Team, T., & Team, T. (2024, January 3). UK teen 'gangraped' in metaverse, cops start probe but 'crime' may go unprosecuted under existing laws. *ThePrint*. https://theprint.in/world/uk-teen-gangraped-in-metaverse-cops-start-probe-but-crime-may-go-unprosecuted-under-existing-laws/1909242/

Theo Farrant. (2024, January 4). *British police launch first investigation into virtual rape in metaverse*. https://news.yahoo.com/british-police-launch-first-investigation-110534353.html

Treleaven, P., Barnett, J., Brown, D., Bud, A., Fenoglio, E., Kerrigan, C., Koshiyama, A., Sfeir-Tait, S., & Schoernig, M. (2023). The future of cybercrime: AI and emerging technologies are creating a cybercrime tsunami. *SSRN Electronic Journal*, 1–34. https://doi.org/10.2139/ssrn.4507244

Tugtekin, U. (2022). *The dark side of metaverse learning environments.* https://doi.org/10.4018/978-1-6684-6513-4.ch004

Vayansky, I., & Kumar, S. A. (2020). A review of topic modeling methods. *Information Systems, 94*, 101582.

Wang, S., & Wang, W. (2023). A review of the application of digital identity in the metaverse. *Security and Safety, 2*, 1–10. https://doi.org/10.1051/sands/2023009

Weinberger, M. (2022). What is metaverse? – A definition based on qualitative meta-synthesis. *Future Internet, 14*(11), 1–16. https://doi.org/10.3390/fi14110310

Wu, J., Lin, K., Lin, D., Zheng, Z., Huang, H., & Zheng, Z. (2023). Financial crimes in Web3-empowered metaverse: Taxonomy, countermeasures, and opportunities. *IEEE Open Journal of the Computer Society, 4.*, 37–49 https://doi.org/10.1109/OJCS.2023.3245801

Yang, Q., Zhao, Y., Huang, H., Xiong, Z., Kang, J., & Zheng, Z. (2022). Fusing blockchain and AI with metaverse: A survey. *IEEE Open Journal of the Computer Society, 3.* https://doi.org/10.1109/OJCS.2022.3188249

Zhang, M., Yang, L., He, S., Li, M., & Zhang, J. (2021). Privacy-preserving data aggregation for mobile crowdsensing with externality: An auction approach. *IEEE/ACM Transactions on Networking, 29*(3), 1046–1059. https://doi.org/10.1109/TNET.2021.3056490

Chapter 11

Challenges and Future Directions for the Use of AI and Security Intelligence in Tourism Industry

Mohammad Badruddoza Talukder[a], *Firoj Kabir*[b], *Mohammad Abu Horaira*[a] *and Sanjeev Kumar*[c]

[a]*International University of Business Agriculture and Technology, Bangladesh*
[b]*Daffodil Institute of IT, Bangladesh*
[c]*Lovely Professional University, India*

Abstract

This chapter examines the challenges and future directions concerning using artificial intelligence (AI) and security intelligence within the tourism industry. It aims to identify critical hurdles the industry faces in integrating AI and security intelligence solutions while outlining future directions for enhancing security measures in the tourism sector. A comprehensive review of secondary sources, including academic literature, industry reports, and online resources, was conducted. Relevant information regarding integrating AI and security intelligence in the tourism industry was synthesized to identify critical challenges and potential future directions for analysis. The findings reveal several challenges, including data privacy concerns, technological barriers, lack of standardized frameworks, and human resource constraints hindering the effective integration of AI and security intelligence in the tourism sector. Moreover, the study identifies potential future directions, such as adopting advanced AI algorithms, collaborating with cybersecurity experts, and developing tailored security solutions to address industry-specific needs. The study is limited by the availability of literature and the interview scope. Additionally, the rapidly evolving nature of technology and security threats poses challenges in providing exhaustive insights into future developments. This research offers valuable insights

The AI Metaverse Revolution: Transforming Multi-Business Scenarios (Volume 1), 165–178

doi:10.1108/978-1-83662-582-720251011

for tourism industry stakeholders, policymakers, and technology providers to navigate the complexities of integrating AI and security intelligence solutions. It provides valuable insights that can inform decision-making processes and guide strategic investments in technology and security infrastructure to ensure the sustainability and growth of the tourism sector.

Keywords: AI; security intelligence; tourism industry; challenges; future directions

Introduction

The tourism and hospitality industry faces increasing competition and guest demands for personalized, seamless experiences. The hospitality sector is turning to AI to optimize operations, improve guest service, and enhance the guest experience to meet these challenges (Kumar et al., 2024). AI has the potential to revolutionize the hospitality industry by providing the sector with the tools they need to deliver exceptional service while also reducing costs and increasing efficiency. With the rapid advancement of AI technologies, tourism in emerging markets embraces AI applications to enhance tourist experiences and footprints (Rane et al., 2023). Recent developments in machine and deep learning (DL) have revolutionized cognitive computing and natural language processing, laying the foundations for proliferating AI tourist-friendly applications in nations like China. Fig. 11.1 shows that AI is poised to reshape emerging tourist markets through biometric authentication, surveillance and monitoring systems, fraud detection and prevention, crisis management and emergency response, risk assessment and predictive analytics, augmented reality (AR), virtual reality (VR), etc. Consequently, savvy tourism entrepreneurs are pondering using facial, image, and speech recognition applications to mitigate costs and barriers, enhancing their productivity (Zhou et al., 2022).

In emerging markets, AI provides a technological solution to the economic and social challenges governments, firms, and people face at the bottom of the economic pyramid. Integrating data from multiple sources (e.g., websites, social media, and traditional channels) can help firms build data management platforms, develop sound business strategies, lower barriers to doing business, create innovative business models, and spur economic development. The tourism industry in developing countries may use innovative AI-based solutions to enhance autonomous tourist products and service delivery, implement production automation, and develop mobile AI apps for services and credit access (Türkmendağ, 2022). AI-based technologies can create opportunities and expand markets by enhancing productivity, business process automation, financial solutions, and government services.

Literature Review

AI has developed over decades and is now present in various industries. In the early 1950s, John Von Neumann and Alan Turing transferred machines to

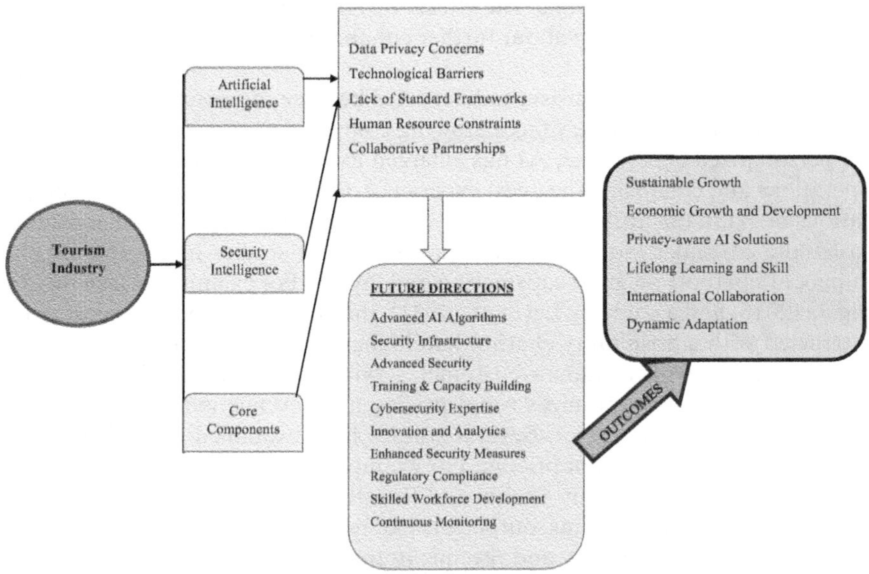

Fig. 11.1. Challenges and Future Directions for the Use of AI and Security Intelligence in Tourism Industry. *Source*: Authors' compilation.

binary logic, which built AI's scientific and technical foundation. John McCarthy coined the term "artificial intelligence" at an academic conference in 1956, initially defining it as the automation of intelligent behavior focusing on math and logic problems (Penn, 2020). In the 1980s, the focus of AI moved to knowledge and rule-based expert systems; it was essentially considered a form of "advanced computing." Early AI paradigms centered on high-level cognitive processes, such as the potential to engage in multi-step reasoning, comprehend the semantics of the natural language, and formulate novel strategies to accomplish objectives. At the beginning of the 1990s, the AI paradigm shifted to machine learning (ML), namely, how computer programs learn from experience and task performance. AI development boomed in 2010 with open access to massive volumes of data and accelerated learning algorithms (Alam, 2021). These circumstances led to an innovation with multiple levels of representation: DL, which combines big data and computer hardware, has extended AI applications in industries such as healthcare, marketing, tourism, and education. AI has more recently transformed various sectors and permeated daily life. In healthcare, AI is revolutionizing diagnostics, drug discovery, and patient care, enhancing the accuracy and speed of medical decisions. AI has also made strong inroads in education, allowing personalized learning and supporting educators in assessment and content development (Tedre et al., 2021). The entertainment and gaming industry benefits from AI-driven content recommendations, immersive virtual reality experiences, and AI-generated art and music. At a personal level, AI has become an integral part of consumers' lives, from voice assistants and chatbots to AI-driven content curation on eight social media. The effects of AI are pervasive, and its ongoing evolution promises to bring about further enhancements in numerous industries and everyday experiences.

The use of AI in the tourism industry has become increasingly prevalent in recent years. As this industry faces growing competition and guest expectations for personalized experiences, AI has emerged as a powerful tool for improving operations and enhancing the guest experience. One of the most common applications of AI in the hospitality industry is using chatbots and virtual assistants to handle customer inquiries and requests. Several studies have explored the impact of chatbots on guest satisfaction and loyalty. For example, in a survey by Sigala (2018) and a study by Lei et al. (2021), the authors explored if guests who interacted with a hospitality chatbot had higher satisfaction ratings than those who interacted with a human customer service representative (Van Schoors et al., 2024). AI also optimizes room pricing and revenue management in the hotel accommodation sector. Several studies have examined the effectiveness of ML algorithms for room pricing. For example, a survey by Pereira and Cerqueira (2022) and a study by Shehhi and Karathanasopoulos (2020) found that machine-learning algorithms outperformed traditional revenue management models in terms of accuracy and revenue optimization (Binesh et al., 2024).

Definitions of AI

AI, the term itself calls to mind humans: "artificial" refers to a human-created object, while "intelligence" captures an agent's ability to think on its own (Kim et al., 2024). Two types of definitions have, therefore, emerged. The first is human-centered; it focuses on experimental validation and empirical science. This human-centered approach states that a technical system needs intelligence to think, act, learn, and perform tasks as a person would. From this view, AI can be a computer, a computer-controlled robot, or software that obtains and analyzes real-time data and mimics human effort. By studying or simulating the brain's cognitive processes, AI (instead of people) can execute tasks through software and algorithms. Such algorithms can be used to predict or detect events. For example, tourism websites have adopted AI algorithms to forecast tourist arrivals (Ferhat Şeker & Bozkurt, 2024).

AI Applications in the Tourism Industry

As the hospitality industry becomes increasingly competitive, AI will become even more critical for improving efficiency and providing a personalized guest experience. Due to the large amounts of data generated and the potential for personalized experiences, the hospitality industry is ideal for implementing AI (Das et al., 2024). This section will explore some of the specific applications of AI in the hospitality industry, including chatbots and virtual assistants, revenue management, and personalized guest experiences. See Table 11.1.

Chatbots and virtual assistants are among the most common applications of AI in the hospitality industry. Chatbots and virtual assistants typically handle

Table 11.1. AI Applications in the Context of Hospitality and Tourism Usage.

Usage Context (Specific Firms or AI Applications)	Description
AI-based chatbots/virtual agents (e.g., Starbucks barista, Subway order bot, ChatGPT on the Expedia app)	AI-based chatbots, available 24/7/365, can answer customers' questions or submit service requests
Search/booking engines (e.g., Allora's hotel search/booking engine)	Based on AI and ML, hospitality and tourism search/booking engines are standard
AI-based robotics (e.g., Hilton's concierge robot "Connie")	AI-based robotics enable consumer interaction in hotels, restaurants, and airports (Bhuiyan et al., 2024)
Kiosks/self-service (e.g., facial recognition check-in kiosks)	Kiosks/self-service technologies use facial recognition software and biometric data to offer convenient hospitality and tourism services (Sharma & Aggarwal, 2024)
VR/AR (e.g., ETIPS AR travel app, VR travel booking service)	VR/AR offers consumers a digital environment that makes their experiences more enjoyable
Autonomous vehicles (e.g., Domino's autonomous pizza delivery)	Autonomous vehicles are widely used for service delivery

Source: Authors' compilation.

customer inquiries, requests, and complaints, freeing hospitality staff to focus on more complicated tasks. Chatbots and virtual assistants can also provide a personalized experience for guests by using data analytics to learn about their preferences and habits (Bhuiyan, 2024). For example, a hospitality industry's chatbot may recommend local restaurants or tourist attractions based on a guest's search history or provide personalized recommendations for room amenities based on previous bookings. Furthermore, chatbots and virtual assistants can provide customer support 24 hours a day, seven days a week, improving response times and overall customer satisfaction. Revenue management is another application of AI in the hospitality industry. Revenue management entails real-time adjustments to room rates based on factors such as demand, seasonality, and customer behavior (Milton, 2024). The personalization of visitor experiences is another application of AI. Hospitality businesses, for example, can use AI-powered mobile apps to provide personalized recommendations for nearby attractions and events based on a guest's preferences and previous bookings (Wang, 2024). For a comparison of benefits and challenges of AI in the hotel industry, see Table 11.2.

Table 11.2. The Benefits and Challenges of AI in the Hotel Industry.

Benefits	Challenges
Enhanced efficiency	Technical challenges
Cost reduction	Privacy and data security (Wilkowska & Ziefle, 2012)
Smooth operation	Dependability on machine
Uplift guest experiences	Lack of human interaction (Xu et al., 2023)
Exact work as instruction	Failure of system

Source: Authors' compilation.

Evaluation of AI Applications

The evaluation of AI applications in the hospitality and tourism industry is essential to the research by Huang et al. (2022), who reviewed existing research and some, but not all, of the current applications of AI in the hospitality and tourism industry and proposed a new evaluation framework to inform the susceptibility of AI adoptions. Here is a visual representation of the different types of AI and the various AI applications utilized in the industry (Talukder et al., 2023). The types of AI represented include solutions for searching/booking engines, virtual agents or chatbots, robots and autonomous vehicles, kiosks or self-service screens, and AR/VR. Evaluating listed AI applications is crucial in determining their effectiveness and impact on the industry. By understanding the strengths and limitations of each AI application, hospitality and tourism businesses can make informed decisions about which technologies to implement to enhance their operations and services (Buhalis et al., 2024).

AI Systems and Their Use in Travel and Tourism

AI systems have several applications in tourism. From the consumer perspective, AI helps users find more relevant information, gives them greater mobility, improves decision-making, and ultimately provides a better tourism experience. From a business perspective, AI can be used in almost every aspect of management, especially promotion and productivity. AI systems in the tourism industry can be stand-alone or embedded in existing applications and systems (Kumar et al., 2024). These include recommender systems, personalization and techniques, conversational systems (chatbots and voice assistants), forecasting tools, autonomous agents, language translation applications, and smart tourism destinations. For example, a guest may interact with a robot that incorporates a conversational system and, depending on the requirements, a recommender system, a personalization technique, or an autonomous agent. The dialog with the user may be based on a chatbot or voice assistant (Noonia et al., 2024).

Tourism and AI

The relationship between AI and tourism is multifaceted and dynamic. As tourism evolves in the digital age, AI has emerged as a critical technological driver shaping various aspects of the industry. Here is an in-depth exploration of this relationship:

1. *Crowd management*: AI-powered systems can predict and manage the flow of tourists in popular destinations, ensuring they do not become overcrowded.
2. *Chatbots and virtual assistants*: AI-powered chatbots assist customers in real-time, answering queries, making bookings, or offering suggestions, thereby streamlining customer service operations (Binesh et al., 2024).
3. *Language translation*: Real-time AI-driven translators break down language barriers, making travel more accessible for tourists in foreign countries.
4. *Biometrics*: Airports and border controls use AI-driven biometric systems, like facial recognition, to enhance security and speed up processes.
5. *Predictive analytics*: Tourism businesses use AI to analyze data and predict future travel trends, helping them optimize inventory and marketing strategies.
6. *VR & AR*: Tour operators and travel agencies use VR and AR to offer virtual tours, allowing tourists to experience a destination before deciding to visit (Talawar et al., 2024).
7. *Dynamic pricing*: Airlines, hotels, and other service providers use AI-driven dynamic pricing models that consider various factors like demand, seasonality, and competitor prices to offer personalized rates (Manoharan et al., 2024).

AI and Tourist Decision-making

- 85% of tourists tried and enjoyed AI-recommended cuisines, highlighting AI's potential to enhance culinary tourism (Jin & Zhang, 2025).
- 88% of air passengers found virtual assistants helpful in enhancing their travel experience (Jiménez-Barreto et al., 2023).
- 70% of tourists prefer AI-driven personalized experiences (Saxena et al., 2024).
- Chatbots handle customer queries 50% faster than human operators (Nicolescu & Tudorache, 2022).
- 8 out of 10 eco-tourism agencies reported a positive impact from AI recommendations on promoting sustainable choices (Chi et al., 2022).
- 80% of tourists felt that AI interactions significantly enhanced their travel experience (Solakis et al., 2024).
- AI accurately detected sentiments in hotel reviews with a 95% accuracy rate.
- Biometric systems in airports resulted in 60% faster security clearance for passengers (Rubio-Andrada et al., 2023).
- 65% of participants changed their travel destination preference after experiencing it through VR (Alyahya & McLean, 2022).

Based on previous studies, these key findings shape tourist decision-making in various aspects of the tourism industry.

Impacts of AI on Hospitality

Since hospitality is one of the primary industries in tourism, the impact of AI on hospitality is analyzed more thoroughly by examining the technologies and applications used in the hospitality sector (Ben Saad, 2024). In the field of operations, AI allocates rooms and other resources according to guest value, helps in the preventive management of the facilities, bases the animation offered on past behaviors and predictions of tourist arrivals, adapts the cuisine available to the tastes of the existing customers, enables room cleaning robots, helps select the appropriate employee for the facilities and the products offered, improves energy management of the facilities and tourist consumption, allows the creation of an environment in which the guest can feel at home, provides guests with access to their digital services, and supports finance management by taking into account expected revenues and arrivals (Talukder et al., 2024b).

In the final stage, the systems are integrated when AI is fully developed and implemented in the hospitality industry. They can interoperate, and almost all the tasks that humans currently perform will be able to be performed by robots, AI, and natural language systems. However, this does not mean that the hospitality industry will be run without the presence of humans. Humans will continue to have two main functions. First, humans will develop a small set of tasks that are extremely difficult to automate, even with the development of the capabilities of robotics and AI. Second, the presence of humans will be used as a distinction, and luxury will be a differential factor. In other words, if humans are inefficient from an economic perspective, their presence will be justified from a differentiation perspective or through an increase in quality, as is currently the case in gas stations (Zhang et al., 2024).

AI-related Challenges in Travel and Tourism

AI has and will have many positive effects on travel and tourism. However, there are some challenges and risks that have to be addressed. This chapter analyzes three main issues in detail: the tourists' perspective of AI, the substitution of humans for machines, and the ethics and biases in AI. Finally, there will be some suggestions for future research at the end of this chapter. Such are:

1. *Issues related to tourists' adoption and use of AI*

The first challenge with AI is the tourists' thoughts, attitudes, and perceptions of these technologies. As with any other technology or innovation, tourists can be grouped into the categories mentioned by Rogers (2010): innovators, early adopters, early majority, late majority, and laggards (Soliman et al., 2024). Taking into account the risks and benefits of AI, Tussyadiah and Miller (2019) found three types of users: laggards (who perceive high levels of risks and low levels of benefits for AI), aficionados (who perceive high levels of benefits and low levels of risks for AI), and realists (who are aware of both the likely benefits and risks of AI). These authors found that people with negative sentiments toward AI have never used such technologies. Regarding user adoption of robots, as with other technologies, the main drivers are perceived usefulness and performance. However, Gretzel (2011) warns that there is a need to move from research on intentions of use to actual use, use patterns, and nonuse (Manoharan et al., 2024).

2. *The substitution of humans*

The substitution of the human workforce by machines has been taking place since the First Industrial Revolution. However, machines could only replace humans in simple, routine tasks for a long time. With the growth of AI and AI-empowered technologies, a new generation of machines (such as service robots) has appeared to compete with and replace humans in almost every possible task. This means that the tourism sector, which has been immune to this situation for a long time, is now at risk. Bowen and Morosan (2018) estimate that 25% of the hospitality workforce could be replaced by robots in the next decade, thus categorizing the adoption of robots as a paradigm shift (Talukder et al., 2024a). Some authors have named AI the most significant threat to humankind (Kumar et al., 2024). Worker displacement has been one of the main concerns regarding the impact of AI in tourism not only because of the loss of jobs but also because of the worker's loss of a sense of belonging. There has been an intense debate in the academic literature over which jobs are more susceptible to being performed by machines. Sigala (2018) states that machines are good at complex reasoning and algorithm-based and repetitive tasks, while humans are best at generalization, perception, creativity, and interaction with the natural world (Gupta et al., 2023).

3. *Ethics and biases in AI*

The expected impact of AI on all aspects of life and society is massive. As part of the Fourth Industrial Revolution, its effect is comparable to that of machines and computers. This creates specific ethical challenges that need to be discussed. Two of these have already been mentioned, that is, loss of privacy and fear of a society entirely guided by technology. Another important and relevant risk associated with the widespread use of AI concerns bias. All humans are biased (including those who create AI algorithms), and prejudice is natural in humans, for example, bias relating to race, gender, age, and economic status. The problem is that AI is much more powerful than humans and might facilitate the amplification of the biases embedded in algorithms. This could potentially mean that as AI learns, it learns to implement biased structures that are then replicated (Bearman & Ajjawi, 2023).

4. *Expected future developments*

Businesses will be able to understand their customers better and, thus, design products, services, and experiences that are better tailored to their needs. It will also be possible for businesses to create personalized packages dynamically according to client interests. Technologies will replace and complement specific jobs, thus reducing overall operational costs and leading to savings that can be partially passed on to customers. It also means that businesses can offer affordable services that might previously have been prohibitively expensive. Technology can also enhance particular jobs or free workers from specific tasks, improving service and customer support (Talukder & Hossain, 2021). Language and cultural differences will not be barriers to tourism but additional attractions. Technologies will allow customers to receive the best possible service while guaranteeing privacy as much as possible (Talukder & Kumar, 2023).

Recommendations

Building upon the essential insights from the thorough literature review, the subsequent discussion provides overarching recommendations applicable to stakeholders across various tourism industry sectors. Such are:

- *Enhance customer service with Chatbots*: Considering chatbots' efficiency, travel agencies, airlines, and hotels should consider integrating AI-powered chatbots for customer service, bookings, and FAQs.
- *Capitalize on AI for culinary tourism*: Food is integral to the travel experience. Platforms can integrate AI to recommend local cuisines or restaurants, enhancing the culinary experience.
- *Invest in predictive analytics*: The accuracy with which AI can predict trends, like cruise demands, suggests that stakeholders should invest more in predictive analytics to anticipate better and cater to tourist demands.
- *Improve security with biometrics*: Airports and other high-security zones should consider integrating biometric systems to enhance security and improve the traveler's experience.
- *Incorporate virtual reality*: With a significant portion of participants changing their destination preference after a VR experience, tourism boards and agencies can use VR for promotional activities, allowing potential tourists to "experience" a place before visiting.
- *Invest in AI-personalized experiences*: Given the high percentage of tourists preferring AI-driven experiences, businesses should invest in technology that offers personalized recommendations, itineraries, and services.
- *Drones as tourism enhancers*: Given the unique value addition of drones, tourism spots can offer aerial tours or use drone footage for promotional activities.

In summary, while the potential of AI in transforming the tourism industry is evident, it is essential to approach its integration thoughtfully, ensuring ethical concerns are addressed, and the human touch is retained where necessary.

Conclusion

Integrating AI in the tourism sector reshapes the traveler's experience in multifaceted ways. The literature shows that AI-driven personalization stands out as a prominent tool in enhancing tourist satisfaction, with most travelers expressing a preference for such tailored experiences. Equally notable is the efficiency introduced by AI systems, as demonstrated by chatbots and predictive analytics, optimizing both the operational aspects for businesses and the travel experience for tourists. However, as with any technological integration, balance is critical. The increasing automation in the hospitality sector, while providing efficiency, has also underscored the irreplaceable value of human touch. Ethical considerations, especially surrounding data privacy and potential job displacement, emerge as crucial facets to address as the industry evolves. From a broader perspective, AI is not merely a tool for operational enhancement but also a catalyst for sustainable and ethical tourism. As VR, drones, and biometric systems further penetrate the industry, the tourism landscape will continually evolve, promising richer experiences for travelers and more sustainable and efficient business operations.

References

Al Shehhi, M., & Karathanasopoulos, A. (2020). Forecasting hotel room prices in selected GCC cities using deep learning. *Journal of Hospitality and Tourism Management*, *42*, 40–50. https://doi.org/10.1016/j.jhtm.2019.11.003

Alam, A. (2021). *Possibilities and apprehensions in the landscape of artificial intelligence in education.* 2021 International conference on computational intelligence and computing applications (ICCICA) (pp. 1–8). https://doi.org/10.1109/ICCICA52458.2021.9697272

Alyahya, M., & McLean, G. (2022). Examining tourism consumers' attitudes and the role of sensory information in virtual reality experiences of a tourist destination. *Journal of Travel Research*, *61*(7), 1666–1681. https://doi.org/10.1177/00472875211037745

Bearman, M., & Ajjawi, R. (2023). Learning to work with the black box: Pedagogy for a world with artificial intelligence. *British Journal of Educational Technology*, *54*(5), 1160–1173. https://doi.org/10.1111/bjet.13337

Ben Saad, S. (2024). The digital revolution in the tourism industry: Role of anthropomorphic virtual agent in digitalized hotel service. *International Journal of Contemporary Hospitality Management*, *36*(11), 3751–3773. https://doi.org/10.1108/IJCHM-09-2023-1485

Bhuiyan, K. H., Ahmed, S., & Jahan, I. (2024). Consumer attitude toward using artificial intelligence (AI) devices in hospitality services. *Journal of Hospitality and Tourism Insights*. https://doi.org/10.1108/JHTI-08-2023-0551

Bhuiyan, M. S. (2024). The role of AI-enhanced personalization in customer experiences. *Journal of Computer Science and Technology Studies*, *6*(1), 162–169. https://doi.org/10.32996/jcsts.2024.6.1.17

Bhuiyan, K. H., Ahmed, S., & Jahan, I. (2024). Consumer attitude toward using artificial intelligence (AI) devices in hospitality services. *Journal of Hospitality and Tourism Insights*, *7*(2), 968–985. https://adoi.org/10.1108/JHTI-08-2023-0551

Binesh, F., Belarmino, A. M., Van Der Rest, J.-P., Singh, A. K., & Raab, C. (2024). Forecasting hotel room prices when entering turbulent times: A game-theoretic artificial neural network model. *International Journal of Contemporary Hospitality Management*, *36*(4), 1044–1065. https://doi.org/10.1108/IJCHM-10-2022-1233

Bowen, J., & Morosan, C. (2018). Beware hospitality industry: The robots are coming. *Worldwide Hospitality and Tourism Themes*, *10*(6), 726–733. https://doi.org/10.1108/WHATT-07-2018-0045

Buhalis, D., Efthymiou, L., Uzunboylu, N., & Thrassou, A. (2024). Charting the progress of technology adoption in tourism and hospitality in the era of industry 4.0. *EuroMed Journal of Business*, *19*(1), 1–20. https://doi.org/10.1108/EMJB-11-2023-0310

Chi, O. H., Gursoy, D., & Chi, C. G. (2022). Tourists' attitudes toward the use of artificially intelligent (AI) devices in tourism service delivery: Moderating role of service value seeking. *Journal of Travel Research*, *61*(1), 170–185. https://doi.org/10.1177/0047287520971054

Das, I. R., Talukder, M. B., & Kumar, S. (2024). Implication of artificial intelligence in hospitality marketing. *Utilizing smart technology and AI in hybrid tourism and hospitality.* IGI Global. https://doi.org/ 10.4018/979-8-3693-1978-9.ch014

Gretzel, U. (2011). Intelligent systems in tourism. *Annals of Tourism Research*, *38*(3), 757–779. https://doi.org/10.1016/j.annals.2011.04.014

Gupta, S., Modgil, S., Lee, C.-K., & Sivarajah, U. (2023). The future is yesterday: Use of AI-driven facial recognition to enhance value in the travel and tourism industry. *Information Systems Frontiers*, *25*(3), 1179–1195. https://doi.org/10.1007/s10796-022-10271-8

Huang, A., Chao, Y., De La Mora Velasco, E., Bilgihan, A., & Wei, W. (2022). When artificial intelligence meets the hospitality and tourism industry: An assessment framework to inform theory and management. *Journal of Hospitality and Tourism Insights*, *5*(5), 1080–1100. https://doi.org/10.1108/JHTI-01-2021-0021

Jiménez-Barreto, J., Rubio, N., Mura, P., Sthapit, E., & Campo, S. (2023). "Ask Google Assistant Where to Travel" tourists' interactive experiences with smart speakers: An assemblage theory approach. *Journal of Travel Research*, *62*(4), 734–752. https://doi.org/10.1177/00472875221094073

Jin, F., & Zhang, X. (2025). Artificial intelligence or human: When and why consumers prefer AI recommendations. *Information Technology & People*, *38*(1), 279–303. https://doi.org/10.1108/ITP-01-2023-0022

Kim, H., So, K. K. F., Shin, S., & Li, J. (2024). Artificial intelligence in hospitality and tourism: Insights from industry practices, research literature, and expert opinions. *Journal of Hospitality & Tourism Research*, 10963480241229235. https://doi.org/10.1177/10963480241229235

Kumar, S., Talukder, M. B., & Tyagi, P. K. (2024). The impact of artificial intelligence on improving efficiency in service and implementing best practices in service marketing. In V. Nadda, P. Tyagi, A. Singh, & V. Singh (Eds.), *AI innovations in service and tourism marketing* (pp. 57–79). IGI Global. https://doi.org/10.4018/979-8-3693-7909-7.ch004

Lei, H., Khamkhoutlavong, M., & Le, P. B. (2021). Fostering exploitative and exploratory innovation through HRM practices and knowledge management capability: the moderating effect of knowledge-centered culture. *Journal of Knowledge Management*, *25*(8), 1926–1946.

Manoharan, G., Razak, A., Rao, C. V. G., Ashtikar, S. P., & Nivedha, M. (2024). Artificial intelligence at the helm: Steering the modern business landscape toward progress. In R. Kumar, A. Joshi, H. O. Sharan, S.-L. Peng, & C. R. Dudhagara (Eds.), *Advances in computational intelligence and robotics* (pp. 72–99). IGI Global. https://doi.org/10.4018/979-8-3693-2964-1.ch005

Milton, T. (2024). Artificial intelligence transforming hotel gastronomy: An in-depth review of AI-driven innovations in menu design, food preparation, and customer interaction, with a focus on sustainability and future trends in the hospitality industry. *International Journal for Multidimensional Research Perspectives*, *2*(3), 47–61. https://doi.org/10.61877/ijmrp.v2i3.126

Nicolescu, L., & Tudorache, M. T. (2022). Human-computer interaction in customer service: The experience with AI chatbots – A systematic literature review. *Electronics*, *11*(10), 1579. https://doi.org/10.3390/electronics11101579

Noonia, A., Beg, R., Patidar, A., Bawaskar, B., Sharma, S., & Rawat, H. (2024). Chatbot vs intelligent virtual assistance (IVA). In R. Rawat, R. K. Chakrawarti, S. K. Sarangi, P. Vyas, M. S. Alamanda, K. Srividya, & K. S. Sankaran (Eds.), *Conversational artificial intelligence* (1st ed., pp. 655–673). Wiley. https://doi.org/10.1002/9781394200801.ch36

Pereira, L. N., & Cerqueira, V. (2022). Forecasting hotel demand for revenue management using machine learning regression methods. *Current Issues in Tourism*, *25*(17), 2733–2750. https://doi.org/10.1080/13683500.2021.1999397

Penn, J. (2020). *Inventing intelligence: On the history of complex information processing and artificial intelligence in the United States in the mid-twentieth century [[object object]]*. https://doi.org/10.17863/CAM.63087

Rane, N., Choudhary, S., & Rane, J. (2023). Sustainable tourism development using leading-edge Artificial Intelligence (AI), Blockchain, Internet of Things (IoT), Augmented Reality (AR) and Virtual Reality (VR) technologies. *SSRN Electronic Journal*. https://doi.org/10.2139/ssrn.4642605

Rogers, E. M. (2010). *Diffusion of innovations* (4th ed.). Simon and Schuster.

Rubio-Andrada, L., Celemín-Pedroche, M. S., Escat-Cortés, M.-D., & Jiménez-Crisóstomo, A. (2023). Passengers satisfaction with the technologies used in smart airports: An empirical study from a gender perspective. *Journal of Air Transport Management*, *107*, 102347. https://doi.org/10.1016/j.jairtraman.2022.102347

Saxena, S. K., Gupta, V., & Kumar, S. (2024). Enhancing guest loyalty in the hotel industry through artificial intelligence-drive personalization. In S. K. Kulshreshtha & C. Webster (Eds.), *Advances in hospitality, tourism, and the services industry* (pp. 335–350). IGI Global. https://doi.org/10.4018/979-8-3693-2272-7.ch017

Şeker, F., & Bozkurt, A. (2024). What if the Covid-19 pandemic never happened estimation of the tourist arrivals for 2020 via Levenberg-Marquardt optimization and K-Star (K) machine learning algorithms. *Journal of Tourism and Gastronomy Studies*, *1*. https://doi.org/10.21325/jotags.2024.1402

Sharma, I., & Aggarwal, A. (2024). Revolutionizing creative tourism: Integrating AI in marketing for immersive travel experiences. In S. Manohar, A. Mittal, S. Raju, & A. J. Nair (Eds.), *Advances in hospitality, tourism, and the services industry* (pp. 179–197). IGI Global. https://doi.org/10.4018/979-8-3693-2019-8.ch011

Sigala, M. (2018). New technologies in tourism: From multi-disciplinary to anti-disciplinary advances and trajectories. *Tourism Management Perspectives*, *25*, 151–155. https://doi.org/10.1016/j.tmp.2017.12.003

Solakis, K., Katsoni, V., Mahmoud, A. B., & Grigoriou, N. (2024). Factors affecting value co-creation through artificial intelligence in tourism: A general literature review. *Journal of Tourism Futures*, *10*(1), 116–130. https://doi.org/10.1108/JTF-06-2021-0157

Soliman, D. S. A., Shalaby, R. A. E. A. Y., Khourshed, N. F., & Amara, D. F. (2024). The impact of technological innovativeness on the intention to utilize digital transformation: An application of diffusion of innovation in the Egyptian private universities. *Arab Journal of Administration*, *44*(5), 1–20. https://doi.org/10.21608/aja.2024.270485.1587

Talawar, A., Suresh, S., & Alathur, S. (2024). Assessing the moderating effects of involvement on tourist attitudes and intentions through virtual reality applications. *Journal of Hospitality and Tourism Insights*, *7*(2), 1050–1069. https://doi.org/10.1108/JHTI-10-2023-0676

Talukder, M. B., & Hossain, M. M. (2021). Prospects of future tourism in bangladesh: An evaluative study. *I-Manager's Journal on Management*, *15*(Issue 4), 1–8. https://doi.org/10.26634/jmgt.15.4.17495

Talukder, M. B., Kabir, F., Mia, M. N., & Khan, M. R. (2024a). Application of smart technologies in the development and promotion of religious tourism destination. In R. Castanho & M. Franco (Eds.), *Cultural, gastronomy, and adventure tourism development* (pp. 71–88). IGI Global. https://doi.org/10.4018/979-8-3693-3158-3.ch003

Talukder, M. B., Kabir, F., Muhsina, K., & Das, I. R. (2023). Emerging Concepts of Artificial Intelligence in the Hotel Industry: A Conceptual Paper. *International Journal of Research Publication and Reviews*, *4*(9), 1765–1769. https://doi.org/10.55248/gengpi.4.923.92451

Talukder, M. B., & Kumar, S. (2023). Revisit Intention in Hotel Industry of Bangladesh: A Critical Review of Present Literatures' Limitations and Suggestions for Further Study. *Research Gate*, April 2023. [Online]. https://www.researchgate.net/publication/371503587_Revisit_Intention_in_Hotel_Industry_of_Bangladesh_A_Critical_Review_of_Present_Literatures'_Limitations_and_Suggestions_for_Further_Study

Talukder, M. B., Kumar, S., & Das, I. R. (2024b). Perspectives of Digital Marketing for the Restaurant Industry. In G. Erol & M. Kuyucu (Eds.), *Advancements in Socialized and Digital Media Communications* (pp. 118–134). IGI Global. https://doi.org/10.4018/979-8-3693-0855-4.ch009

Tedre, M., Toivonen, T., Kahila, J., Vartiainen, H., Valtonen, T., Jormanainen, I., & Pears, A. (2021). Teaching machine learning in K–12 classroom: Pedagogical and technological trajectories for artificial intelligence education. *IEEE Access*, *9*, 110558–110572. https://doi.org/10.1109/ACCESS.2021.3097962

Türkmendağ, Z. (2022). Artificial intelligence in the delivery of mobile tourism services. In A. B. Waluyo & L. Tan (Eds.), *Advances in hospitality, tourism, and the services industry* (pp. 162–188). IGI Global. https://doi.org/10.4018/978-1-7998-6904-7.ch008

Tussyadiah, I., & Miller, G. (2019). Nudged by a robot: Responses to agency and feedback. *Annals of Tourism Research*, *78*, 102752. https://doi.org/10.1016/j.annals.2019.102752

Van Schoors, R., Bhatt, S., Elen, J., Raes, A., Van Den Noortgate, W., & Depaepe, F. (2024). Design and development of a digital personalized learning track: Bridging the gap between textual and visual programming. *International Journal of Designs for Learning*, *15*(1), 74–95. https://doi.org/10.14434/ijdl.v15i1.35224

Wang, P. Q. (2024). Personalizing guest experience with generative AI in the hotel industry: There's more to it than meets a Kiwi's eye. *Current Issues in Tourism*, 1–18. https://doi.org/10.1080/13683500.2023.2300030

Wilkowska, W., & Ziefle, M. (2012). Privacy and data security in E-health: Requirements from the user's perspective. *Health Informatics Journal*, *18*(3), 191–201. https://doi.org/10.1177/1460458212442933

Xu, W., Dainoff, M. J., Ge, L., & Gao, Z. (2023). Transitioning to human interaction with AI systems: New challenges and opportunities for HCI professionals to enable human-centered AI. *International Journal of Human–Computer Interaction*, *39*(3), 494–518. https://doi.org/10.1080/10447318.2022.2041900

Zhang, B., Zhang, X., Huang, F., & Miao, D. (2024). Cross-domain knowledge collaboration for blending-target domain adaptation. *Information Processing & Management*, *61*(4), 103730. https://doi.org/10.1016/j.ipm.2024.103730

Zhou, X., Yang, Z., Hyman, M. R., Li, G., & Munim, Z. H. (2022). Guest editorial: Impact of artificial intelligence on business strategy in emerging markets: A conceptual framework and future research directions. *International Journal of Emerging Markets*, *17*(4), 917–929. https://doi.org/10.1108/IJOEM-04-2022-995

Chapter 12

AI and Robotics Awareness: Effects on Hotel Employee Turnover

Anshul Garg[a], Gopinath Sangaran[a] and Vincent Pang Fook Huat[b]

[a]*Taylor's University, Malaysia*
[b]*Sauerkraut, Malaysia*

Abstract

As technology evolves, hotels leverage AI to optimise operations, sparking discussions on its impact. Despite benefits, AI adoption raises concerns about employee turnover, job insecurity, and altered perceptions of support. There is a lack of empirical studies on hospitality employees' awareness of AI implications in the academic literature. This study will fill this gap by examining the relationship between hotel AI adoption and employee turnover. Taking a positivist approach, it collects data through questionnaires from full-time employees in a five-star hotel in Malaysia to provide new insights into this area.

Keywords: Artificial intelligence; robotics; hospitality employees; employee turnover; job insecurity; organisational support

Introduction

Technology plays a pivotal role in driving efficiency and enhancing guest experiences in the rapidly evolving hospitality landscape. Embracing technological advancements has become imperative for hotels seeking sustainable competitive advantages (Kim et al., 2008). Artificial Intelligence (AI) is a transformative force in hotel operations, promising speed, accuracy, and effectiveness beyond human capabilities. Despite AI's benefits, its integration raises concerns, particularly regarding the impact on hotel employees. Staff members are crucial in decision-making around technology adoption, including AI (Sun et al., 2020). While AI enhances operational efficiency and guest satisfaction, it also poses threats to job

The AI Metaverse Revolution: Transforming Multi-Business Scenarios (Volume 1), 179–192

doi:10.1108/978-1-83662-582-720251012

security. The potential for job displacement may lead to reduced morale, performance, and increased turnover rates among hotel employees (Khaliq et al., 2022; Koo et al., 2021). Balancing the advantages of AI with its potential disruptions is a critical challenge for hotels striving for sustainability. While AI adoption improves operational efficiency and competitiveness, its implementation requires careful consideration of its impact on the workforce. Hoteliers must address concerns regarding job security and provide adequate support and training to ensure successful integration while fostering a positive work environment. By navigating these challenges effectively, hotels can harness AI's full potential while safeguarding their employees' well-being and maintaining a sustainable approach to hospitality.

This research is important because it can help better understand the true impact of AI on hotel employees and their turnover rates. Additionally, this research can help better understand whether AI is the most influential factor in hotel employee turnover rates. Understanding the impact of AI on hotel employee turnover rates is essential because hotel employees play a vital role in hotel operations, and hotels cannot afford to lose employees. Although AI and robots have become increasingly common nowadays, there are very few studies about the impact of AI and robotics and job insecurity on hotel turnover rates. Therefore, this research will study whether the advent and use of AI in hotels are the most decisive factors in hotel employee turnover rates or other factors such as job insecurity and perceived organisational support. Based on the above discussion, this study addresses the following research objectives and questions.

Research Objectives

1. To understand the relationship between hotel employee turnover rates and the use of AI in the hotel industry.
2. To identify the relationship between perceived organisational support and job insecurity due to the use of AI in hotels towards the turnover rate of hotel employees.
3. To investigate whether awareness of AI and robotics affects the turnover rate of hotel employees.

Research Questions

1. Is there a relationship between the turnover rate of hotel employees and the use of AI in the hotel industry?
2. Do perceived organisational support and job insecurity due to the use of AI in hotels affect the turnover rate of hotel employees?
3. Does awareness of AI and robotics affect the turnover rate of hotel employees?

Literature Review

Technology, Robotics, and AI Awareness

The integration of AI in hospitality has spurred the adoption of robots, impacting organisations, employees, and customers (Zhang et al., 2023). Academic research on this adoption trend is expanding (Budhwar et al., 2022; Vrontis et al., 2021). At a macro level, introducing robots is expected to reduce overall employment, replace certain skill levels, and potentially widen social disparities (Lu et al., 2020; Wu et al., 2023). On a meso level, robot utilisation is forecasted to enhance labour productivity and business efficiency (Cheng et al., 2019). However, at a micro level, adopting robots alters management models and increases job insecurity among employees (Koo et al., 2021; Wu et al., 2022).

The hospitality industry has swiftly embraced information and communication technologies, integrating AI, and robotics across various operations, from front-of-the-house to back-of-the-house tasks (Ivanov & Webster, 2017). AI-powered chatbots and robotic assistants are increasingly utilised to enhance guest interactions and concierge services, enriching the hotel experience. However, introducing AI robots in workplaces can inadvertently affect employees' psychological well-being and attachment to the workplace, potentially leading to decreased commitment and a sense of belonging (Li et al., 2019). Concerns about widespread job displacement and unemployment accompany the global implementation of AI and robotics. Research indicates that rapid advancements in modern robotics and AI can negatively impact employee attitudes and behaviours, potentially contributing to high turnover rates (Chui et al., 2015). Employees may feel undervalued and unappreciated when AI and robotics replace their roles, as supported by Brougham and Haar (2017).

AI and robotics are increasingly prevalent in hotel services, notably in restaurants where robots join service crews to streamline operations through automation. Siciliano and Khatib (2018) noted the rapid transition of robotics from industrial to human-centric applications. Li et al. (2019) found that hotel staff attitudes towards AI correlate with turnover intentions, potentially leading to high turnover rates due to concerns about job loss stemming from simplifying tasks. Advanced technologies may induce insecurity and stress among employees about their prospects and job stability, increasing the likelihood of resignation. Drawing from this existing literature, the following hypothesis is proposed:

> *H1*. The use of AI and robotics awareness in the hotel industry positively impacts the hotel employee turnover rate.

Organisational Environment and Support

Organisational support theory posits that achieving organisational objectives hinges on employers treating their employees generously. When employees feel supported by the organisation, they tend to develop stronger emotional ties. This can lead to increased dedication and a willingness to adapt when the organisation faces challenges (Kurtessis et al., 2015). The theory underscores the significance of organisational support and its impact on employee motivation, highlighting how it influences employees' willingness to work for and contribute to the organisation (Hao & Wang, 2022).

Perceiving organisational support correlates with increased employee dedication and performance, promoting optimal organisational outcomes (Orpina et al., 2022). Astuty and Udin (2020) suggest that perceived organisational support fosters effective commitment and a positive organisational identity. Managers expect heightened dedication and cooperation from employees when adequate support is provided (Arasanmi & Krishna, 2019). Conversely, employees feeling undervalued are prone to dissatisfaction and uncooperative behaviour, perceiving themselves as owed compensation without future rewards (Knapp et al., 2017).

Research indicates that higher perceived organisational support is associated with increased job satisfaction and decreased turnover intentions (Kurtessis et al., 2015). This perception reflects employees feeling valued and cared for by the organisation (Arasanmi & Krishna, 2019), leading to improved performance, collaboration, and colleague appreciation (Orpina et al., 2022). Managers' responses to employee errors and providing constructive feedback are crucial for enhancing performance (Hewagama et al., 2019). Perceived organisational support, encompassing assistance and favours within the organisation, fosters a positive work environment valued by employees, including those in the hospitality industry (Arasanmi & Krishna, 2019; Jiang et al., 2019).

Wang and Wang (2020) emphasised the importance of businesses providing appropriate organisational support to mitigate the risks of burnout and attrition. This highlights the important role of organisational circumstances and support from the organisation in determining the turnover rate of hotel employees. Hotels that foster a positive organisational atmosphere and provide adequate support are less prone to turnover intentions and rates, even in the context of AI integration into hotel operations. This study demonstrates that organisational commitment is how perceived alternative job opportunities are utilised to decrease turnover intention.

> *H2*. Organisational environment and support significantly impact the hotel employee turnover rate.

Job Insecurity

One of the biggest sectors in the hospitality industry is food and accommodation. Since this industry focuses heavily on the quality of service performed, every hotel employee is expected to perform well and provide the best service to the guests they serve. This high level of expected job performance can affect employees' stress regarding their jobs. This high level of job stress can cause short- and long-term effects, including job insecurity. Job insecurity is defined as the perceived fear of losing the current job due to unexpected and uncontrollable events that can interrupt the continuity of one's work experience (Shoss, 2017; Sverke et al., 2002).

Job insecurity has garnered significant attention in academic research, spurred by shifts in labour markets and organisational dynamics (De Angelis et al., 2021). Economic unpredictability and heightened market competition have led to downsizing and reorganisation, intensifying employee concerns about job loss and future employment prospects (Sverke et al., 2002). The widespread implementation of AI and robots worldwide raises valid concerns about potential job displacement and widespread unemployment (Li et al., 2019).

Moreover, the impact of job insecurity on workers' mental health, well-being, and organisational performance has become increasingly recognised

(Shoss, 2017). Job insecurity manifests in symptoms of burnout, conflicts between work and personal life, and diminished life satisfaction (Richter et al., 2010). Studies indicate negative associations between job insecurity and job satisfaction, organisational commitment, and overall well-being, highlighting its role as a stressor (Etehadi & Karatepe, 2018; Sverke et al., 2002).

According to research, it is estimated that about 25% of Singapore's jobs are at high risk of computerisation (Lee, 2017). It is also estimated that by 2025, blue-collar and white-collar workers will be at risk of being laid off due to automated and networked AI applications (Li et al., 2019). Moreover, the individual feels insecure when the organisation introduces new technology, which eventually results in the unemployment of less skilled employees (Koo et al., 2021). Therefore, building on previous research, the first hypothesis was developed.

H3. Job insecurity positively impacts hotel employee turnover rate.

Employee Turnover

Employee turnover refers to the rate at which workers leave their positions within a specified timeframe compared to the average number of employees. Turnover encompasses the termination of employment in a hotel for any reason and can impact the establishment positively or negatively, depending on the departing employee's performance level (Sangaran & Garg, 2012). High and low performers tend to have the highest turnover rates, while intermediate performers typically remain longer. Turnover can be voluntary, referring to employees leaving their jobs on their own accord. Involuntary turnover refers to employers terminating the employment relationship, often with more negative effects for the employee. Dysfunctional turnover refers to satisfactorily performing employees leaving voluntarily. When employees depart, the organisation must find and hire replacements, which consume time, energy, and costs. Replacing humans with AI and robotics could trigger any of the turnover categories, leaving the establishment or industry in an uncertain state in managing their operations or business (Brougham & Haar, 2020).

Turnover in the Hotel Industry

Employees leave organisations for various reasons, with job dissatisfaction often being a primary factor. Job satisfaction, an essential attitude towards work, significantly impacts turnover, absenteeism, and performance. Research indicates that employees with higher job satisfaction are less likely to be absent and tend to stay longer in their positions (Sangaran & Kumar, 2015). With the inclusion of AI and robotics, the industry can face resistance if employees have poor job security. Employees need to be engaged further with the decisions and operational plans using AI and robotics. These factors collectively shape employees' perceptions of their jobs and affect their decision to remain in their current roles or explore other opportunities (Brougham & Haar, 2020). Fig. 12.1 displays the conceptual framework for the study.

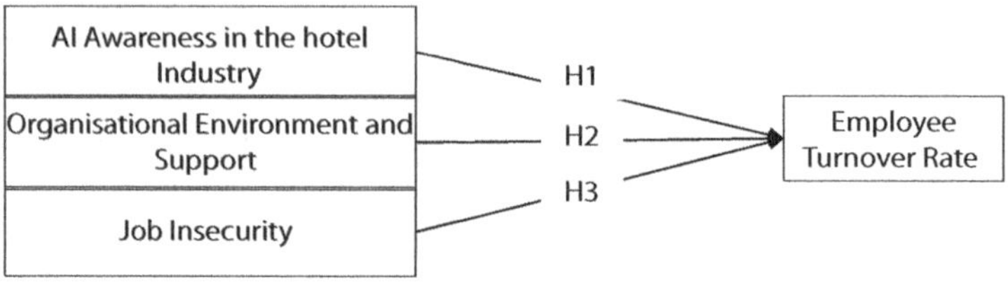

Fig. 12.1. Conceptual Framework of the Study.

Research Methodology

The research design serves as the framework for data gathering, estimation, and analysis in alignment with the study's research questions (Sekaran & Bougie, 2016). This study adopts a positivist paradigm, characterised by a systematic, empirical, quantitative, and deductive approach, to comprehensively explore social or human phenomena. A quantitative research methodology is chosen to address the research objectives and hypotheses due to its suitability for evaluating relationships between variables using numerical data. Employing a deductive approach, hypotheses are formulated based on existing theories (Graneheim et al., 2017). The research utilised a quantitative approach, employing convenience random sampling and a self-reported survey questionnaire for data collection.

A structured online survey questionnaire was developed, incorporating items derived from a comprehensive literature review. The questionnaire comprised two main sections. The first section gathered respondents' demographic information, including age, gender, work duration, and monthly income. The second section delved into the key constructs outlined in the research framework. This section consisted of items measuring various dimensions using a five-point Likert scale, ranging from 'strongly disagree' (1) to 'strongly agree' (5). Within this second section, there were a total of 13 items on independent variables, namely, AI awareness in the hotel industry (5 items), organisational environment and support (4 items), and job insecurity (4 items). These independent variables were assessed to evaluate the dependent variable, employee turnover rate, which consisted of five items.

In the context of the study conducted at one of the premier hotel in Malaysia, researchers collected a total of 267 responses from employees. However, 62 responses were excluded from the analysis. Among these exclusions, 35 respondents consistently provided identical answers across all Likert scale questions, while 27 respondents only partially completed the questionnaire. After refining the data, the remaining 205 responses were used for further analysis. For this study, SPSS version 25 was employed for data analysis. Descriptive analysis was conducted to examine the demographic characteristics of the respondents. Additionally, reliability tests were performed on the instrument to ensure that all constructs were devoid of random error. Furthermore, correlation and multiple regression analyses were conducted to evaluate the proposed hypothesis. These statistical analyses allowed for a comprehensive examination of the relationships between variables and testing of the research hypotheses.

Findings and Analysis

Demographic Profile

In this study, Table 12.1 represents a total of 205 respondents participated. Among the valid sample sizes collected, 40.5% identified as male, 58% as female, and 1.5% chose not to reveal their gender. Most respondents fell within the age range of 20–25 years, accounting for 77.6% of the total, followed by the 26–30 age group at 10.7%, and 6.3% were above 41 years. Regarding work duration in the hotel, the most significant proportion of respondents (37.5%) had been working for less than 1 year, while 25.5% had been employed for more than 10 years. Additionally, 19% had worked at their current hotel for 1–2 years, and 17.5% had a tenure of 3–4 years. Regarding monthly income, most participants (56.6%) reported earning between RM 1,500 and 2,000, followed by 20% of staff earning more than 3,000 Malaysian Ringgit.

Reliability of the Study

Cronbach's coefficient alpha is commonly used to assess internal consistency reliability. According to Kline (2015), Cronbach's alpha value of 0.7 and above is

Table 12.1. Demographics of the Study ($n = 205$).

Variable	Category	Frequency (F)	Percentage (%)
Gender	Male	83	40.5
	Female	119	58
	Prefer not to say	3	1.5
Age	20–25	159	77.6
	26–30	22	10.7
	31–35	7	3.4
	36–40	4	2.0
	Above 41	13	6.3
Work duration in the hotel	Less than 1 year	77	37.5
	1–2 years	40	19.5
	3–4 years	36	17.5
	5–10 years	52	25.5
Monthly income (RM)	1,500–2,000	116	56.6
	2,001–2,500	25	12.2
	2,501–3,000	23	11.2
	3,001 and above	41	20.0
		205	100%

Table 12.2. Cronbach Alpha Coefficients for all Constructs.

Construct	Cronbach Alpha (α)	Number of Items
AI awareness in the hotel industry	0.763	4
Organisational environment and support	0.697	5
Job insecurity	0.754	5
Employee turnover rate	0.645	4
Overall	0.849	18

considered reliable, while Sekaran and Bougie (2016) suggested that a value of 0.5 is a lower acceptable limit. In the study, Table 12.2 presents Cronbach's alpha coefficients for all constructs. All measures demonstrated satisfactory reliability, with Cronbach's alpha values between 0.645 and 0.763, which falls within the recommended range of 0.70 (Pallant, 2020). This indicates that the measures were free of random error, and reliability coefficients estimate the amount of systematic variation (Churchill & Iacobucci, 2005). The overall Cronbach's alpha value was 0.849, indicating excellent reliability. The higher Cronbach's alpha values suggest that all items were internally consistent, and the higher overall Cronbach's alpha value indicates that convergent validity was achieved.

Correlation Analysis

In the current study, correlation analysis was employed to measure the closeness of the relationship between two or more variables and to assess the joint variation of these measures (Churchill, 1995; Pallant, 2020). Specifically, correlation analysis was used to examine the correlation between the independent variables: AI awareness in the hotel industry, organisational environment and support, and job insecurity, with the dependent variable, employee turnover rate. The results of the correlation analysis, as presented in Table 12.3, were found to be significant at the 0.01 level. Upon examination of the correlation coefficient matrix between the study variables, it was observed that no correlation coefficient reached a value of 0.90 or above. This finding supports the discriminant validity of the study, indicating that all constructs are distinct from one another (Amick & Walberg, 1975). Furthermore, a strong positive correlation between the variables was identified.

Regression Analysis

Regression analysis is a statistical technique used to derive an equation that relates the criterion variable to one or more predictor variables. It considers the frequency distribution of the criterion variable when one or more predictor variables are held fixed at various levels (Churchill, 1995). In the study context, the authors performed a regression analysis to test the hypotheses about understanding the employee turnover rate. One concern when performing regression analysis is multicollinearity, which is defined as the extent to which other variables in the analysis can explain a particular variable. Multicollinearity exists when two or more independent variables are highly correlated (Zhang, 2009). To address multicollinearity, the authors conducted a check using the correlation matrix and examined the variance inflation factor (VIF) values and tolerances. For standardised data, a tolerance value of less than 0.2 or 0.1 and a VIF value of 10 or above indicate harmful collinearity. Additionally, the Durbin-Watson statistic, which ranges from 0 to 4 with a midpoint of 2, is used to detect autocorrelation in the residuals from a regression analysis. A value between 1.5 and 2.5 is considered ideal for indicating independent observations (Zhang, 2009). These checks help ensure the validity and reliability of the regression analysis results.

Table 12.4 indicates that regression analysis was conducted with 'Employee Turnover Rate' as the dependent variable and 'AI awareness in the hotel industry', 'Organizational environment and support', and 'Job insecurity' as independent variables. This regression analysis aimed to predict the 'Employee Turnover Rate' implications. The results show that AI awareness in the hotel industry ($\beta = 0.399$), organisational environment and support ($\beta = 0.600$), and job insecurity ($\beta = 0.471$) exhibit a positive relationship with perceived

Table 12.3. Correlations of the Study Variables.

Variables				
Scales	**1**	**2**	**3**	**4**
AI awareness in the hotel industry	1			
Organisational environment and support	0.473**	1		
Job insecurity	0.495**	0.408**	1	
Employee turnover rate	0.452**	0.503**	0.357**	1

**All the correlations are significant at the 0.01 level (two-tailed).

Table 12.4. Regression Analysis.

Dependent Variable: Employee Turnover Rate						
Independent Variables	***β***	***t*- Value**	***p*-Value**	**Tolerance**	**VIF**	**Hypothesis**
AI awareness in the hotel industry	0.399	0.452	0.000	0.640	1.563	*H1* – significant
Organisational environment and support	0.600	0.600	0.000	0.465	2.151	*H2* – significant
Job insecurity	0.471	0.357	0.000	0.513	1.950	*H3* – significant

Notes: Durbin-Watson = 1.723, $R^2 = 0.187$, $F = 11.352$, $p \leq 0.01$.

usefulness, leading to the acceptance of hypotheses *H1*, *H2*, and *H3*. Furthermore, the results indicate that the coefficient of determination (R^2) was 0.187, indicating that the independent variables can explain approximately 18.7% of the variability in the employee turnover rate. The F value of 11.352 was significant at $p < 0.01$, suggesting that the regression model is significant. The Durbin-Watson value was also calculated to be 1.723, which falls within the ideal range of 1.5–2.5, indicating no significant autocorrelation in the residuals. Moreover, the VIF was below 3 for all independent variables, indicating no multicollinearity problem. Overall, the regression analysis results suggest that AI awareness in the hotel industry, organisational environment and support, and job insecurity positively relate to perceived usefulness and implications of employee turnover rate.

Discussion and Conclusion

AI, aimed at streamlining operations and improving customer experience, has become increasingly prevalent in the hospitality industry. However, this technological advancement has also brought about uncertainty in the hotel industry work environment, particularly regarding employee job security. This study contributes empirical evidence by examining the impact of AI technology on hotel employees, focusing on identifying the pivotal role of job insecurity, organisational environment and support, and turnover intention. By exploring these factors, the study sheds light on the intricate dynamics between AI implementation and its effects on employees within the hotel sector (Koo et al., 2021).

Many scholars have delved into the ramifications of AI technology in the workplace on hotel employee turnover rate (Khaliq et al., 2022; Koo et al., 2021), employment rates (Lu et al., 2020; Wu et al., 2023), labour productivity and economic efficiency in businesses (Cheng et al., 2019), job insecurity among employees (Koo et al., 2021; Wu et al., 2022) have provided valuable insights, enriching our understanding of related fields. Furthermore, several studies have yielded negative conclusions when examining the impact of AI technology in the workplace. For instance, research by De Angelis et al. (2021) and Li et al. (2019) has highlighted reduced employee job satisfaction, organisational commitment, and increased turnover intention. These findings have predominantly been derived from employees' perceptions and cognitive perspectives (Wang et al., 2023).

Despite the increasing volume of empirical research on the influence of AI technology in the workplace, there remains a gap in exploring the relationship between AI and employee turnover. Employees are essential stakeholders for organisations, and providing them with proper treatment and social responsibility can yield positive outcomes such as improved work attitudes, loyalty, job security, satisfaction, emotional attachment, and participation in innovation while also reducing turnover intention (Wang et al., 2023). However, recent empirical studies on the effects of AI technology in the workplace have primarily overlooked this aspect.

This study investigates the impact of AI and robotics awareness, perceived organisational support, and job insecurity resulting in hotel employee turnover rates. The findings underscore the importance of enhancing hotel staff's understanding of AI and robots. It is evident that increased awareness leads to a more favourable perception of organisational support, subsequently reducing job insecurity stemming from AI utilisation (Riggle, Edmondson, & Hansen, 2009). Organisations can enhance employee confidence and job satisfaction by providing information about AI technologies and their potential impact on job roles. Additionally, over 40% of respondents believe prioritising staff development is crucial to mitigating increased employee turnover. This highlights the significance of fostering a supportive organisational environment prioritising employee growth and well-being, ultimately contributing to lower turnover rates.

It is important to note that this research was explicitly targeted at targeted hotel employees and management, ensuring that the survey findings accurately represent this specific population. One key finding of this investigation is that respondents generally believe introducing AI technology will benefit the hotel business. Many individuals expressed views that aligned with the idea that AI will assist employees in their tasks and enhance service quality. However, a significant concern voiced by respondents was the apprehension of potential job displacement in the future due to advancements in AI technology.

This focused approach enhances the credibility of our results as they are based on the firsthand experiences and opinions of individuals directly involved in the hotel industry. Overall, this study provides valuable insights into the perceptions of AI within the hotel business, highlighting both positive and negative predictions about its impact on employees. It underscores the need for further research into practical strategies for effectively utilising AI while addressing concerns about its potential consequences.

Limitations and Suggestions for Future Research

Several limitations of this study provide avenues for future research. Firstly, the data were collected from a single geographical area within one country and only one hotel. Therefore, future studies should aim to include multiple hotels from various countries with diverse economic backgrounds to validate the results further and enhance their generalisability.

Additionally, future research could explore AI's role in the hospitality industry and its impact on strategic decision-making processes. By addressing these knowledge gaps, future studies can better understand AI's implications within the industry and provide valuable insights for managers and policymakers. Furthermore, considering the rapid advancement of AI technology, longitudinal studies could be conducted to assess how perceptions and attitudes towards AI in the hospitality industry evolve. This would provide valuable insights into the long-term implications of AI adoption and its effects on employee turnover rates and organisational dynamics. Overall, future research endeavours should aim to overcome these limitations and contribute to a comprehensive understanding of the role of AI in the hospitality industry, ultimately informing strategic decision-making processes and enhancing organisational effectiveness.

References

Amick, D. J., & Walberg, H. J. (1975). *Introductory multivariate analysis: For educational, psychological, and social research.*

Arasanmi, C. N., & Krishna, A. (2019). Employer branding: Perceived organisational support and employee retention – The mediating role of organisational commitment. *Industrial and Commercial Training, 51*(3), 174–183. https://doi.org/10.1108/ict-10-2018-0086

Astuty, I., & Udin, U. (2020). The effect of perceived organizational support and transformational leadership on affective commitment and employee performance. *The Journal of Asian Finance, Economics and Business, 7*(10), 401–411. https://doi.org/10.13106/jafeb.2020.vol7.no10.401

Brougham, D., & Haar, J. (2017). Employee assessment of their technological redundancy. *Labour & Industry: A Journal of the Social and Economic Relations of Work, 27*(3), 213–231. https://doi.org/10.1080/10301763.2017.1369718

Brougham, D., & Haar, J. (2020). Technological disruption and employment: The influence on job insecurity and turnover intentions: A multi-country study. *Technological Forecasting and Social Change, 161*, 120276. https://doi.org/10.1016/j.techfore.2020.120276

Budhwar, P., Malik, A., De Silva, M. T. T., & Thevisuthan, P. (2022). Artificial intelligence – Challenges and opportunities for international HRM: A review and research agenda. *International Journal of Human Resource Management, 33*(6), 1065–1097. https://doi.org/10.1080/09585192.2022.2035161

Cheng, H., Jia, R., Li, D., & Li, H. (2019). The rise of robots in China. *Journal of Economic Perspectives, 33*(2), 71–88. https://doi.org/10.1257/jep.33.2.71

Chui, M., Manyika, J., & Miremadi, M. (2015). Four fundamentals of workplace automation. *McKinsey Quarterly, 29*(3), 1–9.

Churchill, G. A. (1995). *Marketing research: Methodological foundations* (6th ed., Vol. 1). Houghton Mifflin.

Churchill, G. A., & Iacobucci, D. (2005). *Marketing research: Methodological foundations* (9th ed.). South Western Educational Publishing.

De Angelis, M., Mazzetti, G., & Guglielmi, D. (2021). Job insecurity and job performance: A serial mediated relationship and the buffering effect of organizational justice. *Frontiers in Psychology, 12*, 1–15. https://doi.org/10.3389/fpsyg.2021.694057

Etehadi, B., & Karatepe, O. M. (2018). The impact of job insecurity on critical hotel employee outcomes: The mediating role of self-efficacy. *Journal of Hospitality Marketing & Management, 28*(6), 665–689. https://doi.org/10.1080/19368623.2019.1556768

Graneheim, U. H., Lindgren, B., & Lundman, B. (2017). Methodological challenges in qualitative content analysis: A discussion paper. *Nurse Education Today, 56*, 29–34. https://doi.org/10.1016/j.nedt.2017.06.002

Hao, Y., & Wang, G. (2022). The effect of supportive organizational climate on employee turnover intention: A cross-level analysis. *Journal of Human Resource and Sustainability Studies, 10*(03), 334–355. https://doi.org/10.4236/jhrss.2022.103021

Hewagama, G., Boxall, P., Cheung, G. W., & Hutchison, A. M. (2019). Service recovery through empowerment? HRM, employee performance and job satisfaction in hotels. *International Journal of Hospitality Management*, *81*, 73–82. https://doi.org/10.1016/j.ijhm.2019.03.006

Ivanov, S. H., & Webster, C. (2017). *Adoption of robots, artificial intelligence and service automation by travel, tourism and hospitality companies – A cost-benefit analysis*. Social Science Research Network. https://papers.ssrn.com/sol3/Delivery.cfm/SSRN_ID3007577_code657096.pdf?abstractid=3007577&mirid=1

Jiang, W., Huang, S., & Hou, P. (2019). Emotional intelligence, emotional labor, perceived organizational support, and job satisfaction: A moderated mediation model. *International Journal of Hospitality Management*, *81*, 120–130. https://doi.org/10.1016/j.ijhm.2019.01.009

Khaliq, A., Waqas, A., Nisar, Q. A., Haider, S., & Asghar, Z. (2022). Application of AI and robotics in hospitality sector: A resource gain and resource loss perspective. *Technology in Society*, *68*, 101807. https://doi.org/10.1016/j.techsoc.2021.101807

Kim, T. G., Lee, J. H., & Law, R. (2008). An empirical examination of the acceptance behaviour of hotel front office systems: An extended technology acceptance model. *Tourism Management*, *29*(3), 500–513. https://doi.org/10.1016/j.tourman.2007.05.016

Kline, R. B. (2015). The mediation myth. *Basic and Applied Social Psychology*, *37*(4), 202–213. https://doi.org/10.1080/01973533.2015.1049349

Knapp, J. R., Smith, B., & Sprinkle, T. A. (2017). Is it the job or the support? Examining structural and relational predictors of job satisfaction and turnover intention for nonprofit employees. *Nonprofit and Voluntary Sector Quarterly*, *46*(3), 652–671. https://doi.org/10.1177/0899764016685859

Koo, B., Curtis, C., & Ryan, B. (2021). Examining the impact of artificial intelligence on hotel employees through job insecurity perspectives. *International Journal of Hospitality Management*, *95*, 102763. https://doi.org/10.1016/j.ijhm.2020.102763

Kurtessis, J. N., Eisenberger, R., Ford, M. T., Buffardi, L. C., Stewart, K. A., & Adis, C. (2015). Perceived organizational support: A meta-analytic evaluation of organizational support theory. *Journal of Management*, *43*(6), 1854–1884. https://doi.org/10.1177/0149206315575554

Lee, K. F. (2017). Automation, computerization and future employment in Singapore. *Journal of Southeast Asian Economies*, *34*(2), 388–399. https://www.jstor.org/stable/44684969

Li, J., Bonn, M. A., & Ye, B. H. (2019). Hotel employee's artificial intelligence and robotics awareness and its impact on turnover intention: The moderating roles of perceived organizational support and competitive psychological climate. *Tourism Management*, *73*, 172–181. https://doi.org/10.1016/j.tourman.2019.02.006

Lu, V. N., Wirtz, J., Kunz, W. H., Paluch, S., Gruber, T., Martins, A., & Patterson, P. G. (2020). Service robots, customers and service employees: What can we learn from the academic literature and where are the gaps? *Journal of Service Theory and Practice*, *30*(3), 361–391. https://doi.org/10.1108/jstp-04-2019-0088

Orpina, S., Jalil, N. I. A., & T'ng, S. T. (2022). Job satisfaction and turnover intention among Malaysian private university academics: Perceived organisational support as a moderator. *South East Asian Journal of Management*, *16*(1), 26–50. https://doi.org/10.21002/seam.v16i1.1002

Pallant, J. (2020). *SPSS survival manual: A step by step guide to data analysis using IBM SPSS* (7th ed.). Routledge.

Richter, A., Näswall, K., & Sverke, M. (2010). Job insecurity and its relation to work-family conflict: Mediation with a longitudinal data set. *Economic and Industrial Democracy*, *31*(2), 265–280. https://doi.org/10.1177/0143831x09358370

Riggle, R. J., Edmondson, D. R., & Hansen, J. C. (2009). A meta-analysis of the relationship between perceived organizational support and job outcomes: 20 years of research. *Journal of Business Research, 62*(10), 1027–1030. https://doi.org/10.1016/j.jbusres.2008.05.003

Sangaran, G., & Garg, A. (2012). Magnetizing & retaining the finest talent in hospitality sector, an empirical study of determinants of job satisfaction and effects on employee turnover in the hotels of Kuala Lumpur City Center. *International Journal of Hospitality and Tourism Systems, 5*(2), 1–8.

Sangaran, G., & Kumar, J. (2015). The effects of job satisfaction towards employee turnover in the hotel industry: A case study of hotels in Kuala Lumpur City Center. *Journal of Tourism and Hospitality, 04*(01), 1–5. https://doi.org/10.4172/2167-0269.1000142

Sekaran, U., & Bougie, R. (2016). *Research methods for business: A skill-building approach* (7th ed.). Wiley.

Shoss, M. K. (2017). Job insecurity: An integrative review and agenda for future research. *Journal of Management, 43*(6), 1911–1939. https://doi.org/10.1177/0149206317691574

Siciliano, B., & Khatib, O. (2018). Humanoid robots: Historical perspective, overview, and scope. In A. Goswami & P. Vadakkepat (Eds.), *Humanoid robotics: A reference* (pp. 3–8). Springer. https://doi.org/10.1007/978-94-007-6046-2_64

Sun, H., Lee, P., Law, R., & Zhong, L. (2020). The impact of cultural values on the acceptance of hotel technology adoption from the perspective of hotel employees. *Journal of Hospitality and Tourism Management, 44*, 61–69. https://doi.org/10.1016/j.jhtm.2020.04.012

Sverke, M., Hellgren, J., & Näswall, K. (2002). No security: A meta-analysis and review of job insecurity and its consequences. *Journal of Occupational Health Psychology, 7*(3), 242–264. https://doi.org/10.1037/1076-8998.7.3.242

Vrontis, D., Christofi, M., Pereira, V., Tarba, S. Y., Makrides, A., & Trichina, E. (2021). Artificial intelligence, robotics, advanced technologies and human resource management: A systematic review. *International Journal of Human Resource Management, 33*(6), 1237–1266. https://doi.org/10.1080/09585192.2020.1871398

Wang, J., Xing, Z., & Zhang, R. (2023). AI technology application and employee responsibility. *Humanities and Social Sciences Communications, 10*(1), 356. https://doi.org/10.1057/s41599-023-01843-3

Wang, Q., & Wang, C. (2020). Reducing turnover intention: Perceived organizational support for frontline employees. *Frontiers of Business Research in China, 14*(1). https://doi.org/10.1186/s11782-020-00074-6

Wu, T., Li, J., Wang, Y., & Zhang, R. (2023). The dualistic model of passion and the service quality of five-star hotel employees during the COVID-19 pandemic. *International Journal of Hospitality Management, 113*, 103519. https://doi.org/10.1016/j.ijhm.2023.103519

Wu, T., Li, J., & Wu, Y. J. (2022). Employees' job insecurity perception and unsafe behaviours in human-machine collaboration. *Management Decision, 60*(9), 2409–2432. https://doi.org/10.1108/md-09-2021-1257

Zhang, L.-X., Li, J.-M., Wang, L.-L., Mao, M.-Y., & Zhang, R.-X. (2023). How does the usage of robots in hotels affect employees' turnover intention? A double-edged sword study. *Journal of Hospitality and Tourism Management, 57*, 74–83. https://doi.org/10.1016/j.jhtm.2023.09.004

Zhang, W. (2009). *The motivations, constraints and decision-making of Beijing outbound tourists* [PhD dissertation]. The University of Waikato, Hamilton, New Zealand. https://hdl.handle.net/10289/3580

Chapter 13

Guest-Centric AI: A Theoretical Inquiry of Guest Experiences on the Integration of AI Chatbots Among Luxury Guest Accommodations

Chen Weimei, Rupam Konar and Neethiahnanthan Ari Ragavan

Taylor's University, Malaysia

Abstract

Luxury hotels prioritise exceptional, personalised service. Recently, the industry has seen a rise in the use of robots to enhance customer experiences, particularly through efficient check-ins. Consumers have responded positively, expecting more AI-driven services in luxury hotels. AI chatbots are becoming central to operations, helping guests with inquiries, room service, and travel guidance. However, research on AI chatbot features, such as adaptability, responsiveness, and reliability, remains limited, especially in the luxury hotel sector. Additionally, the influence of information quality (e.g. relevance, security, and privacy) on customer satisfaction and intention to continue using these services is underexplored. While AI chatbots have been studied in education, banking, and healthcare, their role in hospitality requires further investigation. This chapter develops a conceptual framework through a systematic review of relevant academic theories, focusing on the factors shaping guest experiences with AI in luxury hotels. By critically evaluating these theories, the chapter aims to enhance understanding of the relationship between AI technologies and guest satisfaction within luxury accommodations.

Keywords: Luxury hotels; theoretical inquiry; AI chatbots; guest-centric artificial intelligence; guest experience

The AI Metaverse Revolution: Transforming Multi-Business Scenarios (Volume 1), 193–204

Published under exclusive licence by Emerald Publishing Limited
doi:10.1108/978-1-83662-582-720251015

1. Introduction

With the growing popularity and development of artificial intelligence (AI) technology, the luxury guest accommodation industry is gradually increasing its interest in its application. Emerging AI chatbot technology is already playing an important role in luxury guest rooms. These chatbots could interact with guests and provide personalised services, answer questions, booking services, and other features (Parmar et al., 2019), thus enhancing the guest experience. This trend is backed by the continuous advancement of natural language processing (NLP) and machine learning in AI technology (Patel & Trivedi, 2020). Chatbots perform a variety of tasks such as order verification, shipment tracking, and resolving service queries. Several academic surveys have highlighted their continuous availability, autonomous knowledge acquisition, and system upgrades to improve guest satisfaction. With advances in machine learning and NLP, chatbots can understand user text or speech and engage in natural dialogue in areas such as education, finance, healthcare, and consulting (Aslam, 2023). Luxury hotels continue to integrate technology to enhance the customer experience and optimise operational efficiency from booking to departure through smart room control systems, smart security systems, and smart booking systems (Stringam & Gerdes, 2021). It is important to study the use of guest-centric AI chatbots in luxury guest accommodations and their impact on the guest experience.

In an era where the complexity of the customer experience demands closer examination, particularly in the context of AI chatbot integration, it is essential to address both the benefits and challenges of this technology. Although AI chatbots are thought to increase efficiency and save costs, studies have shown the low willingness of guests to use this technology and that most consumers prefer to interact with human agents (Balasubramanian & Konar, 2022; Cheng et al., 2022), and according to Press (2019), 87% of consumers prefer a human agent to a chatbot for interaction. However, the luxury guest accommodation industry has always been committed to delivering quality service and exceptional experiences to attract more guests and increase brand value. The introduction of AI technology has provided the luxury guest accommodation industry with a new service model and experience that allows for more efficient and personalised service (Nam et al., 2021). Therefore, an in-depth exploration of the application of guest-centric AI in luxury guest accommodation can help luxury guest accommodation companies better understand and utilise this new technology to improve service quality and competitiveness.

In addition, guest experience, as one of the core competencies in the luxury guest accommodation industry, directly affects guest satisfaction and loyalty. And AI chatbots, as a new type of interaction, have great potential for enhancing the guest experience (Sidaoui et al., 2020). Through in-depth research on the application of AI in luxury guest accommodation and its impact on the guest experience, it can provide more specific and effective guidance and suggestions for luxury guest accommodation enterprises to help them optimise their service processes, improve their service level, and thus increase guest satisfaction and loyalty.

Therefore, this study aims to explore the application of guest-centred AI chatbots in luxury guest accommodation and to analyse in depth the mechanism of their impact on the guest experience. Through the study of this important issue, it can not only promote the application and development of AI technology in the luxury guest accommodation industry but also provide theoretical support and practical guidance for improving guest experience and service quality and promote the development of the luxury guest accommodation industry in the direction of more intelligent, personalised, and quality.

2. Definition of Guest Experience

The concept of guest experience is crucial in the hospitality industry and covers the interactions and impressions of guests from before they check in to after they leave the hotel. The cumulative effect of each interaction guests has with the hotel and its team members during their stay determines how they feel about the overall experience. The guest experience is created by considering six dimensions: sensory, emotional, cognitive, practical, lifestyle, and relational, to provide a holistic and interconnected experience. It is a key indicator of quality service in the hospitality industry, influencing customer loyalty and attracting new guests (Ehimen et al., 2020). The guest experience specifically relates to guest interactions and encounters in the hotel environment. In the end-to-end lodging domain, factors such as aesthetic, social, escapist, behavioural, and sensory factors can significantly influence the guest experience, leading to loyalty and authenticity, and effectively understanding and controlling these aspects can increase guest satisfaction and loyalty and contribute to the prosperity of the industry.

3. Characteristics and Importance of the Guest Experience in Luxury Hotels

The primary focus of luxury hotels is to provide unique and luxurious accommodation options with first-class facilities to meet the needs of both corporate and leisure travellers. The importance of guest experience in luxury hotels cannot be overemphasised, as it has a profound impact on customer behaviour, satisfaction, and loyalty. The guest experience in luxury hotels is significantly influenced by various factors such as hedonism, ambience, escapism, personalisation, and convenience (Shahid & Paul, 2022). These factors have a significant impact on positive word-of-mouth and customers' willingness to return to the hotel. Furthermore, the integration of AI in luxury hotels through the implementation of personalised guest experiences and chatbots has helped improve operational efficiency and customer satisfaction, thus transforming the traditional hotel concept. Factors that significantly influence customer well-being, attitudes, and behavioural intentions in luxury hotels include the authenticity of the hospitality experience, perceived luxury value, and memorable travel experiences (Oguz, 2020). In conclusion, luxury hotels can improve visitor well-being and remain competitive by prioritising personalised experiences, optimising operations, and improving convenience.

4. Applicability of Existing Research Guest Experience in Luxury Hotels

Existing research on guest experience in luxury hotels highlights the significant impact of AI on improving guest satisfaction. Luxury hotels are committed to improving the guest experience by providing unique, luxurious accommodations and high-quality services to business and leisure travellers. In addition, the use of social media by luxury hotels plays a crucial role in engaging potential guests and improving communication strategies, especially during crises like the COVID-19 pandemic (Gómez-Suárez et al., 2023). Consumers seek emotional and sensory connections with luxury brands, emphasising the importance of personalised and memorable experiences in the hospitality industry. The study also highlights the importance of service quality factors such as quality of interaction, quality of physical environment, and quality of outcomes in influencing the customer experience in luxury hotels. Together, these findings emphasise the importance of AI, social media engagement, and service quality in shaping the luxury hotel guest experience (Buehring & O'Mahony, 2019). Therefore, existing research needs to be dug deeper and adapted to the specific needs of luxury guest accommodation.

5. The Evolution of Hotel AI Chatbots

While AI is one of the major sources of innovation and is rapidly gaining popularity across a wide range of services, it is also one of the areas of computer science that can improve the efficiency of business in the hospitality industry. AI is a major driver of innovation and is rapidly gaining popularity across various services. As a key area of computer science, it has the potential to significantly enhance business efficiency in the hospitality industry, particularly through advancements in AI technology and the growing adoption of AI chatbots. Initially, the application of AI in the hospitality industry focused on back-end operations such as revenue management and predictive analytics (Grobbelaar & Verma, 2024). However, as AI chatbots utilise NLP and machine-learning techniques to understand user input and provide relevant responses, they bring many advantages to the hospitality industry, including features such as 24/7 service availability, fast response times, and multilingual services (Lukanova & Ilieva, 2019). In recent years, AI-powered chatbots have become more sophisticated as language models and datasets have advanced, becoming an integral part of a variety of hospitality environments.

The hospitality industry is increasingly integrating AI into its operations, products, and services, and AI has the potential to improve efficiency, enhance the customer experience, and create new business opportunities. Many hotels use chatbots for online customer service. These chatbots can answer frequently asked questions, help with the booking process, or suggest activities and amenities. For example, Hilton Hotels & Resorts' Connie (an intelligent entity like Apple's Siri) performs a variety of tasks, such as greeting guests in different languages, recommending interesting places and attractions, answering guest queries, refining responses based on the frequency of guest interactions, and assisting with check-in

(Solomon, 2016). Wynn Las Vegas is integrating Amazon Echo to digitise hotel rooms, providing guests with voice control of room lighting, temperature, TVs, and curtains, in addition to a variety of amenities using Echo's personal assistant service (Wynn Las Vegas, 2016). Clarion Hotel Amaranten in Stockholm also uses Amazon Echo as a chatbot butler to help guests book taxis, provide room service, assist with online information, and more (Maruti Techlabs, 2018).

6. Functionality and Importance of AI Chatbots in Luxury Hotels

AI chatbots play a variety of roles in luxury guest rooms, for example, the AI chatbot acts as a service assistant to provide round-the-clock service support to guests. It can answer guests' questions, provide information queries, and process reservations and orders, among other services (Buhalis & Cheng, 2020). It can also play the role of a personalised butler, based on guests' historical data and preferences, the AI chatbot can provide personalised recommendations and suggestions to guests, such as recommending restaurants, attractions, and shopping (Pillai & Sivathanu, 2020). However, the functions of AI chatbots in luxury hotels also have diversity, the first is the query information function, and guests can query the hotel facilities, services, room layout, and other information through the AI chatbot to understand the hotel situation in advance. Secondly, it is the question-and-answer function, when guests encounter problems, they can ask the chatbot, such as cannot find the room and need to delay the checkout, the robot will answer and provide solutions in time. As well as providing guests with personalised service functions, according to the guest's preferences and preferences, the chatbot can recommend restaurants, activities, attractions, etc., to enhance the guest experience. In addition, chatbots can be integrated with other smart devices such as smart home systems to provide guests with more convenient control and experience (Parmar et al., 2019). To enhance the guest experience, AI chatbots can interact with guests, and the AI chatbots in some luxury guest accommodations support voice interaction, allowing guests to communicate with the bots through voice commands to enhance the interaction experience. Text communication and interaction is also possible, providing guests with functions such as asking questions and placing bookings; quick response is also a unique feature of AI chatbots. Overall, AI chatbots play multiple roles in luxury guest accommodations, providing rich and diverse service functions. Its interaction modes and experiences with guests are rich and diverse, and it can provide personalised, convenient, and fast services to enhance the overall level of guest experience.

7. Factors Affecting the Level of Guest-aware AI Chatbot Integration

Guests' perception of AI chatbots is influenced by various factors related to the level of system quality, service quality, and information quality. Customer's perception of service quality is the key to determine the success of chatbot services (Liu et al., 2023).

Service quality refers to the extent to which the services provided by a company can meet customer expectations. In luxury guest accommodation, good service quality is the key to enhancing the guest experience. Previous studies have shown that there is a close relationship between service quality and guest experience (Ali et al., 2021). Quality service enhances guest satisfaction and loyalty and improves the overall guest experience. The mechanisms influencing service quality of AI chatbots include assurance, reliability, interactivity, and understandability.

Assurance: Professional problem solving and communication skills of AI chatbots when helping customers solve problems. If chatbots can provide professional and trustworthy services, then user expectations of chatbot services are expected to be widely met. Users are significantly more satisfied when they perceive an AI chatbot to have higher assurance (Kushwaha et al., 2021).

Reliability: The ability of AI chatbots to perform promised services reliably and accurately. AI chatbots are reliable because they deliver software-driven services consistently. AI chatbots are immune to fatigue, emotion, and bias. Advanced deep learning chatbots can predict guest preferences and improve service quality over time (Misischia et al., 2022).

Interactivity: Interaction and engagement between the user and the AI-powered chatbot system, such as booking and checking out functions that mimic human dialogue. AI chatbots' human-like speech is a popular feature. Real-time chatbots respond. Chatbots' 24/7 availability assures constant and timely assistance, thereby improving the guest experience. Chatbots evaluate and learn from vast volumes of user-generated data to personalise guest encounters in luxury hotels. They answer questions and make appointments in real time (Jiang et al., 2022).

Understandability: AI chatbots can understand the meaning of content or commands sent by customers in voice or text form. Customers want AI chatbots to understand their queries and capture their emotions in the discussion. After converting the voice system to text and back, the AI chatbot's voice- and text-processing procedures are the same, which can satisfy diverse guests. Users are more likely to acknowledge that the chatbot meets their original expectations if most of its information is understandable (Li et al., 2021).

System quality refers to the characteristics of the AI chatbot's system such as availability, responsiveness, and adaptability. In luxury guest accommodations, good quality of the AI system can enhance the guest experience. Previous studies have found a significant positive relationship between system quality and guest experience.

Availability: Involves the ease with which a user can access a chatbot in the process of completing a task. Chatbots' direct and fast access to information is their main advantage in marketing services. Additionally, AI chatbots improve customer service efficiency, agility, accessibility, reliability, predictability, and transferability. The success of a chatbot depends on the quality of the system. Meeting customer expectations requires 24/7 availability and delivering accurate information at the right time. Users stated that the information system should work perfectly on all Internet connections (Trivedi, 2019).

Responsiveness: Timeliness of service and length of the system's response time. The value of AI chatbots also comes from the quality and appropriateness of the response. AI chatbots are highly effective in delivering prompt responses, and research has shown that measuring the perceived quality of AI chatbot service in hotels, while guests appreciate the efficiency and immediacy of chatbot responses (Gursoy et al., 2019).

Adaptability: AI chatbots ensure that chatbots can provide reliable assistance in all situations. Chatbots can be embedded into various devices in different scenarios to adapt to changing environmental functions. For example, chatbots can be embedded in travel apps, hotel booking platforms and airport self-services to provide tourists with information, advice and booking services. Additionally, chatbots can be embedded into company websites, apps, and social media pages to provide real-time customer support and Q&A services. This helps reduce customer support costs and improve customer satisfaction. When a guest makes a reservation through a chatbot, the hotel can send messages to assist the guest before, during, and after check-out (Buhalis & Cheng, 2020).

Information quality refers to the relevance and completeness of the information provided by the AI chatbot to the guest during the service, the security of the information at the first level, and privacy guarantees, among other characteristics. In luxury guest accommodations, information quality is critical to the guest experience. Previous studies have shown that there is a strong relationship between information quality and guest experience.

Relevance: An AI chatbot provides relevant information and content for a customer's question or command. After spending time and effort on technology and services, users anticipate highly relevant information. The user may lose trust in the chatbot and seek other information if it gives irrelevant or erroneous information. Relevance measures system data quality. Information that meets users' needs is high-quality. The quality of the information obtained determines their chatbot satisfaction (Nguyen et al., 2021).

Completeness: Access to credible, accurate, comprehensive, and timely information can significantly enhance user satisfaction. The chatbot's crippled, partial, and erroneous information will harm client satisfaction with the hotel. Some clients constantly ask the AI chatbot for a response and complain about the service. Thus, chatbots' complete information can boost client satisfaction (Ashfaq et al., 2020).

Security/privacy: The degree of security and protection of customer information of AI chatbots. With the rise of computer power and technologies like machine learning and NLP, information systems like chatbots have collected, stored, and processed vast amounts of data, including private and sensitive information. Customers care about personal data security and want service providers to keep chatbot interactions secure (Liu et al., 2023).

8. Theoretical Investigation: The Impact of AI Chatbot Integration on Guest Satisfaction

AI chatbots play an important role in improving service quality (e.g. assurance, reliability, interactivity, and comprehensibility) and ultimately impacting guest satisfaction in the hospitality industry (Liu et al., 2023). AI applications such as personalised guest experience, chatbots, and virtual assistants can improve guest satisfaction in luxury hotels by streamlining operations and providing personalised services (Mei et al., 2024). The combination of AI with staff service quality influences the overall service quality assessment, customer satisfaction, and loyalty in hotels. Service quality is a key determinant of guest satisfaction, and the dimensions of assurance, reliability, interaction, and understanding significantly affect guest satisfaction in hotels. Therefore, the use of AI to improve service quality while maintaining a balance of human interaction is essential to ensure high levels of guest satisfaction in the hospitality industry (Liu et al., 2023).

Furthermore, AI chatbot system quality, including adaptability, responsiveness, and availability, significantly affects guest interactions and behaviours in the hospitality industry (Liu et al., 2023). These dimensions positively influence communication quality, interaction quality, and willingness to pay for hotel services (Chi & Nam, 2022). The service quality of AI chatbots influences customer loyalty through perceived value, trust, satisfaction, and loyalty, highlighting the importance of system quality in building long-term relationships with guests. Maintaining and improving chatbot quality is critical due to the challenges of anticipating user requests and language changes over time, emphasising the need for continuous improvement and adaptation to meet guest expectations and provide a seamless experience (Ackerman et al., 2022).

The impact of AI chatbot message quality (e.g. relevance, completeness, and security/privacy) on customer satisfaction is an important aspect to consider in the customer service domain (Chang et al., 2024; Liu et al., 2023). Customer satisfaction has the potential to influence customer behaviour, including the likelihood of them making repeat purchases and revisiting a website. In addition, enhanced delight can be achieved by considering factors such as the degree of relevance and completeness. Ensuring the accuracy and relevance of the information provided by AI chatbots relies heavily on the importance of data quality. The importance of data quality lies in its accuracy, comprehensiveness, reliability, relevance, and timeliness. Similarly, Liu et al. (2023) emphasised the importance of variables such as accuracy, comprehensiveness, coherence, reliability, and soundness in assessing data quality. In addition, the characteristics of AI chatbots can have an impact on consumer relationships. Exploring the process by which AI systems analyse data and derive knowledge from it to achieve specific goals, there is a correlation between information quality and pleasure and chatbot trust, but the extent of the effect may be attenuated (Atlan, 2023; Balasubramanian et al., 2022).

9. Conclusion

Luxury guest rooms increasingly use AI chatbots. Research has examined how this integration affects guests. In the literature, chatbot integration is discussed in terms of service quality (assurance, reliability, interactivity, and comprehensibility), system quality (adaptability, responsiveness, and availability), information quality (relevance, completeness, and security/privacy), and guest satisfaction. The following key findings and perspectives are derived by analysing the importance and impact mechanisms of service quality, system quality, and information quality dimensions on guest experience, as well as AI chatbot roles, functions, and interaction patterns in luxury guest accommodations.

Firstly, service quality, system quality, and information quality are important factors influencing guest experience. Chatbots meet the personalised experience needs of luxury guests by providing personalised, convenient, and efficient services that enhance brand recognition and loyalty. In addition, the effectiveness of chatbot integration depends on several factors, including technological maturity, the human–machine interaction experience, and privacy protection. Only when all these aspects are better addressed can a positive impact on the guest experience be truly realised. Guest acceptance of chatbot integration varies, and some guests may be less interested or sceptical due to unfamiliarity with the new technology or personal preferences (Konar et al., 2024).

Secondly, as an emerging technology, AI chatbots play the role of service assistants and personalised housekeepers in luxury guest accommodation, providing guests with information enquiries, booking services, question answers, and personalised recommendations. AI chatbots interact with guests in a variety of modes, including text and voice interactions, and can provide instant responses and personalised services to enhance guests' satisfaction and experience.

Finally, the positive impact of AI chatbot integration on luxury guest accommodations is widely recognised in the literature, but the challenges of AI chatbots in terms of technological maturity and user experience are also noted. Some studies conclude that chatbot integration can enhance the guest experience, while others conclude that guest acceptance varies, and more research is needed to explore this.

Therefore, future research could delve further into the specific mechanisms by which service quality, system quality, and information quality affect the guest experience to reveal the principles and patterns behind them. Researchers can work on optimising the algorithms and techniques of AI chatbots to improve their intelligence and service levels to meet changing guest needs. Future researchers can explore personalised service models based on big data and AI technology to provide more accurate personalised services by analysing guests' preferences and behaviours to further enhance the guest experience. While promoting the application of AI technology, it is also necessary to consider the social and ethical issues it may bring, such as privacy protection and data security. Future research should focus on exploring and solving these aspects.

References

Ackerman, S., Anaby-Tavor, A., Farchi, E., Goldbraich, E., Kour, G., Rabinovich, E., Raz, O., Route, S., Zalmanovici, M., & Zwerdling, N. (2022). *High-quality conversational systems*. http://arxiv.org/abs/2204.13043

Ali, B. J., Gardi, B., Othman, B. J., Ahmed, S. A., Ismael, N. B., Hamza, P. A., Aziz, H. M., Sabir, B. Y., & Anwar, G. (2021). Hotel service quality: The impact of service quality on customer satisfaction in hospitality. *International Journal of Engineering, Business and Management*, *5*(3), 14–28. https://doi.org/10.22161/ijebm.5.3.2

Ashfaq, M., Yun, J., Yu, S., & Loureiro, S. M. C. (2020). I, Chatbot: Modeling the determinants of users' satisfaction and continuance intention of AI-powered service agents. *Telematics and Informatics*, *54*, 101473. https://doi.org/10.1016/j.tele.2020.101473

Aslam, F. (2023). The impact of artificial intelligence on chatbot technology: A study on the current advancements and leading innovations. *European Journal of Technology*, *7*(3), 62–72. https://doi.org/10.47672/ejt.1561

Atlan. (2023, September 6). *Achieving high data quality during cloud data migrations: A 2024 guide!* Retrieved April 1, 2024, from Atlan website: https://atlan.com/high-data-quality-during-cloud-data-migrations/

Balasubramanian, K., & Konar, R. (2022). Moving forward with augmented reality menu: Changes in food consumption behaviour patterns. *Journal of Innovation in Hospitality and Tourism*, *11*(3), 91–96.

Balasubramanian, K., Kunasekaran, P., Konar, R., & Sakkthivel, A. M. (2022). Integration of augmented reality (AR) and virtual reality (VR) as marketing communications channels in the hospitality and tourism service sector. In *Marketing communications and brand development in emerging markets Volume II: Insights for a changing world* (pp. 55–79). Springer International Publishing.

Buehring, J., & O'Mahony, B. (2019). Designing memorable guest experiences: Development of constructs and value generating factors in luxury hotels. *Journal of Hospitality and Tourism Insights*, *2*(4), 358–376. https://doi.org/10.1108/JHTI-11-2018-0077

Buhalis, D., & Cheng, E. S. Y. (2020, January 08–10). *Exploring the use of chatbots in hotels: technology providers' perspective* (pp. 231–242). Information and communication technologies in tourism 2020: Proceedings of the international conference in surrey, United Kingdom. Springer.

Chang, J. Y. S., Konar, R., Cheah, J. H., & Lim, X. J. (2024). Does privacy still matter in smart technology experience? A conditional mediation analysis. *Journal of Marketing Analytics*, *12*(1), 71–86.

Cheng, X., Zhang, X., Cohen, J., & Mou, J. (2022). Human vs. AI: Understanding the impact of anthropomorphism on consumer response to chatbots from the perspective of trust and relationship norms. *Information Processing & Management*, *59*(3), 102940. https://doi.org/10.1016/j.ipm.2022.102940

Chi, N. T. K., & Nam, V. H. (2022). The impact of AI chatbot on long-term relationships between customers and hotels. *VNU University of Economics and Business*, *2*(6), 1–10. https://doi.org/10.57110/vnujeb.v2i6.123.

Ehimen, S., Ikechukwu Uduji, J., & Christian Ugwuanyi, C. (2020). *Hotel guests' experience, satisfaction and revisit intentions: An emerging market perspective*. https://doi.org/10.46222/ajhtl.19770720-108

Gómez-Suárez, M., Veloso, M., & Quinones, M. (2023). *The influence of the Covid-19 pandemic on social media engagement of luxury hotels* (pp. 134–141). National brand and private label marketing conference. Springer.

Grobbelaar, W., & Verma, A. (2024). Future Employments in the Hospitality Industry. In *Artificial Intelligence for Smart Technology in the Hospitality and Tourism Industry* (1st Edition, pp. 77–104). CRC Press.

Gursoy, D., Chi, O. H., Lu, L., & Nunkoo, R. (2019). Consumers acceptance of artificially intelligent (AI) device use in service delivery. *International Journal of Information Management*, *49*, 157–169. https://doi.org/10.1016/j.ijinfomgt.2019.03.008

Jiang, H., Cheng, Y., Yang, J., & Gao, S. (2022). AI-powered chatbot communication with customers: Dialogic interactions, satisfaction, engagement, and customer behavior. *Computers in Human Behavior*, *134*, 107329. https://doi.org/10.1016/j.chb.2022.107329

Konar, R., Bhutia, L. D., Fuchs, K., & Balasubramanian, K. (2024). Role of virtual reality technology in sustainable travel behaviour and engagement among millennials. In *Promoting responsible tourism with digital platforms* (pp. 1–19). IGI Global.

Kushwaha, A. K., Kumar, P., & Kar, A. K. (2021). What impacts customer experience for B2B enterprises on using AI-enabled chatbots? Insights from Big data analytics. *Industrial Marketing Management, 98*, 207–221. https://doi.org/10.1016/j.indmarman.2021.08.011

Li, L., Lee, K. Y., Emokpae, E., & Yang, S.-B. (2021). What makes you continuously use chatbot services? Evidence from Chinese online travel agencies. *Electronic Markets, 31*, 1–25. https://doi.org/10.1007/s12525-020-00454-z

Liu, Y. L., Hu, B., Yan, W., & Lin, Z. (2023). Can chatbots satisfy me? A mixed-method comparative study of satisfaction with task-oriented chatbots in mainland China and Hong Kong. *Computers in Human Behavior, 143*, 107716. https://doi.org/10.1016/j.chb.2023.107716

Lukanova, G., & Ilieva, G. (2019). Robots, artificial intelligence, and service automation in hotels. In *Robots, artificial intelligence, and service automation in travel, tourism and hospitality* (pp. 157–183). Emerald Publishing Limited. https://doi.org/10.1108/978-1-78756-687-320191009

Maruti Techlabs. (2018, February 15). How hotels are using artificial intelligence to provide an awesome user experience – Part 2. *Chatbots Magazine*. https://chatbotsmagazine.com/how-hotels-are-using-artificial-intelligence-to-provide-an-awesome-user-experience-part-2-85b2a6008578

Mei, C. W., Konar, R., & Kumar, J. (2024). The role of AI chatbots in transforming guest engagement and marketing in hospitality. In V. Nadda, P. Tyagi, A. Singh, & V. Singh (Eds.), *Integrating AI-driven technologies into service marketing* (pp. 595–620). IGI Global. Scientific Publishing. https://doi.org/10.4018/979-8-3693-7122-0.ch029

Misischia, C. V., Poecze, F., & Strauss, C. (2022). Chatbots in customer service: Their relevance and impact on service quality. *Procedia Computer Science, 201*(C), 421–428. https://doi.org/10.1016/j.procs.2022.03.055

Nam, K., Dutt, C. S., Chathoth, P., Daghfous, A., & Khan, M. S. (2021). The adoption of artificial intelligence and robotics in the hotel industry: Prospects and challenges. *Electronic Markets, 31*(3), 553–574. https://doi.org/10.1007/s12525-020-00442-3

Nguyen, D. M., Chiu, Y. T. H., & Le, H. D. (2021). Determinants of continuance intention towards banks' chatbot services in Vietnam: A necessity for sustainable development. *Sustainability (Switzerland), 13*(14), 7625. https://doi.org/10.3390/su13147625

Oguz, U. (2020). *The role of authenticity in the luxury hotel experience: A mixed-methods study of the hotel sector in the United Kingdom*. https://doi.org/10.23889/SUthesis.59516

Parmar, S., Meshram, M., Parmar, P., Patel, M., & Desai, P. (2019). Smart hotel using intelligent chatbot: A review. *International Journal of Scientific Research in Computer Science, Engineering and Information Technology*, 5(2), 823–829.

Patel, N., & Trivedi, S. (2020). *Leveraging predictive modeling, machine learning personalization, NLP customer support, and AI chatbots to increase customer loyalty*. https://www.researchberg.com/index.php/eqme/article/view/46

Pillai, R., & Sivathanu, B. (2020). Adoption of AI-based chatbots for hospitality and tourism. *International Journal of Contemporary Hospitality Management, 32*(10), 3199–3226.

Press, G. (2019). *AI Stats news: Chatbots increase sales by 67% but 87% of consumers prefer humans*. https://www.forbes.com/sites/gilpress/2019/11/25/ai-stats-news-chatbots-increase-sales-by-67-but-87-of-consumers-prefer-humans/?sh=2f8e2b4348a3

Shahid, S., & Paul, J. (2022). Examining guests' experience in luxury hotels: evidence from an emerging market. *Journal of Marketing Management, 38*(13–14), 1278–1306. https://doi.org/10.1080/0267257X.2022.2085768

Sidaoui, K., Jaakkola, M., & Burton, J. (2020). AI feel you: Customer experience assessment via chatbot interviews. *Journal of Service Management, 31*(4), 745–766. https://doi.org/10.1108/JOSM-11-2019-0341

Solomon, M. (2016). *Technology invades hospitality industry: Hilton Robot, domino delivery droid, Ritz-Carlton Mystique*. https://www.forbes.com/sites/micahsolomon/2016/03/18/high-tech-hospitality-hilton-robot-concierge-dominos-delivery-droid-ritz-carlton-mystique/?sh=5413203d120b

Stringam, B. B., & Gerdes, J. H. (2021). Hotel and guest room technology. *University of South Florida (USF) M3 Publishing*, *17*(9781732127593), 6.

Trivedi, J. (2019). Examining the customer experience of using banking chatbots and its impact on brand love: The moderating role of perceived risk. *Journal of Internet Commerce*, *18*(1), 91–111. https://doi.org/10.1080/15332861.2019.1567188

Wynn Las Vegas. (2016). *Wynn Las Vegas announces the addition of Amazon echo to all hotel rooms*. https://www.prnewswire.com/news-releases/wynn-las-vegas-announces-the-addition-of-amazon-echo-to-all-hotel-rooms-300377995.html

Chapter 14

Business Resilience via Forward-Looking Approach: Metaverse as a Potential Innovation

Sneha Biswas and Rituparna Chatterjee

Pailan College of Management & Technology, Kolkata, India

Abstract

Even in difficult times, business sustainability depends on expanding deliberately. COVID-19 has made conditions difficult while rendering it necessary to investigate cutting-edge strategies for corporate sustainability. Using modern technologies in an organization concept has grown essential in this situation. Under these circumstances, including the forward-looking approach (FLA) into the company model will become essential. Metaverse is a rapidly developing global technology that offers clients cutting-edge amenities at a higher return on investment (HROI). It is discovered throughout an investigation of the futuristic technology known as metaverse as well as its potential effects on humanity. In addition to evaluating consumer benefits, the study evaluated commercial prospects for shareholders along with entrepreneurs. The study identifies the variables that will shape the metaverse's future and makes predictions regarding its complete promised deployment in various businesses. It should be noted that the survey gathered responses from people all across the world, including India, who varied in their age groups and degree of familiarity with upcoming technologies. The feedback indicates that in order to have a more significant effect as well as be used more effectively, these cutting-edge technologies must be made widely accessible at a reasonable cost and also raise a great deal of user consciousness. This document outlines

The AI Metaverse Revolution: Transforming Multi-Business Scenarios (Volume 1), 205–216

Published under exclusive licence by Emerald Publishing Limited
doi:10.1108/978-1-83662-582-720251016

the metaverse's predicted business opportunity along with timelines gives interpretation methods.

Keywords: Forward-looking approach; metaverse; higher return on investment; modern technologies; consumer consciousness

1. Introduction

In the face of unprecedented challenges brought about by the COVID-19 pandemic, the pursuit of business sustainability has become increasingly paramount (Das et al., 2022). Despite the adversity, the imperative to expand deliberately remains, compelling organizations to explore innovative strategies for corporate resilience and growth (Jamader, Chowdhury, & Shankar Jha, 2023). In this era of uncertainty and rapid digital transformation, the integration of modern technologies into organizational frameworks emerges as a critical imperative for navigating the evolving business landscape (Jamader, 2022). Amidst this backdrop, the concept of the metaverse has garnered significant attention as a burgeoning global technology with the potential to revolutionize various facets of human interaction and enterprise operations (Das et al., 2019). The metaverse, characterized by its immersive digital environments and interconnected virtual spaces, holds promise for delivering cutting-edge amenities to consumers while offering higher returns on investment (HROI) for businesses. This research paper delves into the exploration of the metaverse and its potential implications for corporate sustainability and growth (Jamader et al., 2022). In Fig. 14.1 by adopting a FLA and incorporating the metaverse into the organizational model, businesses can position themselves strategically to leverage the transformative power of this futuristic technology (Jamader et al., 2019). Drawing upon insights from a comprehensive investigation into the metaverse, this paper evaluates its prospective impact on humanity and assesses its commercial viability for shareholders and entrepreneurs (Nayak et al., 2022). Through the analysis of diverse variables shaping the future of the metaverse, including consumer preferences, technological advancements, and market dynamics, this study endeavors to delineate the anticipated business opportunities and timelines associated with its widespread adoption across industries (Jamader, Chowdhury, & Shankar Jha, 2023). Crucially, the research methodology employed in this study encompasses a global perspective, gathering responses from individuals worldwide, including diverse demographic groups and varying degrees of familiarity with emerging technologies (Jamader et al., 2021).

The findings underscore the importance of democratizing access to cutting-edge technologies and enhancing user awareness to maximize their impact and efficacy (Jamader, Chowdhury, & Shankar Jha, 2023). By providing a comprehensive overview of the predicted business opportunities within the metaverse and elucidating various data collection, analysis, and interpretation methodologies, this paper aims to contribute to the discourse on corporate sustainability in the digital age and inform strategic decision-making for businesses navigating the complexities of the modern marketplace (Sagayam et al., 2022).

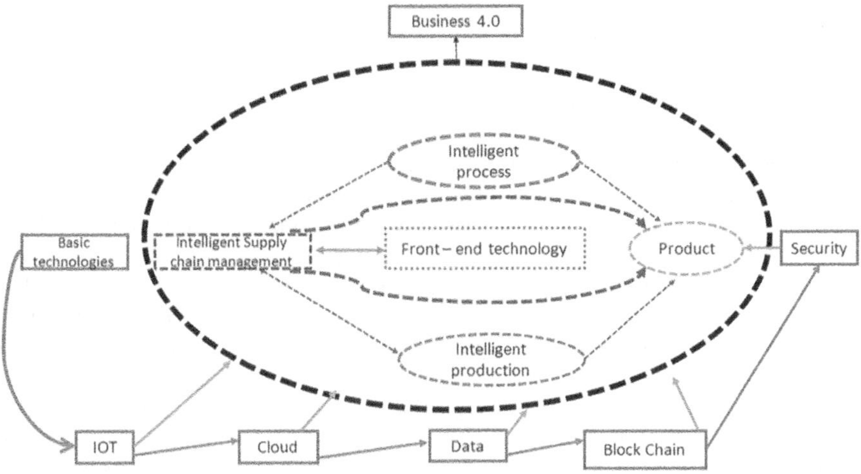

Fig. 14.1. Forward-looking Approach.

2. Literature Review

2.1. Understanding Business Resilience

The ability of an organization to be resilient in the face of environment that is always shifting and unpredictable has emerged as a crucial concern for businesses that are concerned with achieving long-term success (Jamader et al., 2024).

- *The dynamic capabilities and resilience of the organization:*

In the groundbreaking 2007 book, David J. Teece (2007) redefines our understanding of organizational resilience, spotlighting the transformative influence of dynamic capabilities. Dynamic capabilities, characterized by an organization's adaptive prowess, integration abilities, and adeptness at reconfiguring internal and external competencies, emerge as the linchpin for effectively navigating the complexities of contemporary business environments. Teece challenges the conventional static portrayal of resilience, presenting it as an ongoing and dynamic process rather than a fixed state. He underscores the criticality of flexibility and adaptability in building organizational resilience, asserting that businesses endowed with the capability to flexibly modify their resource base are better positioned to weather disruptions and seize emerging opportunities. Teece's alignment with the resource-based view underscores the significance of dynamic capabilities in managing and manipulating valuable resources, fostering continuous adaptation and innovation. Importantly, Teece's insights extend to strategic management, highlighting that organizations prioritizing the development of dynamic capabilities not only react effectively to external disruptions but also proactively shape and influence their business environment, ultimately creating a sustainable competitive advantage. In conclusion, Teece's work propels organizations toward an adaptive and proactive stance, emphasizing the continuous cultivation of dynamic capabilities as a fundamental strategy for sustained success amid the turbulence of the contemporary business landscape.

- *Enhancing organizational resilience through supply chain strategies:*

In their 2021 article, Ali, Mahfouz, et al. (2021) and Ali, Suleiman, et al. (2021). delve into the intersection of supply chain robustness and organizational resilience, emphasizing the intrinsic link between the two components in contemporary business dynamics. The research underscores the vital role of flexible supply chain strategies in mitigating disruptions and enhancing overall business resilience. The findings stress that the architecture of supply chains should prioritize cooperation and flexibility, moving away from rigid models to foster adaptability in the face of changing circumstances. Cooperative partnerships and agile frameworks emerge as pivotal elements, advocating for strong collaborative ties with suppliers and stakeholders. The study's implications extend to supply chain management practices, urging organizations to proactively design and adjust supply chain architectures to align with the dynamic business environment. Overall, Naim and Tan's insights provide a roadmap for organizations to not only fortify supply chains against disruptions but also contribute significantly to enduring organizational resilience.

- *The management of risk and the capacity for change:*

Niu and Zou (2019) research establishes a critical link between risk management and organizational resilience, contending that an effective risk management system is indispensable for an organization's capacity to endure unforeseen challenges. Emphasizing the integral role of risk management in building resilience, their study advocates for a comprehensive strategy that involves recognizing, analyzing, and proactively reducing risks. Zou and Ward challenge the notion that resilience can exist independently of a well-structured risk management approach, asserting that an organization's ability to withstand disruptions is intricately tied to its proactive management of potential threats. The research underscores the importance of preparing organizations for unanticipated problems, urging businesses to adopt an anticipatory stance through rigorous risk identification and analysis. In navigating today's complex and uncertain landscape, Zou and Ward's insights guide organizations toward an integrated approach that not only safeguards against risks but actively contributes to enduring adaptability and sustainability.

- *The relationship between organizational culture and resilience:*

Brown (2022) explained the pivotal role of organizational culture as a mediator in the development of resilience within an organization. Their research underscores that a culture characterized by supportiveness and adaptability significantly contributes to an organization's ability to rebound from temporary setbacks. The findings accentuate the critical importance of fostering a resilient mindset throughout all levels of the organization. This perspective emphasizes that beyond structural and procedural considerations, the intangible fabric of organizational culture plays a vital role in shaping the collective response to challenges. The study advocates for the cultivation of a culture that not only supports its members during times of adversity but also promotes adaptability, acknowledging the dynamic nature of the contemporary business landscape. Acknowledging and actively fostering such a resilient culture emerges as a strategic imperative for organizations seeking to enhance their overall capacity for recovery and sustained success.

2.2. Exploring FLAs in Business

In the dynamic and uncertain landscape of today's business environment, FLAs have gained prominence as essential strategies for organizational success.

- *Sensemaking in organizations:*

Karl E. Weick's (2001) seminal work on sensemaking in organizations holds pivotal significance in unraveling the intricacies of how organizations comprehend and interpret their environments. Weick's exploration delves into the notion that FLAs necessitate an ongoing process of sensemaking. According to Weick, this continuous sensemaking allows organizations to adeptly interpret signals from their surroundings, facilitating a proactive stance in shaping their future. By emphasizing the importance of understanding and making sense of the evolving context, Weick's insights underscore the dynamic nature of organizational adaptation. This conceptual framework has become foundational in strategic management, guiding organizations toward a more responsive and anticipatory approach in navigating the complexities of the business landscape. Weick's work resonates as a critical guide for organizations seeking to not only comprehend their present circumstances but also actively engage in shaping their trajectories forward.

- *Scenario planning and future preparedness:*

Peter Schwartz's (2012) influential work on scenario planning in 2012 has significantly shaped how organizations approach future preparedness. Schwartz advocates for scenario planning as a strategic tool that empowers businesses to navigate an uncertain future effectively. This methodology prompts organizations to envision and explore diverse, yet plausible, future scenarios. By doing so, businesses gain a more comprehensive understanding of potential trajectories and uncertainties. The core idea is to develop strategies that prove robust across multiple possible futures, fostering adaptability and resilience. Schwartz's contribution underscores the proactive role of scenario planning in strategic management, providing organizations with a structured framework to anticipate and respond to the dynamic nature of the business environment. This approach becomes particularly vital in an era marked by rapid changes, uncertainty, and the need for organizations to be agile in their response to emerging challenges and opportunities.

- *Innovation and proactive adaptation:*

Clayton M. Christensen's (2013) groundbreaking work has been instrumental in reshaping perspectives on innovation and proactive adaptation in business. Christensen introduces the concept of disruptive innovation, arguing that successful organizations must not only embrace innovation but also proactively disrupt their own established models. The core idea is to anticipate industry shifts and technological advancements, recognizing that clinging to existing practices may lead to obsolescence. Christensen's FLA urges businesses to be proactive in exploring and adopting disruptive technologies and business models, enabling them to stay ahead of the competition. By advocating for a mindset that actively seeks to challenge and reinvent existing paradigms, Christensen's work continues to influence strategic thinking, encouraging organizations to navigate the complexities of a rapidly evolving business landscape through innovation and proactive adaptation.

- *Big data analytics for future insights:*

In their influential work, Viktor Mayer-Schönberger and Kenneth Cukier (2013) underscore the transformative role of big data analytics in shaping FLAs for businesses. The authors highlight how organizations leverage advanced data analytics to extract valuable insights from massive datasets, enabling a deeper understanding of emerging trends and patterns. The emphasis on big data in this context reflects a paradigm shift where businesses move beyond traditional methods to embrace data-driven decision-making processes. By harnessing the power of big data analytics, organizations can anticipate future developments, make informed strategic decisions, and gain a competitive edge in a rapidly evolving business landscape. Mayer-Schönberger and Cukier's work continues to emphasize the pivotal role of big data in providing organizations with the tools to proactively navigate and capitalize on the wealth of information available for future insights.

- *The fourth transformation (Scoble & Israel, 2016):*

In "The Fourth Transformation" (2016), Robert Scoble and Shel Israel provide illuminating insights into the transformative impact of augmented reality (AR) and virtual reality (VR), technologies that serve as pivotal components in the evolution of the metaverse. The book delves into the profound changes brought about by AR and VR, emphasizing their influence across various industries. Scoble and Israel explore how these technologies are not only reshaping traditional sectors but also creating new and innovative opportunities, particularly in fields such as education, healthcare, and entertainment. By showcasing real-world examples and potential applications, the authors contribute to a deeper understanding of the broader implications of AR and VR in the context of the metaverse. "The Fourth Transformation" acts as a comprehensive guide, offering readers valuable perspectives on the intersection of immersive technologies and the evolving landscape of the metaverse, shaping discussions around the potential future trajectory of virtual and augmented realities.

- *Metaverse and its implications for businesses (Kumar et al., 2023):*

In the recent research paper titled "Metaverse and its implications for businesses" (Kumar et al., 2023), Kumar and colleagues delve into the potential ramifications of the metaverse for businesses. The study systematically explores how companies are adapting their strategies to incorporate the metaverse into their operations. By examining cases of successful metaverse integration, the research sheds light on practical implementations and identifies challenges that organizations may encounter on this transformative journey. Kumar et al.'s work contributes to the evolving understanding of the metaverse's impact on businesses, providing valuable insights for practitioners, strategists, and scholars seeking to comprehend and navigate the implications of this emerging virtual space.

- *Metaverse and the future of work (Wang et al., 2022):*

In the academic study titled "Metaverse and the future of work" (Wang et al., 2022), the authors delve into the transformative impact of the metaverse on the future of work. The research investigates how virtual environments and immersive technologies within the metaverse have the potential to reshape traditional work structures. The study explores how these technological advancements can enhance collaboration and open new avenues for remote work. Beyond the opportunities, the paper also addresses the challenges associated with integrating the metaverse into work environments. By examining the evolving relationship between the metaverse and the future of work, Wang et al.'s study contributes to the scholarly understanding of the implications, both positive and challenging, that the metaverse brings to the way we work and collaborate in the digital age.

- *The role of metaverse in corporate training and development (Wang et al., 2022):*

In the study titled "The role of metaverse in corporate training and development" (Wang et al., 2022), Wang and co-authors delve into the application of the metaverse in the realm of corporate training and development. The research explores how virtual simulations and immersive learning experiences within the metaverse can contribute to enhancing employee training, skill development, and knowledge transfer. The paper discusses the advantages of utilizing the metaverse as a training platform, shedding light on its potential impact on workforce development. By investigating the role of the metaverse in corporate training, Wang et al. provide valuable insights into the transformative possibilities that immersive technologies can bring to the realm of professional development, offering practical considerations for organizations looking to leverage the metaverse for training and up skilling initiatives.

2.3. Technology, Resilience, and Business Continuity

In the dynamic and interconnected world of business, the role of technology in fostering resilience and ensuring continuity during disruptions has become increasingly critical.

- *Business continuity management: a critical review of the literature (Elliott et al., 2014):*

In the paper titled "Business continuity management: A critical review of the literature" (Elliott et al., 2014), the authors conduct a comprehensive review to establish a foundational understanding of business continuity management. The review encompasses an examination of various strategies and frameworks aimed at achieving organizational resilience. The authors highlight the critical role of technology integration, emphasizing the significance of information technology (IT) systems, data recovery, and redundancy in bolstering business continuity. By synthesizing literature on business continuity management, Elliott et al. contribute to a deeper understanding of the multifaceted approaches and technological considerations crucial for organizations seeking to enhance their resilience in the face of disruptions and uncertainties.

3. Gain of the Novel Method

The primary benefit of this approach lies in the researchers' adeptness at capturing the dynamic nature of manufacturing workflows including the interdependence of methods based on lean. This approach better captures the process of developing an efficient industrial system as follows: logical, incremental steps that result in small gains. The biggest corporation developed a unique and unmatched production approach over a period of time. Its several processes combined into a single, seamless flow allow for the faultless mass manufacturing of a variety of manufactured goods with no loss of quality. This could only be achieved by first establishing a dependable one-piece circulation, which is contingent upon many conditions being satisfied. It is necessary to codify to improve every aspect of work. The production line can be timed by utilizing standard work to determine the output rate at each site. This enables the achievement of the goals as follows:

$$PL = \cap_i = 1_n P_2.$$

PL denotes the production line operation and P_1, P_2, …, P_n represent the operations of individual workstations within the production line.

The authors of this chapter delve into the intersection of Industry 4.0 lean production systems and the digital skills prevalent in the V4 countries (the Visegrád Group, consisting of Czech Republic, Hungary, Poland, and Slovakia). They aim to address two key issues within this realm: first, the integration of

Industry 4.0 technologies to enhance value creation, and second, the relationship between lean production principles and the emergence of Industry 4.0. By comparing the core concepts of lean production systems with the definition of Industry 4.0, the authors assert that lean manufacturing principles will not become obsolete with the rise of Industry 4.0. Instead, they argue that lean principles will become even more crucial, serving as essential guidelines for effectively harnessing Industry 4.0 technology. They foresee Industry 4.0's potential to significantly augment the growth of lean production, or its evolution thereof (Barman et al., 2024).

One notable aspect highlighted is the facilitation of information flow throughout the value chain by Industry 4.0 tools, allowing for swift acquisition and dissemination of customer demand data. In smart factories enabled by Industry 4.0, production processes can be streamlined to reduce waste and accelerate manufacturing. Real-time monitoring of material movement is emphasized as a means to minimize inventory across the value chain. However, the authors anticipate that the adoption of Industry 4.0 technologies will likely entail a transformation in traditional lean production practices. They predict a decline in the utilization of physical tools such as Kanban cards and Andon systems, as Industry 4.0 technologies become more prevalent. Nevertheless, the authors argue that if Industry 4.0 technologies are implemented in alignment with lean production principles and effectively contribute to achieving the company's objectives, their adoption would be justified and would significantly enhance the production system. Turning their focus to the V4 nations, particularly the automobile sector, the authors note that the most significant value addition occurs in this industry, with considerable automation observed in manufacturing processes. However, they highlight a disparity in research and development investment between the V4 nations and Western Europe, which impacts the level of technological advancement. Despite this, they note a trend toward digitalization, particularly in areas such as social networks and data sharing, suggesting a gradual adoption of digital technologies across major organizations in the region.

4. Conclusion

In conclusion, the integration of modern technologies, particularly the metaverse, into corporate sustainability strategies has become imperative, especially in the challenging times brought about by the COVID-19 pandemic. The FLA is essential for businesses to expand deliberately and thrive in the face of adversity. The metaverse presents a rapidly evolving global technology offering innovative amenities and a HROI for clients. Through a comprehensive investigation of the metaverse and its potential impacts on humanity, this study has revealed promising prospects for both consumers and stakeholders. By incorporating feedback from individuals worldwide, including India, it has become evident that widespread accessibility and affordability of cutting-edge technologies are crucial for maximizing their impact and effectiveness. The study identifies key variables shaping the future of the metaverse and provides insights into its anticipated deployment across various industries. It emphasizes the importance of raising user awareness and making these technologies more accessible to drive meaningful adoption and utilization. In summary, the metaverse represents a significant business opportunity with the potential to revolutionize industries and enhance sustainability efforts. By embracing a FLA and leveraging the transformative power of the metaverse, businesses can navigate challenges, seize opportunities, and thrive in an increasingly digital world.

5. Future Work

Future work in this area could focus on several key areas to further explore and enhance the potential of integrating the metaverse into corporate sustainability strategies:

Exploring emerging applications: Conduct further research to identify and explore emerging applications of the metaverse in various industries beyond the scope of the current study. This could involve conducting case studies or pilot projects to evaluate the feasibility and effectiveness of implementing metaverse technologies in different business contexts. User experience and adoption: investigate the user experience and adoption barriers associated with metaverse technologies. This could involve conducting user surveys or usability testing to identify challenges and opportunities for improving user engagement and adoption rates.

Economic and social impact assessment: Assess the economic and social impact of widespread adoption of metaverse technologies. This could involve conducting economic impact studies to quantify the potential benefits and costs associated with integrating the metaverse into business operations, as well as exploring the social implications of virtual environments on human behavior and interaction. Policy and regulation: examine the policy and regulatory implications of metaverse adoption, particularly in areas such as data privacy, intellectual property rights, and virtual asset management. This could involve collaborating with policymakers and industry stakeholders to develop guidelines and best practices for responsible metaverse usage.

Technology development and innovation: Continue to monitor and analyze advancements in metaverse technologies, such as VR, AR, and blockchain. This could involve staying abreast of new developments in hardware and software platforms, as well as exploring opportunities for innovation and collaboration within the metaverse ecosystem.

Long-term strategy and planning: Develop long-term strategic plans for integrating metaverse technologies into corporate sustainability strategies. This could involve working with business leaders and sustainability experts to identify key objectives, milestones, and performance metrics for metaverse implementation, as well as developing roadmaps for phased adoption and deployment.

By addressing these areas of future work, researchers and practitioners can further advance our understanding of the potential of the metaverse to enhance corporate sustainability efforts and drive positive societal impact.

Declarations

Funding: The authors declare that they do not have any funding or grant for the manuscript.

Conflict of interest: The authors declare that they do not have any conflict of interests that influence the work reported in this paper.

References

Ali, M., Mahfouz, A., & Arisha, A. (2021). Analytical framework for resilience assessment in supply chain: A dynamic capability approach. *Supply Chain Management: An International Journal*, *26*(1), 37–52. https://doi.org/10.1108/SCM-02-2020-0070

Ali, M. H., Suleiman, N., Khalid, N., Tan, K. H., Tseng, M. L., & Kumar, M. (2021). Supply chain resilience reactive strategies for food SMEs in coping to COVID-19 crisis. *Trends in Food Science & Technology*, *109*, 94–102.

Barman, A., Barman, M., & Jamader, A. R. (2024). Ecological impacts of the Himalayan region in West Bengal. In S. N. Biswas & P. Kumar (Eds.), *Mountain tourism and ecological impacts: Himalayan region and beyond* (pp. 47–61). IGI Global.

Brown, D. D. (2022). *The dynamics of organizational culture and work climate for employee innovative work behavior in highly regulated industries* [Doctoral dissertation, University of Maryland University College].

Christensen, C. M. (2013). *The innovator's dilemma: When new technologies cause great firms to fail*. Harvard Business Review Press.

Das, P., Jamader, A. R., Acharya, B. R., & Das, H. (2019, May). HMF based QoS aware recommended resource allocation system in mobile edge computing for IoT. In 2019 *International conference on intelligent computing and control systems (ICCS)* (pp. 444–449). IEEE.

Das, P., Martin Sagayam, K., Rahaman Jamader, A., & Acharya, B. (2022). Remote sensing in public health environment: A review. In S. Biswas, C. Chowdhury, B. Acharya, & C. M. Liu (Eds.), *Internet of things based smart healthcare: Intelligent and secure solutions applying machine learning techniques* (pp. 379–397). Springer.

Elliott, M., Golub, B., & Jackson, M. O. (2014). Financial networks and contagion. *American Economic Review*, *104*(10), 3115–3153.

Jamader, A. R. (2022). A brief report of the upcoming & present economic impact to hospitality industry in COVID19 situations. *Journal of Pharmaceutical Negative Results*, *13*, 2289–2302.

Jamader, A. R., Chowdhary, S., Jha, S. S., & Roy, B. (2023). Application of economic models to green circumstance for management of littoral area: A sustainable tourism arrangement. *SMART Journal of Business Management Studies*, *19*(1), 70–84.

Jamader, A. R., Chowdhary, S., & Shankar Jha, S. (2023). A road map for two decades of sustainable tourism development framework. In G. E. Bayram, A. Sharma, & J. Kumar (Eds.), *Resilient and sustainable destinations after disaster: Challenges and strategies* (pp. 9–18). Emerald Publishing Limited.

Jamader, A. R., Das, P., & Acharya, B. (2022, January 1). *An analysis of consumers acceptance towards usage of digital payment system, Fintech and CBDC*. Fintech and CBDC.

Jamader, A. R., Das, P., & Acharya, B. R. (2019, May). BcIoT: Blockchain based DDoS prevention architecture for IoT. In *2019 International conference on intelligent computing and control systems (ICCS)* (pp. 377–382). IEEE.

Jamader, A. R., Das, P., Acharya, B., & Hu, Y. C. (2021). Overview of security and protection techniques for microgrids. In G. B. Narejo, B. Acharya, S. S. Ranjit Singh, & F. Newagy (Eds.), *Microgrids* (pp. 231–253). CRC Press.

Jamader, A. R., Dasgupta, S., & Baibhaw, G. (2024). The resilient brand management framework as a responsive business strategy in the industry 4.0 era. In J. Kumar, M. Arora, & G. Erkol Bayram (Eds.), *Exploring the use of metaverse in business and education* (pp. 113–130). IGI Global.

Jamader, A. R., Immanuel, J. S., Ebenezer, V., Rakhi, R. A., Sagayam, K. M., & Das, P. (2023). Virtual education, training and internships in hospitality and tourism during Covid-19 situation. *Journal of Pharmaceutical Negative Results*, 286–290.

Kumar, A., Shankar, A., Shaik, A. S., Jain, G., & Malibari, A. (2023). Risking it all in the metaverse ecosystem: Forecasting resistance towards the enterprise metaverse. *Information Technology & People*, *40*(1), 1–23.

Mayer-Schönberger, V., & Cukier, K. (2013). *Big data: A revolution that will transform how we live, work, and think*. Houghton Mifflin Harcourt.

Nayak, D. K., Mishra, P., Das, P., Jamader, A. R., & Acharya, B. (2022). Application of deep learning in biomedical informatics and healthcare. In P. K. Pattnaik, A. Vaidya, S. Mohanty, S. Mohanty, & A. Hol (Eds.), *Smart healthcare analytics: State of the art* (pp. 113–132). Springer.

Niu, Y., & Zou, Z. (2019). Corporate investment, Tobin's Q and liquidity management under time-inconsistent preferences. *Annals of Economics and Finance*, *20*(2), 721–736.

Sagayam, K. M., Das, P., Jamader, A. R., Acharya, B. R., Bonyah, E., & Elngar, A. A. (2022). *DeepCOVIDNet: COVID-19 detection of chest image using deep learning model*. https://doi.org/10.21203/rs.3.rs-1725511/v1

Schwartz, P. (2012). *The art of the long view: Planning for the future in an uncertain world*. Crown Currency.

Scoble, R., & Israel, S. (2017). *The fourth transformation: How augmented reality and artificial intelligence change everything*. Patrick Brewster Press.

Teece, D. J. (2007). Explicating dynamic capabilities: The nature and microfoundations of (sustainable) enterprise performance. *Strategic Management Journal*, *28*(13), 1319–1350.

Wang, X., Wang, J., Wu, C., Xu, S., & Ma, W. (2022). Engineering brain: Metaverse for future engineering. *AI in Civil Engineering*, *1*(1), 2.

Chapter 15

Virtual Tourism: Traversing the Kaleidoscope of Virtual Reality

Neetha Mary Avanesh[a] and Minu Zachariah[b]

[a]*School of Business and Management, Christ (Deemed to be University), Bengaluru, India*
[b]*Department of Management Studies and Research Centre, B.M.S. College of Engineering, Bengaluru, India*

Abstract

The influx of artificial intelligence (AI) in tourism have paved way for the phenomenal growth in virtual tourism. An attempt has been made to understand the current state of virtual reality (VR) adoption in the tourism sector, its pros, the VR tools available in tourism, a few VR companies and their business models, the interplay of VR with various tourism sectors for the promotion of physical tourism, the major challenges being faced, and recommendations to manage the challenges. The authors believe that the outcome of the study would provide practical insights for myriad stakeholders for enhancing growth in the tourism sector.

Keywords: Virtual tourism; artificial intelligence; virtual reality; tourism sector; business models; physical tourism

1. Introduction

AI and VR have played a vital role in reviving the tourism sector post corona virus pandemic. In 2020, there had been a steep fall in global travel due to travel bans, border closures, event cancellations, quarantine requirements and fear of disease spread, resulting in huge losses for the tourism industry as a whole, and loss of employment for many who were engaged in this sector (Kaushal & Srivastava, 2021). This accentuated the need for digital innovations. The changing mindset

The AI Metaverse Revolution: Transforming Multi-Business Scenarios (Volume 1), 217–227

doi:10.1108/978-1-83662-582-720251017

of the masses towards technological adoption, cross-collaboration among international operators and advancements in VR, augmented reality (AR), and other immersive technologies offered personalised, engaging, accessible, and cost-effective experiences to travellers (Lee et al., 2021). This led to the birth of virtual tourism as a closer alternative to physical tourism.

2. Virtual Tourism

Virtual tourism refers to the use of technology to provide individuals with a simulated experience of visiting different locations without physically being present there. In other words, virtual tourism combines the concepts of VR and tourism, wherein the travellers could experience the beauty of their preferred destination without leaving the comfort of their homes. Virtual tourism is also referred to as digital travel or virtual travel. Virtual tourism provides viewers with an immersive tourism experience with the aid of VR, still images, video, audio, narration, and other multimedia formats. In some cases, the tourist might be required to use a headset or simulator or wear gloves or may be made to experience slight motion, as in the case of a roller-coaster simulator, or a feeling, as in the case of being sprayed with cold air or water, depending on the innovative experience that is being designed (Stainton, 2023).

VR systems in tourism can be classified based on their level of immersion, namely, non-immersive, semi-immersive, and fully immersive VR systems (Beck et al., 2019). In non-immersive VR, the users can interact with the virtual environments using 360-degree videos, virtual tours, and interactive web-based experiences. These can be done through a computer screen, without the aid of any specialised VR hardware like headsets. Semi-immersive VR is often used for more interactive and engaging virtual tours, with the aid of headsets. Fully immersive VR systems call for advanced VR hardware like high-quality VR headsets with motion tracking, haptic feedback devices, room-scale tracking systems, and so on. It enables the users to virtually walk through streets, explore landscapes, and interact with virtual elements.

Some of the applications of virtual tourism are listed below:

i. *AR apps*: These apps are known to integrate digital, visual, audio, and other content into real-world environment for the benefit of users. In tourism, they can act as interactive guides, providing information about landmarks, historical sites, virtual reconstructions of ancient ruins, and so on.
ii. *VR tours*: Travel and tourism companies and government organisations have tried to attract tourists by offering VR tours. With the aid of VR headsets, tourists can explore the virtual environments that replicate real-world destinations. Many museums, cultural institutions, online platforms, and websites are known to offer VR tours to their users.
iii. *360-degree videos*: These videos enable the user to experience a panoramic view of their desired location by capturing a 360-degree view.
iv. *Gaming environments*: Virtual tourism experiences are also being integrated into the gaming environment to capture the attention of gamers towards those landmarks.

v. *Live streaming*: Live streaming platforms offer real-time interaction wherein the travellers can attach themselves with the virtual guides through live streams to get a personalised virtual touring experience.
vi. *Digital twins*: The digital replicas of physical locations are often referred to as digital twins. Many of the cities or landmarks created as digital twins can be explored by digital travellers, which would, in turn, provide them with an immersive real-world experience.

3. Virtual Tourism Industry Overview

According to the Virtual Tourism Market Research Report 2022, the global virtual tour market was valued at USD 301.5 million in 2021. As per the VR in Tourism Market Report 2024, the application of VR in tourism is bound to expand at a compound annual growth rate of 33.0% from 2023 to 2030 (Dharmadhikari, 2024). The rising virtual events, the increasing technological advancements, and the increasing demand for immersive experiences among millennials have fuelled the growth. The Asia Pacific region had dominated the market in 2023, accounting for nearly 38% of the global revenue. Nevertheless, North America had captured the largest market share in the VR tourism market due to its advanced technology, high consumer awareness, and well-established tourism industry.

According to Cognitive Market Research, the 3D virtual tours and simulations has captured the largest market share in the VR tourism market. The ability to deliver immersive and visually compelling experiences, the demand among customers for richer and more engaging travel content, and the widespread availability of 3D devices have played a vital role in its gaining popularity. Furthermore, hotel applications have been found to capture the largest market share in the VR tourism market. The virtual hotel tours, 360-degree views of rooms coupled with booking convenience, and personalising stays through VR-driven hotel applications had contributed to its widespread adoption.

After assessing the rising market potential in virtual tourism, many companies are at the forefront of developing VR hardware and software solutions for the tourism sector. VizioFly, World Travel VR, Ascape VR, Zco Corporation, Cubix, VARS, Giga Works, Groove Jones, Cubix, The Amsterdam VR Company, Infinito VFX, Immersion VR UK, 3D Walkabout, Ignition Immersive, First Airlines, Google, Oculus, Immersive, Ascape VR, Be More Colorful, Samsung Electronics Co. Ltd., Microsoft Corporation, HTC Corporation, and Sony Corporation are a few of the key players in the AR/VR segment relating to travel and tourism.

4. Advantages of Virtual Tourism

Virtual tourism offers an array of benefits to different stakeholders. Firstly, it offers the prospective travellers a real-time experience pertaining to their destination even before they book it. Secondly, it makes travel accessible to physically challenged individuals or those with any other limitations that might prevent them from engaging in physical travel. Thirdly, it provides the travellers the convenience of exploring destinations from the convenience of their own homes, along with their near and dear ones. Fourthly, it proves to be a cost-effective mechanism as it eliminates expenses related to transportation, accommodation, dining, and so on. Fifthly, virtual tourism provides a safe alternative during times of pandemic, natural calamities, and other crises situations such as terrorist attacks or international conflicts. Sixthly, virtual tourism is used as a strong marketing tool by advertisers to attract tourists on social media. Furthermore, it contributes towards environmental sustainability by reducing carbon emissions; air, land, and water pollution; and natural resource wastages. Furthermore, it mitigates over tourism and its negative effects on local communities and ecosystems.

5. Virtual Tourism Tools and Technology

Virtual tourism leverages on various tools and technologies to provide an immersive and engaging user experience (Duda, 2020). A few of the commonly used tools (Fig. 15.1) include:

i. *VR*: VR headsets like Oculus Rift, HTC Vive, and PlayStation VR and applications such as Google Earth VR, Wander, and YouVisit help in engaging the tourists by offering a 360-degree tour in the virtual environment (Putra et al., 2021).
ii. *AR*: AR apps like Google Lens, Wikitude, AR City, and so on and AR glasses developed by Microsoft HoloLens and Magic Leap enhance the

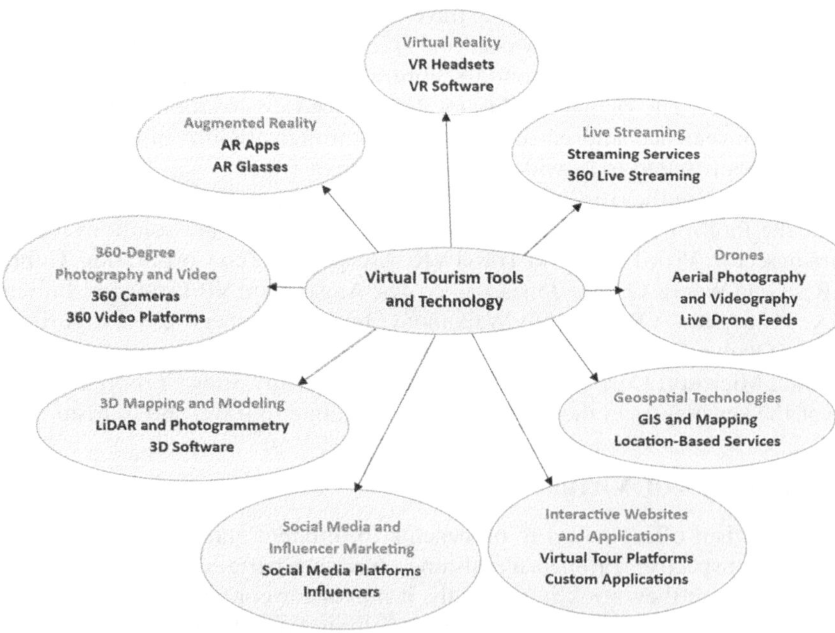

Fig. 15.1. Virtual Tourism Tools and Technology. *Source*: Developed by authors.

users' virtual journey by projecting virtual elements into the user's field of vision.

iii. *360-degree photography and video*: With the aid of 360 cameras like GoPro MAX, Insta360, and Ricoh Theta and 360 video platforms such as YouTube 360, Facebook 360, and Vimeo 360, there has been a phenomenal increase in the consumer reach with respect to virtual tourism.

iv. *3D mapping and modelling*: Technologies such as LiDAR and photogrammetry and 3D software tools like SketchUp, Blender, and Unity 3D help in creating 3D models of real-world location

v. *Interactive websites and applications*: Websites and applications like Matterport, Kuula, and Roundme offer interactive virtual tours with clickable hotspots, navigation tools, and multimedia integration. Further destination-specific apps help in customising the applications based on client requirements.

vi. *Live streaming*: Platforms such as YouTube Live, Facebook Live, and Twitch provide real-time broadcasts of tours, events, and 360 live streaming services for the benefit of virtual tourists.

vii. *Drones*: Drones not only facilitate aerial photography and videography but also provide live feeds on destinations.

viii. *Social media and influencer marketing*: Virtual tourists could also make use of the information shared by travel influencers and social media platforms such as Instagram, TikTok, and so on to decide on the virtual destinations or experiences they would like to engage in (Pecníková et al., 2021).

ix. *Geospatial technologies*: Geographic information systems (GIS) and services like Google Maps and ArcGIS provide detailed maps and geographic data for virtual exploration. Many apps provide location-based services to the virtual tourists which enhance their remote travel experiences through real-time information and interactive features.

6. Virtual Tour Companies and Business Models

Virtual tour companies specialise in delivering virtual experiences to the clients, generally travel agents, and their collaborating partners. These virtual tourism companies either create their own virtual tours with the help of experts and sell it to the clients or provide a platform that acts as market place enabling to stream tours that helps them in improving their business.

There is no uniform business model as to how virtual tourism companies operate. However, one of the approaches is to provide platform that acts as market place to host virtual tourism multimedia by providing format for creators who can post their virtual experiences and invite travellers to join them as 'Airbnb Online Experience' company does. Another approach adopted by Google Arts and Culture is to operate as repositories, wherein consumers could source information relating to arts and culture (Reali, 2024). Some companies publish a virtual tour free online but earn revenue through online ad programmes. Few others sell premium virtual tour products and market it online. Consumers can search for such products, go through the product offerings, and compare and purchase it. Premium virtual tour creators can make money from the travel agents or tour operators for a fee, but if they are using platform for posting virtual tours, they have to pay commission for providing market place.

7. Virtual Tourism Companies and Services

Cristobal Reali (2024) conducted a study on virtual tourism companies all over the globe and highlighted their contributions. It was found that each virtual tour company had unique services to offer as follows:

'Airbnb online experiences' is a virtual tour company, under the renowned Airbnb brand has provided a virtual tour platform to enable travellers get virtual tourism experience of places and activities with the help of experts through Zoom at the centre of its operations. They have collaborated with partners like Tonkean, Automate.io, Guesty, and many others to provide excellent virtual tour experiences. This platform acts as a marketplace for online experiences enabling developers/creators earn money, while Airbnb gets commission for providing the platform to host virtual tour of places or activities. They also have self-service help centre to for host, experienced hosts, guests, and travel admins. One unique feature of Airbnb platform is that it focuses on social interactions.

'Google art and culture' is a virtual tourism branch of giant tech company google. It provides comprehensive platform that is capable of hosting high-quality images and videos of cultural artefacts and art works across the globe by building network of partnerships. The platform has features to host multimedia materials that include images, interactive games, videos, and written copies. Their web-based platform has mobile port usable by both Android and iPhone users. One unique feature of Google Arts and Culture is they have introduced an app with AR that allows users to view real size art work with their smart phones in their own environment, keeping them engaged. It is a non-commercial initiative by google.

YouVisit, a virtual tour company now acquired by EAB, offers immersive experiences for the brands and their audiences by creating 360 virtual tours, ultimate virtual tours, and interactive web content on Aria platform. Besides this, it offers online contact form and guides to get started, frequently asked questions. They have self-service help centre provide technical support when required. YouVisit provides Aria platform to create interactive realistic ours of buildings, activities, and other aspects of a tour.

'VR Gorilla' is a VR production studio that creates VR experiences from scratch by filming and creating great VR materials immersing the clients with their powerful story telling elements. They use state-of-art cameras and software to deliver mind boggling footage and charge the clients for photoshoots, video-recording sessions, and VR post-production by collaborating with companies like DSM, Erasmus MC, Amsterdam UMC, Jeroen Bosch Hospital, and many others. They offer online contact form and maintain open lines of communication.

'Haptical', a California-based company headquartered at Nevada city, created web portal specifically devoted for delivering VR- and AR-related updated news, including for those interested in virtual tourism.

'TimeLooper' is a company which is pioneer in interpretive experience design and delivers mesmerising virtual tours. This is possible as they leverage from combining web and mobile technologies to provide high-quality videos, GIS mapping, holographic imaging, 3D renders, and VR and AR technology to immerse viewers. The business model operates offers both free and premium content. The company produces high-quality videos and contents through self-financing and sells its virtual tours to clients across the globe. They hold their viewers captive through their story telling, thus luring them in exploring virtual tour in entirety.

'Wild Within VR' is a North American Organisation that launched one of the products that enables travellers to experience nature as if they were there themselves by using interactive 360 video footage that is compatible with VR headsets. Their virtual tours of two adventures, namely, British Columbia and Canada, are most sought after even today.

'Unbound' a virtual tourism company provides viewers immersive 360 experience of peculiar attractions in popular destinations. It uses AR technology to virtual experiences making it more engaging for viewers. They generated stable revenue through direct sales.

Virtually Visiting is a virtual company floated by a team of travel and technology experts dedicated to adventure seekers by providing 360 virtual tours.

8. Interplay with Various Sectors to Promote Physical Tourism

Traditionally physical tourism was organised by the travel agents and tour operators by collaborating and coordinating with various other sectors like transportation, accommodation, entertainment, attractions, food, and beverages. They operated with the aid of information technology to carry out these transactions. People mostly relied on the information provided by travel agents and tour operators and had to choose the facilities they provided and had to be contented with the arrangement made by these agencies. Though with advanced technology virtual tourism was possible, it did not kick start in the way it was expected to be, as people could not accept the fact that virtual tourism will give them the pleasure that they would gain from physical tourism. However, restrictions due to the spread of COVID-19 to prevent the spread of the virus was the turning point, wherein virtual tourism gained the momentum as people didn't have much options left (Reali, 2024). Slowly, virtual tourism gained acceptance and paved way to boost physical tourism as well. The travel and tourism sector introduced virtual tourism as a strategy to promote physical tourism, wherein the tourists can decide on their package after virtually accessing all the facilities that are available based on the destination they would like to travel and, therefore, are not subjected to shocks during their journey.

Now public can enjoy virtual tourism and beyond, wherein they can visit these tourist spots physically if they desire, based on various factors taken into consideration like affordability, health, etc. This is possible as virtually they can go through all the options and facilities available to travel to the destination of their choice and get the tourism package tailormade as per their requirement.

The following virtual tours of tourist spots and facilities have helped them decide whether to be contended with virtual tourism or go beyond that to convert into physical tourism.

Promoting tourism through virtual experience of landmark destinations: VR in travel and tourism industry has enabled the viewers to explore the tourist destinations by providing them 360-degree view of every part of the location through interactive images or videos with enough contents in a unique and immersive way. They can view this with the help of the headset on a mobile or computer device. VR is used in tourism industry by the travel agents as a marketing tool as it gives prospective clients virtual travel experience of landmark destinations by imagining being in that location that, in turn, drives them to visit the place physically to have real-life experience.

Virtual flight and other modes of transport experiences: Prospective passengers embark upon a replica of aeroplane cabin, cruise trip, etc., get to know food served there, safety precautions taken, and other services provided and could check whether it is value for their money and decide on the modes of transport spread across their tour. The main goal is to provide them realistic experience while travelling to the destination and back and during their tour to various landmark locations. First Airlines, a Tokyo-based company, has created the first VR airline. Many are now following suit.

Virtual tour of hotels: The users are provided with a complete 360-degree interactive tour of the hotels in the chosen location, wherein they can view both interiors and exteriors that gives them an idea of the various facilities provided and the cost they could incur for their stay so that they could decide whether it will fit into their budget. Generally, the VR hotel tours are uploaded to websites and social media for prospective clients to view any time. This also pressurises the hotels to create an impression and enable the user in brand engagement.

Virtual tour of entertainments and attractions: VR tour of entertainment programmes and attractive tourist spots can be viewed so that it will encourage travellers to visit that place if it interests them.

Virtual tour of foods and beverages: The prospective user should be provided a tour of hotels or restaurants to view varieties of food and beverages available in the locality and the cost. This helps them decide on the restaurant they need to visit during their tour.

Virtual tour of certain emergency services: The clients should be provided virtual tour of certain emergency services like hospitals, police, fire force, etc., are to be provided to the visitor to protect him from certain unawares happening during his onward journey and back.

Virtual booking interface: A virtual booking interface is a recent development within tourism VR. Users can plan their vacation, book tickets for travel, accommodation, food & beverages, entertainment programmes, and tourist spot visits and for other amenities if required during their stay in their preferred destination as and when they virtual view and convinced. It is still in its infancy stage and yet to catch up to become more common in years to come. It is the travel agencies normally taking up this responsibility to enhance their business.

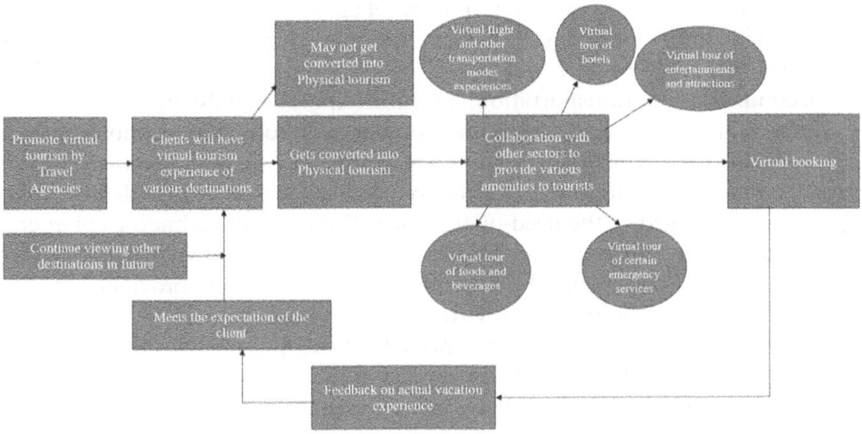

Fig. 15.2. Virtual Experiences of Tourists at Various Stages that May or May Not Be Converted into Physical Tourism. *Source*: Developed by authors.

With all this virtual tour, if the potential tourists are convinced, they go-ahead booking tickets to proceed with their onward journey to the tourist destination and more, so if the vacation experience to these tourists were delightful, they plan again and again to visit different destinations by following the same process.

The illustrative model given below (Fig. 15.2) would help in understanding the process better.

9. Virtual Tourism Challenges

Virtual tourism poses myriad challenges to different stakeholders.

Tourists: Virtual tourism does not give the client complete experience as they get exposed to physical tourism experiences. Technology-related issues can screw up the pleasure, and the travel agents might not be showing what we intend to see (Gately, 2024). They miss out the real experience of feeling the natural environment, tasting local food delicacies, physical shopping experience, and as there is no change of place meaning, there is no relaxation of mind also. Besides this, the virtual tourist does not get opportunity to interact with other tourists or locals leaving no memorable moments to cherish about. Virtual tourism kills the thrill or curiosity of having first-hand experience of viewing the chosen destination. The tourist will not be able to appreciate the creator. Some people have cyber sickness and may have to avoid virtual tourism.

Destination communities: The locals will not be able to socialise with the tourists and learn about their life style and behaviours. They lose business and employment opportunities they otherwise gain through physical tourism. Even now virtual tourism has not been accepted by the people of some countries and high level of promotion and encouragement to provide virtual tour of the services desired by the tourists. Furthermore, there could also be a risk of cultural misrepresentation based on oversimplification in virtual domain.

Travel agencies or tour operators: For travel agencies or tour operators, virtual tours provide limited monetisation potential unless it is converted into physical tourism. There could be potential loss of income from traditional tourism sectors like accommodation, transportation, adventure sports, and dining.

Technology providers: As virtual tourism has been rooted in technology, there is a constant requirement for technology companies to be innovative. Ensuring accessibility and offering user friendly products across diverse demographic groups have emerged as the need of the hour. The need for technological upgradation and maintenance calls for huge investment in technology which may not be feasible for all companies. Furthermore, these technology providers need to safeguard user data and privacy in virtual tourism platforms.

Policymakers: There is an ardent need to develop guidelines and standard operating procedures for tourism operations in the virtual domain. Effort needs to be taken to ensure that there is no misrepresentation of facts, and all ethical standards are being met. Furthermore, the potential social impact on societies heavily reliant on physical tourism needs to be addressed, and sufficient measures have to be designed so as to ensure that the growth of physical tourism is not at stake.

10. Strategies to Address Challenges

Firstly, effort has to be taken to encourage collaboration between government bodies, technology providers, tourism businesses, and local communities to ensure an authentic and immersive virtual experience, without curbing the growth of physical tourism. Secondly, the content being represented through virtual tourism has to be vetted by designated bodies to ensure authenticity in what is being displayed virtually. Thirdly, providing digital literacy programmes would help tourists and local stakeholders adapt to virtual tourism technologies. Fourthly, the travel agents can design themed virtual tours focusing on themes such as history, art, cuisine, adventure, religion, and so on. Furthermore, they could devise hybrid travel packages highlighting pre and post travel experiences. The post travel experience could offer virtual tours of destinations clients have already visited, allowing them to relive their experiences with friends and family. They could also create a new revenue stream from the corporate sector by engaging in corporate events like organising virtual corporate retreats, team-building activities, and conferences. Fifthly, there has to be strong regulatory framework to ensure data privacy and ethical disclosure. Furthermore, virtual tourism should be promoted emphasising on its role in reducing carbon footprint and supporting sustainable tourism practices. Sixthly, the government machinery and private sectors should also offer financial support and incentives for developing virtual tourism infrastructure and content.

11. Conclusion

The phenomenal growth in virtual tourism has given a new direction to the tourism sector. Virtual tourism is, indeed, a boon for people who either cannot afford physical tourism or is unable to visit tourist spots due to some other reason. However, for the overall development of the tourism sector, virtual tourism should not only complement but also act as a promotional tool to boost physical tourism. In other words, the tourist experience can be truly memorable when virtual tourism is supplemented by physical tourism. Furthermore, the potential tourist should be allowed to virtually tour not only attractive places but also explore various modes of transportation, types of accommodates, food & beverages, entertainment, and so on. This would, in turn, help the client to decide on various amenities required and demand tailormade package tours from the travel agents. The benefits of the virtual tourism can be accrued entirely only when it is widely accepted all over the globe and if all incumbents are available for partnership and are willing to provide the videos and contents for circulation among the prospects either directly or indirectly. In short, virtual tourism backed by VR can be instrumental in nurturing an inclusive, sustainable, and enriching travel experience for traveller's world over.

References

Beck, J., Rainoldi, M., & Egger, R. (2019). Virtual reality in tourism: A state-of-the-art review. *Tourism Review*, *74*(3), 586–612.

Dharmadhikari, S. (2024, March 27). *Virtual reality in tourism market report 2024* (Global edition). Cognitive Market Research. https://www.cognitivemarketresearch.com/virtual-reality-in-tourism-market-report

Duda, T. (2020). Virtualization of experience – Evaluating new communication tools in tourism and guiding. *Communication Papers. Media Literacy and Gender Studies*, *9*(19), 25–39.

Gately, J. (2024). *Virtual tourism examples | Explore the world from home in 2024*. https://enjoytravellife.com/virtual-tourism-examples-travel/#section3/

Kaushal, V., & Srivastava, S. (2021). Hospitality and tourism industry amid COVID-19 pandemic: Perspectives on challenges and learnings from India. *International Journal of Hospitality Management*, *92*, 102707.

Lee, S. A., Lee, M., & Jeong, M. (2021). The role of virtual reality on information sharing and seeking behaviors. *Journal of Hospitality and Tourism Management*, *46*, 215–223.

Pecníková, J., Mališová, D., & Moškořová, K. (2021). *Urban culture in pandemic era: Opportunities for using virtual marketing tools in local tourism* (pp. 379–392). Modern management tools and economy of tourism sector in present era, SKRIPTA.

Putra, A. S., Akhirianto, P. M., & Aisyah, N. (2021). Designing a virtual Jakarta tourism application on android OS and virtual reality tools. *International Journal of Science, Technology & Management*, *2*(5), 1460–1467.

Reali, C. (2024, May 5). *Everything you need to know about virtual tourism companies*. https://mize.tech/blog/everything-you-need-to-know-about-virtual-tourism-companies/#:~:text=Virtual%20tourism%20refers%20to%20a,multimedia%20format%20offered%20to%20travelers

Stainton, H. (2023, February 19). What is virtual tourism and is it the future? *Tourism Teacher*. https://tourismteacher.com/virtual-tourism/

Virtual Tour Market Share, Size, Trends, Industry Analysis Report, 2022–2030. (2022, November). *Polaris market research*. https://www.polarismarketresearch.com/industry-analysis/virtual-tour-market

Chapter 16

Demystifying Opportunities and Risk for Businesses: A Qualitative Enquiry

Manpreet Arora[a] *and Jeetesh Kumar*[b]

[a]*Central University of Himachal Pradesh, India*
[b]*Taylor's University, Malaysia*

Abstract

This qualitative enquiry, titled 'Demystifying Opportunities and Risks for Businesses in the Metaverse', explores the metaverse's dual nature, highlighting its transformative potential and associated challenges for businesses. The study examines key opportunities, such as enhanced customer engagement, new revenue streams through digital ownership (NFTs), and the creation of immersive virtual workspaces, all of which promise to revolutionise industries ranging from retail and education to entertainment. However, it also addresses significant risks, including privacy concerns, regulatory uncertainties, and technological barriers. Through a comprehensive analysis, the enquiry aims to provide businesses with a nuanced understanding of balancing innovation with responsible implementation, ensuring they can harness the metaverse's potential while mitigating risks effectively. This abstract is a foundation for business leaders to make informed decisions in navigating this emerging digital landscape.

Keywords: Metaverse; risks; opportunities; multi-business sectors; augmented reality; digitalisation; immersive experiences

Introduction

The metaverse holds increasing importance in today's business landscape, offering transformative potential in how businesses operate, engage with consumers, and innovate. As a digital ecosystem, it merges with virtual and augmented realities

The AI Metaverse Revolution: Transforming Multi-Business Scenarios (Volume 1), 229–240

Published under exclusive licence by Emerald Publishing Limited
doi:10.1108/978-1-83662-582-720251018

(Wang et al., 2023). The metaverse has opened new avenues for companies to interact with consumers in immersive and interactive environments. This shift is significant in today's scenario because modern consumers seek more personalised and experiential brand interactions. Businesses have the potential to leverage the metaverse to increase virtual showrooms, host immersive events, and offer services that engage consumers in a way that traditional digital platforms cannot. These experiences boost consumer loyalty and enhance brand visibility in a saturated digital market.

Furthermore, the metaverse introduces innovative business models and new revenue streams, mainly through blockchain and NFTS. Digital ownership is becoming a central component of the metaverse economy (Lee et al., 2021), enabling businesses to sell virtual goods and services that appeal to tech-savvy companies. For example, the brands can release limited edition digital items, collaborate with virtual influencers, or participate in virtual marketplaces, all providing fresh opportunities to monetise their presence. The ability to conduct transactions in virtual environments through cryptocurrencies and NFTS allows businesses to create new product lines and consumer experiences not constrained by the physical world. In addition to the consumer engagement, the metaverse is reshaping the workplace collaboration. With the rise of remote and hybrid working models, companies increasingly use virtual platforms to facilitate team interactions and project collaborations. Virtual meeting rooms like those offered by platforms such as Meta's, Horizons Workrooms, and Microsoft's Mesh give businesses a way to create life-like interactions without needing physical presence. These spaces encourage collaboration, reduce the need for travel, and can lead to higher productivity through better engagement between the team members. As businesses adapt to the post-pandemic world, the metaverse offers a vital tool to maintain and enhance workplace dynamics. However, the importance of the metaverse extends beyond just customer and employee engagement. It also contributes to sustainability and corporate social responsibility. While concerns are rising about environmental impacts, companies are exploring ways to reduce their carbon footprints, and the metaverse offers an innovative solution. Virtual events, trade shows, and digital platforms reduce the need for physical production and logistics. It also minimises the environmental impact. This aligns businesses with sustainability goals and allows them to demonstrate a commitment to CSR, which is increasingly important for consumers and investors.

In summary, the metaverse is becoming a pivotal aspect of modern business technology. Its ability to create immersive customer experiences, unlock new revenue streams, enhance remote collaboration, and contribute to sustainability makes it a valuable tool for companies seeking growth and differentiation. As the technology supporting the metaverse continues to evolve, its significance in shaping the future of business is expected to grow, offering endless possibilities for those willing to invest in its potential (Damar, 2021).

While full of promise, the metaverse is a double-edged sword for businesses. On one hand, it offers immense opportunities for innovation, customer engagement, and new revenue streams. However, it also presents significant risks and challenges that must be carefully navigated. This duality makes the metaverse a space of potential and peril for companies eager to explore its possibilities. On the positive side, the metaverse allows businesses to tap into new levels of customer interaction by creating immersive, experimental environments. Companies can offer virtual experiences that engage users in creative and personalised ways, something traditional online platforms need help to achieve. For example, the virtual store's interactive events in the branded virtual spaces enable deeper customer engagement, building loyalty, and enhancing brand recognition. These opportunities are particularly appealing in retail, entertainment, and education industries, where experiences can be more meaningful than transactions. In addition, the metaverse unlocks new markets for digital goods and services such as virtual fashion, real estate, and art, with the rise of NFTS further enriching this digital economy.

However, the other side of the sword reveals significant risks. One of the pressing concerns is security and privacy. The metaverse relies on a large amount of personal data, including biometric information, which is gathered from virtual reality and augmented reality devices (Wang et al., 2022). If these systems are breached, companies risk losing sensitive data and facing significant reputational damage. Moreover, the decentralised nature of metaverse platforms powered by blockchain technology means that digital assets like NFTS and cryptocurrencies are vulnerable to hacking or fraud. Ensuring robust cybersecurity measures in such complex digital ecosystems can be daunting for businesses, notably smaller enterprises with limited resources. Another critical challenge is the lack of a regulatory framework governing the metaverse. Issues related to digital ownership, intellectual property rights, taxation, and user protection are still evolving, and the businesses operating in these spaces may find themselves navigating legal grey areas. The decentralised global nature of the metaverse complicates regulatory compliance, and businesses could be subject to conflicting laws from different jurisdictions. This legal uncertainty could expose the business to fines, lawsuits, or unforeseen liabilities, creating financial and operating risks.

Additionally, the metaverse comes with technological and market adoption risks (Gadekallu et al., 2022). Despite its potential, the infrastructure supporting the metaverse is still in development, and many consumers do not yet have access to the advanced technologies required for immersive experiences. For businesses investing heavily in metaverse platforms, there is a risk that consumer adoption may be slower than expected. It can also lead to financial losses. Moreover, technological barriers such as expensive VR headsets, high-speed Internet requirements, and complex software systems may limit access to the metaverse. It makes it an exclusive space rather than a mass market phenomenon. Ethically, the metaverse raises concerns about its impact on mental health, digital addiction, and social inequalities. The immersive nature of the virtual world could lead users to spend excessive time online, potentially affecting their mental well-being. Moreover, the digital divide may widen as the metaverse becomes more prevalent, with marginalised communities needing more resources to participate fully in this digital ecosystem. This could lead to greater inequality, which businesses must be mindful of while developing metaverse strategies.

Opportunities for Businesses in the Metaverse

Enhanced Customer Engagement

One of the most exciting business opportunities is the potential for immersive customer engagement. The metaverse enables companies to create interactive three-dimensional environments where consumers can engage innovatively with products and services. Retailers, for example, can set up virtual stores, while consumers can try on clothes using avatars or preview products in realistic simulations before purchasing. The heightened level of engagement is expected to increase consumer experience and loyalty. Various international brands like Nike, Gucci, and Samsung have already begun exploring such possibilities, allowing consumers to interact in a highly personalised and immersive manner.

New Revenue Streams

The metaverse also opens up new revenue generating avenues. The concept of digital ownership, made possible through blockchain-based assets such as non-fungible tokens, allows businesses to sell virtual products and services. This ranges from digital fashion and art to virtual reality real estate. Many companies are experimenting with NFT-based merchandise, offering exclusive and limited-edition digital goods that appeal to collectors and tech-savvy consumers. Furthermore, the metaverse also enables subscription-based and pay-per-use business models. Platforms can monetise user engagement through inward experiences such as concerts, educational seminars, or exclusive virtual events.

Collaborative and Remote Workplaces

The COVID-19 pandemic accelerated the adoption of remote working, and the metaverse is poised to revolutionise this further by offering immersive virtual workplaces. Platforms like Meta's Horizon, Workrooms, and Microsoft's Mesh create collaborative environments where employees can meet, interact, and collaborate as if they were in the exact physical location. This will not only create opportunities for companies to foster teamwork, innovation, and productivity, but potentially, it will also reduce real-world overhead costs, rentals, and travelling expenses.

Marketing and Brand Building

The metaverse provides fertile ground for brand building and innovative marketing campaigns. Virtual worlds allow experiential marketing beyond traditional digital advertising (Kim, 2021). Brands can create memorable experiences for their audiences, engaging them through games, virtual events, or branded content in immersive storytelling. Partnerships with influencers or creators in the metaverse are another valuable marketing strategy. These creators can help businesses reach their niche audiences more authentically and engagingly than traditional platforms like social media.

Risks for Businesses in the Metaverse

One of the primary risks associated with the metaverse is the potential for security and privacy breaches. The metaverse involves much personal data captured by VR and AR devices. Sharing these data is secure from hackers, and the user's privacy is respected; it is a significant challenge for every business to meet up with. Moreover, as the metaverse operates on decentralised platforms powered by blockchain, businesses must protect their digital assets against cyber threats. If they are not adequately secured, NFTs, cryptocurrencies, or user data could be vulnerable to theft, leading to financial losses and reputational damages.

Furthermore, the legal frameworks governing the metaverse are still evolving, creating business ambiguity. Specific issues like intellectual property rights, taxation, digital ownership, and user protection need clear regulatory guidance. The metaverse operates across global jurisdictions, complicating regulatory compliance as the businesses might face conflicting regulations from different regions. Furthermore, the decentralised nature of the metaverse creates a regulatory vacuum where established laws may only partially apply. Although the metaverse is highly promising, the technological infrastructure supporting it is still in its early stages. High-speed internet, sophisticated hardware, and seamless integration of AI and blockchain are necessary to ensure a fully functioning and engaging metaverse. However, many users and businesses may need access to the required equipment or technical know-how to navigate the complexities of the metaverse.

Developing and maintaining the metaverse platforms can also be prohibitive for smaller businesses, limiting their access and participation to only those with substantial resources. While large corporations and early adopters are enthusiastic about using the metaverse as a mainstream consumer, adoption is still far from guaranteed. The novelty of the metaverse may only immediately resonate with some demographics, particularly with older and less tech-savvy consumers. Businesses risk over-investing in metaverse platforms before widespread consumer adoption, potentially leading to financial losses. Furthermore, the trends in technology can be very unpredictable. The metaverse might experience fluctuations in popularity or fail to develop as envisioned shortly, putting the businesses that invest heavily in the businesses or the platforms at risk. The metaverse has also raised many ethical questions, particularly around issues like digital addiction, mental health, and social inequality. The immersive nature of the metaverse could lead to problems like overreliance and virtual environments where the users spend excessive time in digital words at the expense of real-life interactions.

Additionally, the digital divide could deepen existing inequalities. Access to the metaverse may be limited to wealthier, technologically equipped individuals and businesses, while marginalised communities are left behind. Companies operating in the metaverse must be conscious of these ethical concerns and take proactive steps to address them.

Benefits and Challenges of Metaverse Across Different Sectors

The metaverse is the digital ecosystem which combines virtual and augmented realities and has the potential to revolutionise multiple industries, from education to tourism to manufacturing to entertainment. At the same time, each sector stands to benefit from the immersive and interactive possibilities of the metaverse. It also faces unique challenges that must be addressed for sustainable growth and development (Park & Kim, 2022).

Education

In education, if we talk about the benefits, the metaverse can create immersive learning experiences beyond traditional classroom settings (Hwang & Chien, 2022). Virtual reality allows the students to explore historically scientific simulations or complex concepts hands-on, engagingly. Students can also participate in virtual classrooms, interact with avatars of teachers and peers, and explore the topics through interactive simulations, enhancing their understanding and retention. For example, medical students can practice surgeries in virtual operating rooms, and history students can virtually visit ancient civilisations. Simultaneously, the primary challenges in education include the cost and accessibility of metaverse technologies. Only some students can access hardware such as VR headsets and high-speed Internet, which needs full participation. Additionally, concerns about overreliance on technology may distract from interpersonal skills and critical thinking (Xu et al., 2022). The data privacy and security are also paramount while dealing with sensitive information in any educational setting.

Tourism

The metaverse offers transformative possibilities for the tourism industry by enabling virtual travel experiences (Gursoy et al., 2022). Virtual tours of popular destinations, museums, or landmarks allow the users to explore new places from the comfort of their homes. This is particularly beneficial for those who may not be able to travel due to financial, physical, or time constraints. Hotels, airlines, and travel agencies can also use metaverse to offer virtual purviews of destinations, accommodations, and travel experiences, providing potential travellers a sense of place before booking. But on the same hand, if we talk about the challenges, the metaverse could reduce the demand for physical travel, impacting the traditional tourism sector. This shift may affect the jobs and local economies dependent on tourism. Creating high-quality, immersive virtual environments also requires significant investment in digital infrastructure. There is also a question about monetising virtual tourism and balancing it with the real-life travel experience without undermining the latter.

Manufacturing

The manufacturing industry can leverage the metaverse to create virtual factories and simulations, allowing for the testing and optimising of the production processes without needing physical prototypes. This can significantly reduce the cost and time associated with product development. Workers can also be trained in virtual environments to operate machinery or perform tasks, reducing risk and improving efficiency. Integrating AI and IoT within the metaverse could enable real-time monitoring of factory operations and predictive maintenance, minimising downtime.

On the other hand, if we talk about the challenges, adopting the metaverse in manufacturing faces barriers such as the high cost of VR and AR technology implementation. Moreover, digital security risks, including cyber-attacks or connected systems, will threaten manufacturing operations. There is also a need for specialised skills to manage and integrate virtual environments into traditional manufacturing processes, and it requires a significant investment in employee training and education.

Service Industry

In the service industry, particularly customer service and retail, the metaverse can provide personalised and interactive customer experiences. For instance, retailers can create virtual stores where customers can try new clothes and products in 3D before purchasing. Customer service interactions become more engaging and efficient with avatars and virtual assistance. It will also lead to enhanced satisfaction. Additionally, the virtual workspaces in the metaverse enable collaboration between employees across different locations, improving team dynamics and productivity. But there are specific challenges also. The service industry must address digital accessibility issues as not all customers can access technologies needed to participate in the metaverse. Maintaining data security, mainly while dealing with the consumer information, is also significant concern (Zhao et al., 2022). Furthermore, there is a challenge of creating seamless and intuitive virtual environments that do not alienate customers who may prefer traditional in-person service interactions.

Gaming Industry

The gaming industry is one of the most advanced sectors in the metaverse, with many virtual worlds and immersive games already in existence. The metaverse allows for the creation of expensive interactive gaming experiences where players can explore virtual environments, interact with each other, and create a trade virtual asset like NFTS. Multiplayer games can become more social and interconnected, with the players using avatars to engage in virtual economies, communities, and societies. The rise of Play to Earn models is also revolutionising how players monetise their gaming experiences. While the gaming industry thrives in the metaverse, it also faces challenges related to addiction and overreliance on virtual environments. Additionally, issues like harassment or toxic behaviour in virtual spaces must be addressed to ensure player safety. Monetisation strategies like cryptocurrencies also raise concerns about financial regulation and market stability. Lastly, creating a more immersive and interactive gaming experience requires continual technological advancements, which may be costly for the developers.

Music and Television Industry

The metaverse offers exciting possibilities for the music and television industry by providing new platforms for content distribution and fan engagement. Virtual consults, musical festivals, and events in the metaverse allow the artist to reach global audiences without geographical limitations. For example, artists can perform live in virtual environments where fans interact through the avatars, creating unique and personalised concert experiences. For the television industry, immersive storytelling and interactive content can be delivered through the metaverse. Metaverse helps allow the viewers to become part of the story rather than passive observers. For the music and television industry, the challenge lies in developing and maintaining the technology needed to support immersive experiences. There are also intellectual property rights concerns, particularly around the unauthorised reproduction and distribution of content in the day's centralised digital space. Additionally, figuring out effective monetisation strategies like ticketing sales for virtual events or subscription models for interactive content requires innovative approaches to maintain traditional revenue streams.

Sustainability and Corporate Social Responsibility of Metaverse

Sustainability is an increasingly important aspect of business strategy, and the metaverse can support these goals by reducing the environmental footprints of physical products and services. For example, virtual events or fashion shows eliminate the need for travel and physical production, significantly reducing carbon emissions. Businesses can also use the metaverse to create awareness of social and environmental issues, aligning with CSR goals in innovative ways.

The emergence of the metaverse presents both unique opportunities and challenges for sustainability and corporate social responsibility in business practices. As businesses increasingly explore the possibilities of immersive digital worlds, they must also consider their activities' broader environmental, social, and ethical implications within these spaces. By integrating sustainability and CSR into metaverse strategies, companies can create value and demonstrate a commitment to responsible innovation in this new digital frontier.

Reducing Environmental Impact

A promising aspect of the metaverse is the potential to contribute to sustainability by reducing the need for physical products, events, and travel. Businesses can lower their carbon footprints and resource consumption by shifting activities like meetings, conferences, shopping, and entertainment into the virtual realm. For example, virtual events and exhibitions eliminate the need for international travel, large venue rentals, and physical logistics, all contributing significantly to greenhouse gas emissions. Similarly, virtual product trials can minimise the environmental costs of manufacturing, packing, and shipping the physical samples. Moreover, the shift towards digital ownership via blockchain technologies like non-fungible tokens could reduce the production of physical goods, especially in industries like fashion and entertainment. Brands can design and sell digital clothing, accessories, or art in the metaverse, which requires no material, transportation, or waste management. The shift to digital goods aligns with sustainability principles as it reduces the ecological burden tide to the production and disposal of physical products. While the metaverse offers ways to reduce environmental impact, it also poses challenges. The metaverse relies on vast digital infrastructures that require significant energy consumption, particularly for data centres, blockchain technology, and high-performance computing to support immersive experiences. Cryptocurrency mining and NFT transactions have been criticised for their substantial carbon footprints. As businesses transition to the metaverse, they must address these concerns by exploring energy-efficient technologies, renewable energy sources, and carbon offset initiatives to mitigate the environmental costs associated with digital platforms.

Promoting Inclusive and Equitable Access

Incorporating CSR into the metaverse means addressing the issues of digital equity and inclusion. While the metaverse presents exciting opportunities for innovation and engagement, not all individuals or communities have equal access to the technologies needed to participate. The digital divide, where specific populations need access to high-speed Internet or advanced computing systems, poses a significant barrier to entry. As a result, marginalised communities, especially in developing regions, may be excluded from the economic and social benefits of the metaverse. Companies operating in the metaverse are responsible for addressing this inequality by promoting digital literacy and providing more affordable access to the necessary technologies. Partnering with governments, NGOs, and educational institutions to create programs that enhance tech accessibility is crucial for ensuring the metaverse is inclusive. Businesses can also use their platforms to create awareness around social issues and advocate for equity, offering virtual spaces for underrepresented voices to participate in the conversations that can shape the future of digital societies. But if we talk about the challenges, promoting inclusivity in the metaverse is a complex task, especially since the infrastructure required for participation is costly. Even VR headsets and computing power have become more affordable. There is a risk that early adoption will be dominated by affluent customers and businesses, leaving behind those who cannot afford the technological entry costs. Companies must invest in accessible design and pricing strategies to democratise access to the metaverse, ensuring the economic disparities do not widen as digital societies develop.

Ethical Governance and Data Privacy

A significant aspect of CSR in the metaverse revolves around the ethical governance of virtual spaces as users engage more deeply with the metaverse. They share vast amounts of personal data, including biometrics, purchasing behaviour, and even emotional responses tracked by VR and AR devices. Businesses must protect user privacy and handle data responsibly, following the ethical guidelines prioritising transparency, consent, and security. The decentralised nature of the metaverse, often powered by blockchain, creates challenges in governing these digital spaces. A centralised authority makes ensuring compliance with data protection regulations, intellectual property rights, and digital ownership laws more accessible. To uphold the CSR principles, companies must proactively establish frameworks for responsible governance, collaborating with industry stakeholders, governments, and regulatory bodies to set the standards that protect the users.

Additionally, businesses should consider how they manage digital identities and avatars, ensuring they are not used for harassment, discrimination, or unethical marketing practices. The promotion and protection of vulnerable populations such as children from exploitation and harmful content is critical in creating a safe metaverse environment. Furthermore, it is a very challengeable thing to balance innovation with data privacy. To balance innovation with data, privacy is a crucial challenge for businesses operating in the metaverse. Collecting the data to offer personalised services is an integral part of the metaverse appeal, but it can easily slip into overreach or misuse without proper oversight. In trading, compliance with global data protection laws is complicated by cross jurisdictional nature metaverse. Establishing clear regulations and ethical guidelines for the data, user protection, and virtual identities is essential to maintain trust.

Enhancing Social Impact and Community Engagement

The metaverse offers opportunities for businesses to engage in CSR through social impact initiatives. Companies can use their presence in virtual worlds to promote causes such as environmental sustainability, mental health, social justice, and diversity. For example, businesses can host virtual events to raise awareness or funds for global issues like climate change, poverty alleviation, or racial equality. They can also create inclusive digital communities where users can collaborate on social impact projects, participate in meaningful conversations, and access the resources for self-improvement or activism. Another CSR initiative is promoting well-being in the metaverse, particularly mental health. Immersive experiences can be designed to offer stress relief activities, promote mindfulness, and provide support for mental health challenges. Virtual environments can offer therapy sessions, wellness retreats, or educational content on mental health topics, helping businesses contribute positively to their communities while addressing real-world issues.

On the other hand, businesses must be cautious of CSR washing, where they appear to support social causes in the metaverse without taking meaningful or sustained actions. Initiative transparency is critical, as users can quickly identify when companies are using CSR for marketing purposes rather than genuine social good. Furthermore, ensuring that social impact campaigns in the metaverse translate into real-world benefits is essential, so businesses must align their virtual initiatives with tangible, measurable outcomes.

Future-oriented Corporate Social Responsibility

The metaverse offers a chance to redefine CSR by embracing future-oriented concepts such as regenerative economies, circularity, and long-term sustainability. In the metaverse, businesses can experiment with new models of production and consumption that prioritise environmental regeneration over-exploitation. For example, creating digital-only products could serve as a blueprint for reducing waste and promoting circularity in the physical world. Additionally, the metaverse allows companies to engage in forward-thinking social responsibility efforts, such as creating virtual environments that model sustainable cities, regenerative ecosystems, and collaborative economies (Chen & Cheng, 2022). These spaces can serve as educational tools and inspiration for real-world action, encouraging businesses and individuals to adopt more sustainable and socially responsible practices. However, ensuring that these future-oriented initiatives in the metaverse do not remain in the realm of idealism but are backed by real-world actions is essential. Businesses must avoid creating a disconnect between virtual promises and physical world practices. The challenge lies in ensuring that the innovation and experimentation fostered in metaphors are grounded in real-world strategies that promote sustainability and responsibility.

Conclusion

Metaverse offers a unique platform for advancing sustainability and corporate social responsibility by reducing environmental impact, promoting inclusivity, enhancing ethical governance, and creating positive social impact. However, businesses must navigate complex challenges such as energy consumption, data privacy, digital equity, and ethical governance to ensure that these activities. The matter was aligned with the broader – goals of the businesses. By thoughtfully integrating sustainability and CSR into metaverse strategies, companies can create a positive and responsible digital presence that benefits their bottom line and contributes to the greater good. As the metaverse continues to evolve, businesses that take leading, embedding sustainability and CSR into a new digital landscape will be better positioned to succeed ethically and financially.

References

Chen, Y., & Cheng, H. (2022). The economics of the metaverse: A comparison with the real economy. *Metaverse*, *3*(1), 19.

Damar, M. (2021). Metaverse shape of your life for future: A bibliometric snapshot. *Journal of Metaverse*, *1*(1), 1–8.

Gadekallu, T. R., Huynh-The, T., Wang, W., Yenduri, G., Ranaweera, P., Pham, Q. V., da Costa, D. B., Liyanage, M., & Liyanage, M. (2022). *Blockchain for the metaverse: A review*. arXiv preprint arXiv:2203.09738.

Gursoy, D., Malodia, S., & Dhir, A. (2022). The metaverse in the hospitality and tourism industry: An overview of current trends and future research directions. *Journal of Hospitality Marketing & Management*, *31*(5), 527–534.

Hwang, G. J., & Chien, S. Y. (2022). Definition, roles, and potential research issues of the metaverse in education: An artificial intelligence perspective. *Computers and Education: Artificial Intelligence*, *3*, 100082.

Kim, J. (2021). Advertising in the metaverse: Research agenda. *Journal of Interactive Advertising*, *21*(3), 141–144.

Lee, L. H., Braud, T., Zhou, P., Wang, L., Xu, D., Lin, Z., Kumar, A., Bermejo, C., & Hui, P. (2021). *All one needs to know about metaverse: A complete survey on technological singularity, virtual ecosystem, and research agenda*. arXiv preprint arXiv:2110.05352.

Park, S. M., & Kim, Y. G. (2022). A metaverse: Taxonomy, components, applications, and open challenges. *IEEE Access*, *10*, 4209–4251.

Wang, H., Ning, H., Lin, Y., Wang, W., Dhelim, S., Farha, F., Ding, J., & Daneshmand, M. (2023). A survey on the metaverse: The state-of-the-art, technologies, applications, and challenges. *IEEE Internet of Things Journal*, *10*(16), 14671–14688.

Wang, Y., Su, Z., Zhang, N., Xing, R., Liu, D., Luan, T. H., & Shen, X. (2022). A survey on metaverse: Fundamentals, security, and privacy. *IEEE Communications Surveys & Tutorials*, *25*(1), 319–352.

Xu, M., Ng, W. C., Lim, W. Y. B., Kang, J., Xiong, Z., Niyato, D., Yang, Q., Shen, X., & Miao, C. (2022). A full dive into realizing the edge-enabled metaverse: Visions, enabling technologies, and challenges. *IEEE Communications Surveys & Tutorials*, *25*(1), 656–700.

Zhao, Y., Jiang, J., Chen, Y., Liu, R., Yang, Y., Xue, X., & Chen, S. (2022). Metaverse: Perspectives from graphics, interactions and visualization. *Visual Informatics*, *6*(1), 56–67.

Chapter 17

The Dark Side of the Metaverse: Privacy, Security, and Safety Concerns

Vaishali Dhiman and Manpreet Arora

School of Commerce and Management Studies, Central University of Himachal Pradesh, India

Abstract

The metaverse is a new, exciting digital world where people can interact, work, and play in a virtual reality (VR) that feels almost real. While it has many amazing possibilities, there are also some serious problems that come with it. This conceptual exploration aims to shed light on the often-overlooked negative aspects associated with this emerging technology. This chapter explores the potential risks and dangers in the world of metaverse like privacy issues, data security risks, and the potential for people to become addicted to this digital world, which can harm their mental health. Additionally, this chapter has discussed the prevention against dark side of metaverse and ethical concerns and provided recommendations to mitigate risks associated with metaverse like identity theft, cyberbullying, and the confusion between what is real and what is virtual. By examining these negative aspects, this chapter aims to encourage a balanced conversation about the metaverse, suggesting that there is a need for strong rules and ethical guidelines to reduce its harmful effects and ensure that it is a safe and fair place for everyone.

Keywords: Metaverse; dark verse; virtual space; privacy concern; safety concern; security concern

The AI Metaverse Revolution: Transforming Multi-Business Scenarios (Volume 1), 241–254

doi:10.1108/978-1-83662-582-720251019

Introduction

Metaverse is a fully immersive digital domain that offers a significant technical innovation, immersive virtual experiences that could transform social interactions, commerce, entertainment, and education (Carrión, 2024; Kiong, 2024; Kumar et al., 2024a, 2024b). The concept of "Metaverse" is popularized as it combines the physical world with digital world. The term metaverse means an interconnected virtual shared place formed by the merging of virtually improved physical reality and physically persistent virtual spaces (Chen et al., 2024; Dhiman & Arora, 2024; Kim, 2021) that has progressed from a futuristic vision to a near-term reality. This digital frontier, driven by advances in technologies such as VR, augmented reality (AR), artificial intelligence (AI), and blockchain, has the potential to alter how we communicate, work, learn, and play (Arora et al., 2023; Arora & Sharma, 2022, 2023). The metaverse aspires to deliver an immersive, interactive experience that blurs the distinction between the physical and digital worlds, allowing for unprecedented innovation and communication.

The metaverse has a wide range of potential applications (Arora, 2024a, 2024b; Chandel & Arora, 2024). It has the ability to transform social relationships by creating virtual venues where individuals may connect, talk, and collaborate despite their physical distance (Arora, 2020; Mihalic, 2024; Narin, 2021; Rathore & Arora, 2024). In terms of economics, the metaverse has the potential to transform retail experiences by allowing customers to browse and buy virtual and actual things in immersive surroundings. Education could be improved by using virtual classrooms and labs to deliver dynamic and interesting learning experiences (Arora, 2024a, 2024b; Kye et al., 2021; Sim et al., 2024). Entertainment and games are also set to benefit considerably, providing users with completely new worlds to explore and interact with.

Dark Side of Metaverse

Despite its fascinating potential, the metaverse poses substantial problems and concerns that must be addressed in order for it to be successfully and safely integrated into our daily lives (Singh et al., 2024; Tugtekin, 2023; Wang et al., 2022). One of the most urgent problems is "Privacy." To personalize experiences and facilitate smooth interactions, the metaverse collects large amounts of data. These data comprises not just personal information but also behavioral patterns and biometric information gathered via VR and AR gadgets. Such massive data collection raises worry about unauthorized surveillance, data harvesting, and the potential exploitation of personal information. In today's digital landscape, protecting user privacy is critical for preserving confidence and making users feel protected (Aks et al., 2022; Canbay et al., 2022; Chen et al., 2024). Security is another key concern in the metaverse (Chen et al., 2022; Huang et al., 2023; Zhao et al., 2023). As an advanced and interconnected virtual environment, the metaverse is subject to a wide range of cybersecurity risks, including hacking, malware, and ransomware assaults. Cybercriminals may exploit flaws in the metaverse's infrastructure to gain unauthorized access, steal sensitive data, or disrupt services. Furthermore, the integration of virtual economies and digital currencies creates new opportunities for fraud and scams, bringing major financial dangers to consumers. User safety is a major concern which includes not only privacy and security concerns but also physical and psychological well-being (Davis & Lee, 2023; Hayes et al., 2024; Sharma et al., 2024). The immersive aspect of the metaverse may exacerbate problems with online harassment and abuse. The anonymity afforded by digital avatars can encourage harmful actors to engage in bullying, stalking, and other forms of harassment, which can have serious psychological consequences for victims. Furthermore, prolonged usage of VR and AR technology can cause physical health problems such as motion sickness, eye strain, and addiction. The blurring of borders between virtual and real worlds can have an influence on mental health, mandating standards and best practices for safe metaverse use. Addressing these possible threats necessitates a holistic strategy that combines strong privacy safeguards, advanced security measures, and detailed safety plans (Kumar et al., 2023; Talapuru et al., 2023; Yayla et al., 2024). Implementing clear and transparent privacy policies, utilizing privacy-enhancing technologies, and educating users on best practices for preserving their information are all critical steps toward ensuring user privacy. Improved cybersecurity through advanced tools, regular audits, and user training can assist decrease security risks. Promoting a safe and inclusive environment through community guidelines, support resources, and good usage habits is critical for ensuring user well-being.

Terms Associated with Dark Side of the Metaverse

(i) *Cyberbullying and harassment*: Cyberbullying and harassment can occur in the metaverse through verbal abuse, threats, or spreading harmful rumors using digital avatars. To prevent this, platforms must enforce strict policies against such behavior and provide tools for users to report incidents. Educating users on respectful online conduct is also essential (Englander et al., 2017; Kiriakidis & Kavoura, 2010).

(ii) *Virtual theft and scams*: In the metaverse, virtual theft can involve stealing digital assets or identities, and scams can trick users into sharing personal information or making fraudulent transactions (Kristiansen et al., 2024; Smith, 2013). Prevention includes using secure authentication methods, encryption for sensitive data, and educating users to recognize and avoid suspicious activities.

(iii) *Exploitation and predatory behavior*: Some individuals may use the anonymity of the metaverse to exploit others, such as grooming minors or engaging in illegal activities. Platforms should implement strict age verification measures, moderation systems to detect predatory behavior, and reporting mechanisms for users to flag suspicious activities.

(iv) *Misinformation and fake content*: In a post-truth scenario, misinformation spreads rapidly as emotional appeals and personal beliefs often overshadow objective facts and rational discourse (Arora, 2020; Arora et al., 2024). Misinformation and fake content can spread rapidly in the metaverse

(Talapuru et al., 2023), influencing perceptions and behaviors. In the metaverse, the dark side of misinformation becomes more pronounced as immersive and interactive digital environments can be manipulated to distort reality, amplifying the impacts of false narratives. It could also potentially lead to widespread deception and harm. Platforms should implement content moderation strategies, including fact-checking tools and community reporting mechanisms, to combat misinformation and ensure accurate information dissemination.

(v) *Addiction and mental health concerns*: Excessive use of the metaverse can lead to addiction and affect users' mental health. Metaverse platforms can lead to addiction by offering highly engaging experiences (Bojic, 2022; Cerasa et al., 2022; Paquin et al., 2023; Usmani et al., 2022; Yadav & Dhanda, 2024). So, the platforms should promote healthy usage habits, provide tools for users to manage screen time, and offer resources for mental health support. Educating users about the potential risks of overuse is essential.

(vi) *Security vulnerabilities and data breaches*: Security vulnerabilities in metaverse platforms can lead to data breaches, exposing users' personal information to hackers (Farid et al., 2023; Pooyandeh et al., 2022; Sharma et al., 2024; Wylde et al., 2023). Platforms must prioritize cybersecurity measures such as encryption, regular security audits, and prompt patching of software vulnerabilities to protect user data from unauthorized access.

In nutshell, while the metaverse has enormous potential to revolutionize many parts of our life, it also poses substantial privacy, security, and safety concerns. By proactively addressing these concerns, stakeholders can make the metaverse a safer and more secure place, ensuring it to be a constructive and transformational force in society. This chapter investigates the key potential risks and dangers that users may face in the world of metaverse and also makes possible recommendations to avoid these risks, promoting a trustworthy and resilient digital future.

Literature Review

The existing literature on the dark side of metaverse shares several dark aspects. It highlights the need for a cautious approach to its development and adoption. One of the important concerns is the potential for addiction and escapism. Studies highlight that immersive environments within the metaverse can be so engaging that users may develop addictive behaviors, spending excessive time in the virtual world at the expense of real-world responsibilities and relationships. This phenomenon has been documented in studies on Internet and Gaming edition, which similarly apply to metaverse experiences (Barreda-Ángeles & Hartmann, 2022; Bojic, 2022; Bojić et al., 2024; Jones, 2023; Usmani et al., 2022). Another important issue in regard to the world of metaverse is privacy. Metaverse platforms collect vast amount of data which is personal in nature to create personalized and interactive experiences. There is always a higher probability of misusing of the data, leading to privacy breaches and surveillance, as highlighted by various privacy advocates and researchers (Blackwell et al., 2019; Blascovich et al., 2002; Blascovich & Bailenson, 2006; Brey, 2008; Hine et al., 2024; O'Brolcháin et al., 2016; Stanney et al., 1998; Tseng et al., 2022; Vondráček et al., 2023). Therefore, the potential for misuse of personal information is very much heightened in the immersive environments where more detailed and sensitive data is collected. Mental health issues are also very much prominent as the dark side of metaverse. Increased use of virtual environment can contribute to anxiety, depression, and social isolation (Boursier et al., 2020; Epting, 2021; Martončik & Lokša, 2016; Sikorska et al., 2021; Yuen et al., 2013). Studies have shown that excessive use of digital platform negatively impact mental health, and these effects are likely to be increased in more immersive and engaging environmental settings.

Singh et al. (2024) proposed that the "darkverse" of the metaverse presents significant challenges for hospitality and tourism customers. While promising immersive experiences, it raises concerns about privacy, security, and ethical dilemmas. Issues like data exploitation and virtual addiction could undermine user trust and safety. Navigating these complexities is essential for businesses aiming to harness the metaverse's potential while safeguarding user well-being.

Grover (2024) stated that in the midst of the digital revolution of the 21st century, we have to deal with a challenging environment where our digital dependencies and analog sensations collide. Smartphones are little technological wonders that hold everything we need for daily life, including groceries, clothes, and medications. However, despite this ease, there are still pressing concerns in our thoughts around data ownership, security measures, and safety. In a time where technology is always changing, the average user is always concerned about the security of their data. Unquestionably, technology has brought humanity many benefits, but it also has a negative side, as seen by the rise in online fraud and scams.

Kamoun et al. (2024) stated in their study that the metaverse is about to provide an immersive virtual space where individuals may interact, play, socialize, work together, and transact business. The metaverse may not be fully developed yet, but it has already been abused to start fraudulent operations that endanger people's safety and well-being and damage institutions.

Alauthman et al. (2024) mentioned that through the use of cutting-edge exponential technologies like VR, AR, and extended reality, the metaverse symbolizes the evolution of the Internet. With the increasing prevalence of Web 3.0 environments, new types of threats and cybersecurity vulnerabilities are emerging. In order to handle cybersecurity in the metaverse, a thorough framework covering five essential domains, data privacy, identity management, digital asset protection, network and device security, and user education was proposed in their study. An examination of the threat vectors associated with the metaverse is given, encompassing social engineering, cross-reality assaults, weaknesses in decentralized applications, and synthesized media. Based on the distinctive characteristics of metaverse ecosystems, technical restrictions, governance guidelines, and educational initiatives are suggested for each cybersecurity domain.

XinYing et al. (2024) stated that the emergence of the metaverse has generated a great deal of attention. User interaction and aberrant behavior within the metaverse are examples of the behavioral side of the metaverse. Many risks to people and society have been brought about by such technologies. The number of recorded incidences of sexual assault, racism, harassment, hate speech, and bullying is on the rise. These incidents have given birth to the roles of security and privacy on deviant behavior in the metaverse.

Liu et al. (2023) proposed that the goal of metaverse, the next evolution of the Internet, is to create a fully immersive, incredibly realistic, and autonomous virtual environment. People can work, socialize, and have fun in this area. Researchers' attention has been drawn to the realization of the metaverse as a result of the ongoing development and emergence of many technologies across time. But the security and privacy issues that plague the Internet also exist in the metaverse, and there will be even more grave issues there.

Dwivedi et al. (2023) mentioned that with the power to revolutionize multiple areas of work and living at a societal level, the metaverse may give rise to the next universal computing model. Even while the metaverse is expected to bring about a lot of positive changes, its drawbacks have not been fully investigated. Most opinions on it are based on logical assumptions drawn from historical data points connected to related technologies, which leaves them rather devoid of scholarly and professional viewpoint. The dark side views of the metaverse discussed are technological and consumer vulnerability, privacy and diminished reality, human–computer interface, identity theft, financial crimes, terrorist activities, financial crimes, abuse, pornography, social inclusion, mental health, sexual harassment, and metaverse-triggered unintended consequences.

Ghamya et al. (2023) argued that how secure is this metaverse? Things are never flawless, as we all know, and there have always been flaws. This raises many questions, including whether our data are safe in the metaverse, privacy concerns, digital boundaries, and social engineering, as anyone can use our identifiable avatar to enter into a highly confidential event. Despite its supremacy, this makes the metaverse a little scary. It is necessary to do this by raising people's awareness and building a more stable, safe metaverse.

Discussion

Potential Risks and Dangers in the World of Metaverse

(i) *Privacy concerns in metaverse*: Privacy concerns in the virtual world of metaverse originate from large amounts of data recording, which includes personal, behavioral, and biometric information. This information can be used for unauthorized surveillance and data harvesting, posing serious threats to user privacy (Chen & Wen, 2021). Ensuring strong privacy safeguards is critical for preserving user confidence and safety in these immersive digital settings. Some of the privacy issues are described briefly, including:

Data collection and surveillance

The metaverse mainly relies on user data to personalize experiences and improve engagement. These data comprise personal information, behavioral patterns, and even biometric data collected by VR and AR equipment. The vast data collecting may result in unauthorized surveillance and data harvesting by companies and third parties, jeopardizing user privacy.

Identity theft and impersonation

In the metaverse, users design digital avatars that align to their real-world personalities. This relationship facilitates identity theft and impersonation (Thompson & Garcia, 2023). Stolen identities can be exploited for fraudulent acts that harm the victim's image and their financial security.

(ii) *Security concerns in metaverse*: Security risks in the metaverse include hacking, virus, and ransomware attacks that can compromise sensitive data and interrupt services. The integration of virtual economies also raises the possibility of fraud and frauds, endangering user finances. Improving cybersecurity measures is critical for safeguarding the metaverse's infrastructure and user data. A few of the security concerns are briefly discussed below:

Cybersecurity risks

The metaverse, as a complex network of interconnected virtual environments, is vulnerable to a variety of cybersecurity risks such as hacking, malware, and ransomware. Cybercriminals can exploit flaws in the metaverse's infrastructure to gain unauthorized access, steal critical data, or disrupt operations.

Hacking and malware

Because of its complexity and interconnectedness, the metaverse is an attractive target for hackers and malware attacks. Cybercriminals might use vulnerabilities in virtual world infrastructure to steal sensitive data, interrupt services, or install harmful malware.

Scams and frauds

The metaverse has become an incubator for fraud and scams as virtual economies and digital currencies are integrated. Users may become victims of phishing attempts, fraudulent investment schemes, and counterfeit virtual products, resulting in financial losses and a lack of faith in the platform.

(iii) *Safety concerns in metaverse*: Safety issues related to the metaverse include the possibility of online harassment and abuse, which is further complicated by the anonymity of digital avatars. Users may potentially have physical health difficulties, such as VR motion sickness and eye strain, as well as psychological effects from prolonged use. To preserve user well-being in these immersive virtual environments, strong safety measures and support mechanisms must be established. A few safety considerations are described briefly below.

Harassment and violence

The metaverse's anonymity and immersive nature could lead to problems with harassment and abuse. Bullying, stalking, and other types of online harassment can have serious psychological consequences for users. Creating effective moderation and reporting procedures is critical to ensuring a safe and inclusive environment.

Psychological and physical well-being

Excessive usage of VR technology can have negative consequences for mental and physical well-being. VR motion sickness, eye strain, and addiction are serious issues. Furthermore, the blurring of borders between virtual and real worlds might have an influence on users' mental health, prompting the creation of standards and best practices for healthy metaverse use.

Preventions Against Dark Side of Metaverse

The metaverse is a virtual world where people can interact, work, and play through digital avatars. It combines VR, AR, and the internet to create immersive experiences. With its growing popularity, it's essential to understand how to keep this digital space safe and secure.

(i) *User authentication and verification*: User authentication is the process of ensuring that a user is who they claim to be. In the metaverse, this can involve using passwords, biometric data like fingerprints or facial recognition, and multi-factor authentication. These methods help protect user accounts from unauthorized access and ensure that only legitimate users can enter the virtual world.
(ii) *Secure data transmission*: To keep data safe while it travels across the internet, encryption techniques are used. Encryption turns information into a code that only authorized parties can decode. In the metaverse, this ensures that personal data, financial transactions, and other sensitive information remain confidential and secure from hackers.
(iii) *Content moderation and filtering*: Content moderation involves monitoring and managing the content within the metaverse to prevent harmful, illegal, or inappropriate material. Automated systems and human moderators work together to filter out such content, ensuring a safe and welcoming environment for all users.
(iv) *Cybersecurity protocols*: Cybersecurity protocols are rules and practices designed to protect the metaverse from cyber-attacks. These include firewalls, anti-virus software, and regular security updates. Implementing strong cybersecurity measures helps prevent data breaches, malware infections, and other cyber threats.
(v) *Ethical frameworks*: Ethical frameworks are critical in shaping a responsible and inclusive metaverse. Ensuring ethical AI involves designing and implementing AI systems with a focus on fairness and bias avoidance. This approach aims to mitigate potential biases in algorithms that could otherwise perpetuate discrimination or inequality within virtual environments. Inclusive design principles are equally essential, aiming to create virtual spaces that accommodate diverse user needs and preferences. By prioritizing accessibility and inclusivity, developers can prevent discriminatory practices and foster a welcoming environment for all participants.

Recommendations to Mitigate Risks Associated with Metaverse

To avoid potential risks and create a trustworthy digital future in the metaverse, it is critical to develop strong privacy safeguards, such as transparent data usage policies and privacy-enhancing technologies. Regular cybersecurity audits, enhanced security tools, and user education can all help mitigate security concerns. Furthermore, creating a safe environment with clear community norms, support resources, and healthy usage behaviors will protect users' well-being. Some of the potential recommendations and suggestions are described briefly, including:

Robust privacy protection

Create clear and thorough privacy policies outlining data collecting, usage, and sharing methods. Provide user-friendly consent forms and data control tools to ensure transparency.

Privacy-enhancing technologies

Use technologies like anonymization and differential privacy to secure user identities. Use decentralized identity management solutions to provide consumers control over their personal data.

Awareness and education for users

Hold regular user education campaigns to enlighten users about privacy dangers and recommended practices for protecting their data. Awareness campaigns play a vital role in reinforcing these teachings and expanding public consciousness about online safety. These campaigns focus on highlighting specific threats like phishing attacks, emphasizing the importance of using strong, unique passwords, and promoting safe behaviors such as verifying sources before sharing information. By raising awareness about these issues, campaigns aim to cultivate a culture of vigilance and responsibility among metaverse users, fostering a safer digital ecosystem overall.

Strengthen security measures

To increase security measures in the metaverse, the encryption technologies must be implemented to protect the user data. Regular system updates and patching are critical for quickly addressing problems. Concurrently, performing frequent security audits and vulnerability assessments aids in identifying and mitigating possible threats, while developing a strong incident response strategy assures quick action in the event of a security breach. Furthermore, providing thorough cybersecurity training through sessions and resources enables users to recognize and prevent typical cyber risks such as phishing and malware, resulting in a more secure metaverse environment.

Technical solutions

Encryption, blockchain, and decentralized identity management are examples of technological solutions that can improve data safety and security in the metaverse. Implementing these technologies can help protect user information, maintain data integrity, and give users more control over their personal data.

Promoting safety, well-being, and healthy usage practices

To ensure safety and well-being in the metaverse, clear community norms outlining appropriate behavior must be established, as well as rigorous moderation and reporting procedures in place to quickly address incidents of harassment and abuse. Furthermore, providing support resources like as counseling services and hotlines guarantees that users have access to help when they need it, while developing safe spaces inside the metaverse encourages a supportive environment. Encouraging good usage habits through screen time management tools and educating users on the potential physical and psychological consequences of extended metaverse use is crucial.

Legal and regulatory frameworks for data protection

To ensure data privacy in the metaverse, complete legal and regulatory frameworks must be developed that address the particular issues faced by these virtual settings. Regulations like the general data protection regulation and the California Consumer Privacy Act lay the groundwork, but new rules may be required to expressly address metaverse-related issues.

Conclusion

The concept of the metaverse, often portrayed as a boundless virtual realm offering unprecedented experiences, also brings forth significant risks and challenges that necessitate careful consideration by both businesses and users. Referred to as the "darkverse," this virtual landscape introduces concerns related to privacy, security, and ethical implications that extend beyond specific industries like tourism. Users contend with potential privacy issues concerning the collection, usage, and protection of personal data within virtual environments, which could be exploited or compromised. Furthermore, the vulnerability of virtual spaces to cyberattacks poses risks such as data breaches or service disruptions, highlighting the critical need for robust cybersecurity measures. Ethical dilemmas surrounding digital identity, virtual addiction, and the influence on real-world behaviors underscore broader societal impacts that must be addressed. To mitigate these risks effectively, proactive measures are essential. Implementing stringent data protection protocols, deploying advanced cybersecurity solutions, and establishing clear ethical guidelines for virtual interactions are imperative steps. Moreover, fostering education and awareness among users about the risks and benefits of the metaverse, advocating for adaptive regulatory frameworks, and promoting collaboration among industry stakeholders and policymakers can collectively safeguard against the darker aspects of virtual environments. By approaching these challenges comprehensively and collaboratively, businesses and users can harness the transformative potential of the metaverse while ensuring a secure and ethical digital landscape for all participants.

References

Aks, S. M. Y., Karmila, M., Givan, B., Hendratna, G., Setiawan, H. S., Putra, A. S., Winarno, S. A., Kurniawan, T. A., Simorangkir, Y. N., Taufiq, R., Herawaty, M. T., & Asep (2022, August). *A review of blockchain for security data privacy with metaverse*. 2022 International Conference on ICT for Smart Society (ICISS) (pp. 1–5). IEEE.

Alauthman, M., Ishtaiwi, A., Al Maqousi, A., & Hadi, W. (2024, February). *A framework for cybersecurity in the metaverse*. 2024 2nd International conference on cyber resilience (ICCR) (pp. 1–8). IEEE.

Arora, M. (2020). Post-truth and marketing communication in technological age. In S. A. Dadwal (Ed.), *Handbook of research on innovations in technology and marketing for the connected consumer* (pp. 94–108). IGI Global.

Arora, M. (2024a). Metaverse metamorphosis: Bridging the gap between research insights and industry applications. In J. Kumar, M. Arora & G. Erkol Bayram (Eds.), *Research, innovation, and industry impacts of the metaverse* (pp. 275–286). IGI Global.

Arora, M. (2024b). Virtual reality in education: Analyzing the literature and bibliometric state of knowledge. *Transforming Education with Virtual Reality*, 379–402.

Arora, M., Kumar, J., & Valeri, M. (2023). Crises and resilience in the age of digitalization: Perspectivations of past, present and future for tourism industry. In *Tourism innovation in the digital era* (pp. 57–74). Emerald Publishing Limited.

Arora, M., & Sharma, R. L. (2022). Integrating gig economy and social media platforms as a business strategy in the era of digitalization. In *Integrated business models in the digital age: Principles and practices of technology empowered strategies* (pp. 67–86). Springer International Publishing.

Arora, M., & Sharma, R. L. (2023). Artificial intelligence and big data: Ontological and communicative perspectives in multi-sectoral scenarios of modern businesses. *Foresight*, *25*(1), 126–143.

Arora, M., Sharma, R. L., Dhiman, V., & Rathore, S. (2024). Managing (Mis-/) disinformation through big data analysis: Resorting to sustainable strategies to counter infodemic. In *Sustainable strategic business infrastructure development and contemporary digital practices in industry 5.0* (pp. 57–72). Apple Academic Press.

Barreda-Ángeles, M., & Hartmann, T. (2022). Hooked on the metaverse? Exploring the prevalence of addiction to virtual reality applications. *Frontiers in Virtual Reality*, *3*, 1031697.

Blackwell, L., Ellison, N., Elliott-Deflo, N., & Schwartz, R. (2019). Harassment in social virtual reality: Challenges for platform governance. *Proceedings of the ACM on Human-Computer Interaction*, *3*(CSCW), 1–25.

Blascovich, J., & Bailenson, J. (2006). Immersive virtual environments and education simulations. In *Virtual decisions* (pp. 229–253). Routledge.

Blascovich, J., Loomis, J., Beall, A. C., Swinth, K. R., Hoyt, C. L., & Bailenson, J. N. (2002). Immersive virtual environment technology as a methodological tool for social psychology. *Psychological Inquiry*, *13*(2), 103–124.

Bojic, L. (2022). Metaverse through the prism of power and addiction: What will happen when the virtual world becomes more attractive than reality?. *European Journal of Futures Research*, *10*(1), 22.

Bojić, L., Agatonović, M., & Guga, J. (2024). The immersion in the metaverse: Cognitive load and addiction. In *Augmented and virtual reality in the metaverse* (pp. 211–223). Springer Nature Switzerland.

Boursier, V., Gioia, F., Musetti, A., & Schimmenti, A. (2020). Facing loneliness and anxiety during the COVID-19 isolation: The role of excessive social media use in a sample of Italian adults. *Frontiers in Psychiatry*, *11*, 586222.

Brey, P. (2008). Virtual reality and computer simulation. In K. E. Himma, J. D. Herman & T. Tavani (Eds.), *The handbook of information and computer ethics* (pp. 361–384) John Wiley & Sons, Inc.

Canbay, Y., Utku, A., & Canbay, P. (2022, October). Privacy concerns and measures in metaverse: A review. 2022 15th international conference on information security and cryptography (ISCTURKEY) (pp. 80–85). IEEE.

Carrión, C. (2024). Research streams and open challenges in the metaverse. *The Journal of Supercomputing*, *80*(2), 1598–1639.

Cerasa, A., Gaggioli, A., Marino, F., Riva, G., & Pioggia, G. (2022). The promise of the metaverse in mental health: The new era of MEDverse. *Heliyon*, *8*(11), 1–7.

Chandel, M., & Arora, M. (2024). Metaverse perspectives: Unpacking its role in shaping sustainable development goals – A qualitative inquiry. In *Research, innovation, and industry impacts of the metaverse* (pp. 62–75). IGI Global.

Chen, C., Li, Y., Wu, Z., Mai, C., Liu, Y., Hu, Y., Zheng, Z., & Kang, J. (2024). Privacy computing meets metaverse: Necessity, taxonomy and challenges. *Ad Hoc Networks*, *158*, 103457.

Chen, L., & Wen, Q. (2021). Data privacy and security issues in the metaverse: A comprehensive review. *Journal of Cyber Security*, *5*(2), 45–60.

Chen, Z., Gan, W., Sun, J., Wu, J., & Yu, P. S. (2024, May). *Open metaverse: Issues, evolution, and future*. Companion proceedings of the ACM on web conference 2024 (pp. 1351–1360).

Chen, Z., Wu, J., Gan, W., & Qi, Z. (2022, December). *Metaverse security and privacy: An overview*. 2022 IEEE international conference on big data (big data) (pp. 2950–2959). IEEE.

Davis, K., & Lee, S. (2023). Psychological impacts of the metaverse: Harassment and mental health. *Journal of Digital Psychology*, *6*(4), 97–112.

Dhiman, V., & Arora, M. (2024). Current state of metaverse in entrepreneurial ecosystem: A retrospective analysis of its evolving landscape. In *Exploring the use of metaverse in business and education* (pp. 73–87). IGI Global.

Dwivedi, Y. K., Kshetri, N., Hughes, L., Rana, N. P., Baabdullah, A. M., Kar, A. K., Koohang, A., Ribeiro-Navarrete, S., Belei, N., Balakrishnan, J., Basu, S., Behl, A., Davies, G. H., Dutot, V., Dwivedi, R., Evans, L., Felix, R., Foster-Fletcher, R., Giannakis, M., … Yan, M. (2023). Exploring the darkverse: A multi-perspective analysis of the negative societal impacts of the metaverse. *Information Systems Frontiers*, *25*(5), 2071–2114.

Englander, E., Donnerstein, E., Kowalski, R., Lin, C. A., & Parti, K. (2017). Defining cyberbullying. *Pediatrics*, *140*(Supplement_2), S148–S151.

Epting, S. (2021). Vulnerable groups, virtual cities, and social isolation. *Technology in Society*, *67*, 101711.

Farid, F., Bello, A., Jahan, N., & Sultana, R. (2023). *Cyber security management in metaverse: A review and analysis*. Proceedings of the computational methods in systems and software (pp. 183–193).

Ghamya, K., Yadav, C. C., Pranav, D. V. S., Reddy Madhavi, K., & Patel, A. (2023, March). *Metaverse: The potential threats in the virtual world*. Proceedings of fourth international conference on computer and communication technologies: IC3T 2022 (pp. 59–67). Springer Nature Singapore.

Grover, A. (2024). Navigating the digital era: Exploring privacy, security, and ownership of personal data. In *Digital technologies, ethics, and decentralization in the digital era* (pp. 201–227). IGI Global.

Hayes, A., Robinson, S., Bai, A., & Noonan, R. (2024, March). *This is not a game: Users want a safe and ethical metaverse*. Society for information technology & teacher education international conference (pp. 1272–1283). Association for the Advancement of Computing in Education (AACE).

Hine, E., Rezende, I. N., Roberts, H., Wong, D., Taddeo, M., & Floridi, L. (2024). Safety and privacy in immersive extended reality: An analysis and policy recommendations. *Digital Society*, *3*(2), 33.

Huang, Y., Li, Y. J., & Cai, Z. (2023). Security and privacy in metaverse: A comprehensive survey. *Big Data Mining and Analytics*, *6*(2), 234–247.

Jones, J. (2023). How will video games in the metaverse affect adolescent children?. *Journal of Student Research at Indiana University East*, *5*(2), 16–25.

Kamoun, F., Iqbal, F., Zeresenay, S., Khalid, Z., Ikuesan, R., & Abraham, S. (2024). Metaverse forensics: A preliminary analysis of opportunities and challenges. In F. Kamoun, F. Iqbal, S. Zeresenay, Z. Khalid, R. Ikuesan & S. Abraham (Eds.), *Forecasting cyber crimes in the age of the metaverse* (pp. 182–208). IGI Global

Kim, J. (2021). Advertising in the metaverse: Research agenda. *Journal of Interactive Advertising*, *21*(3), 141–144.

Kiong, L. V. (2024). *Metaverse made easy: A beginner's guide to the metaverse: Everything you need to know about metaverse, NFT and GameFi*. Liew Voon Kiong.

Kiriakidis, S. P., & Kavoura, A. (2010). Cyberbullying: A review of the literature on harassment through the internet and other electronic means. *Family & Community Health*, *33*(2), 82–93.

Kristiansen, S., Jensen, A. V., Nimgaard, M., & Ludvigsen, E. (2024). Virtual item trade scams: A typology of young victims. *International Review of Victimology*, 02697580241258786.

Kumar, A., Shankar, A., Shaik, A. S., Jain, G., & Malibari, A. (2023). Risking it all in the metaverse ecosystem: Forecasting resistance towards the enterprise metaverse. *Information Technology & People*.

Kumar, J., Arora, M., & Erkol Bayram, G. (Eds.). (2024a). *Exploring the use of metaverse in business and education*. IGI Global.

Kumar, J., Arora, M., & Erkol Bayram, G. (Eds.). (2024b). *Research, innovation, and industry impacts of the metaverse*. IGI Global.

Kye, B., Han, N., Kim, E., Park, Y., & Jo, S. (2021). Educational applications of metaverse: Possibilities and limitations. *Journal of Educational Evaluation for Health Professions*, *18*.

Liu, K., Zheng, T., Zhou, T., Liu, C., Liu, F., & Cai, Z. (2023, November). *The security and privacy concerns on metaverse*. International artificial intelligence conference (pp. 287–305). Springer Nature Singapore.

Martončik, M., & Lokša, J. (2016). Do world of warcraft (MMORPG) players experience less loneliness and social anxiety in online world (virtual environment) than in real world (offline)?. *Computers in Human Behavior*, *56*, 127–134.

Mihalic, T. (2024). Metaversal sustainability: Conceptualisation within the sustainable tourism paradigm. *Tourism Review*. https://doi.org/10.1108/TR-09-2023-0609

Narin, N. G. (2021). A content analysis of the metaverse articles. *Journal of Metaverse*, *1*(1), 17–24.

O'Brolcháin, F., Jacquemard, T., Monaghan, D., O'Connor, N., Novitzky, P., & Gordijn, B. (2016). The convergence of virtual reality and social networks: Threats to privacy and autonomy. *Science and Engineering Ethics*, *22*, 1–29.

Paquin, V., Ferrari, M., Sekhon, H., & Rej, S. (2023). Time to think "Meta": A critical viewpoint on the risks and benefits of virtual worlds for mental health. *JMIR Serious Games*, *11*, e43388.

Pooyandeh, M., Han, K. J., & Sohn, I. (2022). Cybersecurity in the AI-based metaverse: A survey. *Applied Sciences*, *12*(24), 12993.

Rathore, S., & Arora, M. (2024). Sustainability reporting in the metaverse: A multi-sectoral analysis. In *Exploring the use of metaverse in business and education* (pp. 147–165). IGI Global.

Sharma, S., Singh, J., Gupta, A., Ali, F., Khan, F., & Kwak, D. (2024). User safety and security in the metaverse: A critical review. *IEEE Open Journal of the Communications Society*, *5*, 5467–5487.

Sikorska, I. M., Lipp, N., Wróbel, P., & Wyra, M. (2021). Adolescent mental health and activities in the period of social isolation caused by the COVID-19 pandemic. *Advances in Psychiatry and Neurology/Postępy Psychiatrii i Neurologii*, *30*(2), 79–95.

Sim, J. K., Xu, K. W., Jin, Y., Lee, Z. Y., Teo, Y. J., Mohan, P., & Cai, Y. (2024). Designing an educational metaverse: A case study of NTUniverse. *Applied Sciences*, *14*(6), 2559.

Singh, R., Iqbal, J., Kukreja, P., Yadav, M., & Ramkissoon, H. (2024). Metaverse? It is virtual hell! Understanding the dark side of the metaverse (darkverse) for hospitality and tourism customers. *Tourism Review*.

Smith, R. G. (2013). Identity theft and fraud. In *Handbook of internet crime* (pp. 273–301). Willan.

Stanney, K. M., Mourant, R. R., & Kennedy, R. S. (1998). Human factors issues in virtual environments: A review of the literature. *Presence*, *7*(4), 327–351.

Talapuru, S., Dantu, R., Upadhyay, K., Badruddoja, S., & Zaman, S. (2023, November). *The dark side of the metaverse: Why is it falling short of expectations?* 2023 5th IEEE international conference on trust, privacy and security in intelligent systems and applications (TPS-ISA) (pp. 287–296). IEEE.

Thompson, A., & Garcia, B. (2023). Identity theft and authentication in the metaverse. *Digital Security Journal*, *8*(3), 72–85.

Tseng, W. J., Bonnail, E., McGill, M., Khamis, M., Lecolinet, E., Huron, S., & Gugenheimer, J. (2022, April). *The dark side of perceptual manipulations in virtual reality*. Proceedings of the 2022 CHI conference on human factors in computing systems (pp. 1–15).

Tugtekin, U. (2023). The dark side of metaverse learning environments: Potential threats and risk factors. In *Shaping the future of online learning: Education in the metaverse* (pp. 57–67). IGI Global.

Usmani, S. S., Sharath, M., & Mehendale, M. (2022). Future of mental health in the metaverse. *General Psychiatry*, *35*(4).

Vondráček, M., Baggili, I., Casey, P., & Mekni, M. (2023). Rise of the metaverse's immersive virtual reality malware and the man-in-the-room attack & defenses. *Computers & Security*, *127*, 102923.

Wang, Y., Su, Z., Zhang, N., Xing, R., Liu, D., Luan, T. H., & Shen, X. (2022). A survey on metaverse: Fundamentals, security, and privacy. *IEEE Communications Surveys & Tutorials*, *25*(1), 319–352.

Wylde, V., Prakash, E., Hewage, C., & Platts, J. (2023). Post-Covid-19 metaverse cybersecurity and data privacy: Present and future challenges. In *Data protection in a post-pandemic society: Laws, regulations, best practices and recent solutions* (pp. 1–48). Springer International Publishing.

XinYing, C., Tiberius, V., Alnoor, A., Camilleri, M., & Khaw, K. W. (2024). The dark side of metaverse: A multi-perspective of deviant behaviors from PLS-SEM and fsQCA findings. *International Journal of Human–Computer Interaction*, 1–21.

Yadav, V., & Dhanda, N. (2024). The metaverse and mental health: The future. *Decentralized Systems and Distributed Computing*, 337–354).

Yayla, A., Warkentin, M., & Dincelli, E. (2024). *Introduction to the minitrack on the dark and bright sides of the metaverse*.

Yuen, E. K., Herbert, J. D., Forman, E. M., Goetter, E. M., Comer, R., & Bradley, J. C. (2013). Treatment of social anxiety disorder using online virtual environments in second life. *Behavior Therapy*, *44*(1), 51–61.

Zhao, R., Zhang, Y., Zhu, Y., Lan, R., & Hua, Z. (2023). Metaverse: Security and privacy concerns. *Journal of Metaverse*, *3*(2), 93–99.

Index

Printed and bound by CPI Group (UK) Ltd, Croydon, CR0 4YY

01/06/2026

14890759-0003